Professor Eli F. Heckscher's book on Mercantilism has been out of print for several years. Since it is the only existing comprehensive study in its field and, for some fifteen years, has been used as a textbook in economic history all over the Western World, the publishing of a new and revised edition has been planned for some years. At his death in December 1952 Professor Heckscher had almost finished his revision.

In order to keep down the cost of the new edition the text has not been reset. Minor alterations have been made, and in some cases whole chapters have been rewritten, e.g., the chapter on power as the main objective of mercantilist economic policy. But in most cases the amendments are to be found at the end of each of the two volumes. This enables the reader to compare Heckscher's original interpretation with his later conception, and as the *addenda* generally give his reasons for the reinterpretation there can be little doubt that this greatly enhances the value of the revised edition for the scholarly reader.

Another interesting addition is a chapter on Lord Keynes and Mercantilism. To a very great extent Lord Keynes's interpretation of Mercantilism, as given in his *General Theory of Employment, Interest and Money*, was based on the first edition of Heckscher's book. On many points Heckscher could not accept this interpretation; his criticism of it should be of great interest not only to economic historians but also to economists, as it to some degree implies a criticism of the validity of the Keynesian theory and points out the limitations of its applicability as a general economic theory.

MERCANTILISM

MERCANTILISM

by

ELI F. HECKSCHER

Authorized Translation
by
MENDEL SHAPIRO

Revised Edition Edited
by
E. F. SÖDERLUND

VOLUME TWO

LONDON : GEORGE ALLEN & UNWIN LTD
NEW YORK : THE MACMILLAN COMPANY

First published in Swedish in 1931

The English translation, prepared from the German edition and revised by the author, published in 1935

Revised 2nd Edition 1955

PRINTED IN GREAT BRITAIN
BY BRADFORD AND DICKENS
LONDON W.C.1

CONTENTS

VOLUME II

PART II

Mercantilism as a System of Power

PART III

Mercantilism as a System of Protection

PART V

Mercantilism as a Conception of Society

I: THE CONCORD BETWEEN MERCANTILISM AND
    LAISSEZ-FAIRE

II: THE NATURE OF THE MERCANTILIST CONCEPTION
    OF SOCIETY

PART II

MERCANTILISM AS A SYSTEM OF POWER

I

THE ESSENCE OF THE SYSTEM OF POWER

State interest

It is natural to consider mercantilism as the economic system of nationalism. This conception is also elaborated by Edgar Furniss in *The Position of the Laborer in a System of Nationalism* (1920), one of the most closely reasoned expositions of the subject. And to the extent that mercantilism showed indifference towards anything unrelated to its own country, the view is substantiated. In principle and in practice it denied all those universalist factors such as the church and the empire which had fashioned medieval society. If the mercantilist concentrated on encouraging the sale and consumption abroad of native products, he was not thinking of the well-being of foreign consumers, but in accordance with his general approach to the situation, he saw in it an advantage for his own country. To this extent one is perfectly justified in considering mercantilism as a nationalist system.

It must, however, be pointed out that this approach does not lead to any fundamental explanation of the essence of mercantilism. Its peculiarities are revealed when compared with the doctrines of free trade as first enunciated by Hume and later elaborated theoretically by Ricardo. From certain points of view, free trade provides the strictest contrast with mercantilism. But paradoxical as it may seem, free trade on its first premises was likewise entirely preoccupied with the interests of the native country. Only in its consequences was it cosmopolitan.

In the construction given to the theory of foreign trade by Ricardo, the factors of production—land, labour and capital—of a country were presumed to be mobile only within the country, but not over its boundaries. From the point of view of economic policy, however, the most important aspect to note is that it was out of a concern for the interests of their own country that free trade theorists demanded free exchange with other countries.

*　　*　　*　　*　　*　　*　　*

Had it been otherwise their views would obviously not have had much prospect of success in any country, and certainly not in England. This outlook was expressed in Hume's essay on *Jealousy of Trade* (1752), which contains his definitive judgment on mercantilist commercial policy. The conclusion to the essay runs as follows: "I shall therefore venture to acknowledge, that *not only as a man, but as a British subject*, I pray for the flourishing commerce of Germany, Spain, Italy, and even France itself. I am at least certain, that Great Britain, and all those nations, would flourish more, did their sovereigns and ministers adopt such enlarged and benevolent sentiments towards each other."[1]

The interests of the native country were the deciding factor in determining policy both under free trade and under mercantilism. The differences between the two lay in another direction.

It is only when we come to the question of what constitutes the national interest that we arrive at something concrete. Most discussions on nationalism and national problems are obscured through the lack of theoretical clarity on this point.

In attempting an analysis of mercantilism on these lines, it must be admitted at the outset that the economic eminence of their respective countries was emphasized by English and French writers, often in the most exaggerated and grandiloquent manner. Nevertheless it appears to me that the expressions "nationalism" and "national considerations" are inaptly foisted on mercantilism. There is something in the expression "nationalism" which, in my opinion, is later than mercantilism. Nationalism is a child of 18th and 19th-century romanticists, an outcome of the belief in the predetermined natural peculiarities and individual destiny of nations. Such ideas were almost entirely alien to peoples of the 16th and 17th centuries. The collective entity to them was not a nation unified by common race, speech, and customs: the only decisive factor for them was *the state*. In most cases the state concerned included many varied national elements, and it was considered possible to deal tolerantly with these national and linguistic dissimilarities so long as they did not conflict with the interests of the state. Extremely typical of this are the Swedish parliamentary 17th-century records of the deliberations of the House of Nobles, the first of the four Estates constituting the Swedish Parliament until 1866. It follows from these records that speeches were made in Parliament both in German and Dutch;

---

[1] Hume, *Essays Moral, Political and Literary*, Part 2, No. 6: Of the Jealousy of Trade (ed. T. H. Green and T. H. Grose, Lond., 1898, I 348). The italics are mine.

and the secretaries of the House of Nobles showed no hesitation in reproducing them in the language in which they were made. To bring out the contrast, we may imagine how a modern representative assembly would react if a member used any other but the native tongue and if such speeches were recorded in the minutes. Mercantilism was the exponent of the prevailing conception of the relationship between the state and nation in the period before the advent of romanticism. It was the state and not the nation which absorbed its attention.

To put the case in this manner at once throws more light on the attitude of mercantilism to organized society. The state must have *one* outstanding interest, an interest which is the basis for all its other activities. What distinguishes the state from all other social institutions is the fact that, by its very nature, it is a compulsory corporation or, at least in the last instance, has the final word on the exercise of force in society; it has the "authority of authorities" (*Kompetenz-kompetenz*), to borrow the terminology of that eminent German constitutional jurist, Jellinek. *Power* must therefore be the first interest of the state, which it cannot resign without denying its own existence. *La raison d'état*—the history of which since Machiavelli, its modern starting-point, has been described by Friedrich Meinecke in his book *Die Idee der Staatsräson in der neueren Geschichte* (1924)—is simply the claim of the state that regard for its power must, if necessary, precede all other considerations.

Mercantilism would similarly have had all economic activity subservient to the state's interest in power. Here we have a parallel to the ideas put forward in the first part: mercantilist efforts at unification endeavour to secure the state's power *internally* against particularist institutions, and the question here is the *external* power of the state in relation to other states.

Keeping in mind that the state cannot dispense with its external power if there is no guaranteed super-state juridical system, it is only natural that all social forces must when necessary either serve or give precedence to the interests of the state. That economic activity should be made subservient to it is thus not peculiar to that period. Consequently we have not yet penetrated to the root of the problem, to the actual peculiarities of mercantilism.

It is true that several mercantilists considered it an exclusive feature of their times that interest in power should be applied to the economic sphere. Cunningham was thus able to find support in contemporary statements when he represented mercantilism as an economic system of power *par préférence*. Bacon, in his history of Henry VII, has a very characteristic passage on this point (1621/22): "The King also, having care to make his realm potent, as well by sea as by land, for the better maintenance of the navy, ordained, 'That wines and woads from the parts of Gascoign and Languedoc, should not be brought but in English bottoms,' bowing the ancient policy of this estate, from consideration of plenty to consideration of power."

But still it may be asserted that, on this point, mercantilism was not fundamentally different from the policy which was later to supersede it. This is particularly clear in the remarks of Adam Smith. He showed himself in profound agreement with measures precisely in the sphere of the policy of power, which, in view of his general attitude, would not on other grounds have met with his approval. Best known is his judgment on the Navigation Acts. He not only gave these laws his explicit approbation, but even called them "perhaps the wisest of all the commercial regulations of England", indeed, giving as a reason his clear opinion that "defence is of much more importance than opulence". In spite of the fact that many clauses in the Acts were actuated by purely national feelings, they appeared to him to be "as wise as if they had been dictated by the profoundest wisdom". Nor did Adam Smith confine himself to this, which he considered the most important instance. In another connection he writes: "If any particular manufacture was necessary, indeed, for the defence of the society, it might not always be prudent to depend upon our neighbours for the supply; and if such manufacture could not otherwise be supported at home, it might not be unreasonable that all the other branches of industry should be taxed in order to support it." No one could have made it clearer that economic activity ought to be subordinated to the state's striving for external power.[2]

*The analysis must therefore be carried a stage further if we are to arrive at any understanding of the features peculiar to mercantilism in its attitude towards the state's striving for power. The most vital aspect of the problem is whether power is conceived as an *end in itself*, or only as a means for gaining something else, such as the well-being of the nation in this world or its everlasting salvation in the next.

[2] Bacon, *The History of the Reign of King Henry the Seventh* (*Works*, Lond. 1803, V 63).—Adam Smith, *Wealth of Nations*, Book 4, chaps. 3 & 5 (ed. Cannan, I 427 ff., II 23); similarly his attitude to bounties on fisheries, which had his qualified approval on principle, although he did not like the manner in which they were applied in practice.
* See below II 359-63, *Addendum* §1.

Even though there is not always a clear line of demarcation between these two conceptions, there can be no doubt that an essential distinction is discernible here, a distinction which had its reactions on all aspects of the problem. Adam Smith's argument was undoubtedly that the endeavours towards opulence must make such sacrifices as security demanded. For him, power was certainly only a means to the end, as can be seen clearly enough from the title of his book, and from the rare and almost insignificant exceptions to the general rule which he permits for the sake of defence. Mercantilists usually believed the reverse, and mercantilism as a system of power was thus primarily a system for forcing economic policy into the service of power as an end in itself. To some extent means and ends changed places.

With that epigrammatic touch of which he was so fond, Colbert expressed the principles of his policy in a letter to his cousin, the Intendant at the naval base of Rochefort (1666). "Trade," he wrote, "is the source of [public] finance and [public] finance is the vital nerve of war." In this passing remark, Colbert indicates clearly the relationship between means and ends. The end was war, and essential to its purpose was a healthy state of finance, which in turn presupposed an active and vital economic system. This statement of opinion really expressed Colbert's fundamental outlook, as may be seen in the whole of his work, which was most emphatically directed to subjecting economic forces to Louis XIV's military policy. The well-known antagonism between Colbert and Louvois did not arise on the question of whether the development of external power should be the state's highest ambition, but on how far the financial resources for developing this power should be frittered away in premature military adventures instead of being allowed to mature. Colbert's memorandum of advice to Louis XIV of the year 1664, even though not so lucid as his above observation, is another illustration of his attitude. He explained that it was essential to the lofty ambitions which the king set himself "to limit all the industrial activity of Your subjects, as far as possible, to such professions as may be of use in furthering these great aims, that is to agriculture, trade (les marchandises, i.e., trade and manufacture), war at sea and on land". Everything else ought to disappear. The utterances upon the measures to be taken in actual contingencies reveal this attitude even more clearly than do the general statements. Into these, too, Colbert crams considerable information.

Colbert was thoroughly convinced that the eagerness of the Dutch to fetch goods from the countries of origin and "to acquire

the trade of the whole world into their own hands . . . and
to rob other nations of the same" had political motives. On the
question of whether France should choose England or Holland
for an ally, Colbert went on to say: "Upon this they base the
principal doctrine of their government, knowing full well that
if they but have the mastery of trade, their powers will continually wax on land and sea and will make them so mighty
that they will be able to set up as arbiters of peace and war in
Europe and set bounds at their pleasure to the justice and all the
plans of princes." Two years later Colbert wrote to the French
ambassador in The Hague: "It is certain that their whole power
has hitherto consisted in trade; if we could manage their trade,
they might find it more difficult in the future to carry out their
preparations for war than they have hitherto done."

This conception of Dutch progress and its reasons and motives
was naturally dependent on Colbert's views of France's own
policy. They are best expressed in a memorandum on the finances
of the country prepared for the king in 1670. The following
extract illustrates his view on the relationship between economic
matters and questions of policy: "It seems as if Your Majesty,
having taken in hand the administration of your finances, has
undertaken a monetary war against all European states. Your
Majesty has already conquered Spain, Italy, Germany, England,
and several other countries, and has forced them into great
misery and poverty. At their expense Your Majesty has waxed
rich and so acquired the means of carrying out the many great
works Your Majesty has undertaken and still daily undertakes.
There remains only Holland, which still struggles with all its
great power. . . . Your Majesty has founded companies which
attack them (the Dutch) everywhere like armies. The manufactures, the shipping canal between the seas, and so many other
new establishments which Your Majesty sets up are so many
reserve corps which Your Majesty creates from nothing in order
that they may fulfil their duty in this war. . . . This war, which
must be waged with might and main, and in which the most
powerful republic since the Roman Empire is the price of victory,
cannot cease so soon, or rather it must engage Your Majesty's
chief attention during the whole of Your life." Ending the
memorandum with a budget estimate, Colbert was so obsessed
with the importance of his commercial creations that he lowered
the claim for direct military needs by a total of eleven million
livres, while he increased the amount for trading companies by one
million—for it was they, in reality, which in Colbert's mind

constituted the armies in the most important war. Even after the military war with the Netherlands in 1679, he wrote to one of his intendants that Marseilles was "a city which must be employed in a constant trading war against all foreign commercial cities."[3]*

It may perhaps be thought that all this proves very little, in so far as the minister of finance of the most ambitious monarch of the time simply had to make a virtue of necessity, and that his remarks cannot therefore be considered a reliable index of the prevalent opinion of the age, or indeed of his own personal opinion. It is certainly true that no statesman of the time was so hard pressed to create means for military and other political expenditure as Colbert, and it is no exaggeration to say that the enormous effort which the situation required of him shortened his life. But the examples quoted are evidence that his outlook was deep-rooted; and, moreover, it was shared by many others who, unlike him, were not weighed down by a political burden of the same magnitude and could therefore express their opinions with greater freedom. A few examples will illustrate the point.

First it is clear that such tendencies as those of Colbert must have produced similar tendencies in other places even where they had not hitherto existed. In a memorandum on a commission on trade taken from the papers of Lord Shaftesbury, the most highly gifted among contemporary English statesmen, we read "that which makes the Consideration of Trade of far greater import now than ever is that the Interest of Commerce, though formerly neglected, is of late years Become an Express Affair of State as well with the French as with the Hollander and Swede. And because it is understood by latter experience to be more Conducing towards an universal Monarchy (either for the gaining or preventing of it) then either an Army or Territory, though never so great, of which Instances out of several kingdoms might easily be Produced, In regard It is Trade and Commerce alone that draweth store of wealth along with it and its Potency at sea By shipping which is not otherwise to be had." That is Colbert's own opinion expressed from the other side. Significant, too, is a statement from the same period (1668) of the Duke of York, later James II, quoted by Samuel Pepys, in whose presence it was made. The discussion turned on Turenne's prospects, after he had turned Catholic, of becoming more powerful than Colbert, "the latter to promote trade and the sea, which, says the Duke of York, is that that we have most cause to fear". Thus Turenne's military successes were obviously considered less

[3] *Lettres de Colbert* III : I 37, VI 3, 264, II 610, VII 250-4, II 706 resp.
* See below II 363-4, *Addendum* §2.

important by comparison. A very similar remark is ascribed to Napoleon, the most important representative of the economic policy of power. He is said to have remarked to Oberkampf, the founder of the French cotton industry, during the time of the Continental System: "We both are fighting the English, but yours is the better war."[4]*

It is interesting, however, to consider the customary explanation of the unbroken interest in economic advantage shown during the mercantilist era. Viner's essay, quoted above, provides a battery of quotations in which power, commerce and plenty make up the combined aim for economic activity. I find this evidence convincing. Yet, one must not neglect the many instances in which the welfare of subjects has been seen as the indispensable basis for the power of the state, statements maintaining the opposite causal relationship being rare. Bacon's reasoning in this matter is considered in Addendum §1, and other expressions, less noteworthy though perhaps more representative, may be added here. Several observations from the mid-16th century typify this attitude, for instance, the execrable but representative poem by Sir William Forrest entitled *Pleasaunt Poesye of Princelie Practise*:

> "That Kynge (bee sure) can neauer bee poore;
> wheare as his Commons lyuethe welthelye."

The *Discourse of the Common Weal of this Realm of England*, ascribed to John Hales, contains one section entitled "How the King can not have treasure when his subjects have none". In precisely the same way the French tailor-statesman Barthélemy de Laffemas, the commercial adviser of Henry IV, wrote in 1601: "A king is never rich when his subjects are poor."

In the German cameralist literature, this point of view was simply overwhelming. Indeed the task of the cameralists consisted in filling the "chamber" of the prince, in other words, they were to ensure that the sources of his income did not run dry. Even in a comparatively modern representative of this huge band, Wilhelm von Schrötter (Schröder), who was strongly influenced by western Europe, this attitude is to be found in its pure form. In his work *Fürstliche Schatz- und Rent-Cammer* (1686) he wrote: "Therefore must a prince first procure for his subjects

---

[4] Shaftesbury: Quot. Beer, *The Old Colonial System 1660–1754* (N.Y. 1912) I: 1 242 f.—Duke of York: Pepys, *Diary*, 20 December 1668 (ed. H. B. Wheatley, Lond. 1924, VIII 184).—Napoleon: Levasseur, *Histoire des classes ouvrières et de l'industrie en France de 1789 à 1870* I (Paris 1903) 421.

* See below II 364, *Addendum* §3.

a good livelihood if he will take anything from them." The second was the reason for the first. According to Schrötter a special council, "highest and absolute" (*summum et absolutum*), should be created independent of all others to deal with the prince's revenues. The means of filling the state treasury, which was the end, consisted in the orthodox method of seeking revenue in the riches of the subject and a great circulation of money or capital. A later publisher of von Schrötter placed as a motto on the title-page of the book the picture of a sheep-shearing, and added the following verse, which though it has wrongly been ascribed to Schrötter himself, expresses his point of view by no means inadequately:

> Useth the wise prince thus his flock,
> Well will they live, and wool shall he stock.
> But let him strip its fell forthwith,
> No future profit doth it give.[5]

This drastic outlook—comparing a nation to a flock of sheep which is shorn for the benefit of the prince—might appear characteristic of the adviser of a German absolutist prince; but as a matter of fact, it is not at all foreign to the mercantilist doctrines of western European countries, and von Schrötter had a forerunner in Thomas Mun (*England's Treasure by Forraign Trade*, written about 1628, published 1664). He said: "For if he [the Prince] should mass up more money than is gained by the over-balance of his foreign trade, he shall not *Fleece*, but *Flea* his Subjects, and so with their ruin overthrow himself for want of future shearing."[6]

The fact that much which was basic in mercantilist doctrine was closely related to the concept of power is important;

[5] Wenn eines klugen Fürsten Herden
Auf diesem Fuss genützet werden,
So können sie recht glücklich leben
Und dem Regenten Wolle geben.
Doch wer sogleich das Fell abzieht,
Bringt sich um künftigen Profit.

[6] Forrest, reprinted (as an extract), *England in the Reign of King Henry the Eighth* I (ed. S. J. Herrtage, Early English Text Soc., Extra Ser. XXXII, Lond. 1878) lxxxix.—*Discourse of the Common Weal* (ed. Lamond) 35.— B. de Laffemas, *Les discours d'une liberté générale et vie heureuse pour le bien du peuple* (Paris 1601) 15.—[von Schrötter], *Fürstliche Schatz- und Rent-Cammer* Preface § 11, ch. 2 § 12, ch. 4 § 9, ch. 50 § 2 (1st ed. Lpz. 1686, Preface 22, text 23, 47, 245 *et passim*.)—Poem: quot. (as though written by von Schrötter himself): A. Oncken, *Geschichte der Nationalökonomie* I (Lpz. 1902) 231.—Mun, *England's Treasure by Forraign Trade* chap. 18 (ed. W. J. Ashley, N.Y. 1895, 92 f.).

but insofar as economic welfare was a dominant factor in mercantilist thinking, it would have been quite consistent to strive for as high an absolute standard of living as possible for the population of a country. However, there was a notion prevalent even among later mercantilists, that the goal could be achieved just as well, if not better, by weakening the economic power of other countries instead of strengthening one's own. If wealth is considered as an aim, this is the height of absurdity, but from the point of view of political power it is quite logical. If power means increase in the strength of one country as against that of others, absolute economic progress loses its value. Hume's argument in his essay on *Jealousy of Trade* of 1752 therefore misses the point completely, in so far as it purports to be a criticism of an outlook motivated by ideas of pure political power. That such an outlook should have appeared to Hume the acme of foolishness is quite another matter. To mercantilists it did not appear so.

Many examples can be given of how mercantilists regarded the economic weakening of other countries. In one of his essays, Bacon quite logically advised (1625) "that princes do keep due sentinel that none of their neighbours do overgrow so, by increase of territory, by embracing of trade, by approaches, or the like, as they become more able to annoy them than they were". The notion that well-being consists of a relationship between the condition of different countries has never, to my knowledge, been expressed so clearly as by one of the typical later German mercantilists or cameralists, P. W. von Hörnigk, Becher's brother-in-law, in his book entitled *Oesterreich über alles, Wann es nur will* (1684). "Whether a nation," he said, "be to-day mighty and rich or not depends not on the abundance or scarcity of its powers or riches, but principally on whether its neighbours possess more or less than it. For power and riches have become a *relative* matter, dependent on being weaker and poorer than others." This observation, stating explicitly that riches do not make a country rich, makes Hörnigk, it may almost be said, the Tertullian of mercantilism.

It is interesting to note how this train of thought recurs among the subtle, theoretical English mercantilists of the end of the 17th century. For them the stock of money was the important point. On the question of when a nation could rest from its perpetual striving after a favourable balance of trade, Sir William Petty makes the reply (in *Verbum Sapienti*, written in 1665 and published in 1691): "When we have certainly more Money than any of our Neighbour States, (though never so little,) both in Arithmetical and Geometrical proportion, (i.e.) when we have more years provision aforehand, and more present effects." Roger Coke, one of the most independent of the English mercantilists, uses almost the same words (1675): "And therefore if our Treasure were more than our Neighbouring Nations, I did not care whether we had one-fifth part of the Treasure we now have."

The most characteristic observation, however, originates with the most famous of them all, no less a person than John Locke. He discussed (1691) not only the amount of money or precious metal necessary for a country, but also how that amount was to be created. "Nor indeed, things rightly considered, do Gold and Silver drawn out of the Mine equally Enrich, with what is got by Trade. He that would make the lighter Scale preponderate to the opposite, will not so soon do it, by adding encrease of new Weight to the emptier, as if he took out of the heavier what he adds to the lighter, for then half so much will do it. Riches do not consist in having more Gold and Silver, but in having more in proportion, than the rest of the World, or than our Neighbours, whereby we are enabled to procure to ourselves a greater Plenty of the Conveniences of Life than comes within the reach of Neighbouring Kingdoms and States, who sharing the Gold and Silver of the World in less proportion, want the means of Plenty and Power, and so are Poorer." It might be thought that it would have been tempting to an exponent of the quantity theory of money, such as Locke was to base his reasoning on the consideration that the purchasing power of the precious metals was lowered by increased production, but not if they were imported only from other countries. This is, however, not the case; throughout he considered the advantage to consist in the relative superiority over neighbouring countries.[7]*

Static conceptions

The whole of this mercantilist outlook provides one reason for the commercial wars, carried on almost without interruption from the end of the 17th century down to 1815. In the last instance,

---

[7] Bacon, *Essays or Covnsels Civill and Morall*, No. 19, "Of Empire," in the 1625 ed. (ed. W. A. Wright, Lond. 1920, 77).—[Hörnigk] ch. 7 (1723 Regensburg ed., 20).—Petty, *Verbum Sapienti* ch. 10 (*Econ. Writings*, ed. C. H. Hull, I 119). The geometrical and arithmetical proportions are an idea originating in Aristotle, see A. Nielsen, *Die Entstehung der deutschen Kameralwissenschaft im 17. Jh.* (Jena 1911) 48 *et passim*.—Coke, *Treatise III: England's Improvements* 44 f.—Locke, *Some Considerations of the Consequences of the Lowering of Interest, etc.* (in Several Papers relating to Money, Interest, and Trade, etc., Lond. 1696, 15).—Cp., however, 238 ff. below.

* See below II 364-5, *Addendum* §4.

the ideas were based on a *static* conception of economic life: the view that there was a fixed quantity of economic resources in the world, which could be increased in one country only at the expense of another. Any attempt at economic advance by one's own efforts in one country must therefore have appeared pointless, unless it consisted in robbing other countries of part of their possessions. Scarcely any other element in mercantilist philosophy contributed more to the shaping of economic policy, and even of foreign policy as a whole.

It is true that some writers, foremost amongst them Werner Sombart,[8] have not only failed to realize this, but have even regarded mercantilism as dominated by a dynamic view of society, by way of contrast with the *laissez-faire* doctrine, which is regarded as static in its outlook. To a large extent, these opposing interpretations are due to a confusion between the use of the terms static and dynamic, as applied to methods of study on the one hand, and to the nature of social life on the other. This confusion has led to serious misunderstandings and should therefore be dispelled.

In speaking of the static attitude of *laissez-faire*, what one undoubtedly has in mind is the fact that classical economic theory is static, in the sense that it deals with the stages of economic equilibria, without having discovered the laws of transition from one stage to another. In this respect it resembles neo-classical theory as well, though not, of course, the modern theories of "dynamic" equilibrium. As to its view of the factors tending towards economic change, it is also appropriate to point out that *laissez-faire* theory had too little regard for what could be effected by investing, so to speak, capital in human beings, that is, by increasing human efficiency in industry, through cutting down the hours of labour and improving the material and non-material conditions of life.

But quite irrespective of this, the *laissez-faire* doctrine was based upon a belief in human progress to an almost exaggerated degree. It was consequently dynamic to the core, in the sense that it attached the greatest possible importance to the factors working for what was considered as economic progress. Adam Smith led the way with the third book of his famous work, entitled *Of the different Progress of Opulence in different Nations*. He there sought to

---

[8] Sombart, *Der moderne Kapitalismus*, 3rd ed. II (Lpz. 1919) 918.—Like so much else that has been written in German literature on classical theory, this conception originates in List's very suggestive but also very perverse exposition of the "school" in *Das nationale System der Politischen Ökonomie* (1840).

elucidate the reasons for the obstruction or facilitation of economic progress. In other words, he set himself a purely dynamic problem. Two quotations should illustrate the point: "A revolution of the greatest importance to the public happiness, was in this manner brought about by two different orders of people, who had not the least intention to serve the public. To gratify the most childish vanity was the sole motive of the great proprietors. The merchants and artificers, much less ridiculous, acted merely from a view to their own interest, and in pursuit of their own pedlar principle of turning a penny wherever a penny was to be got. Neither of them had either knowledge or foresight of that great revolution which the folly of the one, and the industry of the other, was gradually bringing about." "The capital, however, that is acquired to any country by commerce and manufacture, is all a very precarious and uncertain possession, till some part of it has been secured and realized in the cultivation and improvement of its lands."[9]

It would, in fact, have been remarkable if the 18th century, with its unshakable belief in the perfectibility of man, had overlooked economic progress; and nothing could be farther from the truth. It is precisely this line of thought that was followed by the active and influential economists of the 19th century, and they are largely responsible for the naïve optimism with regard to progress which has rightly been considered as typical also of the last century. This was in strictest contrast to a static conception of economic life.

As to mercantilism, on the other hand, it is true to say that it was hardly concerned with economic equilibria, and that it was definitely bent on discovering the methods of deriving as much profit as possible for the individual country. Further it is true that this was a great change from the medieval ideal of a suitable subsistence, which in practice presupposed no change in the social *status quo* of class and individual. *Within* the state, mercantilism consequently pursued thoroughgoing dynamic ends. But the important thing is that this was bound up with a static conception of the total economic resources in the world; for this it was that created that fundamental disharmony which sustained the endless commercial wars. Both elements together implied that the position of a particular country could change and was capable of progress, but that this could only happen through acquisitions from other countries. This was the tragedy

[9] Adam Smith, *Wealth of Nations*, Book 3; the passages quoted are to be found in ch. 4 (ed. Cannan I 389f., 393), but the whole section should be read.

of mercantilism. Both the Middle Ages with their universal static ideal and *laissez-faire* with its universal dynamic ideal avoided this consequence. Without grasping this it is impossible to understand mercantilism either in theory or practice.

It is easy to find confirmation of this mercantilist conception of the static nature of economic life. One of the earliest observations along these lines is to be found in Montaigne's famous *Essays* (1580) which, even then, were widely read: "The profit of one man," he said, "is the damage of another . . . no man profiteth but by the loss of others." This is then proved by showing that owing to changes in supply and demand, the one only profits at the expense of the other. It was probably with this in mind that Montchrétien, the author of the well-known, rather than distinguished, *Traicté de l'Oeconomie politiqve*, stated a few decades later (1615): "It is said that no one ever loses without another gaining. This is true and is borne out in the realm of commerce more than anywhere else." And again, ten years later Bacon wrote: "It is likewise to be remembered that, forasmuch as the increase of any Estate must be upon the Foreigner, (for whatsoever is somewhere gotten is somewhere lost), there be but three Things which one Nation selleth unto another."[10]

No one has produced so polished an exposition of the static conception of economic life as Colbert. He, moreover, applied the conception in practice in a most ominous manner. His observations therefore merit fuller consideration.

His most important remarks are to be found in a paper of 1669 in which he discusses the question of the choice of France between an English or a Dutch alliance. A quotation from this memorandum has already been given above. The argument is set out in very logical sequence and the most typical passages are the following: "From all our knowledge and after scrupulous investigation it may be asserted without doubt that the trade of all Europe is carried on in about 20,000 ships of all sizes. . . . It is easy to see that this number cannot be increased so long as the population in all countries and consumption are always equal. . . . This is the position therefore in which European trade has hitherto found itself and still finds itself at present. . . . After setting out this information, which is reliable, we must concentrate on the first fundamental point that by this alliance England seeks primarily to increase her trade. Such increase can

[10] Montaigne, *Essais* Book I, ch. 22 (ed. F. Strowski, Bordeaux 1906, I 135).— Montchrétien, *Traicté de l'Oeconomie politiqve* (1st ed. Rouen 1615, [II] 38).— Bacon, *Essays* No. 15, "Of Seditions and Troubles" (ed. Wright, 59).

only take place by providing more employment for her subjects' ships and raising their number. This cannot come about except either through the discovery of new, hitherto unknown, trade or through the decrease in the number of ships of one of the other nations. The discovery of new trade is very uncertain and an argument based on the assumption of such an accident is ruled out; or rather it may be said that an accident of this kind will definitely not occur. And even if it did occur, it would not bring about new consumption of necessaries or luxuries. At the most it would make it easier for one nation rather than for another to attract these goods which are already consumed and which constitute a part of the consumption of all Europe. The intended increase of English trade must therefore occur through the decrease in the number of vessels of one of the other nations. . . . And so we necessarily come to the conclusion that England cannot increase the scope of employment for the ships of her subjects or increase their number other than by a diminution of those of the Dutch." This was taken as proved and it followed ominously and logically that the trade war must continue. "It must be added that trade causes perpetual strife both in time of war and in time of peace between all the nations of Europe to decide which of them shall have the greatest share."

Writing on public finance in the following year, Colbert adapted the same argument to the precious metals as he had employed in 1669 for commercial shipping. He identified himself with the notion which we have already observed in other mercantilists " . . . as there is only a fixed quantity of silver circulating in the whole of Europe, which is increased from time to time by import from the West Indies, it may certainly be proved that there is no more than 150 million *livres* of silver circulating among the public. It is not possible to increase (the stock of one country) by 20, 30, or 50 million without at the same time taking the same quantity from neighbouring states. Thus arises this two-fold increase (*élévation*), which has been so clearly discernible for several years past: on the one hand the power and greatness of Your Majesty increases, on the other that of your enemies and ill-wishers falls." Locke and Colbert, the Minister of an absolutist monarch and the founder of the philosophy of the constitutional state, thus ágreed implicitly: it was in fact a matter of recognized mercantilist doctrine.[11]

---

[11] *Lettres de Colbert* VI 264 ff., VII 239 resp.—We must add, however, that at least *one* English author rejected this static conception. The author was Roger Coke, who, in spite of his bizarre manner of writing, looked further

The foundation for the power theory to be found in mercantilist doctrine ought thus to have been made clear.

Variations

The above should not be understood to mean that all mercantilist statesmen and writers were dominated by the policy of power with the same extreme one-sidedness as was Colbert in most cases. In the introduction to this work it has already been shown that such an assumption distorts the facts.

The relation between political and military power and economic power was often reversed, in contrast with the view just illustrated. Where that was so the striving towards political power was considered a means for mastering the riches of the whole world. Such was particularly the case in the older colonial policy with its eternal hunt for precious metals and its unscrupulous employment of military power, standing as it did half-way between piracy and peaceful trade.

Many authors pass imperceptibly from one view to the other. The existence of the second of the two is evidenced sufficiently by the fact that so pronounced an advocate of the policy of power as Richelieu expounds this view-point clearly in his *Political Testament*. One section bears the title "Concerning trade as dependent upon dominion over the seas". He ends, as usual, with the reference to the Dutch, but unlike Colbert, to their wealth, not their power. "The wealth of the Dutch . . . is an example and an irrefutable proof of the value of trade."[12]

Perhaps even more common was the placing of political power and specifically economic aims side by side, striving for the latter as ends *per se*, but simultaneously making them serve the ends of power. It is this approach that Viner has documented so richly.

---

ahead than the majority of his contemporaries. He has not yet received the attention which he deserves. Coke said, "that saying That *there is but such a Trade in the world*, is only true by accident, not necessarily; for many thousands of people might increase Trade in the world if they had means, which being denied, they cannot do" (*Treatise* III 20, italics in the original). If the assertions that mercantilism had an underlying dynamic idea were based on such utterances as these, they might have been correct. Such ideas, however, pave the way precisely to *laissez-faire*.

[12] Richelieu, *Testament politique*, ch. 9 sec. 6 (quotn. 4th ed., Amst. 1691, II 133).—In the introduction by G. Hanotaux to another writing of Richelieu, published by him, he ascribes to the political testament a very high degree of authenticity. A statement in an immediately preceding section in the same chapter, with approximately the same idea as the statement quoted, agrees almost literally with a signed paper of Richelieu's (*Maximes d'état et fragments politiques du Card. de R., Extr. d. documents inédits*, Paris 1830, xviii). The same view of the *Testament* is shared by other French historians.

A distinguished representative of this eclectic point of view, as it were, was Sir Josiah Child. In rebutting the attacks on the Navigation Acts, he wrote (his own italics): " . . . I cannot deny but that this may be true, if the present profit of the generality be barely and singly considered; but this Kingdom being an Island, the defence whereof hath always been our Shipping and Sea-men, it seems to me *absolutely necessary that Profit and Power ought jointly to be considered.*" Similarly, though with rather stronger emphasis on the idea of power, an anonymous pamphleteer wrote a few years later (1672): "The undoubted Interest of England is Trade, since it is that alone which can make us either *Rich* or *Safe*; for without a powerful Navy, we should be a Prey to our Neighbours, and without Trade, we could neither have Sea-Men nor Ships." Likewise, Charles Davenant, at the turn of the following century, introduced power as an item among a number of more obvious elements in the national wealth: "what tends to make a people safe at Home, and considerable Abroad, as do Fleets and Naval Stores." When he defended the import of Indian textiles by the East India Company, his reason for sacrificing the considerations of sale of English goods and employment of the people was—at least if he is to be taken literally— the necessity of foreign trade for purposes of political power. "England could subsist," he wrote, "and the Poor perhaps would have fuller Employment, if Foreign Trade were quite laid aside; but this would ill Consist with our being great at Sea, upon which (under the present Posture of Affairs in Europe) all our Safety does certainly depend."[13]

In its direct, explicit form the policy of power was certainly cast for widely varying roles by the sundry authors and men of affairs. It was hardly to be expected, as Viner has correctly pointed out, that the merchants who wrote most of the mercantilist pamphlets would be chiefly interested in the power of the state. It was almost inevitable that their prime interests should be in commerce, and of course, in the advantages they might expect from the various measures. For statesmen, and in particular one such as Colbert, it was just as natural that considerations of power should take precedence over all others. Finally, it might also have been expected that the leaders of absolute states would have been more

---

[13] Child, *New Discourse of Trade*, ch. 4 (Lond. ed. of 1698, 114 f.).—Letter to Sir Thomas Osborne (1672); quot. Beer, *Old Colonial System* I 16.—Davenant, *Discourses on the Publick Revenues etc.* (Lond. 1698) II 60; *An Essay on the East India Trade* (1697, repr. with separate pagination as an appendix to the previous, 33).

strongly influenced by this viewpoint than those of countries like England or the Netherlands where merchants exerted a dominant influence on economic policy. Thus although a monistic interpretation might be misleading, we must not be too sceptical about this approach since many manifestations of mercantilist policy were directly inimical to commerce: all manner of obstructions were put in the way of imports, and thus indirectly in the way of exports. These obstacles nevertheless received the approbation of the authors of tracts and pamphlets on commercial policy, despite the fact that the measures actually opposed their interests. This particular case offers an example of the general truth that a doctrine may be ideologically or theoretically determined and thus accepted in principle even by persons whose interests are incompatible with it. Quite consistent with this observation is the claim that the policy of power is of greatest interest when seen in the light of mercantilist thought in general.

A survey of the measures of a practical nature which were instituted to serve the ends of the policy of power will serve to make this discussion more realistic. These measures were the diametric opposite of those which came later; even the Navigation Acts which Adam Smith had defended were finally destined to disappear. The following chapter discusses the methods used to facilitate the carrying out of the policy of power.

METHODS OF THE POLICY OF POWER

Two methods

In the practical application of the principles of the policy of power, mercantilism followed two different methods; the first consisted in deflecting economic activity directly towards the particular ends demanded by political, and more especially military, power; the second in creating a kind of reservoir of economic resources generally, from which the policy of power could draw what it required. The significance of this important distinction is revealed when analysed theoretically from the economic point of view.

The direct use made of the policy of power was deliberately to influence the supply and the accumulation of stores of goods in the desired direction and to cause corresponding changes in prices. The import of goods necessary for war was directly ordered or encouraged by premiums, while their export was forbidden or burdened with dues. In this way the country's stock of these commodities was increased. By similar, though somewhat more complicated, regulations, the number of ships or sailors, the rural population or the total population, could be increased. This was the first method. If the second method were adopted, the total national income, not the supply of particular goods or services, was taken as a starting-point. It was then considered that taxation would be the state's weapon for accumulating the particular means required, i.e. for exerting an effective demand for such goods and services as were needed for defence or for the policy of power in general, and also that this demand would be sufficient for the purpose. If the problem was tackled in this second way, considerations of power became a motive for stimulating the general economic prosperity of the country, for this was considered the best guarantee for ensuring a powerful state. Money and the precious metals had a peculiar role to play under either of the two methods. The attempt was made by their means to serve both the direct political ends of state power and even more the indirect ends, for they were considered necessary for fostering general economic prosperity.

Where the striving after power assumed the second form, it was bound up with general economic policy in quite a different way from the first. The ever-growing importance of general commercial considerations in public discussion and statesmanship must have made people more and more inclined to fall back upon general economic resources for political ends. The many-sided and varying demands imposed by the state in its striving after power also contributed to the decline of the direct, principally military method, for it became wellnigh impossible to prepare beforehand everything required by statecraft. Only in one sphere did the first method still assert its influence down to the beginning of the 18th century, and retain its formal position till even much later. This referred to one of the foremost items of the policy of power. It seems appropriate to describe first this earlier type of state policy of power.

Defence on land

For reasons into which we need enter no further, this type was to be found mainly in England, not only in such matters as were peculiar to a maritime and colonial power, but also in others. A beginning had already been made before the end of the Middle Ages in the province of land defence. During Edward IV's reign, endeavours were made to compel a better supply of wood for bows and arrows. All merchants importing goods from Venice or any other place which hitherto had exported bow staves were required to bring four such staves with them for every ton of goods (1472). A decade later (1483/84) the same obligation was imposed in the import of wine. This policy, moreover, lasted longer than might be assumed, in fact at least a century, for even in the 1570's the Hanseatic merchants complained that this obligation, in their opinion, entailed costs out of proportion to the value of the goods. Sir Thomas Gresham, Elizabeth's right hand in all continental affairs, wrote triumphantly in 1562 to William Cecil (later Lord Burghley) regarding his own deliveries of saltpetre and bow staves, "it is a thing better than any treasure", which was, at the same time, a declaration that this kind of tangible preparation was better than money.[1]

Soon after, when changes in military technique relegated bows and arrows to the museum—Lord Burghley wrote towards the end of Elizabeth's reign, "the strength of the wars being altered from bows and arrows to ordnance"—a very similar policy was pursued with regard to the new armaments. Early in the 16th century the export of various copper alloys had been forbidden. The original statute was then renewed and extended in 1541/42, the reason given being that "All other Realms and

[1] Statutes: 12 Ed. IV c. 2; 1 Rich. III c. 11.—R. Ehrenberg, *Hamburg und England im Zeitalter der Königin Elisabeth* (Jena 1896) 133, 136.—Gresham's Letter: in Burgon, *Life of Sir Thomas Gresham* II 11.

countries be full of Artillery and munitions, and this Realm is like to lack". The Mines Royal arose in Elizabeth's reign as one of the first joint stock companies, founded principally with an eye to artillery requirements. This attitude was always maintained in later times, although the export prohibition appears to have become practically ineffective. A proclamation against the export of cannons occurred even as late as 1681.[2]

The saltpetre industry, as the basis for the manufacture of gunpowder, was later given most careful attention. Saltpetre was produced from the excrement of man, horses, and doves. The eagerness to secure this for military purposes occasioned many conflicts,[*] which played their part in the long struggle against the system of privileges under Elizabeth and the two early Stuarts (see Chapter VI in previous part). Both the production of saltpetre, and even more the supervision of "saltpetre mines", as they were somewhat euphemistically called, were granted to various individuals innumerable times in the period between Elizabeth's accession and the Puritan Revolution and occasionally even later—the "saltpetre men" as they were called—who were employed directly to investigate the saltpetre mines and thus made themselves even more than usually unpopular.

In spite of this unpopularity, the military requirements were so generally recognized that these privileges were to some extent given an exceptional position. During the struggles against patents in 1601 Lord Burghley's younger son, Robert Cecil, later Lord Salisbury, who was at the time Elizabeth's Secretary of State, frankly admitted that to meddle in these matters "generally troubleth the Subject", and he also informed the people that the queen would have the validity of these privileges legally investigated. But at the same time, he emphasized that the country had an insufficient supply of gunpowder. After several attempts to tax the extortions, which had little effect, James I promised in 1606 to abolish the patents; a promise which was presumably not seriously intended. When his last Parliament made the Statute of Monopolies in 1623/24 the basis of the system of patents and privileges, both saltpetre and gunpowder production, as well as artillery and munition works, were excepted from the prohibitions against monopoly. In the following

---

[2] Statutes: 21 Hen. VIII c. 10 (1529); 33 Hen. VIII c. 7 (1541/42); 2 & 3 Ed. VI c. 37 (1548).—Cecil's statement, etc.: Scott, *Joint Stock Companies to 1720* I 113 f.—Mines Royal and Artillery works: H. Hamilton, *The English Brass and Copper Industries to 1800* 25, 75 note 3, 276 *et passim*.—Export prohibitions on cannons: Holdsworth, *History of English Law* VI 305.

[*] See below II 365, *Addendum* §5.

year, however, Common Law judges ruled that anyone could produce saltpetre on his own property. This did not deter Charles I from issuing patents of monopoly and instituting a regulatory system. A proclamation issued shortly before his accession prohibited not only the export of the much-desired deposits but also that stables, dove-cots, privies, etc., be covered with stones, boards, chalk, sand, or earth so as to render more difficult their employment for saltpetre; and this ruling was maintained. The policy was continued during the following period although its administration was neither consistent nor forceful; in 1656 the "saltpetre men" were forbidden to trespass on private property. The preoccupation of the government with the problem of ensuring an adequate production of saltpetre survived the Puritan Revolution so that in 1689 prohibitions against the export of this article were drawn up, and new patents of monopoly for its production granted in 1691 and 1692. Whether the results were commensurate with these efforts may well be questioned. These regulations, however, are of interest in that they represented the most far-reaching attempt to serve general military ends by using the weapons of economic policy.[3]

Shipping

The method of the policy of power under consideration here achieved its greatest success in the sphere of shipping. In this aspect of its activity, too, England was by far the most important country, though it is true that the policy, centring around direct military requirements, was to be found in its most concentrated form in the Scandinavian countries at an earlier stage of development. The way in which it was applied there was to compel the building of private ships which could be adapted in time of war. Such were the so-called "mounted", or armed, merchantmen in Sweden and the defence ships in Denmark. It is obviously analogous to the English policy in the matter of supply of artillery on land. The ships which satisfied certain military demands were given customs reductions and these acted as

[3] Sources for the policy regarding saltpetre, etc. *i.a.*: early charters: in Price, *English Patents of Monopoly* 149 f., 157, 163.—Cecil's speech of 1601: in *Tudor Econ. Docs.* II 291.—James I's declaration: 1606: in *Journals of the House of Commons* I 317 f.—Statute of Monopolies (21 Jac. I c. 3) §10.—Proclamation of 1624: in Cunningham II[3] 291 note 2.—Proclamation of 1625: in *Foedera* (ed. Rymer) 1st ed. XVIII 23 ff., Hague ed. VIII : II 16 ff.—Other measures under Charles I: *Calendar of State Papers, Domestic 1634-35*, 387 f.— Charters: Scott II 471–74; *Select Charters of Trading Companies* (ed. Carr) 234–8; cf. lxxix ff.—See also: esp. Cunningham II[3] 60 f., 263; Holdsworth *op. cit.*[3] Lipson *Econ. Hist. of England* III (5th ed.) 358 f.

bounties on the building of such ships. In this way the country was meant to be better prepared for defence in case of naval warfare. These measures were first taken towards the beginning of the 17th century, in Sweden from 1617 onwards, and in Denmark some few years later. Sweden clung to the policy longer than any other country, in fact for a whole century, under the name of *helfrihet* (i.e. total freedom from customs duties, though in actual fact there was only a reduction of one-third). England also pursued the same policy, to some extent, but considerably later. It first introduced such regulations during the Restoration in 1662, and they became more prominent after the Revolution of 1688. At this period English shipping policy, with its underlying military motives, had already been fully developed and the idea of encouraging the use of armed merchantmen never played more than an insignificant part in England, for the obvious economic reason that she was the strongest naval power.[4]

English shipping policy, dictated by interests of defence, and to some extent also the policy of continental countries, was, however, one step removed from the kind of policy discussed so far, which was directly concerned with creating military supplies. For it sought support for its military aims in normal, private economic activity, such as was not directed by military ends, and so approximated somewhat to the *second* of the two methods of the policy of power, namely the one which sought the source of political power in a prosperous economic system. But it did not altogether coincide with the second method, for it was concerned not with the *general* stimulation of industry, but only with its encouragement along certain definite lines—shipping, ship-building, and fishing.

The practical embodiment of this programme were the measures which have become famous through the English Navigation Acts. These aimed at reserving the country's shipping, and particularly the long-distance shipping, to the native trading fleets. The next step was to place a premium on native ship-building by laying down that ships were to be built in the country. Furthermore, sailors of native stock were to be bred by means of appropriate regulations for the nationality of the crew and the ships' officers. This system was more or less common to all Europe. It occurred, for example, in Aragon as early as the 13th century, then it came to England towards the end of the 14th century. It was adopted by the Hansa in the 15th century,

[4] Heckscher, "Produktplakatet och dess förutsättningar" (*Historiska studier tillägnade Harald Hjärne*, Ups. 1908, 698–704).

and, at the end of the century by Castile, in the 17th century by
France and Denmark, and in the 1720's by Sweden through the
so-called *produktplakat*.[5] The policy may have been actuated by
different motives in the various countries at different times, but
its importance here is its connection with the mastery of the seas,
wherein England led the world.

The preambles to English Acts of Parliament are proverbially
misleading as expressions of the real motives of policy. But in this
case there can be no doubt of their authenticity; for the motives
given therein recurred in all public and private utterances of the
century, wherever the question of English shipping was brought
up. The language used was so uniform and almost stereotyped
that it sounds very much like an ever-recurring refrain, whether
the measures in question were the long-distance sea trade and the
voyages of discovery, the trading companies, colonial trade, shipbuilding, fishing, supply of naval stores, training of sailors, or
anything which had even a remote connection with naval power.
It is true that this should by no means be taken as though more
commercial considerations were entirely wanting. They were
usually mentioned together with the others; only the interest in
power was never allowed to wane.

It may be enough to give the following examples chosen from
an overwhelming number, especially as few facts in English
economic history are better known, as a result chiefly of the
writings of Cunningham.

Even the earliest English Navigation Act, that of 1381, contained
a reference to the decay of the navy and the necessity of employing the usual means for assisting it. The same idea recurs in
Henry VII's law of 1485, with regard to which Bacon made the
statement quoted above on the reorientation of policy from one
of abundant provisions to one of power. From Henry VIII
onwards until Queen Anne's reign, throughout two centuries,
this *Leitmotiv* reappears with a monotony of repetition in one
Act of Parliament after another, and very often, too, in other
official statements. In one of the statutes of Henry VIII (1531/32),
the decline of the navy is deplored, the navy which "had been
not only a great defence and surety to this Realm of England
in time of War, but also a high commodity to all the Subjects",
so that the kingdom would suffer great danger and the nation
would deteriorate if there were seafaring men no more. In
Elizabeth's time, legislation was even more vigorous in this

[5] Heckscher, "Produktplakatet och des förutsättningar" (*Historiska studier
tillägnade Harald Hjärne*, Ups. 1908, 780).

sphere. In one of these laws (1580/81) it was complained that soon there would no longer be "a great number of Mariners and Seamen fit for the Service of her Majesty and her said Realm for the Defence thereof in time of Wars". When the Levant trade was about to be regulated, Elizabeth's minister, Walsingham, wrote to her (?) offering reasons for the conceding of privileges to the Levant Company. "First, you shall set a great number of your greatest ships in work whereby your navy shall be maintained, one of the principallest strengths and defence of this realm." Under James I the same theme was varied slightly so as to flatter his by no means trifling pride. An Act of 1603/4, providing for the production of sail cloth, discusses "His Highness' Navy, the chiefest strength of this Realm (next unto God and his Highness)". In the instructions to a Commission for Trade set up towards the end of his reign, in 1622, it was stated that "because the Maintenance of our Navy and the shipping of our kingdom, is a principal means to advance the Honour Strength Safety and Profit thereof, we will and require you . . ." and there followed a large number of commercial measures that were to be taken. Preoccupation with interests of power was not peculiar to one or another political regime. The reasons given for the 1651 Navigation Act of the Commonwealth were "the Increase of the Shipping and the Encouragement of the Navigation of this Nation, which under the good Providence and Protection of God, is so great a means of the Welfare and Safety of this Commonwealth". The 1660 Navigation Act of the Restoration period, the most detailed and most decisive of them all, repeated this wording almost literally. And to conclude this tedious enumeration, the 1705 colonial law of Queen Anne alludes to "the Royal Navy and the Navigation of England wherein under God the Wealth Safety and Strength of this Kingdom is so much concerned".[6]

One of the most important aspects of this policy concerned fishing, which was considered a unique training for sailors. It is, however, superfluous to enter into a detailed description of the regulations for its encouragement, for, with one exception, they were identical with those instituted in other spheres. Identical,

[6] Statutes: 5 Rich. II st. 1 c. 3; 1 Hen. VII c. 8; 23 Hen. VIII c. 7; 23 Eliz. c. 7; 1 Jac. I c. 24; 12 Car. II c. 18; 3 & 4 Anne c. 9.—Navigation Act of the Commonwealth (Acts 1651 c. 22): in *Acts and Ordinances of the Interregnum, 1642–1660* ed. C. H. Firth & R. S. Rait (Lond. 1911) II 559 ff.—Walsingham: pr. in Epstein, *Early History of the Levant Company* 245.—The 1622 instruction: in *Foedera* (ed. Rymer) 1st ed. XVII 414, Hague ed. VII: IV 14.

too, was the theoretical nature of the policy. But the exception mentioned is of considerable interest and forms one of the most picturesque phenomena in mercantilist policy; it was the so-called Political Lent.

Political Lent was first introduced in 1549; thereafter it was vigorously maintained for about a century, and did not disappear from the statute book until the 19th century. Its purport was as follows: with certain exceptions which varied from time to time, people were obliged to refrain from eating meat and to eat fish on certain days of the week. As Cunningham points out, this legislation is so interesting because what was originally a religious custom was reinstituted for political purposes, although its former *raison d'être* was completely discarded. In the preface to the first of these Acts it is stated *inter alia* that "Albeit the King's Subjects now having a more perfect and clear light of the Gospel and true word of God . . . and thereby perceiving that one day or one Kind of Meat of it self is not more holy more pure or more clean than an other, for that all days and all Meats be of their nature of one equal purity cleanness and holiness . . . ; Yet forasmuch as diverse of the Kings Subjects turning their Knowledge therein to satisfy their sensuality . . . : The King's Majesty . . . considering . . . specially that Fishers . . . may thereby the rather be set on work . . ." causes the particular regulations to be passed. That the object was to increase the country's readiness for defence on the seas is manifest in the next Act on the same subject, the most important of the Elizabethan Navigation Acts, called an *Act touching certain Politique Constitutions made for the Maintenance of the Navy* (1562/63). There Political Lent is regulated by still more detailed prescriptions, closely bound up with the aim of naval defence, though the need for economizing meat is also mentioned. In the long series of statutes and proclamations regarding Political Lent, references to the need of preparation for naval defence are constantly repeated.[7]

The naval policy of power had yet another aspect. It en-

---

[7] Statutes quoted: 2 & 3 Ed. VI c. 19; 5 Eliz. c. 5 §§ 11–14, 22–23.— The final repeal took place through 3 Geo. IV c. 41 § 2 (1822) and 31 & 32 Vic. c. 45 § 71 Sched. 2 (1868).—A law which had once repealed the system for a short period (39 Eliz. c. 10, 1596/97), contains an interesting and rather damaging criticism of it. The remainder of the relevant legislation is reproduced or mentioned in Cunningham I⁴ 499 f., II³ 67–73; and the remainder of the English fishing policy may also be studied there.—For the rest, the literature on this subject is too great for me to be able to refer to it here with any completeness.

deavoured to secure for the country an abundant stock of naval stores (*fournissements de la marine*). In doing so it fell back upon the older of the two methods discussed here, procuring the particular articles apparently necessary for defence by direct measures. This policy was directed mainly against the northern Powers, particularly Sweden-Finland, the main source of supply, which was thoroughly determined to take advantage of its monopolistic position, especially with regard to the production of tar. Colbert met this by stimulating native production, and partly also by attempting to wrest the Baltic trade from the Dutch, though this attempt was chiefly dictated by his over-whelming desire to deal a blow at Dutch shipping. England, on the other hand, realized more and more that it had in the North American colonies what from the mercantilist point of view was an ideal source of supply of these stores; all the more so because to develop their production of these goods was to restrain them from competing with the mother country in manufactures, particularly the cloth industry, the apple of her eye.[8]

The scarcity of timber prevailing, as it was thought, in most European countries, provided a difficulty which, at any rate in England, was a very real one, for timber was in demand primarily for naval purposes. Oak was always considered necessary for men-of-war and generally for ships carrying arms, and oak was especially scarce. The encouragement of native shipbuilding meant first and foremost an increased consumption of the meagre stock of native timber. And if this stock was insufficient it was necessary to import, which involved an expensive outlay on freight and tonnage, whereas to import ships would not only obviate both freight and tonnage costs, but would in fact economize freights and place more tonnage at the country's disposal. Importing timber, moreover, did not make the country any the less dependent on foreign supplies than importing ready-built ships would have done. If, in spite of these difficulties, native shipbuilding was stimulated, it is a proof that considerations of power actually had to be subjected to the general or com-mercial mercantilist interests and that defence was not always furthered by measures which had it for their motive. In this case

[8] On England, see *i.a.*, Cunningham II[3] and Beer, *Old Colonial System*, *passim*.—On France, see e.g. *Lettres de Colbert* III: 1 76 ff., 223, 240, III: 11 54 f., VII 242 f. ; Martin, *La grande industrie sous Louis XIV* 184–7 ; on the Baltic Sea trade P. Boissonnade and P. Charliat, *Colbert et la Compagnie de commerce du Nord*; on Colbert's Compagnie des fournissements de la marine, see also a speech of the deputy for Nantes at the Conseil de Commerce of 1701 ; repro-duced in *Correspondance des contrôleurs généraux* (ed. Boislisle) II 498.

the import of raw materials was regarded as useful, while the import of finished goods was frowned upon. This policy was decisive, although English naval strength might have been better served by directly contrary measures. Apparently, however, people were ignorant of this contradiction. In so far as they were at all conscious of it, they may have believed that economic prosperity, which was considered the outcome of shipbuilding at home, was a source of political power according to the second of the two methods distinguished at the beginning of this chapter. It goes without saying that attempts were made to maintain and to increase the stocks of timber in the country itself, but with negligible success in the majority of countries.[9]

In the relation between political power and economic policy, the colonies played a great part. The situation was outlined by Sir John Seeley half a century ago and has been vigorously confirmed by the more recent historian of English colonial policy, the American G. L. Beer. According to the Old Colonial System the task of the mother country was to protect the colonies, but in return they were to grant her commercial advantages; more especially they were to direct their production along those lines which the mother country considered most advantageous to herself. To this extent it was commercial and not political interests which predominated, with the exception that the system was to provide a means for colonial defence. But two other aspects may be distinguished in the system and their main end was the power of the state. Both were connected with the principle of self-sufficiency, which was chiefly dictated by considerations of political power.

Self-sufficiency

The fact that the colonies differed widely in their geographical and economic make-up from the mother country made them well suited for supplementing its needs. They opened up the possibility of providing a system of supply within a self-contained empire. To make the colonies thus the complement of the mother country, the latter guaranteed their products a preferential or even a monopolistic position in her markets, and in extreme cases went so far as to wipe out completely any native manu-

---

[9] On this question it will be sufficient to refer to the most complete exposition on the subject: R. G. Albion, *Forests and Sea Power, the Timber Problem of the Royal Navy 1652–1862*: (Harvard Econ. Studies XXIX, Cambr., Mass., 1926); the effects of the shipbuilding policy 74 f., 115, 244 f., the policy in forestry, ch. 3 party. 117–38.—On the question of fuel in France cp. for instance Martin, *La grande industrie sous Louis XIV* 313 f., *do. do. sous Louis XV* 149, 151 f., as well as the deputy for Nantes 1701 (see previous note).

facture competing with the one which it was desired to foster in the colonies. The best example of this is the policy directed against tobacco growing in England, which was systematically and vigorously uprooted, partly by the use of armed force, throughout several decades in the supposed interests of the southern states of North America.

The policy of self-sufficiency had a second economic function, and that was to prevent the colonies from so developing their potentialities that they would be able to stand on their own feet and become politically independent. The English Staple Act of 1663, one of the keystones of the Old Colonial System, referred in explicit terms to the need for developing "a greater correspondence and kindness" between the colonies and the mother country; but at the same time required the former to remain "in firmer dependence upon it", etc.—a droll combination of two inconsistent points of view. As far as Ireland was concerned, friendship was hardly ever so much as mentioned. Lord Strafford, who ruled the island in the 1630's with a rod of iron, wrote frankly, "I am of Opinion that all Wisdom advises to keep this Kingdom as much subordinate and dependent upon England as is possible, and holding them from the Manufacture of Wool . . . and then inforcing them to fetch their Clothing from thence and to take their Salt from the King (being that which preserves and gives value to all their native staple Commodities), how can they depart from us without Nakedness and Beggary?"[10]

Both attitudes are extremely important in colonial policy, even though they were hardly as well considered as they might appear.

To consider first the latter point of view, the need for political subjection of the colonies: if it were true that the colonies could be kept in perpetual subjection, under the conditions prescribed by Strafford, this postulates three things, and in practice it is very unlikely that all three conditions should be fulfilled. If

[10] Staple Act: 15 Car. II c. 7 § 4.—*The Earl of Strafforde's Letters and Despatches*, ed. Knowler, I 193: quoted in Cunningham II³ 368 note 2.—Seeley's *Expansion of England* (1883): of the two series of lectures it embodies, the fourth lecture of the first series contains the phrase: "England gave defence in return for trade-privileges."—For the general policy, see Beer, *Origins of the British Colonial System* and *The Old Colonial System* (not completed) part^y ch. 3 in the first and ch. 1 in the second. For the tobacco policy party, *Origins* 403–8 and *Old. Col. Syst.* I 140–7.—Perhaps the best short survey for France is still Pigeonneau's "La politique coloniale de Colbert" (*Annales de l'école libre des sc. pol.* I, 1886, 487–509).

we assume in the first place that the economic side of the argument were sound, it does not follow that the colonists, eager for liberty, would allow themselves to be frightened off from revolting. In fact it is conceivable that they would put up with "nakedness and beggary" for the sake of what in their eyes were a higher end. But actually the economic argument itself is not without flaws, and for two reasons : if an industry which has natural advantages in a country has been forcibly restrained, it does not follow that it cannot arise once the restrictive measures disappear. And finally even though it were really true that such manufactures could not arise in colonies which had grown independent, because they had formerly been artificially restrained, would it therefore really be likely that the colonists could no longer procure their supplies from their former mother country? Mercantilist doctrine taught that export was the only desirable economic transaction and goods were exported to enemy countries even in war time. It is thus extremely improbable that export to independent colonies would be forbidden, and in fact the actual course of development proves that it was by no means the case. After the American colonies gained their independence, they continued to draw their supplies from England, and England did not for one moment contemplate withholding her goods from them. But if this argument is not sound, it is sufficient to invalidate the whole train of reasoning; and that it was false is proved by the course of history.

In the second place, with regard to the principle of self-sufficiency, its military value could not be particularly great if it were applied in practice to a system comprising a European country and its transoceanic colonies. For if the country were not mistress of the seas, she could not in case of need draw her supplies any better from her own colonies than from foreign countries, in fact far less easily than from her immediate neighbours. This axiom was borne out in the 18th century as regards France, when England laid an embargo on all French colonial products. Besides, where there was a shortage of tonnage it might be more difficult, even for a country which dominated the seas. to draw its supplies from distant colonies than from foreign ports closer at hand. Thus even England found difficulties in procuring timber from her colonies, because to obtain it thence involved from three to five times as much freightage costs as to obtain it from the ports of the North Sea and the Baltic. In addition there was the greater cost of labour, sometimes six times as great, and the less efficient commercial organization.

There was, however, one set of conditions under which the policy of drawing supplies from the colonies could spell greater safety than import from foreign countries, i.e. when foreign states placed embargoes on their own exports for political or other reasons; for such obstructions were out of the question when the goods came from a territory subject to the same government. And these conditions were not altogether absurd, for it is well known, for example, that Sweden under Charles XII was an unknown factor in this respect—there was no knowing how she would act. It was, further, of outstanding practical importance, that the Baltic, the enclosed sea from which naval stores were drawn, could be blockaded very easily by any adjacent or other maritime power, whereas this was impossible in the Atlantic Ocean on to which the colonies bordered. There is thus a kernel of common sense in the endeavours of the Old Colonial System to build up its political power on a self-sufficient territory comprising the mother country and its overseas possessions; but the weight of this argument has certainly been much over-estimated.[11]

Autarchical aims appear still more self-contradictory in mercantilism, because the old idea of blockade, the cutting off of the enemy's supplies, is inconsistent with the conception that a country's gain lies in export, and that import constitutes a loss. The result is then a kind of "self-blockade", the most stupendous example of which is Napoleon's Continental System. The work to be carried out in the interests of defence by the policy of self-sufficiency could thus not be very great; for enemies were on the look-out for the opportunity to flood a country with goods. It follows that in reality it was based on a strictly economic doctrine and *not* on any considerations of power. It is not impossible to find instances of a consciousness of this character of the policy. Richelieu, a statesman who was continually engaged in war, is silent on the need for protection against blockade when discussing in detail that France ought to manage without importing from her neighbours. Montchrétien's view on the economic problems of war is revealed, e.g. in his desire to send expensive furs to the enemy "so as to draw thence gold and silver and other advantages and, after he has been thus enfeebled, to be able to

[11] Cp. Albion 238 f., 240.—An English proclamation of 1625 concerning saltpetre calls it a country's good fortune not to be dependent on the "dangerous, chargeable and casual Supply thereof from Foreign Parts" (*Foedera*, ed. Rymer, 1st ed. XVIII 23, Hague ed. VIII: 1 16). The second of these three adjectives obviously refers to the naïve view that native production was not "chargeable"; the first is explained by the third, which is therefore what remains of the argument.

conquer him more easily and to become his master". The measures and aims which are taken to have been dictated by political considerations of power reveal themselves in such observations as a cloak for economic ideals.[12]

Population

There were still other and more important aspects of economic life which were brought into contact with the state's interest in power; the policy regarding population was particularly affected by it. It usually manifested itself merely in a general attempt to increase population, which was also actuated by many other economic motives (economic in the narrower sense of the word) as will be elaborated in the following part. In the continual struggle against the enclosing of pasture lands to the detriment of corn growing, carried on in England throughout the 16th century, the idea that frequently appeared was the need to maintain a peasant population in the interests of national defence. A proclamation of 1548, for instance, stated that "the surety . . . of the Realm must be defended against the enemy with force of men, and the multitude of true subjects, not with flocks of sheep and droves of beasts". And the idea recurs again and again in contemporary literature.[13]

It is of still greater interest that in exceptional cases the policy of power was concerned not merely with the size but also with the quality of the population. It might be thought that quality would already have been considered important for general economic reasons; but actually mercantilists did not give much thought to the effect on production of the quality of the working population, except in the case of individuals with superior craftsmanship. As far as the mass of the working population was concerned, they were counted rather than weighed. Considerations of power occasionally introduced another conception. True, the idea that man and his welfare might be an end in themselves certainly never occurred to anyone; they were merely a means to be used for purposes of the state. But to be suited for such purposes certain human qualities were still considered necessary. This attitude is best expressed by Bacon, as has been indicated in *Addendum* §1 to the previous chapter. His essay "Of

[12] Richelieu, *Testament politique* ch. 9, sec. 6 (1691 ed. 136–9 *et passim*). Montchrétien, *Traicté*, etc. II 131. J. Niehans "Der Gedanke der Autarkie im Merkantilismus, etc. . . ." (*Zürich. Volkswirtsch. Forsch.* XXXVII, Zürich 1945).

[13] Proclamation of 1548: in *Discourse of the Common Weal* (ed. Lamond) 149, cf. xi.—Also: *ib.* 90, 93; "Policies to Reduce this Realme of Englande vnto a Prosperus Wealthe and Estate" 1549 (*Tudor Econ. Docs.* III 311 ff.) ch. 1; H. Latimer, *Seven Sermons before Edward VI* (1549; English Reprints, ed. E. Arber, XIII, Birmingham 1869, 40).

the True Greatnesse of Kingdomes and Estates" inquires, as the title suggests, into the essence of true political greatness, which according to Bacon was a matter of quality not quantity:

"The population may appear by musters, and the number and greatness of cities and towns by cards and maps. But yet there is not anything among civil affairs more subject to error than the right valuation and true judgment concerning the power and forces of an estate. The Kingdom of Heaven is compared, not to any great kernel or nut, but to a grain of mustard seed, which is one of the least grains, but hath in it a property and spirit hastily to get up and spread. So are there States great in Territory, and yet not apt to enlarge or command; and some that have but a small dimension of stem, and yet apt to be the foundation of great monarchies.

"Walled towns, stored arsenals, and armouries, goodly races of horse, chariots of war, elephants, ordnance, artillery, and the like; all this is but a sheep in lion's skin, except the breed and disposition of the people be stout and warlike; nay, number itself in armies importeth not much where the people is of weak courage; for, as Virgil saith, 'It never troubles a wolf how many the sheep be.' "

One of the most popular ideas of the time, then, comes under the lash of his argument:

"Neither is money the sinews of war, as it is trivially said, where the sinews of men's arms, in base and effeminate people, are failing."

He then develops a complete social programme:

"Let States that aim at greatness take heed how their nobility and gentlemen do multiply too fast; for that maketh the common subject grow to be a peasant and base swain, driven out of heart, and in effect but the gentleman's labourer. . . . And you will bring it to that, that not the hundred poll will be fit for an helmet, especially as to the infantry, which is the nerve of an army; and so there will be great population and little strength."[14]

It must be admitted that the *Machtpolitik* aspect of population policy could hardly have been expressed more conclusively.

The ideal behind the distribution of property, it must be emphasized, and the relative strength of various classes was related, in the considerations of power, to medieval aspirations. I refer to the subject dealt with in Chapter VI of the foregoing part (I 271 f.). People were fearful that "the rich eat out the poor", that monopolization might create a small number of rich at the expense of a suitable subsistence for the large majority.

[14] Bacon, *Essays* (ed. Wright 119–22). See also *Addendum* §1.

In Bacon we see the connection between this standpoint and that of the policy of power, applying not merely to the rural population referred to in the last quotation but conceived on much broader lines. "Above all things good policy is to be used, that the treasure and monies in a State be not gathered into few hands; for, otherwise, a State may have a great stock and yet starve. And money is like muck, not good except it be spread"— this phrase was also meant to support the demand to keep money in circulation. "This is done chiefly by suppressing, or, at the least, keeping a strait hand upon, the devouring trades of usury, ingrossing, great pasturages, and the like."[15]

This attitude, it should be added, has been exceptional at all times in the treatment of population problems, and it became increasingly so in the course of the mercantilist period. The military aspect of population was not emphasized at all strongly in later mercantilist thought. The worker came to be regarded altogether as a factor of production, as will be discussed in detail towards the end of the following part (*v.i.* 152–172). The individual played a part in the system only as a servant of economic ends, though these ends, in their turn, could be made subservient to the interests of power. With a large population and low wages it was hoped to effect a large export surplus of manufactures and a large import surplus of gold and precious stones, and this desire became itself a part of the state's policy of power. This brings us close to the *second* of the two methods of the policy of power: the state attempting to strengthen its power through national economic prosperity. The view of the means to that end consequently coloured the policy of power.

Money

The attitude of the policy of power towards money is particularly characteristic of this, for it was naturally conditioned by the general mercantilist conception of money as embodying all economic resources. Again and again the view is repeated, with greater or less clarity, that a state could be without money only on pain of serious political and even more serious military consequences. John Hales, in his *Discourse of the Common Weal*, calls "treasure" the sinews of war because the king could not use other sorts of money (of leather, etc.) abroad.

"Money the sinews of war" (*pecunia nervus belli* or *nervi bellorum*) was a slogan that seldom failed. Bacon, with his more organic view of society, did not approve of it and attacked this most

[15] Bacon, *Essays*, "Of Seditions and Troubles" (No. 15 in 1625 publ., ed. Wright, 60).

popular opinion on the relation between power and economic life.* Sometimes it was said that it was " now " no longer the sharpest sword but the longest purse that won wars, and sometimes the illustration was more detailed. In a typical, anonymous pamphlet of 1671, *The Use and Abuses of Money*, the opinion is given that "The greatest and most weighty reason that money is of public use, is, that it tends to the preservation of a Kingdom; money is the sinews of war, and riches the honour of a Kingdom in Peace. . . . And if Soldiers could be paid without money, or a Crown maintained and kept without Coin, there would be no absolute need of it." As usual, Locke was a particularly good representative of the mercantilist point of view. In support of the thesis that a country must have more money than its neighbours, he wrote "if any of our Neighbours have it in a much greater abundance than we, we are many ways obnoxious to them—([sic]—he must have meant it the other way about). 1. They can maintain a greater force. 2. They can tempt away our People, by greater wages, to serve them by Land or Sea, or in any Labour. 3. They can command the Markets and thereby break our Trade, and make us poor. 4. They can on any occasion ingross Naval and Warlike Stores, and thereby endanger us." The argument was based throughout on the characteristic mercantilist theory of money, and is interesting as a proof of how important considerations of power in money policy appeared even to so advanced a rationalist as Locke. It shows how important this attitude was in the practical policy of mercantilism.[16]

The relation between monetary policy and power was particularly close in the sphere of public finance, for financial resources were of course one of the first prerequisites of military policy. The economic justification for connecting this with the supply of money was possibly greater than when applied to economic life as a whole, for many states, especially on the continent, found great difficulty in reckoning their revenues on a money basis to the same degree as they had to do with their expenditure. Be that as it may, the policy harmonized perfectly with the general mercantilist conception of the role of money in economic activity. Needless to say Colbert was the best representative of this view,

---

[16] *Discourse of the Common Weal* 86 f.—[M. de St. Jean], *Le commerce honorable ou considérations politiques* (Nantes 1647) sect. 2 chap. 3 & 4, part[y]. 150, 162 ff.— *The Use and Abuses of Money* (Lond. 1671) 4 f.—Locke, *Further Considerations Concerning Raising the Value of Money* (2nd ed., Lond. 1695, 15 f.).—Sir F. Brewster, *New Essays on Trade* (Lond. 1702) 28, 31.—J. Law, *Considérations sur le commerce et l'argent* (1705, French ed., La Haye 1720, chap. 7 & 8, e.g. 183).— D. Defoe, *A Plan of the English Commerce* (1728, repr. Lond. 1928, 39 f.) etc.

* See below II 365. *Addendum* §6.

for he was the greatest martyr to financial policy. In the great *Mémoire au Roi sur les Finances* of 1670 quoted above he elaborated the relationship in the greatest detail. He there viewed the connection between the amount of taxation and the total of circulating money or precious stones in a manner typical of mercantilism and its monetary conceptions. He then entered into detailed computation of the way in which a better proportion between the two could be arrived at. In his opinion, the proportion should be 1 : 3, whereas in reality he calculated the total taxation at 70 million *livres* compared with a silver circulation of only 120 millions. In this way he easily arrived at the usual mercantilist precept, that of increasing the amount of money in the country, and with him this precept became a strong fundamental of public finance. How intimate Colbert regarded this relationship and how seriously he went about the matter may be seen in the fact that he not only urged strict economies in the budget, but seriously contemplated placing obstacles in the way of the circulation of silver between the provinces, so that one should not be able to have too little and another too much. For the same reasons he urged that the fortifications in the newly acquired territories be limited and no troops be sent there, so as to prevent money from flowing to neighbouring countries. A statesman more than usually dominated by consideration of power is here seen to allow his practical measures to be profoundly influenced by his views of the connection between cause and effect in the economic field, above all in the field of money.[17]

In this way the policy of power led to the typical mercantilist programme for the organization of economic activity, because the latter was considered a means for the attainment of power. At the same time it is evident that such a programme could often easily come into conflict with the demand that the country must be prepared for war, and in fact many examples have been given above to this effect. Colbert attacked Louvois' war expenditure and military undertakings, because they undermined, in his opinion, the real source of power—economic activity. On the same grounds, others were able to attack the encouragement given for military reasons to individual industries, because this was considered harmful to the general economic development. The English Navigation Acts, for example, therefore did not enjoy universal approbation among mercantilist writers. Roger Coke's vigorous criticism of these Acts is a particularly character-

[17] *Lettres de Colbert* VII 235 ff., 254.

istic example, for it expresses in its most refined form the point of view of political power as a factor in the state's economic policy.

General policy

Like the majority of the mercantilist writers, Coke was strongly influenced by the consideration of power. In the "Definitions" with which he prefaced the first of his series of four pamphlets on trade, he stated, e.g. (1671), "The end of trade is threefold, viz. Strength, Wealth, and Employment for all sorts of People." Thus power took its place among the benefits of trade; and this was consistent with Coke's view that the victory of the Dutch over the Spaniards was due to trade and that his panacea for all evils, increased immigration, meant increased power to the country. But this by no means prevented Coke from vigorously attacking the Navigation Acts. His reason was that supremacy at sea, like domination in any other sphere, was to be won simply and solely through commercial prosperity: "I desire as much as any man, that Navigation and Mariners may be encreased by the Natives of England, and English Ships, as far as the Natives of England in such Shipping can maintain Navigation; yet both must be done in time, as by such means as God and Nature have ordained, viz. by encreasing Trade in England: and if both Trade and Navigation cannot be carried on by the Natives alone, I see not reason why (at least at present) Trade (which is more excellent than Navigation) should not be encreased, though upon the account of foreign Navigation." There follows a long series of maxims regarding changes in the regulation of economic activity, whereby the admission of foreigners to various employments could be made easier and the purchase of ships from abroad rendered possible, and thus not only trade but also shipping could be encouraged. He delivers himself finally of the following reflection: "It is not the royal French fleet, its numbers and greatness, which makes the French King almost as mighty at sea as the English or Dutch; but it is the lack of the latter of such industries as could increase their shipping and the number of their seamen."[18]

Thus the state's policy of power was welded firmly and completely to the general economic policy. We have therefore arrived at the point when it is necessary to turn to the treatment of the economic matters proper in the mercantile system; and this will be the subject of the two parts that follow.

[18] Coke, *Treatise* I "Definitions" (unpaged); II "Preface to the Reader" (unpaged); III 27; the whole of IV, part^y. 75, 80.

PART III

MERCANTILISM AS A SYSTEM OF PROTECTION

I

DIFFERENT ATTITUDES TOWARDS COMMODITIES

To recapitulate briefly the points leading to the present stage: the first part of the present work attempted to elucidate the endeavours towards moulding the state into an economic unit. A subordinate part referred to the administrative question, the attempts to transfer the treatment of problems of economic policy to the state. But our main task was to inquire to what extent the economic sub-division of the state into feudal units—among which the towns, with their essentially local interests, were the most significant—disappeared during the period, or to what extent it remained as a legacy for subsequent regimes. In part this was intended to elucidate the role of economic policy in the development known as the Industrial Revolution, i.e., the effect of the policy on economic institutions developing during the 19th century. It should be noted here that current ideas which have their roots in the 19th century and which have become the successors to liberalism, have intentionally been given a secondary position and those of liberalism given precedence in the discussion.

The second part has likewise dealt with the relations to the aims of the state, not by way of contrast with national disintegration, but with regard to the use to which the resources of the state should be put. More precisely, how far economic life was subordinated to considerations of state power, especially in relation to foreign states, though also in some cases in relation to dependent colonies. So far as a number of primitive measures were concerned, this was a simple matter, for their connection with the aims of political power was unequivocal. This referred to activities directly intended to increase the supply within the country of commodities of military importance. But together with these, were discovered other aspects of economic policy, which became increasingly important in the course of time. The measures expressing these aspects were not dictated directly but indirectly influenced by considerations of power, their direct aim being to foster economic life as a whole, as an aid to political power. But what was considered economically beneficial or harmful to the country depended in turn on the general conceptions of economic matters. It is therefore necessary to look into these conceptions.

In the third and fourth parts, ideas on the interplay of economic forces will be considered, in so far as they influenced economic policy. It will be necessary to investigate the way in which economic activity was intended to serve the particular ends, and the means that were considered suitable from the point of view of society or the state. To understand this, it is necessary to explain the influence of the general ideas of the time on the workings of the economic system. Only such general ideas can explain why action was taken in one or another direction. It is in this way that we arrive at what is specifically economic in mercantilism, what, from the economic point of view, distinguishes it basically from earlier or later doctrines. Henceforth the question arises of the choice of means for particular ends, whereas hitherto only the ends themselves have been dealt with. Now, an economic system is nothing but an adaptation to given non-economic ends, so it follows that we have only now reached what is specifically economic in mercantilism.

Further, the efforts hitherto described arose more or less of necessity, forced by the requirements of the state, whereas there is nothing which arose obviously or of necessity in what follows. A state authority there must be, and this authority will always attempt to master particular institutions and to provide itself with the economic resources necessary to assert itself. It is true that the manner in which it grapples with this problem will not always be the same at different times, but the problem itself is always there. On the other hand, the economic policy determined by the prevailing economic ideal, and the conception of economic life on which that ideal is based are susceptible of unlimited change.

An investigation into what is specifically economic in mercantilism must start from its attitude towards *commodities*. This and the related problems will be dealt with in the third part. The fourth part will then be devoted to the relationship of mercantilism to *money*. The connection between the money aspect and the goods aspect is very close, perhaps even closer in mercantilist conception than in reality. These two aspects of economic life were thus most intimately related. Yet they were treated differently in many respects. The attitude towards goods was taken more or less for granted and was hardly ever made the subject of a thoroughgoing analysis during the actual heyday of mercantilism, but only in the time of its decline in the 18th century. The mercantilist conception of money rested just as much on unguided instinct, but it was increasingly the subject of lively and intensive discussion and so was well thought out and rationalized. For the sake of clarity it is therefore essential to keep the two aspects apart, though we must never lose sight of their inter-relationship.

The attitude of any economic doctrine towards goods might appear to be the same and too obvious to require mention. For one would expect every society to make efforts to provide its members with as plentiful a supply of goods as possible for their requirements. When trading with other groups, it would do this by endeavouring to get the greatest possible value out of the transaction. In other words, the interests of the society, like the interests of the individual, might be thought to lie in buying cheap and selling dear. On closer consideration, this is seen to be merely two aspects of one and the same thing; for the actual payment for one's own goods is made up of the goods of someone else, so that if relatively many commodities are received in exchange for one's own, one is both buying cheap and selling dear at the same time.

To the ordinary observer, however, the matter is not so clear. Moreover, economic life is so complex that the application of this simple argument to concrete cases involves considerable difficulties. It may be said that *laissez-faire* concentrated on the goal described, often with complete indifference to the complications involved. As in other cases, it stood *laissez-faire* in good stead here that it could, in a way peculiar to itself, ignore the economic ideas of the "natural man". These did not dare venture forth in the face of its doctrines, for these doctrines came to appear too irrefutable to stand contradiction.

A parallel to the attitude of *laissez-faire* towards commodities existed in a much earlier period, in the early Middle Ages. What is usually described as medieval economic policy is undoubtedly a relatively late phenomenon, succeeding an earlier state of affairs in which there was less interference from above and greater economic mobility. North of the Alps, the new, so called medieval tendencies were not of much importance before the 13th century, and in the Hansa, for example, the new policy was in full swing only after 1400. It is difficult to determine how far the apparently "liberal" order which had prevailed until then was the expression of a particular economic outlook, for its character is revealed most clearly in the measures of compulsion which set it aside. But it is not inconceivable that it was partly based on ideas which saw an advantage in the expansion of trade and the visit of foreign merchants.[1] The main explanation, however, must

---

[1] The greater freedom in the early Middle Ages in the case of the German towns has been emphasized particularly by von Below's *Probleme der Wirt-*

be sought in another direction. Deliberate encroachment on economic activity was impossible simply because there were no institutions powerful and purposeful enough to identify themselves with such a policy. In so far as there was any such economic policy at all, it differed entirely from the *laissez-faire* of later times. Consequently, an account of the history of economic policy after ancient times need not go further back than to municipal policy in its classical, medieval form.

The first part of the present work has shown, with detailed evidence, how vastly important were the medieval towns in all aspects of economic policy, and how they retained their importance until well into the 19th century. And municipal influence made itself felt just as much in the attitude towards commodities. But even from the point of view of municipal policy, there were three different conceptions of the significance of goods, and all three enjoyed a far-reaching and lasting influence.

In the first place, goods could be regarded purely from the standpoint of exchange. This was how they were regarded in trade, or rather in middlemen's trading. Where the town was a *trading centre*, this view was decisive. Secondly, even when viewed from the standpoint of municipal interests, goods could be treated as was natural to citizens who only consumed but did not produce goods of this kind. For the most essential of all goods, food-stuffs, a town is almost exclusively a *centre of consumption*. It was therefore natural to aim at as plentiful a supply of goods as possible without considering the effect on the producers. That was the second aspect. The third was a function of the town in its capacity as a *production centre*, goods being regarded through the eyes of the producer. Production was then considered to some extent an end in itself, and the goal of production, the catering for wants and consumption, was ignored. These three points of view are mutually exclusive, but they can all be deduced from the principles of a selfish municipal policy, as we have observed in the fourth chapter of the first part. In practice, each of the three exercised a wide influence both in space and time.

The results of all three may easily be described. From the point of view of trade, pure and simple, no sentiment, as it were, enters

schaftsgeschichte (Tübingen 1920) 233–45; cp. the sentiment placed at the head of the oldest code of Strasburg, dating from the 12th century: "Ad formam aliarum civitatum in eo honore condita est Argentina (= Strasburg), ut omnis homo tam extraneus quam indigena pacem in ea omni tempore et ab omnibus habeat" (*Urkunden zur Städtischen Verfassungsgeschichte*, ed. F. Keutgen, Berl. 1901, 93). In Italy, France, and England municipal policy proper begins approximately equally late.

into the attitude towards goods. Their only function is to provide profits in exchange transactions, and for the rest they are a matter of indifference. Next, from the point of view of consumption, at least in the short view, the aim is necessarily to attract and retain the goods as much as possible. To exaggerate somewhat, this aim may perhaps be called a *hunger for goods*. Lastly, from the producers' point of view, goods are regarded with precisely contrary feelings. The danger then lies in having too much, in not being able to dispose of the goods, and in having them remain on one's hands; while the object is to rid oneself of them as fast as possible. Under the influence of such ideas there arises a sort of *fear of goods*.

With regard to prices, too, these three aspects are clearly differentiated. Commerce desires neither cheap goods nor dear goods; it wants to buy them cheap and sell them dear. Here is a point of agreement with the *laissez-faire* outlook, which will be illustrated below in greater detail. In this connection, too, goods are an *indifferent* factor from the standpoint of commerce. The consumers, on the other hand, desire to procure the goods as cheaply as possible. Their gospel is the gospel of *cheapness*. The standpoint of the producers leads to the gospel of *dearness*.

Still, if the attitude towards goods is reflected in a corresponding attitude towards prices, there emerges an important and novel factor. It is true that high or low prices always appear, to the untutored mind, as the result of a scarcity or abundance in the supply of goods. But if prices are expressed by a common measure of value, the monetary system in reality enters as a new contributory factor of the most far-reaching importance. The demand for higher or lower prices then leads to a corresponding monetary policy. Here, therefore, exists a close relationship between the goods aspect and the money aspect of economic policy. This relationship will be discussed in the fourth part, in connection with monetary policy itself.

The following exposition may be considerably simplified if special expressions are adopted at the outset for the three types of economic policy just outlined.

The policy determined by the interests of intermediary trade will be called *staple policy*. Historically the word "staple" has had a double meaning, but one of its meanings, and in fact the more important, indicates precisely the standpoint which it is here taken to characterize. The second meaning of the word staple, with which we are not, at least primarily, concerned, arose from the practice of merchant organizations of creating "factories" or commercial centres abroad, on which members were more or less compelled to focus their business, without any regard for the interests of the local merchants. In this second meaning, the term "staple" is identical with "mart town", and is employed as such both in the Hansa as well as in the various English trading corporations, the Merchants of the Staple and the Merchant Adventurers' Company. The staple policy under consideration here was, on the contrary, pursued by the towns themselves in their own interests.

The policy which has the consumers' interests in mind may be described by a contemporary Spanish expression—the *policy of provision (politica de los abastos)*.[2] This expression will be used to include both what is intentional and what is unintentional in the policy.

For the policy dominated by producers' interests there exists an expression of respectable antiquity in the term *protectionism*. But it is particularly necessary to guard against a possible misunderstanding on this point. As used in this book the word does not refer to the presence or absence of governmental measures as such, interfering with economic activity, for these were common to all three types. Protectionism here is taken to be the outcome of a definite attitude towards goods, the "fear of goods" or the "gospel of high prices".

On closer examination, the three types, in spite of fundamental differences, will be found to present many features in common. For our purpose, the relationship of both the staple policy and the policy of provision to protectionism are of importance. At the outset, however, it is necessary to emphasize their differences.

Finally, it might seem natural to assume that the three kinds of policy were always applied to different groups of commodities— the staple policy to the goods used in the intermediary trade of the particular town, the policy of provision to its food-stuffs, and protectionism to its manufactures. Actually this was partly the case; the staple policy and the policy of provision in particular often went together, and indeed this often gave rise to friction. In the normal way, however, the towns limited themselves for a long time to these two of the three possible methods, so that protectionism, in the sense here used, never or hardly ever occurred at all in the medieval system. This was due to the circumstance, which must be stressed over and over again, that

[2] M. J. Bonn, *Spaniens Niedergang während der Preisrevolution des 16. Jahrhunderts* (Stuttgart 1896) 128.

economic policy is determined not so much by the economic facts as by people's conceptions of these facts. Now during the greater part of the Middle Ages, these conceptions did not favour a protectionist system. After the end of the Middle Ages the position was completely changed. In time a divergence arose between the staple policy and the policy of provision on the one hand and protectionism on the other. Protectionism, as I understand the word here, was a relatively late phenomenon, which gave rise to another policy and another attitude towards commodities.

This must by no means be taken to imply that the older methods had disappeared completely before the 19th century. That is true neither of them nor of any other elements of medieval municipal policy. What took place was that there arose in addition a new phenomenon, which pushed them further and further into the background. The new phenomenon is the policy of protection which, together with monetary policy, represents the most important original contribution of mercantilism to the history of economic policy.[3]

[3] In an essay, "The Heavy Hand of Hegel", in *Nationalism and Internationalism, Essays inscribed to Carlton J. Hayes*, ed. E. M. Earle (N.Y. 1950), in general well disposed to my book, C. W. Cole writes that he finds traces of the influence of Hegel in some of my concepts. This is expressed in what he calls my conception of mercantilism "as a real entity", and my regard for the "fear of goods", etc., as "operative entities, which make people do things rather than treating them as mere descriptive terms applied to what people did." I am entirely unaware of having been in any way influenced by Hegel. Not only is my knowledge of Hegel limited, but his views are quite alien to the school of thought to which I belong. With respect to the shortcomings for which I am criticised—and no specific quotation appears—I can only say that I have tried to do precisely that which Cole sees as correct. The notion of hypostatising is quite incompatible with my way of thinking. I could hardly make this clearer than I have done from the outset, since I am quite ignorant of what is meant.

With respect to the "fear of goods", it may be added that I am in full agreement with E. A. J. Johnson when he states in *Predecessors of Adam Smith* (N.Y. 1937) 238, that the phenomenon in question does not in any sense imply a fear of production, but rather that it is "a fear of redundant stocks of finished goods."

II

STAPLE POLICY

1. INTRODUCTION

Even a simple economic analysis must convince the merchant that the supply and the sale of goods are most intimately related. Pure merchant interests have therefore always aimed at guaranteeing the supply of goods to the particular town or corporation to which the merchant belonged, and likewise their sale. The underlying principle of the staple policy is well expressed in an indignant description which the electoral council of Brandenburg gave of Hamburg's policy in 1582: "The Hamburg people are concerned solely with extorting corn at low prices and on their own terms from the Elector of Brandenburg's subjects, and selling it again afterwards as dear as they please." What the Hamburg merchants were reproached with was their eagerness to secure at the same time both the purchase and the sale of corn, in other words, with the fact that so vital a need as corn occupied their attention only as the basis of a business transaction. The attitude denounced here was the same, in principle, as that which gave rise in the United Provinces to what has often been called the Dutch tendency to free trade, an expression which can easily be misconstrued. Laspeyres, the German economic historian of the last century, has aptly characterized this Dutch trait in the following terms: "The merchant was a free-trader in every respect. He desired no limitation on exports, so that he might export as much as possible, and no limitation on imports so that he might import as much as possible; finally he wanted no limitation on transit so that he might import and then export as much as possible."[1]

In elaborating such a policy the problem could first of all be approached purely topographically, as it were. One could concentrate solely on preventing the goods or the trade in the goods from passing by the particular town, that is, on making the town the *staple* (or entrepôt) for the goods. This factor is never absent

---

[1] Schmoller, "Studien über die wirtschaftliche Politik Friedrichs des Grossen": VI Die ältere Elbhandelspolitik, die Stapelrechte und -kämpfe von Magdeburg, Hamburg und Lüneburg (Schmoller's *Jahrb. f. Gesetzgebung*, etc., VIII, 1884) 1039.—E. Laspeyres, *Geschichte der volkswirtschaftlichen Anschauungen der Niederländer zur Zeit der Republik* (Preisschr. der Jablonowskischen Gesellschaft XI, Lpz. 1863) 162.

in staple policy. To this extent the idea of a staple centre as a part of the organization of foreign trade, which has otherwise been excluded from view in this place, may be included in the meaning of the term. And it was in fact through the organization of staple centres in foreign trade that trade was drawn to the place where the staple was fixed. For this reason the cities usually strove to become staples for the Hanseatic or English trading organizations. The aim of staple policy in this case was served by so-called *passive trade*, whereby the merchants and the population of a particular place allowed the merchants of other countries and other places to bring and fetch goods, instead of themselves carrying their goods to foreign places and fetching others back. Without using any kind of compulsion, Bruges employed these principles of passive trade in earlier times, in the same way as Antwerp did, to an even larger extent, during its unique period of prosperity towards the end of the Middle Ages and in the 16th century. Both of these towns succeeded in this way in attracting merchants from the whole of western Europe. Even in a city such as Venice, with its great shipping interests, the policy of passive trade was maintained for the sale of goods carried by land to transalpine Europe, though in this case it could certainly not be pursued without strict measures of compulsion. The policy aimed at making the city the "place of contract" (*il luogho di contratto*) as it was called in Venice. The English historian of Venice, H. F. Brown, has epitomized this idea in his observation "where the goods are there the merchants will gather". Even a monarch like Gustav Vasa, who rationalized medieval ideas to an unusual extent, placed passive trade in the centre of his programme of foreign trading policy, because he believed that transactions effected with foreigners in one's native ports meant more advantageous terms than it was possible, in his opinion, to get before, when "we were always accustomed to dragging them (the goods) to their own door-step".[2]

---

[2] Most of the sources for the North Italian cities have been inaccessible to me. For this reason the greater part of the data has been taken from A. Schaube's invaluable collection of materials, *Handelsgeschichte der Romanischen Völker des Mittelmeergebiets bis zum Ende der Kreuzzüge* (Below and Meinecke, Handbuch der Mittelalterlichen und Neueren Geschichte, Munich and Berl. 1906), part[y]. chaps. 37–46. The facts are partly to be found in W. Heyd's classic work *Histoire du commerce du Levant au moyen-âge* I–II (ed. franç. p. F. Raynaud, Lpz. 1885/86), and in A. Schulte's *Geschichte des mittelalterlichen Handels und Verkehrs zwischen Westdeutschland und Italien* (I–II, Lpz. 1900; but part[y]. for the later Middle Ages). For Venice, which is not treated in Schulte's work, there are other valuable data, especially in: W. Lenel, *Die Entstehung*

As a rule, however, people were not contented simply with attracting goods to the city; they also tried to concentrate the business within the city in the hands of native craftsmen, merchants, brokers, carriers and shippers. A great part of the staple policy was of this nature and this shows how insignificant were the free-trade elements, in a general sense of the term, in this tendency.

At the same time the policy could easily be made to serve the purposes of the policy of provision, because it was bent upon supplying the city with goods. With regard to imports, staple policy and the policy of provision therefore went hand in hand. They only clashed when the staple policy and the middlemen interests also demanded export. A survey of the fate of the staple policy gives a clearer idea of its real nature.

2. ITS DEVELOPMENT

Tendencies towards a staple policy were clearly manifest even in ancient times. Later, Byzantium apparently had a fully developed staple policy, in connection with state trading. European merchants were not permitted to go to the Orient via Constantinople, nor were they allowed to trade with one another within the city.[3] From there the system passed to the North Italian cities.

In North Italy these tendencies were ubiquitous, both in the coastal and in the inland towns. About the middle of the 12th century, for example, when there were fierce struggles between Lucca and Pisa, one of the disputed points was whether Lucca had the right to exercise staple rights with regard to the traffic from the North to Pisa. It may suffice, however, to restrict ourselves to the two most important examples, Venice and Genoa.

In 1095 the Emperor, Henry IV, confirmed an earlier treaty between Venice and the *Regnum Italicum*, at the same time making the important proviso that his people, i.e. the non-Venetians,

---

der Vorherrschaft Venedigs an der Adria (Strasb. 1897); H. F. Brown, *Studies in the History of Venice* I (Lond. 1907); H. Simonsfeld, *Der Fondaco dei Tedeschi in Venedig* II (Stuttg. 1887) part 1.—For Gustav Vasa, see my article "Natural and Money Economy as Illustrated from Swedish History in the 16th Century" (*Journal of Economic and Business History* III 1930/31, 10, 16).

There is a remarkable agreement with Gustav Vasa's arguments in Wheeler's *Treatise* of 1601, defending the Merchant adventurers (69 f.); Wheeler attempts to show the value of the company's concentration of trade in the "mart town".

[3] L. Brentano, "Die byzantinische Volkswirtschaft" (Schmoller's *Jahrbuch* XLI, 1917) 588; cp. J. Kulischer, *Allgemeine Wirtschaftsgeschichte des Mittelalters und der Neuzeit* (Below-Meinecke's Handbuch) I (Munich and Berl. 1928) 80.

should be given the right to trade as far as Venice, though not beyond (*usque ad vos et non amplius*).[4] From the beginning of the 12th century onwards, it was primarily Genoa which pursued this policy. Its aim was to become the sole staple for what is to-day the south of France, and to exclude the cities of those parts from participating in trade on the open sea and primarily the trade to the Levant. In the course of the century, Genoa extended the same treatment to the cities of the west coast of Italy and particularly to Pisa. The strictest measures of all were naturally taken against the cities on its own *riviera*. In 1153 Savona, one of these cities, had to agree to the arrangement that every ship bound for Sardinia and Barcelona should set sail from Genoa, take with it a number of Genoese merchants, and unload at Genoa on the return journey.

The policy was not adopted in Venice for another hundred years, but when it came, it was pursued with a completeness and consistency that far outstripped Genoa. It persisted, with little or no change, down to the overthrow of the city republic by Napoleon in 1798. During the first half of the 13th century various Venetian measures were passed, combining the aims of the staple policy with those of the policy of provision. For the attempt to hinder the intermediary trade of other cities went hand in hand with the endeavour to provide Venice with those goods which it needed itself, that is, not merely with goods intended for resale. This interconnection, which has been referred to before, was also to be found in the German cities. A treaty of 1230 with Ferrara cannot be interpreted otherwise. It gave the Venetians the right to fetch corn, vegetables, and fish from Ferrara, so long as the price did not exceed a certain amount. The same applied to a treaty of 1234 with Ravenna. This city was allowed to sell corn and salt to Venice only and to send to Venice only such food-stuffs as were brought from the Marks and from Apulia. The same two-fold aspect was obviously present in the prohibition of 1236 concerning Ragusa which was not a foreign, but a dependent, city. It was allowed no dealings with the cities of the north Adriatic, except for the purpose of importing food-stuffs into Venice.

Even at that period there were premonitory signs of the notorious Venetian trading system, which took definite shape in the second half of the 13th century. At this point I shall confine myself to a description of its earlier features. An essential

---

[4] The wording is ambiguous (cp. Lenel 3 f., Schaube 7), but in both possible readings the quotation supports the view of the text.

aspect of the system was to reserve for the Venetians all trade, and chiefly trade with distant countries—principally, that is, the Levant trade. Two different principles appear to have been applied here, depending on whether or not the Venetians believed themselves to be capable of entirely excluding competing cities and countries. If not they only attempted to attract to their own city the merchanting of the goods brought from the Levant by others.

The first method was used in connection with a dependent city such as Ragusa. In 1232 it was given exemption from customs duties on its goods in Venice if they came from Slavonia, in Ragusa's immediate neighbourhood. Otherwise it had to pay increasingly high duties, which varied in direct proportion to the distance goods had come. Finally it was only permitted to send into Venice a limited quota of goods from Syria and Africa. What the Venetians reckoned on here was obviously that the Ragusan merchants would not be able to sell elsewhere such goods as they did not sell in Venice, or that, if need be, they could be prevented from doing so by force. To limit the sale of Levant goods in Venice was therefore the same as to limit the sale of Levant goods by the Ragusan merchants in general. If I am not mistaken this may be taken as an instance of Venetian policy at a time when it believed it had complete control over a market. With a powerful and independent state such as Sicily, or an independent city such as Ancona (1264), tactics of the other type were employed. Under the Hohenstaufen Emperor, Frederick II, and also later in 1257 and 1259, Sicily had to undertake to import foreign goods into Venetian territory. In this case I assume that Sicily and Ancona could not be prevented from importing goods from the Levant and that the next best thing, from the Venetian's point of view, was at any rate to divert the goods to their own city.

The measures mentioned hitherto only regulated imports. The measures designed to reserve the sales for the Venetians were even more numerous. Ravenna (1234) and Ancona (1264) were to renounce the pilgrim traffic entirely in favour of Venice. Ancona and Aquileja (1248) had to agree to import no goods into the inland territory reserved for Venice. Ravenna (1261) had to give up all direct imports from countries across the sea and, with certain exceptions, even from North Italy. Ferrara was forced, after its final defeat in 1240, to accept goods, taken up the Po, from Venetians only (or, possibly, from Venice).[5] It is

---

[5] The original has the abbreviation "a Venec̄". This may mean "a Venetis" (from the Venetians) or "a Veneciis" (from Venice). In the latter case the clause belongs to the next paragraph.

seen that trade, not the goods themselves, was everywhere the goal.

Parallel to this was a tendency towards a staple policy in a purely local sense—the endeavour to attract merchants to Venice or to the particular dependent town which Venice wished to favour.

We have already observed that Venice subscribed to the principle of passive trade with regard to the sale of goods on the land route. This applied principally to Germany. With certain exceptions, Venetians were actually prohibited from travelling to Germany to sell their own goods or to buy German products. Such transactions were all to take place in Venice itself (1278). The relations with western Europe were different as regards both export and import. This trade was reserved from the beginning of the 14th century onwards for the famous Venetian galleys. The attitude towards the German trade was probably occasioned by the contempt of the Venetians for trade by land. Their endeavours to attract trade to Venice manifested themselves in a large number of other measures, and not only in the prohibition forbidding their own merchants from travelling across the Alps for purposes of trade. When a Venetian stronghold was established on the southernmost arm of the Po, Marchamò, ("the sea calls"), its commander was obliged to see that goods passing downstream were, with certain exceptions, sent to Venice only. Goods sent to Venice, moreover, had to be sold there. The chronicler and monk, Salimbene, who was bitterly hostile to the Venetians, wrote towards the end of the 13th century: "If a merchant brings his goods there to be sold, he cannot take them back with him, for he is compelled to sell them there whether he will or no." A law of, to my knowledge, a later date laid down more precisely that two-thirds of the cargo carried by a ship putting in at Venice was to be unloaded there. Trade in Venetian territory outside the city proper was, generally speaking, likewise forbidden. Certain favoured, dependent cities, however, were granted staple rights, sometimes with surprising lack of scruple. The patriarch of Aquileja, e.g. in 1248, had to pledge himself to fetch no wine from his own territory of Istria without transporting it first to the Venetian city, Isola. It was not without justification that Salimbene said of the Venetians, "They are a greedy and stiff-necked people . . . they would gladly subject the whole world to themselves if they could; brutally do they treat the merchants who come into their hands."[6]

[6] Schaube, "Die Anfänge der venetianischen Galeerenfahrten nach der Nordsee" (*Historische Zeitschrift* CI, 1908) 28 ff.—For Salimbene: Simonsfeld II 32 note 6 (according to *Monumenta hist. ad prov. Parmens. et Placent. pertinentia* III 252).

In the German cities, essentially the same tendencies were
present, although political and economic factors afforded them
less scope.[7] Their ambitions were usually much more modest
and most cities were concerned with the trade along particular
routes, mostly along the great rivers. There were therefore not
so many possibilities of further development as in Italy and
especially in Venice. The very geographical situation of the
German cities made a vital difference and was, in fact, obstructive
to economic expansion. The geographical position of the Italian
cities gave them far greater potentialities for intermediary trade
and they could therefore gain such trade much more easily and
without strenuous acts of interference. Situated as they were on
the coast, the Italian cities were usually at the end of the route,
whereas the inland German cities were situated somewhere along
a route which in the normal way passed on. In Venice and Genoa
all that the compulsory staple often meant was that they became places of unloading and sale *instead* of other cities, while
in Cologne and Vienna it meant that the goods had to be unloaded there *additionally*. The compulsory staple in the German
cities therefore led to entirely superfluous unloadings and tran-
shipments. It forcibly created an unnecessary intermediary trade
which was hardly the case in Italy. This damaging effect on
Germany's trade, however, was balanced by the fact that no
German cities had the same political opportunities of enforcing
their power unscrupulously as did the strongest of the Italian cities.

Every German city with staple rights thus attempted to appropriate to itself as much of the up- and down-stream traffic as it
could, and in the city itself the goods were then retained in some

---

[7] The staple policy of the German cities has been dealt with in numerous
works. Here follow some treatises bringing together the more important facts:
M. Hafemann, *Das Stapelrecht, eine rechtshistorische Untersuchung* (Lpz. 1910;
rather mechanical); W. Stieda, Art. "Stapelrecht" in *Handwörterbuch der
Staatswissenschaften* (VII³ 808 ff.; disconnected facts); Schmoller, "Die
ältere Elbhandelspolitik," etc. (see note 1 above); W. Naudé, *Deutsche städtische
Getreidehandelspolitik vom 15.—17. Jahrhundert mit besonderer Berücksichtigung
Stettins und Hamburgs* (Schmoller's Forschungen VIII: v, Lpz. 1889; neither
profound nor incisive in judgment, but graphic); W. Stein, *Beiträge zur Ges-
chichte der deutschen Hanse bis um die Mitte des 15. Jahrhunderts* (Giessen 1900,
32–68; thorough); E. Daenell's well-informed work *Die Blütezeit der Deutschen
Hanse* I–II (Berl. 1905–6); H. Rachel's instructive essay, "Die Handelsver-
fassung der Norddeutschen Städte im 15. bis 18. Jahrhundert" (Schmoller's
Jahrb. f. Gesetzgeb. etc. XXXIV, 1910) 983–1045; B. Kuske, "Handel und
Handelspolitik am Niederrhein vom 13. bis 16. Jahrhundert" (*Hansische
Geschichtsblätter* 1909) 318 f., 325 ff.—See also E. Arup, *Studier i engelsk og tysk
handels historie* §§ 295–306.

way or other for the purpose of providing the citizens with trading profits of various kinds. These attempts took various forms which need not, however, be dealt with separately. They were all an expression of one and the same principle which has already been developed here in sufficient detail. As the foregoing account shows, this principle consisted primarily in preventing goods, at all costs, from going past the city. In this way the mobility of goods was tied down. One drastic example should make this point clear. Lüneburg was situated some distance from the trade route which it dominated, and until 1538 it went so far as to force goods travelling up the Elbe to *leave the river*. They had to be loaded on to waggons and to be carried by land, even to such places as Magdeburg that were situated themselves on the Elbe. Even if the staple lay on the route itself, the compulsion was no less burdensome. In various cities, such as Frankfurt-an-der-Oder and Hamburg, goods were compelled to go in a direction *opposite* to their intended destination. In other words they had to travel upstream to the staple city, were then permitted to return and follow their course downstream. This practice of drawing the goods into the city was supplemented by the fact that they were forced to remain for a time in the city, usually three days (*drei Sonnenscheinen*, as it was often called) so that they could be sold. Frequently this was done even where the goods were already sold and were merely passing the city on their way to the purchaser. In any case, a reloading was usually prescribed and even then the foreign merchant was often not allowed to continue the transport of his goods, even if they remained unsold (*jus emporii*).

The essential points of the two oldest German staple charters will illustrate this further.[8] Vienna's staple, according to Article 23 of the Viennese municipal law of 1221, forbade merchants of Swabia, Regensburg and Passau to travel on with their goods to Hungary and ordered them to sell their merchandise to citizens of Vienna.[9] The Cologne compulsory staple was based on a

---

[8] An ordinance of Charles the Great of the year 805 (*Urkunden* ed. Keutgen—see note 1 chap. 1 of this part—No. 69) according to some writers inaugurated the compulsory staple. But in that case, the word must be taken in quite another meaning than the usual. It was a question of directing commerce according to administrative and military ends. Advantages were not given to specific places.

[9] "Nulli civium de Swevia vel de Ratispona vel de Patavia liceat intrare cum mercibus suis in Ungariam. . . . Nemo etiam extraneorum mercatorum moretur in civitate cum mercibus suis ultra duos menses, nec vendat merces quas adduxit extraneo sed tantum civi" (*Urkunden*, etc. No. 164).

charter of 1259 from the Archbishop of Cologne. This decided
that the city was to be the boundary for trade in all directions.
Merchants from eastern parts were not permitted to pass the
Rhine, while people from Flanders and Brabant who came across
the Maas, and other Low Germans, had likewise to remain on
their side of the Rhine, and also were not to travel up the river
further than Rodenkirchen. Finally, South Germans, from without the archbishopric, were not to travel down the Rhine further
than the last tower of Cologne or the village of Ryle (Riel).[10]
It is true that this could hardly have been enforced.

The staple policy of the Hanseatic League, and of the Hanseatic
cities during the heyday of the League in the 15th century,
deviated somewhat from that of the other German cities and
approximated more closely to the staple policy of Italy. This is
quite comprehensible, because the position of the Hanseatic cities
in the Baltic had many points in common with that of the Italian
cities in the Adriatic and the Mediterranean. They pursued a
very elaborately drawn up monopolistic policy, but it would be
superfluous to labour the description further, for it contained
nothing essentially novel. The best examples appear to be the
Prussian and Livonian cities, particularly Danzig and Riga. In
the first place they endeavoured to cut off the inland cities from
any direct connection with the Baltic and to deny all other cities
access to the inland markets. Novgorod, in fact, could only be
visited by members of the Hansa. The Hansa itself even went so
far as to attempt to exclude the Dutch from sea traffic to the
Livonian coastal towns. A very characteristic expression of this
tendency was the fact that the Dutch and the South Germans
were forbidden to learn Russian.

An interesting development arising from the staple compulsion
common in the north German cities was the "division of cities"
in Sweden, which has already been mentioned in another context.
The two trading ordinances of 1614 and 1617 were chiefly responsible for the separation of all cities into two categories, staple
cities and inland cities (*uppstäder*). Only the former had the right
to trade with foreign countries, and they alone might be visited
by foreigners. The inland cities were directed both to import and
export by way of the staples. Charles IX, the father of Gustavus
Adolphus, wanted to develop this idea much further. According
to him (1595 and 1607) Stockholm was to be the only Swedish
staple in the Baltic, so that all the foreign trade of Sweden and
Finland, with the exception of that part of it which could be sent

[10] *Hansisches Urkundenbuch* I (Halle 1876) No. 523.

via Lödöse on the west coast, was to be monopolized in the capital. In support of his idea he referred explicitly to the example of Danzig and Lübeck. To the great chagrin of its originator, the idea was not carried into effect, although Norrland, the northern part of Sweden, and Finland were referred to Stockholm for their relations with foreign countries, by the so-called Bothnian trading restriction, whose origins went back to the Middle Ages. This system of regulation in Sweden, which persisted for several hundred years, is of theoretical interest because the staple policy, which almost everywhere else was expressed in privileges of varying scope for individual cities, was here elaborated into a uniform system for a whole country.[11]

With local differences, the staple policy occurred in divers countries and in varying degrees. Marseilles in many respects adopted a position resembling that of the Italian cities. It was supported in this position by the French monarchy and particularly by Colbert's deliberate and intensive efforts. As a secondary staple city for the Levant trade, Rouen acquired a similar though not so important a position. The inland cities of France employed the same system as the German. In the province of Poitou, where salt was produced, the salt was held up on its way to the coast in every single city and forced to be offered for sale on the spot. In the Netherlands, Ghent's position as a staple for corn caused much bad blood even in the middle of the 16th century, on account of the lack of scruple with which its position was maintained. Bruges, too, pursued a staple policy for monopolistic ends with the greatest eagerness during its later, and in fact much weaker, epoch. These are only isolated examples of a policy common to most European countries.[12]

Nevertheless there was one important exception to the general rule—England. Staple policy in the continental sense, the concentration of trade in particular cities, occurred there in the Middle Ages only in the forms already discussed in connection with the trading companies. Compared to the firm hold of the policy on most other countries, this was practically insignificant. The explanation is that in England the cities were far less independent, in relation to the state authority, than they were on the con-

---

[11] Heckscher, *Sveriges ekon. hist.* I : 1 251 ff., etc. (see *Registret*), 389, 686.— Cf. above I 134 f.

[12] Marseilles and Rouen: Masson, *Hist. du comm. franç. dans le Levant au 17ᵉ siècle* 71, 130, 166 *et passim.*—Poitou: Boissonnade, *Organisation du travail en Poitou* I 217 f.—Ghent: Pirenne, *Hist. de Belgique* II³ 363 f., III² 121 and the references given therein; cp. Naudé 144–54.

tinent. England's insularity, moreover, prevented her, unlike Sweden, from adopting from the continent forces leading to disintegration.

At the same time, however, we have the paradoxical phenomenon that England of all countries, in spite of the fact that a staple policy in the medieval sense of the word never really obtained a footing there, yet elaborated and preserved the last and most important branch of all staple policy more tenaciously than did any other country. But here too English idiosyncrasies manifested themselves. The primary object was not so much to favour one city or another, but to make the *country as a whole* the staple for the most desired commodities. This was the idea behind the Old Colonial System. It originated in Spain but experienced its greatest expansion in England.

Spain kept jealous watch to make sure that all trade with her colonies was reserved exclusively to itself. In fact it even directed this trade via a particular city, first Seville and later Cadiz, where it was kept in the hands of the notorious *Casa de Contratación*. Basing itself on this practice, England employed the same methods from the outset in its own colonial experiments. John Cabot's charter of 1496 already mentioned Bristol as the port for the voyages of discovery. Corresponding regulations were later repeatedly passed for a large number of companies, usually in the interests of London, as already pointed out in connection with the trading companies (I, 432). This may perhaps be regarded as pure staple policy, for individual cities were thereby favoured. But much more important was the form which the policy assumed in the country as a whole.[13]

In letters patent for the East India Company, issued in 1615, it was hopefully suggested that the "staple" for East Indian products was henceforth to be in the home country. In 1636 it was suggested, equally hopefully, that the staple for colonial tobacco should be concentrated in London. The decisive step, however, was first taken by the Navigation Act of 1660, which became the fundamental basis of the Old Colonial System. According to this Act the colonies could send their most important products, the so-called Enumerated Commodities, only to the

[13] Spain: Haring, *Trade and Navigation between Spain and the Indies*, 3, 9–15 *et passim.*—In the Dutch colonial system Batavia occupied a position which *mutatis mutandis* was reminiscent of that of Seville; see, e.g., Lannoy and van der Linden, *Hist. de l'expansion coloniale des peuples européens* II 259.—John Cabot's charter: *Foedera* (ed. Rymer) O. XII 595 f., repr. in *Tudor Econ. Docs.* II 9 ff.

mother country. By an important law passed three years later, actually called the Staple Act, the same was ordered with regard to the export of European goods to the colonies, with the express purpose of "making this Kingdom a Staple not only of the Commodities of those Plantations but also of the Commodities of other Countries and Places for the supplying of them".

In all European countries possessing colonies there were signs of this policy, but its last great impetus was provided by the English measures at the time of the Revolutionary and Napoleonic Wars. The basis of the English tactics was an instruction of 1798, later elaborated in the English Orders in Council of 1807, which were the counterblast to Napoleon's Continental Decrees. By the Orders in Council, all neutral ships were commanded to put in at an English port. One of the objects was obviously to make England the staple for all colonial merchandise. In many respects it is certainly significant that England brought to fruition, in the form of a national monopoly, one of the most powerful tendencies of municipal policy.[14]

The quotation at the beginning of this chapter, concerning Hamburg's staple policy, conveys in general the best idea of the nature of staple policy. The endeavours of the Hamburg merchants, which so incensed the electoral council of Brandenburg, were none other than an expression of that *laissez-faire* principle of buying in the cheapest market and selling in the dearest. No doubt the staple policy would have been abhorred by adherents of *laissez-faire*, for it created monopolies both in buying and selling; and thus the traders were able to buy *still* more cheaply and sell *still* more dearly than would have been possible under free trade. In itself this difference is certainly most important; but it does not alter the fact that the attitude of the staple policy towards goods was the same as that which dominates all economic activity under free trade. According to its proposed aims, the staple policy constituted a monopoly for the benefit of the particular staple locality *as a whole*. The profits resulting from the measures did not necessarily pass from one group of citizens to another, but were a loss to two groups *outside* the city, i.e. the

[14] Letter of 1615: pr. *Register of Letters of the East India Company* (ed. Birdwood & Foster) 470.—Statement of 1636, quoted in Beer, *Origins of the British Colonial System 1578–1660*, 202; the other examples will also be found there 179–88, 195, 197 ff., 201, 205, 343, 347, etc.—Navigation Act of 1660: 12 Car. II c. 18 §§ 18 & 19.—Staple Act: 15 Car. II c. 7 §4.—Orders in Council: A. T. Mahan, *The Influence of Sea Power upon the French Revolution and Empire 1793–1812* (Lond. 1893) II 233 ff.; Heckscher, *The Continental System* 45 f., 113, 120.

merchants who were forced to sell to citizens of the town where they might have sold to others at greater profit, and those who were forced to buy from the citizens where they might with greater advantage have bought from others. Within the city itself, in theory, no industry was prevented from developing as it might have done under free trade. Trade within the city was carried on in such a manner that every person engaged in it derived the greatest possible profit from the common monopolistic position of all the inhabitants. Compulsion only applied to extra-urban trade. It follows that the staple policy had a different position in principle from the policy of provision and the policy of protection. The two latter wished to remould the industrial life of the city itself. They wanted to encourage some things and hinder others, which larger or smaller groups of citizens considered desirable in their own interests.

If the staple policy crippled what is usually meant by economic progress, it did so through its influence on economic life outside the town. In this respect its effect was probably many times more powerful than that of the other types of policy. The natural function of trade, to cater for human needs, was obstructed to a particularly large extent by the staple policy. Certain of its features which make this very clear have been omitted in this exposition. Thus very frequently the reason for a particular measure was merely the desire to cause injury to competitors and political opponents, even though the staple city itself stood to gain nothing definite. Staple policy was very often used purely as a weapon of the policy of power. The host of staple privileges thus became, next to the hopeless state of the tolls, one of the principal factors in the economic disorder of central Europe, although toll confusion must certainly be regarded as the most important among them.

If economic activity in each country as a whole, especially Germany, suffered through the staple policy, there were certainly also many cases where this reacted on the staple cities themselves. The cities might frequently have found themselves much better off had they never enjoyed a trading monopoly at all; at any rate this is in many cases a justifiable presumption. The Belgian historian, Pirenne, for example, has shown that Ghent did not flourish until it lost all its trading privileges, so oppressive to the rest of north-west Europe, after the insurrection of 1539. Similarly, the German historian, Gothein, has attempted to show, in connection with the Rhine cities, that Cologne and Mainz with their numerous staple rights must have experienced an almost complete decline in trade in the 17th and 18th centuries, as a direct result of their privileges. In the place of this trade there came such a mere handling of goods as was felt to be simply a burden to trade. Frankfurt-am-Main and the towns of the Duchy of Berg on the other hand became important centres of trade without having any staple rights whatsoever.[15]

In principle, however, the staple policy from the point of view of the interests of individual cities could be regarded as consistent. A certain modicum of monopolistic power, if not pushed too far, might have provided many a city with benefits which compensated it for the disadvantages arising from the general deterioration of trade as a whole, though it is extremely probable that they usually over-reached themselves.

3. CONNECTION WITH OTHER TENDENCIES. THE TREATMENT OF "MERCHANT-STRANGERS"

Although the staple policy was distinguished in principle from the policy of provision and protectionism, this does not mean that there were no threads linking the former to the latter. There is certainly an obvious connection between staple policy and the policy of provision, as has already been touched upon and will be discussed again. But at this juncture it is of lesser importance, for both the policy of provision and staple policy will be regarded here chiefly from the standpoint of their importance to the policy of protection. The primary question is, therefore, whether there is any connection between staple policy and protectionism.

To reply to this question we must now turn to a study of the treatment of "merchant-strangers", what was called in Germany *Gästerecht* or *Fremdenrecht*.[16] Such measures were the principal means of preserving trade in the hands of the cities' burghers. The staple compulsion confined itself, in fact, to binding the

[15] Pirenne, *Histoire de Belgique* III² 127 f.—E. Gothein, "Zur Geschichte der Rheinschiffahrt" (*Westdeutsche Zeitschr.* XIV 1895) 252.

[16] There are no comprehensive expositions on this subject. None the less it is treated of in many places, in nearly all the works on the staple policy already quoted, and partly, too, in other works, including: Th. Stolze, *Die Entstehung des Gästerechtes in den deutschen Städten des Mittelalters* (Thesis, Marburg 1901); A. Schultze, "Über Gästerecht und Gastgerichte in den deutschen Städten des M.A." (*Historische Zeitschrift* CI, 1908, 473 ff.—A model exposition; though legal in intention, it throws light upon other aspects of the subject as well); on England: Schanz, *Englische Handelspolitik gegen Ende des Mittelalters* (I 379–433, II 594–613) and Cunningham I⁴; for Sweden: see Heckscher, *Sveriges ekon. hist.* I : 1 241, 246 f., 258, and II : 2 671, 750, 861.

trade to the city. These laws were therefore an almost indispensable supplement to the staple right itself.

It is difficult to determine the age of the legislation against foreign merchants with any degree of precision. Regulations regarding the visits of strangers probably have their roots far back in the past. However, there are certain indications, at least in Germany, that conditions of greater freedom preceded the staple policy itself both here and in other spheres. It is tempting to assume that the restrictive policy originated in the Levant, where complicated measures, actuated by mistrust of foreign infidels, are to be found in large numbers. But the material hitherto investigated provides no ground for this assumption. The Italian regulations concerning strangers' rights appear to be comparatively recent, hardly older than the end of the 12th century, but at that date there were already instances north of the Alps. The oldest charter known is probably that drawn up by the Archbishop of Cologne in 1103 for the merchants of Huy and Dinant in the city of the archbishopric. The charter *Libertas Londoniensis* (or *civitatum*), with its unusually detailed and informative clauses relating to strangers' rights, is dated by its most recent publisher, Liebermann, between 1133 and 1155.[17] From that time onwards, the new laws against strangers grew steadily in importance, and were intensified both in Germany and in Italy in the course of the 13th century, in close connection with the development of the staple policy. The Hansa did not acquire any laws against strangers before the end of the 14th and the beginning of the 15th centuries.

In spite of all variations in different cities and in different periods, the basic features of the rights of strangers were everywhere alike.

In the first place attempts were made to institute careful supervision over the whole life of the "guests". They were permitted to live only with specially prescribed "hosts" or in a hostelry reserved for them. The *Fondaco dei Tedeschi*, the hostel for Germans in Venice, is the best known example of this kind of internment. The regulations there were amazingly strict and at night, for example, the foreign merchants were kept locked up in their hostel. The guests were also often compelled to carry on business only through a native dealer, in Italy known as a *Sensal*,

[17] The document of 1103: *Hansisches Urkundenbuch* III No. 601.—*Libertas Londoniensis* (previously often connected with the "Laws of Edward the Confessor"): *Die Gesetze der Angelsachsen*, ed. F. Liebermann, I (Halle 1898) 673 ff.; cp. III 351.

while at an early date there existed a more extensive prohibition against strangers trading with one another at all, or in general transacting any re-sale. Re-sale was already expressly forbidden in the *Libertas Londoniensis*.

The clause of the Viennese municipal law of 1221 mentioned above already decided that merchants were not to sell goods which they had brought with them to strangers, at least not outside the annual market, but only to citizens of the town. In addition strangers were excluded from retail trade (wholesale trade always enjoyed greater freedom), as well as from direct purchase from producers and from trade outside the town market. The Hansa went much further and prohibited many other forms of co-operation with the foreigners, such as entering into partnership with them, providing freights for their ships and so on. A particularly important extension of the restrictions was in many respects the prohibition in Vienna, towards the end of the Middle Ages (1481 and 1500), forbidding the mercers of the town from selling goods purchased from strangers outside the period of the annual city market. The idea here was to limit the competition of imported goods with those of native craftsmen. Furthermore the period of sojourn, the time for which strangers were allowed to remain in the city, was usually limited. Finally there was a special system of jurisdiction for strangers.

This somewhat detailed description of the laws against merchant-strangers shows that they were a necessary supplement to the staple rights and aimed chiefly at reserving intermediary trade to the citizens of the towns or, where this was considered for some reason or other impossible, at least at interposing a citizen as middleman in any dealings between foreigners.

On the other hand it is equally clear that these laws in several of their prescriptions went *further* than the staple laws. Undoubtedly the system largely originated in the mistrust of the actions of all strangers.[18] But the laws against strangers were not entirely made up either of this or of the tendency towards staple policy. The regulations were obviously intended to limit not only the competition of foreign merchants with the native in intermediary trade, but also their buying and selling *in the city itself*. Even though there is only a small and easily comprehensible step from one to the other, a cursory examination is enough to show that it had far-reaching economic consequences. The

---

[18] "In the imagination of the time, two foreigners could hardly come together without plotting some mischief" (Ashley, *Introduction to English Economic History and Theory* II 16 f.).

measures against foreign competition in intermediary trade hit only the foreigners—buyers and sellers outside the city—to the benefit of the city as a whole. But the only people who profited by the exclusion of the foreign merchants from competition in the trade within the city were the merchant classes of the city, and their profit had to be paid for by urban producers and consumers in the form of higher prices which the native merchants were able to demand for their services, once the foreign competition was excluded. In Sweden, for instance, there was one example of this legislation which caused considerable bad blood, the monopoly held by the merchants of the staple cities for the export of Swedish bar-iron. Foreign agents were not allowed to penetrate to the iron districts at all. The monopolist profits which accrued to the native merchants obviously had to be borne, at least to some extent, by the ironmasters, a fact which they of course never failed to point out. For the same reasons English landowners during the Middle Ages, since they were also sellers of wool, were opposed to the anti-foreign laws. In the same way, of course, consumers in the towns had to pay higher prices in many cases where competition in retail trade was restricted.

If protectionism is conceived broadly so as to include any interference in favour of one social group at the expense of another, then these laws, too, certainly had a protectionist tendency. But if the question refers to the particular views on economic policy to which the word protectionism has here been confined, that expression becomes misleading. For then the deciding consideration is not the tendency of the policy to deflect economic life from the course it would otherwise have taken but the attitude of the policy towards goods. From this standpoint there exists even in the cases last mentioned an essential difference between staple policy and laws against strangers on the one hand, and protectionist policy under the motto "fear of goods" on the other. The laws against strangers, in other words, were certainly a system of protection for *trade*, but not for goods or for production. The investigation must therefore be carried further if we are to determine how the laws which favoured native as against foreign *merchants* developed into a protectionist system which put a premium on native as against foreign *goods*.

It might be thought that there was but a small step from the fear of foreign merchants and their harmful competition to the fear of foreign goods. Actually the distance between the two was considerably greater, and the reason lay in the general economic attitude towards goods, which could only alter gradually.

That the problem is not so simple as one might, at first glance, be inclined to believe may be seen, for example, from a letter patent of King Wenceslas of Bohemia regarding the combined cities of Prague (Altstadt and Neustadt). This letter defended the staple and guest regulations of the two, united cities on the grounds that the citizens had recognized how the cities "could suffer and for a long time had suffered *many unpleasantnesses and losses* because strangers from all countries had brought their tied and untied goods to these cities" (my italics). At first sight it appears as though the aversion to foreign goods is here clearly expressed, but a further study of this document reveals no ground for this belief. For the later clauses in the letter prescribe that strangers who sojourned in the town at least five days were not to be permitted *to carry their goods any further*. And this appears to be in harmony with the reference to both "tied" and "untied" (*legata et non ligata*) goods, for the first of these two types of goods, not being unloaded, was unable to compete with local products. If the quotation is taken quite literally, it is not the goods but the *strangers* who caused the damage in bringing the goods with them. The most that might be said is that the reference to the goods brought by the unwelcome strangers allows another conclusion to be drawn; but even that is, to say the least, uncertain. It is most probable that the ill-will was directed only against competing merchants. Similarly in a contemporary document of the Priory of Ste. Geneviève in Paris, foreign merchants who were not guests of the monastery were forbidden to sell such cloths as they had brought with them, unless they had come there by accident, during a visit that was to last no more than two days. Here again the prohibition was directed not against the textile goods themselves, but against their sale by such foreign merchants who remained too long in the place.[19]

[19] Prague: "universitas civium nostrae antiquae civitatis Pragensis nec non cives novae civitatis Pragensis sub castro videntes, quod ipsae civitates multa detrimenta et dampna recipiant et receperint a temporibus retroactis propter hospites de quibuscunque terris, sua mercimonia legata et non ligata indictas (= in dictas) civitates adducentes . . . statuerunt, ut . . . si (dicti hospites) quinque diebus in dictis civitatibus manserint, tunc debent sua mercimonia disligare coram duobus probis viris et notario . . . et tunc dicta mercimonia nullatenus de civitatibus deducere teneantur": *Deutsche Rechtsdenkmäler aus Böhmen und Mähren*, ed. Rössler I (Prague 1845), Introduction lxxxvii f., note. Schultze, who has drawn attention to this interesting document, interprets it in a manner which, in my opinion, is inaccurate:

These examples, therefore, show that we are still dealing with protection of trade and not of production. The same applies to the practice of medieval toll policy according to which, in the large majority of cases, toll had to be paid only by strangers. The further motive seems to have operated, that strangers were free from the other municipal burdens which rested upon the natives.[20] But it is obvious that this did not lead to any protection of goods as such.

Laws against strangers were most closely connected to municipal policy as a whole and thereby obviously also to the gilds. So long as this connection was limited to the merchant gilds alone, the protection of goods remained as far off as ever. It was only when measures began to be taken in the interests of the gilds against foreign *craftsmen* that the protection of goods was approached. Foreign or rather extra-municipal goods could be brought into the city by native, just as well as by foreign, merchants. But if foreign craftsmen were excluded, this undoubtedly reacted on the supply of foreign goods. The two points, it is true, do not altogether coincide, and measures against foreign craftsmen are not quite identical in effect with measures against foreign goods. However, there was a very close connection between them. By means of their regulations against foreign craftsmen, these measures paved the way for the protection of goods.

There can be no doubt that they actually did have this effect in many cases. Both kinds of regulations, against foreign merchants and against foreign craftsmen, occurred explicitly side by side in the *Libertas Londoniensis*. The example concerning Vienna is perhaps even more significant, where the native mercers were prohibited from selling outside the annual markets goods purchased from foreigners, so as not to injure the monopoly of the native craftsmen. This apparently obvious outcome of the laws against strangers, however, was slow in acquiring so great an

"Schon in der Einführung der Waren selbst wird also hier die möglicherweise die Bürgerschaft schädigende Handlung gesehen" (*op. cit.* 502).—Ste. Geneviève (end of the 13th or beginning of the 14th century): "Que nul marchand estrange, se il n'estoit nostre hoste, ne puisse vendre tiretaines ne sarges que il aporte dehors en la dicte terre, se ce n'estoit en trespassant I jour ou II, au plus": pr. G. Fagniez, *Études sur l'industrie et la classe industrielle à Paris au XIIIᵉ et au XIVᵉ siècles* (Paris 1877) No. 46.

[20] "Omnis qui facit iura ville non dat theloneum", were the words of a decree of 1249 in Freiburg in Üchtland, which were copied with minor variations in one city after the other. See the references collected by Kulischer, *Allgemeine Wirtschaftsgeschichte* I 195 and cp. R. Häpke, *Brügges Entwicklung zum mittelalterlichen Weltmarkt* (Abhandl. z. Verkehrs- und Seegeschichte, ed. D. Schäfer I, Berl. 1908) 34 ff., and other works. Cp. I 68 f. above.

importance as might easily be imagined. When the tendency developed into definite protection of goods, it found itself opposed to the policy of provision which had entirely contrary aims. It found in it a most difficult obstacle to overcome. And so before this line of development is followed any further, we must examine the policy of provision.

III

THE POLICY OF PROVISION

1. ITS FORMATION AND DEVELOPMENT

The economic scope of the staple policy must always have been rather limited. In the first place, intermediary trade could have only been of any importance to a fairly small fraction of the population. The only justification for directing attention primarily to the commercial cities is their great importance as pioneers and leaders of medieval economic policy and not the size of their population relative to that of the rural areas. The problem remains of how the welfare of the remainder, and incomparably larger, section of the population was regulated.

But this is not all. Even the towns with staple rights had no guarantee that these rights would assure them of necessary consumption, although the staple policy could naturally be combined with measures effecting this. The staple rights certainly did give the towns the possibility of "earning" and "profit"; but for these advantages to be realized there must have been a more thorough satisfaction of the requirements of the citizens, that is, a greater amount of goods consumed in the city. In the purely commercial as well as in the other towns, the main function of economic policy must have consisted in making precisely this possible, i.e. in supplying the population with goods by importing from outside and by making available the products of the locality itself. It was never sufficient simply to procure goods for intermediary trade; and the staple policy was therefore unable to cover the whole field, or in fact even the principal part of it.

The guiding consideration of the policy of provision, therefore, was not far to seek. By encroaching on trade beyond the town's or the country's boundaries, it endeavoured to ensure the greatest possible supplies for native consumption.[1]

[1] The references quoted in the previous chapter contain a great deal of matter on this point as well.—On Germany there is in addition a popular and brief work which was occasioned by World War I : von Below, *Mittelalterliche Stadtwirtschaft und gegenwärtige Kriegswirtschaft* (Kriegswirtschaftliche Zeitfragen ed. F. Eulenburg, No. 10, Tüb. 1917).—On Italy Schaube is the main authority. With regard to England, Cunningham has emphasized the difference between the policy of provision and the policy of protection, but his view of the importance in this connection of Edward III's reign has been considerably modified by Unwin's collected essays, approved by Cunningham himself: *Finance and Trade under Edward III* (Manchester University Publications, Histori-

There is such a multitude of measures of interference with trade in various countries and during various periods that any choice of examples may easily appear arbitrary. The objection might be raised that though they show the tendency ascribed to them, they were not typical. In order to give a "random sample", in other words to prove that what is described was the rule and not the exception, it would be necessary to have some quantitative measurement of the occurrence of manifestations of the policy of provision. In the majority of cases this would certainly not be practicable or, at any rate, would involve such difficulties that the attempt would not be worth while. None the less it is possible to obtain results for sufficiently large areas and sufficiently long periods which indicate what the normal was, even though no claim to absolute precision can be put forward. The results of two such investigations will therefore be given first.

Statistical analysis

The famous English collection of documents known as Rymer's *Foedera* (*Foedera, conventiones, litterae et cujuscumque generis acta publica*, etc., ed. Th. Rymer, 1st ed. Lond. 1704/17), quoted frequently above, can be used for such a measurement of the scope of the policy of provision. Although in a somewhat unsystematic and obscure form, it contains regulations which were not Acts of Parliament. The collection is particularly applicable for the present purpose, because it has been made the subject of an excellent digest by Sir Thomas Duffus Hardy, at one time deputy-keeper of the Record Office.[2] It must be considered highly representative, with the one important reservation that far too

cal Series XXXII, 1918). On the subject of corn policy, which is most important in this context, all previous works are superseded by N. S. B. Gras's *The Evolution of the English Corn Market from the 12th to the 18th Century* (Harvard Economic Studies XIII, Cambr. Mass., 1915).—The relevant points in the case of France were certainly first put forward by A. Callery, "Les douanes avant Colbert et l'ordonnance de 1664" (*Revue historique* XVIII, 1882 part^y. 75–80) and H. Pigeonneau, *Histoire du commerce de la France* I² (1887); but as a counterpart to Gras's work, though rather less fertile, is A. P. Usher, *History of the Grain Trade in France 1400–1710* (Harv. Ec. Stud. IX, 1913).—On Sweden, the principal work is K. Åmark, *Spannmålshandel och spannmålspolitik i Sverige 1719–1830* (Stockholm 1915).—The corresponding situation in ancient times has been treated by M. P:n Nilsson, "Dyrtid och dyrtidsorganisation i forntiden" (*Statsvetenskapl. Tidskr.* XXII 1919 1 ff., 77 ff.), concerning which there has been a difference of opinion between the author and myself (*ib.* 324 ff., 345 ff.).—On the theoretical aspect of the question, see my *Världskrigets ekonomi* (Stockholm 1915) 235 ff.

[2] *Syllabus (in English) of the Documents Contained in the Collection known as "Rymer's Foedera"*, ed. T. D. Hardy, I–III (Record Publications, Lond. 1869/85).

much emphasis is laid on Edward III's long reign (1327/77), which showed an almost nervous activity in foreign trade.

The following table has been drawn up from the materials supplied by Rymer, as given in Hardy's Syllabus, for the period ending with the latter part of the 14th century, which marks something of an epoch in English history. The figures show the number of times proclamations were issued for each group of goods; the total is therefore greater than the number of decrees issued, for some of them refer at the same time to a number of commodities.

	Export prohibitions	Export licences	Import facilities	Total A	Import prohibitions	Import licences	Total B
Precious metals, coins, etc.	8	7	1	16	(2)	2	2(4)
Textile raw materials	13	18	—	31	—	2	2
Other raw materials	10	3	—	13	—	—	—
War materials	25	6	—	31	—	3	3
Food-stuffs ..	36	21	1	58	1	12	13
Manufactured goods	7	11	—	18	—	—	—
General and miscellaneous	3	10	—	13	—	2	2
Total ..	102	76	2	180	1(3)	21	22(24)

It will be seen that group A is almost nine times as great as group B. Group A is undoubtedly typical of the policy of provision, while it is far more doubtful whether B really expresses the opposite tendency. At first sight it may appear remarkable that export prohibitions and export licences should both represent the same tendency, and the same applies to import prohibitions and import licences on the other side. Detailed investigation of the facts, however, confirms the view that prohibitions and licences always occurred together. On closer examination this is quite explicable. However unwilling the authorities might have been, they had to allow a certain amount of export (and import). That licences occur for indispensable commercial transactions is not by any means a proof that such transactions were welcomed. It shows on the contrary that the authorities were mistrustful of dealings of a certain kind and that the licences issued were regarded as a special favour granted in order to enable people to carry them out. It is prohibitions of a certain type which give rise to licences of the corresponding type. These may be said to be the exceptions, which prove that such prohibitions were the rule.

In the data on which the table is based, the policy of provision may therefore be said to have altogether predominated. The deviations, constituting group B, appear almost accidental, for on the whole they fall under three groups of goods, the import of which people were usually least inclined to prevent, i.e. foodstuffs, means of defence, and precious metals. Thus the figures appear unusually conclusive.

In reality, however, their significance is rather limited by the fact that in the period which they cover, the reign of Edward III and the last three quarters of the 14th century, is accorded too much importance. The following table makes this clear:

			A	B	Total
Before 1300	..	..	4	4	8
1300/26	..	..	13	3	16
1327/99	..	..	163	15	178
Total	..	..	180	22	202

For this reason it is desirable to compare and check the results with material from other sources. A check of this kind may be obtained from investigation of a Swedish source—the outgoing letters of Gustav Vasa from 1521 to 1560, the twenty-nine volumes of which contain most of the state measures extant passed during his long reign. As in the case of the English sources, it is impossible to be certain of completeness, but in neither case is that objection serious, as the material available is sufficiently ample to eliminate what is merely accidental. For Sweden, the material is even rather more ample, for the number of decrees is 209, whereas the 202 or 204 given for England are more than the number of the separate orders. The disparity in time between the two collections is rather an advantage than the reverse, for under Gustav Vasa, Sweden still had a thoroughly medieval make-up, probably even more so than England a century and a half earlier. An analysis of the Swedish material yields the results[3] as shown in the table on page 84.

The prohibitions on the export of coin are not included. The goods which are contained in the last group have been left out in the others. The number of decrees is 209, of which 112 are export prohibitions and 97 export licences, or about the same proportion as in the English figures, which is a further proof of the interconnection of these two kinds of measures. It is particularly striking that the table includes no import prohibitions

[3] For this and the following, see Heckscher, *Sveriges ekon. hist.* I : I 254-62.

	Export Prohibitions	Export Licences	Total
Food-stuffs in general	33	2 ⎫	
Corn (and malt)	16	18 ⎪	
Butter and other fats	21	22 ⎬ 137	
Fish	18	7 ⎭	
Oxen (and other horned cattle) ..	17	7 ⎫ 50	
Horses	17	9 ⎭	
Copper and iron	6	10 ⎫	
Timber, timber goods (and tar) ..	5	13 ⎬ 45	
Hides, leather (and leather goods)	4	7 ⎭	
"Forbidden Goods"	10	3 ⎫ 21	
"Non-Forbidden Goods"	—	8 ⎭	
Reprisals against individual countries	12	3	15
			268

or import licences at all. Apart from two cases, which formally belong here, but are in reality something quite different, they are also completely absent in the material. The policy of provision is thus represented even more clearly in the Swedish figures than in the English.

General characteristics

These rather rough statistical analyses may be clarified by a more thorough discussion. This discussion will include other countries beside the two for which figures could be given without much difficulty.

The two tables have made it sufficiently clear that the tendency was, in the first place, to *retain* the goods and only in the second place to attract them. For this purpose, export prohibitions were the most convenient measures. Their enormous preponderance has just been shown. Frequently, e.g. in France at the beginning of the 14th century, a *general* prohibition of exports was the normal form of commercial policy, and exports could only be effected through licences. The issue of these licences was then often made dependent on the condition that the price should not rise above a certain level. An important English Act (or treaty) regarding tolls of the same period, usually called *Carta Mercatoria* (1303), defining the rights and duties of foreign merchants in England, shows a very similar bias. It is significant that it was not considered necessary to give explicit permission for imports, probably because these were naturally welcomed. On the other hand a general export licence through privileges was granted to foreign merchants for all goods other than wine, for which a special licence was demanded in every individual case.[4]

In many respects this policy was thus reminiscent of the regulation of foreign trade during the Great War of 1914-18. Even the most remarkable feature of that regulation, the so-called system of compensation, had medieval precursors. An example of it was the particularly important regulation of wine import in England under Edward III. A general licence issued to Bristol in 1364 decided that wine must be imported to the same value as the goods permitted to be exported (wool, cloth, etc.), the duty of importing being imposed upon those who enjoyed the benefit of exporting. About the same time the powerful Company of Vintners of England secured a monopoly not only of the import of wines from Gascony, but also of the export of herrings and cloth, which were to go as payment for that indispensable beverage. In this case the motive was certainly different: the unwillingness to allow precious metals to leave the country. But it is significant that no one thought of placing embargoes on imports for that reason, as protectionism was later to do. In a French general export prohibition of 1304, merchants who had imported non-prohibited goods were allowed to export such goods or money to the value of imports. Gustav Vasa, too, always had the idea of compensation in mind. He allowed export only on condition that equivalent imports were forthcoming, or as payment for such import if it had already taken place. The following statement of 1546 is typical. "Since in truth it may be shown that he has brought solid goods into the realm and desires to continue so to do, as he assures us, we graciously allow him in exchange to ship out of the realm fats and other commodities that bring him profit." The import of goods had always been Gustav Vasa's goal, as may be seen, too, from the following observation: "Also ye may think on it to import good wares into

[4] "Quod omnes predicti mercatores mercandisas suas, quas . . . ad . . . regnum . . . adducere . . . possint, quo voluerint, tam infra regnum . . . quam extra ducere seu portare facere, preterquam ad terras . . . hostium regni nostri . . . , vinis dumtaxat exceptis, que de . . . regno . . . , *postquam infra regnum . . . ducta fuerint,* sine voluntate nostra et licentia speciali non liceat eis educere quoquo modo" (my italics): pr. Gras, *The Early English Customs System* (Harv. Econ. Studies XVIII, Cambr. Mass. 1918) 260.— French export prohibition of 1304: pr. *Ordonnances des Rois de France de la 3ᵐᵉ race*, ed. M. de Laurière I (Paris 1723) 422 f.—For Sweden, besides the paper quoted in the previous note, see the useful collection of references in H. Gaessner, *Schwedens Volkswirtschaft unter Gustav Vasa* I (Berl. 1929) 139 f. (note 10). On the other hand, the author's own conclusions from this material (114) appear to me to be mistaken.

the country in return, whereof the realm and honourable men may enjoy the benefit and use" (1545).[5]

Within the framework of municipal policy there occurred similar measures to those just mentioned. At the same time, the towns had even greater means at their disposal for reserving goods for themselves, chiefly through their supremacy over the surrounding rural country. The so-called *Bannmeilenrecht*, prevailing more commonly among German cities, compelled the population in the neighbouring agricultural areas to sell their produce only in the town's market. The North Italian towns went still further. In 1199 Milan instituted a system for the rationing of foodstuffs—to use the modern expression—by allowing landowners to retain only a specific quantity of corn for themselves.

The system of commercial treaties which flourished especially in Mediterranean cities but also made its appearance further north, reveals tendencies purely of a policy of provision, in direct contrast with the protectionist policy of commercial treaties so common in later times. No attempt was made to force goods on the other contracting party, but on the contrary to secure goods from him. The right which the agreements granted was to procure, not to dispose of, goods.[6] It is perhaps even more characteristic to find examples of export being permitted only with the proviso that the finished products, manufactured from those raw materials which were allowed to be exported, should be reimported into the country of origin. A licence of 1302 allowing wool to be sent from France to the towns of Valenciennes and Maubeuge, at that time belonging to the County of Hainaut, prescribed that the wool and the cloth manufactured thereof in Hainaut were to be sold only to French merchants or other French subjects.[7] It thus insisted upon, and regarded as an advantage, something which, in protectionist times, would have been considered ruinous, namely, the import of finished products, manufactured by foreign labour out of the raw material exported from its own country.

[5] F. Sargeant, "The Wine Trade with Gascony," in Unwin's collection (see note 1 above) 261, 307.—Heckscher, *op. cit.*

[6] Schaube's description includes a host of examples on this point. A contract of this kind between Marseilles and the Count of Ampurias of 1219 is reprinted in *Documents relatifs à l'histoire de l'industrie et du commerce en France*, ed. Fagniez I (Paris 1898) No. 144; cp. also No. 271 of the same collection.

[7] "Ita tamen quod lanae ipsae vel panni faciendi ex eis de dicto comitatu Hanoniae extrahi nequeant nec distrahi seu vendi nisi duntaxat mercatoribus seu gentibus regni nostri" (*ib.* II No. 3).

The policy of provision did not manifest itself so clearly in the customs system, for the duties were first and foremost purely fiscal. It was not for some considerable time that tolls came to be used as a suitable and effective weapon of a well-planned commercial policy. There are, none the less, certain traits in the customs system which display an affinity with the policy of provision.

In 1234 imports into Ravenna were free of duty, while tolls were imposed on exports. The best example which has come to my notice is to be found in some documents drawn up in Cologne in 1171 and 1203 for the citizens of Dinant. They are often considered obscure, but in my opinion they are perfectly lucid if they are regarded as showing tendencies of the policy of provision. The second of the two documents is worth summarizing. On entering the city, visitors were to pay *nothing*; but on leaving they were charged four *pfennigs* for a carriage laden with goods bought in Cologne and half that amount for a cart. The goods themselves were free of export duty, with the exception of several which were specifically enumerated: copper, tin, grease, wax, and lead. It then continues "but for copper that is *sold* they are not to pay anything at all". In the markets they were to pay nothing if they had not *bought* in Cologne, "but if they have sold, they are not to pay anything". There follow certain regulations regarding transit, but the refrain is again brought up "and be it known, that if they *sell* copper or anything else in Cologne, they are not to pay anything at all".[8] It must, however, be repeated that the majority of the medieval toll charges of the German cities are far less clear and more difficult to explain on these lines.

In western Europe, on the other hand, the tendency of the duties is much clearer. Medieval France had only export and no import duties. England usually imposed *ad valorem* duties both on import and export, but even there municipal tolls were to be found with clear tendencies of a policy of provision. Berwick's scale of toll duties of 1303 made, for example, the following stipulations: alum, dyeing-wood, coal, onions and wax only paid dues on export; woad had a 35 pence export and only a 22 pence import duty; wine was the only commodity paying the same amount in both cases.[9] In short, we find in this case almost

[8] "Et sciendum, [si] sive cuprum vel quicquid aliud Colonie vendant, nichil penitus inde dabunt." *Hansisches Urkundenbuch* I No. 61. The document of 1171 (*ib.* No. 22) is in itself much less clear, but with the help of that of 1203 it can be interpreted without difficulty.

[9] Reprinted in Gras, *Early English Customs System* 165.

no exceptions to the general rule that *higher* duties were never imposed on imports than on exports.

Types of goods

As for the kinds of goods which were the object of the policy of provision, the two tables given above are typical of every country. Food-stuffs were everywhere at the centre of the policy: they are a class of goods which is always most important. Trade in corn, meat, bacon, butter and cheese as well as tallow and oil is so often regulated on these principles that it is unnecessary to quote particular instances. A small but significant example is an English export prohibition on corn going to France, with the exception of such as went to the King's own French possessions. The prohibition remained on the statute book for 260 years, from 1360/61 to 1624, though it is true that it had declined in importance in the latter part of this period.[10] Next to food-stuffs as the principal class of goods came such luxuries as malt, beer and above all wine—wine, as already noticed, being singled out in the legislation under Edward III.

In principle, a third group, armaments, was placed on an equal footing with food-stuffs. Their place there is just as explicable. In the English table they occupy the second place, while peaceable Sweden under Gustav Vasa accords them a rather less prominent position. This group includes, e.g. horses—one of the largest groups in the Swedish table as well—falcons (at any rate akin to war materials) and arms, for which an export prohibition existed in England and in the various French provinces, as also in a large number of North Italian cities (Modena, Mantua, Bologna, Ferrara, Parma). Hay, too, may possibly be included under this head (Parma). Although the idea behind this part of the regulations is transparent, they were by no means so obvious to later generations—in fact, it is truer to say that they were anything but obvious. Typical of the change of attitude is the observation made in 1699 by Davenant, the leading English mercantilist of his day, "Our Fore-fathers indeed were against transporting Horses and Mares above such a value, . . . but when those Prohibitions were enacted, the business of trade was not so well understood, as it is at present."[11] This was the mercantilist's protest against the policy of provision in one of its most natural spheres of application.

[10] 34 Ed. III c. 20 and 21 Jac. I c. 28 § 11 resp.; cp. Gras, *Engl. Corn Market* 135.

[11] C. Davenant, *An Essay upon the Probable Methods of Making a People Gainers in the Ballance of Trade* (Lond. 1699) 90.

A fourth group of commodities subject to the policy of provision consisted of raw materials, semi-manufactured goods and other means of production; they usually followed immediately after food-stuffs and war materials. Under this head came, in the first place, raw materials of the textile industry, on which export prohibitions were almost a general rule both in France, England and Italy: wool, flax, rams, combed wool, fuller's earth, dyestuffs, yarn and grey or unfinished cloth; in England, on one occasion (1326), a general export prohibition of textile materials was issued. Hides of various kinds were also of this group and in England, for example, also timber, lead, whetstones, coal and various other articles. It was particularly in England, too, at the beginning of Edward I's reign, that the export of coin and of precious metals was made more difficult, first by royal proclamation, then in 1299 by Act of Parliament (27 Ed. I). Similar regulations existed in other countries. It is obvious that the export prohibition on precious metals must have had the effect of counteracting any efforts to secure a surplus of imports, a reaction which was clearly not realized at that time.

The prohibition on the export of means of production might appear as an attempt to keep production in the country, and would then come within the scope of protectionist policy which is yet to be dealt with. The matter, however, acquires a totally different complexion by the fact that along with these regulations appeared a host of others, imposed to obstruct the export of finished goods. On occasions, export prohibitions were even placed on the principal products of the country or the city, particularly on metals and textile goods, as may be seen from the tables. The Swedish table will be seen to include all the most important Swedish exports, metals, timber and hides. In England, too, we find *inter alia* cloth and worsted (*pannos vocatos Worstedes*, 1362). Genoa allowed the export of iron and steel only by agreement with Narbonne (1224); Bergamo (*circa* 1240) and Bologna (1248) imposed export duties on these goods. Ravenna obtained silk free of duty (1234); but it was only after Genoa had concluded the treaty with Narbonne that it allowed *barchent* (a cotton product) to be exported to that city duty-free and granted Montpellier the same privilege in 1201 as regards *fustagni* (another textile product), but only for a total of 100 bales. Genoa had an export prohibition on linen and French cloth (agreement with Arles 1237), and Bergamo had one for cloth (*circa* 1240). The tolls in Bergamo were very peculiar: it graded its hindrances on export in proportion to the stage of manufacture—the later the stage, the higher the duty. Pig-iron thus had to pay six *sol.* per *carrum* on export, while manufactured iron paid eight; raw chestnuts paid three *den.*, roasted chestnuts six. Such charges give at any rate the impression of a perfectly logical but rather startling *reversal* of the principle of "protection to national labour".

Chronology of the policy

It is not to be wondered at that the policy described above was deeply rooted in the past. It appears to have been fairly common in the city states of ancient times. When Rome grew to be the capital of the world this policy was pursued there more intensively than it has ever been in any other place or at any other period. The nearest parallel to Rome's policy regarding foodstuffs is, perhaps, the measures taken by Napoleon to ensure Paris with provisions when he embarked on his Russian campaign in 1812.

The tradition of antiquity, however, does not appear to have remained unbroken, for before the 12th century there are few indications of such a policy in the new social structures. In Germany, the growth of the *Bannmeilenrecht* must have been one of the first manifestations of a deliberate policy of provision. Little is known of the kind of policy pursued in France by the more or less independent great vassals during the centuries after the fall of the Carolingian empire; but from the measures taken perforce by the reorganized monarchy of the 13th and 14th centuries, it appears probable that local and provincial tendencies of this character had existed. In Spain, too (Castile), where the expression "policy of provision" originated, there are indications of similar tendencies, although, as far as I know, not before the beginning of the 14th century. In England clear traces of an export prohibition on corn are to be found in the twenty-third year of Henry II's reign, 1176/77. In 1203 the Great Winchester Assize of Customs forbade the export of corn and other food-stuffs except by licence.[12] The high-water mark was reached under Edward III, about the middle of the 14th century. As the previous examples have shown, there is particularly abundant material available on North Italy, where one city after another took measures against the export of food-stuffs in the last decades of the 12th and the first decades of the 13th centuries. All in all, the new wave of provision policy may be said to have commenced, after ancient times, in various countries

---

[12] 1176/77: Great Roll of the Pipe, 23 Hen. II, in *Pipe Roll Soc. Publications* XXVI (Lond. 1905) 136, cp. 183, 184, and Gras, *Engl. Corn Market* 134.— 1203: in Gras, *Early English Customs System* 218-21.

during the course of the 12th century and reached its culminating point in the 14th century.

This is not to say that the policy of provision became unimportant after that time. Here, as almost everywhere else, the medieval policy retained its hold over people's minds for a considerable time, until well into the 19th century. It is one of the most striking phenomena in the history of economic policy that during the following centuries two tendencies, contrary in principle, persisted so closely side by side. As far as the general policy of provision is concerned, it is very characteristic that in England, the most progressive country—progressive that is according to the standards set here—it was not until 1721 that an Act was passed containing a general right of free export of the country's produce, and that even this statute contained many exceptions. Even a hundred years later, in 1822, twenty-four sections of statutes and thirty complete statutes which had placed hindrances in the way of export were repealed, all of them dating from the pre-Restoration period. It is true that this, on the whole, was only the formal "purification" of the system of regulation binding English economic life, which generally did not take place before the 19th century. But even in actual practice the export prohibition policy on purely manufactured goods lasted until the end of the 17th century. Thus the export prohibitions on iron, copper and bell-metal were only repealed in 1694.[13] In the majority of other countries with a weaker protectionist tendency, the development appears to have been even slower, although a survey of it would entail greater difficulty.

Its persistence

There was, nevertheless, *one* sphere where the persistence of the policy of welfare was not merely a detail in the general picture, but determined the whole economic development. I refer to food-stuffs and particularly corn. It would be no exaggeration to suggest that this treatment constituted the tragedy in the history of the corn trade in Europe, for it largely explains Europe's difficulties regarding food-stuffs, which occurred even in the last century. A detailed analysis of the circumstances in various countries would demand too much space and, for our purpose, is not necessary. It will be sufficient to sketch the main lines of development in one or two countries.[14]

[13] Statutes: 5 & 6 Will. & Mar. c. 17 (1694); 8 Geo. I c. 15 § 17 (1721); 3 Geo. IV c. 41 § 3 (1822).

[14] The literature on the policy regarding food is naturally large. Besides the references given in note 1 above I shall only refer here to W. Naudé's great collection of data, *Die Getreidehandelspolitik der europäischen Staaten vom 13.*

In France the principles of the policy of provision were first assailed by the physiocrats, though in practice it was considerably later before much was done. A decision of the council of state of 1754 first allowed free "export" from one French province to another. Corn could be exported freely from the country even in the latter part of the *ancien régime* only sporadically. In this respect, even Napoleon represented no sharp break with the past. It was especially his fear of labour unrest which explains a great deal of his policy and prompted him to reject all the physiocratic aspirations, so that he even said "the problem of corn is the most vital and troublesome of all to the ruler. . . . The first duty of the prince as regards corn is to retain it for the nation and not to hearken to the sophistry of the landowners". In this respect the medieval order thus outlived even the French Revolution. It was only after the restoration of the Bourbons that a change of policy could be discerned. As far as is known, the first law to place restrictions on the import instead of the export of corn was that of 1819.[15] Provision policy tendencies were thus extremely long-lived.

Similar restrictions prevailed on the rest of the continent. Even Hamburg, the great staple for the corn trade, was often unable to apply its staple policy in the face of the constant provision policy endeavours of the "commonalty". As late as the last decade of the 17th century the demands of the latter for a complete revival of the medieval order caused various measures to be taken in that direction. It was only in 1748 that free transit was allowed in corn. It is extremely significant that even at so late a period and in one of the greatest continental trading cities it was the export and not the import side of the staple policy which aroused opposition.

Certainly in some of the more agrarian states the policy of provision could not assert itself so prominently. Attacks in those countries were usually directed sometimes against the import, sometimes against the export of corn. Occasionally both were forbidden at the same time. Alternatively the prohibitions varied with the size of the harvests and the fluctuations in price, which

bis zum 18. Jahrhundert (Acta Borussica, Getreidehandelspolitik, I, Berl. 1896). The question is approached from an opposite but in my opinion more correct angle by Below, "Die Fürsorge des Staates für die Landwirtschaft eine Errungenschaft der Neuzeit," in his *Probleme der Wirtschaftsgeschichte* 78–142.

[15] Boissonnade, *Org. du tr.*—prev. chap. note 12—I 107–11 II 536–44; Levasseur, *Hist. d. classes ouvr. et de l'ind. en France avant 1789* II 578 ff.; Heckscher, *The Continental System* 341 f.; Levasseur, *Hist. d. classes ouvr.* (etc.) *de 1789 à 1870* I 574.

certainly played havoc with the regular ordering of production and trade. In 1721 and 1722, under Frederick William I, Prussia became a land of agrarian protectionism and even went so far as to impose the death penalty on the consumption of foreign corn. Nevertheless, export prohibitions occurred during the same reign. Under Frederick II the corn trade was often hampered in both directions, but it may be that the unusually realistic attitude of that king led to better results than were usually achieved by the old policy regarding the corn trade; and Prussia's ability to prevent corn exports from Poland obviously contributed to the same end. Remarkably enough, Denmark adopted agrarian protection a hundred years before Brandenburg-Prussia, but there, too, it alternated with export prohibitions. During most of the 17th century, Denmark stood almost alone in protecting its agrarian produce. In Sweden a similar tendency emerges occasionally about half a century later than in Denmark, to be precise in 1672. The reason given there for the policy was that "the mass of corn imported from foreign countries so depresses the price of corn in the possession of our faithful subjects, that the farmer cannot make ends meet". The decision taken with this in mind was, however, repealed in the following year, and for the greater part of the 18th century Sweden, too, prohibited the export of corn.[16]

England was by far the most important exception. She abandoned the policy of provision regarding food-stuffs definitely and completely before the end of the 17th century. A hundred years previously, English statesmen, in common with those of other countries, had regarded the keeping of corn within the country essential to its welfare. This had resulted in strict prohibitions against the export of corn to the enemy, the latter, during Elizabeth's reign, being Spain. But even before that, representatives of the opposite point of view had voiced their opinions, and in the post-Restoration period they won the day. High

---

[16] Hamburg: Schmoller, in his *Jahrbuch* (prev. chap. note 1) VIII 1082, 1086.—Prussia: Naudé, *Die Getreidehandelspolitik und Kriegsmagazinverwaltung Brandenburg-Preussens bis 1740* (Berl. 1901) 206 ff., 236, 239, 246, 250–3; Naudé (and A. Skalweit), do. do. *1740–1756* (Berl. 1910), 62 ff., 71 ff., 77, 102–20; Skalweit, do. do. *1756–1806* (Berl. 1931) *passim*; H. Rachel, *Die Handels-, Zoll- und Akzisepolitik Preussens 1740–1786* (Berl. 1928) I 707–20 (all in Acta Borussica). —Denmark: L. V. Birck, *Told og Accise* (Copenhagen 1920) 43 f., 140.— Sweden: *Samling utaf Kongl. Bref ang. Sweriges Rikes Commerce, etc.*, ed. A. A. von Stiernman, III (Stockholm 1753) 902; *cp.* Danielsson, *Protektionismens genombrott i svensk tullpolitik* (Stockholm 1930) 48 f.; K. Åmark, *Spannmåls- handel och spannmålspolitik i Sverige* 183 *et passim*.

import duties were placed on corn in 1663, and then in 1673 a tentative measure was adopted, flying directly in the face of all principles of provision policy, export bounties on corn being introduced. Directly after the Revolution of 1688 they became a primary factor of English mercantilism. But although the policy of provision in foreign trade was completely reversed in this case, in theory, at least, the principles of the older policy regarding internal trade in food remained, as may be seen from the description of the internal regulation of trade in England previously given (Ch. VI, Part I). With his customary ruthless criticism of the inconsistencies of the *ancien régime*, Adam Smith emphasized that the bounties on exportation, "under the pretence of encouraging agriculture", "occasion, as much as possible, a constant dearth in the home market", while at the same time adding all possible difficulties to the activity of the native corn dealers. They, according to Adam Smith, could never work against the interests of the large mass of the people, as the exporter of corn was able to do.[17] Lord Kenyon, as late as 1800, treated the older system of regulation as valid, and so even at the beginning of the 19th century there were still some traces of the policy of provision.

It is also interesting to note how the ideas behind the policy of provision persisted in people's minds by the side of mercantilist ideas. In fact a kind of genetic relationship may almost be said to have existed between the policy of provision and *laissez-faire*, a relationship which simply passed over mercantilism. Here, too, it will be sufficient to give just a few examples from mercantilist literature, especially since the question will come up again for treatment in the next part (*v.i.* 227.)

In a frequently quoted essay of the period about 1530, ascribed to Clement Armstrong, under the title of *How to Reforme the Realme in Setting Them to Werke and to Restore Tillage*, it is stated for example: "The works of husbandry encreaseth plenty of victuals and the works of artificiality encreaseth plenty of money." The ideal was thus to have a plentiful stock both of food and money, the policy of provision guaranteeing food, protectionist policy the money, but without plenty of manufactured products. This contrast between the two groups of commodities, "for the back and the belly", later recurs again and again, and in this particular

---

[17] Proclamation of 1591 : reprinted in Cunningham II³ 89 ff.—15 Car. II c. 7 § 1; 25 Car. II. c. 1 § 31; 1 Will. & Mar. Sess. 1 c. 12.—Adam Smith, *Wealth of Nations* ed. Cannan, II 40.

form is a favourite argument with Gerald Malynes at the beginning of the following century. In economic policy itself it was even more decisive on the continent than in England, for on the continent the strength of the protectionist policy lay in textiles, while the policy of provision was applied particularly to food-stuffs. But even in England the general opinion, akin to the medieval idea, that low prices were desirable, held sway. Even late in the 17th century, this is expressed in the ever-recurring formula "*good* cheap", "*better* cheap". A typical representative of mercantilism such as Thomas Mun found it opportune to defend the East Indian trade against the reproach that it increased the price of food (1621). Mun's pupil, the Austrian, Wilhelm von Schrötter (Schröder), like-wise preached the gospel of cheapness and strongly urged that the complete medieval policy of provision be retained for food-stuffs (1686).

When Roger Coke, one of the most original and independent mercantilists, attacked certain parts of the orthodox mercantilist policy, one of the reasons which he gave might just as well have been medieval as liberal (1671): "By God's Law cheapness and plenty is a blessing; and by Civil Law, dearness and extreme prices are complained of and redressed. Whereas this law (against the importation of Irish Cattle) designs to prevent God's blessings, and to cause that which is complained of by the 1 and 2 Ph. and M. 5." This refers to an export prohibition on food (1 and 2 Phil. and Mar. c. 5). During the heyday of mercantilism, the citizens of Stockholm, too, rejected a proposal (1731) which "would create dearth of corn in the country and choke up those veins through which the blessings of God flow to the land and which must therefore cause dismay to every true Christian". "Dearness," they went on, "must be regarded a punishment for sinning, and a calamity; we ought rather pray to God that he keep this from us instead of showing ourselves finical about God's rich blessings, and that the poor man may have his bread and sustenance for lesser money."[18]

The scarlet thread of "provision" ideas is thus discernible through the period that followed, even when contrary tendencies,

---

[18] [Armstrong]—see note 2 part 4 chap. 2—in *Tudor Econ. Docs.* III 127.—Malynes, *Consuetudo, Vel Lex Mercatoria* 213 *et passim*; cp. Wheeler, *Treatise of Commerce* (1601) 59 f.—Mun, *A Discourse of Trade from England unto the East Indies* 33 ff.—[von Schrötter], *Fürstliche Schatz- und Rent-Cammer* chap. 94, chap. 102 § 2 etc.—Coke, *Treatise*, I 58.—Stockholm's citizens: Åmark *op. cit.* 147.

continually to the fore, became under mercantilism the commonplace of opinion and business.

2. CAUSES

All the medieval measures which had the effect of hindering exports and encouraging imports have now been grouped together. It is no exaggeration to say that the horizon of foreign commercial policy in the Middle Ages was limited to these measures. But this is not to suggest that they all originated from the disposition that has been characterized as the "hunger for goods". The motives of the policy have yet to be treated.

There is no doubt that *fiscal* interests must be recognized as one of the important factors. The historian of economic policy will again and again come up against the fact that the financial embarrassment of rulers and states in early days was so chronic that it almost regularly occasioned difficulties in carrying on from one day to the next. Financial difficulties are therefore the most natural explanation for the governmental measures in almost every economic sphere, although quite different reasons were often given for them.

It is not difficult to demonstrate the importance of the fiscal aspect even in the regulation of foreign trade. Cunningham, for example, believed at one time that he could discern far-seeing economic plans in Edward III's policy; but as a result of a series of studies carried out by George Unwin and by his students under his guidance, it has been shown that the predominating idea was quite different. What was decisive in this case was the fact that means had to be created for covering the cost of expensive wars in the immediate future and of the no less expensive luxuries of the Court. In particular was this true of the wool exports which Edward III apparently valued specially highly, because they could be used as a weapon for extortion and as a basis for raising loans. This point of view is undoubtedly of great importance in any explanation of the flourishing anti-export policy during Edward III's reign. The state of affairs in France one half or a full century later was similar, not only under Philip le Bel but also under the other princes of the last few generations of the Capetian dynasty. The same could probably be proved to have been true more or less in most other countries. The first English prohibition known to me against the export of coinage occurred, for instance, under Edward I in 1282, because the king wanted to prevent the Pope from collecting a crusade tax which had already been imposed and partly raised from the English clergy. The King wanted to tax them for his own benefit and in this, incidentally, he was largely successful.[19]

The problem, however, would be over-simplified if it were considered that the anti-export policy could be completely explained by ever-urgent financial necessity. For it is not clear why this necessity should lead precisely to embargoes on exports and not to similar hindrances on imports. At the present day it is the latter that are imposed, and the import duties serve as a source of taxation, and this has always been an argument of modern protectionism; whereas export duties now play a very subordinate part, if they appear at all, and are hardly ever considered a source of revenue. And so it remains to be investigated why the state in the Middle Ages sought to obtain revenue precisely from export duties. The question is primarily whether financial or general economic motives were behind that practice.

To some extent it was undoubtedly a matter of public finance. Imports increased the total of commodities directly available for taxation. Anything within the country always lent itself to the possibility of financial extortion, while goods that had crossed the boundaries were once and for all beyond the reach of the treasury.[20]

Nevertheless, this is far from explaining altogether the anti-export policy. Financial policy also follows the line of least resistance and *ceteris paribus* prefers such measures as harmonize with the general conception of what is socially useful. Import duties would certainly have been applied in many cases, if for other reasons they had not been regarded as undesirable. If purely financial considerations had been decisive, both imports and exports would have been taxed with roughly equal severity. Moreover, a large, and perhaps even the most vital, part of the anti-export policy had hardly any fiscal significance at all. I refer to the large number of export prohibitions which, from the start, were seriously intended, and from which no exemptions by means of licences were granted. With food-stuffs, too, interest in abundant provisions and low prices was so general that fiscal considerations almost always took second place. In one commodity, wine, which closely resembled food-stuffs—according to

[19] Unwin (see note 1 above).—The prohibition on the export of coins: *Foedera*, ed. Rymer, Publication of the Record Commission I: II 608; cp. W. E. Lunt, "Papal Taxation in England in the Reign of Edward I" (*Engl. Hist. Review* XXX, 1915, 398 ff.).

[20] Cp. an analogous explanation of the English King's right to impose tariff duties, in H. Hall, *A History of the Custom-Revenue of England* (Lond. 1885) II 76.

Unwin the only commodity of daily consumption during Edward III's reign which had to be imported into England—the connection between fiscal and other state considerations on the one hand and the policy of provision on the other was clearly manifested, in spite of all occasional variations. For example, when the right to import was granted to the wealthy gild of Vintners of England, the king's desire to use the gild for securing loans to himself had something to do with it. But when, in spite of this, the wine-producing Gascons themselves acquired the monopoly of sending wine into England, the deciding motives were purely political; at that time the Gascons were subjects of the English crown, and their loyalty was necessary during the wars with France. But both in the one regime as in the other, the aim was to place at the disposal of the English middle and upper classes as large a supply of wine as possible at the lowest prices possible; in other words "provision" tendencies were common to both kinds of measures.

Of less importance than the fiscal were the purely *military* considerations, though a large proportion of the export prohibitions applied to trade with the enemy or with such countries as might easily become hostile, and also to such goods as happened to be necessary for military purposes. Examples of the latter have already been given. A prohibition against trading with the enemy occurs in the Carta Mercatoria (1303). The general export licence for foreign merchants contained an exception providing against the export "to countries which were clearly and notoriously enemies" of England. A French decree of the following year contained almost literally the same prohibition. Significant also is the large group of reprisals in the form of export hindrances, revealed by the Swedish material given above (*v.s.* 83 f.).

Even in these cases, however, the anti-export policy is not to be explained simply by a reference to political considerations. It is precisely the curious fact that the same real need was believed to justify two exactly opposite conclusions which is characteristic of the theoretical content of economic policy. That hindrances to export were regarded as a military necessity for the native country and harmful to the enemy indicates that the idea must have been derived from the policy of provision or, to be more precise, at any rate from non-mercantilist sources.

It may perhaps seem absolutely absurd that people could ever have considered abundant provisions in time of war and for purposes of war as anything other than an advantage to a country;

but that they did hold such views is sufficiently revealed by word
and deed during the mercantilist period.

The merchant, John Cary, who was also an esteemed corre-
spondent of no less a person than John Locke, wrote during the
English wars with France towards the end of the 17th century
(1695) concerning England's enemy, "I wish he were better
furnish'd with our Product and Manufactures, and we had his
Money for them, which would much more weaken him, than the
other would enable him to carry on the War." His contemporary,
Charles Davenant, one of the most enlightened mercantilists,
came to exactly the same conclusion concerning the same enemy
countries: "The Ballance arising from Trade being wanting,
which should maintain King and People, there must inevitable
follow, at first private want, and then public Poverty." An
overshadowing example of the practical outcome of mercantilist
ideas regarding the part played by goods in war time is the
Continental System, and, it should be noted, not merely on
Napoleon's side. For his part, he hoped to be able "to vanquish
England by excess". He wanted to deal a death-blow to the
enemy by isolating it, but this as we know referred not to its
imports but to its exports. On the English side, ministers and
politicians in Parliament were able to rejoice because this plan
was a failure, so that in spite of all difficulties they had succeeded
in clothing the enemy armies against their will in English cloth.
Thus Lord Grey stated in the House of Lords in 1812, "It is
well known that the manufactures of Yorkshire make the clothing
for the French army; and not only the accoutrements but the
ornaments of Marshal Soult and his army are formed by the
artisans of Birmingham."[21]

It is obvious, therefore, that the fact that there were military
needs does not in itself explain the policy of provision. A "provision" or at least a non-mercantilist attitude must have been
there before military needs, as in the Middle Ages, could lead
to export prohibitions.

As an argument against this evidence, the objection may be

---

[21] Cary, *An Essay on the State of England, in Relation to Its Trade, etc.* 120 f.—
Davenant, *An Essay upon Ways and Means of Supplying the War* (3rd ed., Lond.
1701) 23.—Hansard's *Parliamentary Debates* XXIII 8; Heckscher, *The Continental
System* 35–8, cp. 344 f. *et passim.*—See, too, Montchrétien's remarks II 43 f.
above. The idea that a country is harmed by imports from an enemy country
is typically expressed in B. de Laffemas, e.g.: "Les villes frontières et ports de
mer d'icelui [Royaume] servent d'appui et aide aux ennemis par les moyens
des marchandises qu'ils y conduisent et débitent" (*Les tresors et richesses pour
mettre l'Estat en splendeur*, Paris 1598, 6).

raised that it does not prove that the policy of provision proceeded from a dogmatic belief in goods, but only that the later and exactly contrary policy was based on the dogmatic striving to dispose of the goods. To my mind this objection is valid. The essential explanation of the policy of provision lies, in other words, in the idea that goods are things of value, of which one can rarely have too much and easily too little, and which should therefore not be so lightly permitted to leave the country. In its application through the policy of provision, the idea has certainly one great defect. The two-fold nature of exchange, the mutual dependence of import and export is overlooked. This weakness, however, is obviously common to both the policy of provision and the policy of protection in its usual manifestations. Moreover it is an oversight so natural to the untrained mind that it scarcely requires special explanation. The idea grew naïvely from the simple realization that goods were useful, as may be seen, e.g., in the following reason being given for a French export prohibition of 1304: "Charity begins at home; it borders on cruelty to deprive the field, wherein the spring rises, of water and to lead the water away to other fields. . . ."[22] There is an important parallel to this in the anti-export policy of World War I. The motives for the policy given at the beginning of the 14th century frequently recur in a somewhat altered form six hundred years later, in the guise of protests against the export of food-stuffs not only from blockaded Germany but also, for example, from neutral Sweden.

As the policy of provision was thus limited in time, and was later succeeded by a policy which tended in the exactly opposite direction, it is natural to search among the actual conditions of the times for factors which might explain why considerations of provision had so strong a hold on the Middle Ages. Such an explanation is not difficult, although it is certainly not to be found where one would be likely to look for it first. In the first place, we shall mention briefly those factors which might appear important even though their importance was probably very small or negligible.

[22] "Quia ordinata caritas rite in quosdam a se ipsis incipit, crudelitatique proximum existat, agro in quo fons nascitur sitiente, exhinc ad aliorum agrorum usum aquam duci, [et quidem] damnosum que foret, ut nostri aemuli et inimici nobis et regno confortentur et consolentur ex ipsis, per hoc Deo et justitiae repugnantes ex iis indebite confortari", in *Ordonnances des rois de France de la troisième race* I (Paris 1723) 422 f. The sentence is probably theological in origin and is also applicable to purposes other than the policy of provision, e.g. Wheeler, *Treatise* 163.

It is tempting to explain the policy of provision on the grounds that it arose during an age of universal scarcity of goods. This is, indeed, how it came about during World War I. The assumption, however, is unjustified with regard to the Middle Ages. The policy of provision, like medieval municipal policy in general, originated in the time of the crusades. That period, however, was characterized by increased traffic by land and sea, and greater opportunities for the making and selling of goods, as may be seen, for example, in the rise of the Champagne fairs and the new transport organizations both on land and sea. That the policy of provision came into being at such a time shows that it was not the particular conditions of the period which created it, but the fact that economic policy in western Europe was only then beginning to take definite shape. A very interesting parallel may be seen in the history of the monetary system, where again one cannot draw conclusions on the prevailing policy from external economic conditions, as will be demonstrated in greater detail in the next part. The endeavours to increase stocks of gold and precious metals reached their highest point not in a period of stagnating gold and silver production, but at a time when Europe more than ever before was flooded with the precious metals from Mexican and Peruvian mines. Thus scarcity of money, in the literal sense of the word, cannot explain the hunt for precious metals; neither can scarcity of goods provide the reason for the policy of provision.

Rather more feasible is the explanation in terms of general *uncertainty*, which was an ever-present danger in the Middle Ages to the undisturbed import of goods. The continual state of war, of course, constituted the principal element of uncertainty, but in addition, too, were the bad harvests and other of nature's whims over which man had not yet made himself master. There is perhaps, after all, a kind of parallel on this point to the "provision" tendencies prevalent during World War I, even in the causes. Uncertainty in the Middle Ages was very pronounced also by reason of the small size of the territories and cities, the possibility of a blockade in food-stuffs being a perpetual danger. To isolate a territory was a very common weapon of warfare. The food problem of World War I was reproduced in miniature, for example, in Basle during the time of the Council of 1431. The territorial lords in the neighbourhood of the city who were hostile to the Council cut off the food supplies, according to von Below's data, of the then over-populated city. If a municipality, or the lord of a territory, blockaded its boundaries against exports, the neighbouring locality had to do the same if it were not to be left entirely high and dry. The narrowness of the boundaries within which political power was in fact exercised during the Middle Ages must always have been a cause of the policy of provision, and also partly explains its disappearance after the rise and consolidation of nation states.

Granted all this, we have however not yet arrived at the essential point in the explanation. It is common knowledge that in later times the danger of blockade has always been used as an argument for the policy not of provision but, on the contrary, of protection. From a long period view, this argument is certainly much more telling, though it is true that for a short time a region could increase its stock of food during a blockade by preventing exports. But even an urban territory, which could not possibly cover its own needs in the most important necessities of life, might benefit by allowing export, for by doing so it would be more likely to induce others to supply it with goods. Rightly conceived, insecurity could therefore hardly justify the policy. The reason why this point was not seen may, however, simply have been shortsightedness. To the extent that the policy of provision was purely municipal, it might be possible to assume that it was to some extent dependent on external conditions, even though it is improbable that the external conditions were really the decisive factor. But in fact the policy of provision was by no means merely a municipal policy, but a phenomenon of universal occurrence. It extended over whole states in which the influence of the cities was fairly small and which had a large territory, so that it could not be narrowness of boundaries which led to the policy of provision in these cases. It is particularly suggestive that the medieval policy regarding food-stuffs was able to persist almost unchanged in a country such as France for three centuries after the end of the Middle Ages. It should moreover be borne in mind that the policy of provision did not merely extend to food, but more or less to all kinds of goods. And so to this extent, the only explanation that remains is the one already given again and again, that municipal economic principles stood out as almost the only clear principles of economic policy, and remained for centuries, even after the political influence of the cities had ceased— in fact, even in such countries where it had never existed. For this reason measures which were natural to the cities were extended to regions for which they were far less appropriate.

For the sake of completeness, it may also be pointed out that the export prohibitions on the ordinary export goods of the country might have had the function of raising the prices of these goods by diminishing the supply, or, in the terminology of modern theory, of making it possible to obtain a monopoly price. There is no doubt that something of this sort did often occur to statesmen of that time. It is true that, ultimately, an anti-import policy would have had the same effect as an anti-export policy; for imports and exports depend on one another. But this more subtle point in foreign trade policy was unknown to the politicians of the time, and for that matter is often equally unknown to politicians of to-day. Consequently, if the aim was to get a better price—a more favourable exchange relationship—for the goods of the native country as against those of the foreign country, it was only natural that they should concentrate directly on export goods and endeavour to render the buyers' access to them more difficult. The whole policy of provision is certainly not explained by this, but the point must not be altogether omitted from the explanation.

The various possible explanations mentioned hitherto nevertheless pass over the really vital fact. The policy of provision developed out of the most ingenuous conception of how things are inter-related. To this extent the policy requires no specific explanation. What does rather require explaining is the *new* outlook which ousted the policy of provision, the "fear of goods", not the "hunger for goods". "Hunger for goods" must normally be the predominant tendency where fundamental economic relationships are easily perceived. The explanation of the policy of provision is then quite simply that the facts were seen much more clearly by medieval observers than by those of later times, because the conditions in precisely this connection were so much simpler.

It was the conditions of *natural economy* which brought out these facts so clearly and simply. And the basic condition for the new trend of thought which superseded the policy of provision was obviously money economy. So long as goods were exchanged for goods, it must have been clear to the meanest intelligence that nothing could be gained if the goods offered brought only a small amount of other goods in exchange. Everyone under natural economy recognized that exchange was the more favourable the larger the amount of goods which could be got in exchange for one's own. But then came the monetary system and drew "a veil of money" over the interconnected factors in exchange. In spite of its enormous importance in helping to increase the satisfaction of wants, money economy has thus done much to render more difficult an accurate conception of the forces in economic life and particularly in exchange. It has become perhaps the most important source of false economic theories. Since the goal of economic activity, the acquisition of goods, was so easily discernible under conditions of natural economy, it was only natural that people stopped there and overlooked the dual nature of exchange. And this led to the idea that to retain one's own goods was profitable under any circumstances.

3. ITS DECLINE AND THE TRANSITION TO PROTECTIONISM

However, the idea gradually gained ground that, starting from the policy of provision, from the "hunger for goods", it was illogical to arrive at a policy of export prohibition. People came gradually to realize that native production together with the possibility of export could actually be a *guarantee* for sufficient provisions, because the greater certainty of selling the goods where exports were free would maintain production on a higher plane. More difficult to learn was the similar fact that increased freedom of export also led to greater imports, for goods were exported soonest to those places where no obstacles stood in the way of the exports. But finally even this idea was grasped. On this basis a consumers' policy, or the policy of provision, could combine "hunger for goods" with the complete freedom of foreign trade in both directions, and could do away entirely with all medieval export regulations. Thus, just as in certain aspects of staple policy discussed above, a kind of *laissez-faire* policy of trade would be reached. As we shall presently see, the early free trade writers, too, clearly expressed the same view. The reaction against the policy of provision, however, arose long before that *laissez-faire* policy, likewise without abandoning the "hunger for goods" as its starting-point. It took place in the middle of the 16th century. At this period, particularly in England, but also in France, there are some remarkable observations expressing this point of view.

The clearest discussion of these problems ever presented in former times is to be found in *A Discourse of the Common Weal of this Realm of England*, probably written in 1549 and ascribed to John Hales; published in a somewhat elaborated form and under a different title in 1581 (*v.s.* 20).

The book takes the form of a conversation between a man of learning ("doctor"), a landowner ("knight"), a merchant, a craftsman ("capper") and a husbandman. They converse on the extension of sheep rearing at the expense of corn growing, a development which was rousing general anxiety at the time. The author himself speaks through the doctor. He attacks the prohibition which forbade the export of corn if the price exceeded "a noble the quarter" and urges that only the repeal of this prohibition could maintain corn growing. He is answered by the capper: "Yet it pleaseth us that be artificers nothing at all, which must buy both bread, corn and malt for our penny." And he went on to explain the discrimination between corn and other commodities in an argument which is in line with the view prevailing for a long time: "Every man hath need of corn, and so they have not of other wares so much." This gave the doctor his opening for a rejoinder, very skilfully bringing out the most important point: "Therefore the more necessary that corn is, the more be the men to be cherished that reared it; for if they see there be not so much profit in using the plough as they see in other feats, think you not that they will leave that trade and fall to the other that they see more profitable?" He then continues: "Trow you, if husbandmen be not better cherished and provoked than they be to exercise the plough, but in process of time so many ploughs will be laid down (as I fear me there be already) that if an unfruitful year should happen amongst us, as commonly doth once in seven year, we should then not only have dearth, but also such scarceness of corn, that we should be driven to seek it from outwards parts, and pay dear for it." When the knight asks what is to be done in bad years if the surplus of good years is exported, the same argument is advanced: "By reason that, through the means aforesaid, more ploughs are set awork than would suffice the Realm in a plentiful year. If a scarce year should fall after, the corn of so many plough, as in a good year would be more than enough, in an unfruitful year at the least would be sufficient to serve the Realm."[23]

About the middle of the century in England, the belief was in the air that the prevailing policy could not achieve what it set out to do. In the same year as the *Discourse of the Common Weal* was probably written, an unknown author wrote an essay addressed to Lord Protector Somerset, which has only been published in our own day. The title given to it was *Polices to Reduce this Realme of Englande vnto a Prosperus Wealthe and Estate.* He fiercely attacked the whole system of regulating food-stuffs, declaring that the prohibition could do nothing to remedy the prevailing higher prices, so long as their causes were not removed.

[23] *A Discourse of the Common Weal*, etc., ed. Lamond, 54–61.

In the following year (1550), Sir John Mason, England's ambassador in France, wrote a letter to Cecil in which he ridiculed every attempt to keep down the prices of food-stuffs: "Nature will have her course, *etiam si furca expellatur*; and never shall you drive her to consent that a *penny*-worth of new shall be sold for a *farthing*. If *good cheap* follow this devise, then hereafter will I think it were good the like were still used; but this I am sure, the thing shall not be so plentiful as it was, and then I report me to you whether it will be better cheap. For who will keep a cow that may not sell the milk for so much as the merchant and he can agree upon?"[24]

Almost two decades later, in 1568, Bodin discussed in his famous treatise on money the possibility of lowering the prices of imports indirectly through exports "for what is brought in in exchange for that which is sent out creates low prices in those goods that were scarce".[25]

These observations are so like those of the *laissez-faire* school that Adam Smith himself might have written them. Indeed one can almost say that he actually did write them. He declared, for example, that "Unless more corn is either usually grown, or usually imported into the country, than what is usually consumed in it, the supply of the home market can never be very plentiful. But unless the surplus can in all ordinary cases be exported, the growers will be careful never to grow more, and the importers never to import more, than what the bare consumption of the home market requires. That market will very seldom be overstocked; but it will generally be understocked, the people, whose business it is to supply it, being generally afraid lest their goods be left upon their hands." There is every reason for emphasizing this agreement between the older criticism of the policy of provision and *laissez-faire*, particularly since *laissez-faire* authors— in Sweden, for example, Anders Chydenius (1765)—had greater sympathy with the policy of provision than with its opposite. Adam Smith even reckoned with the possibility that export prohibitions on corn might be useful in exceptional cases, but he was opposed to import prohibitions in all circumstances.[26] It

[24] "Polices, etc.": *Tudor Econ. Docs.* III 339 ff.—John Mason to Cecil, 4th Dec. 1550: *ib.* II 188.

[25] Bodin, *Discovrs svr le rehavssement et diminvtion des monnoyes* (Paris 1578, unpag.): "ce qui entre en lieu de ce qui sort, cause le bon marché de ce qui défailloit."

[26] *Wealth of Nations*, ed. Cannan, II 39, 41 f.—A. Chydenius, *Källan til Rikets Wan-Magt* and *Omständeligt Swar* §§ 54 & 57 (repr. in Politiska skrifter, ed. E. G. Palmén, Hfors. 1880, 101 f., 200 f., 204); cp. also 318 below for this

is then all the more obvious that a criticism of the policy of provision is conceivable even without any mercantilist tendency.

On this point the mercantilists, however, thought themselves
reformers, as is manifest in many of their remarks. The observation of Bacon on the policy of Henry VII, changing "from
consideration of plenty to consideration of power" (*v.s.* 16)
is a case in point. Colbert, too, in 1670 drew an essential contrast
between the new mercantilist policy and the earlier policy
pursued by the tax farmers, who laid heavy duties on exports
but sought to attract imports by low duties. Among the authors
who pointed out the same thing is, e.g., Sir William Petty. He
suggested that land should be sold to foreigners so that the
country should acquire precious metals, whereas in earlier times
foreigners were prohibited from purchasing land (*circa* 1676).
Here Davenant's remark given above (*v.s.* 88) should also be
added, that the prohibition on the export of horses proved how
scanty was the knowledge of the proper principles of trade in
earlier times (1699).[27]

Even though the two tendencies, the policy of provision and
protectionism, were thus antithetical, there were certain connections between them. These were in reality much stronger
than might have been expected from attitudes so different in
theory. There are at least three points in which this connection
was revealed and was of importance.

The most obvious bond between them is the export prohibition
against *precious metals and coins*. To fit this prohibition into a
system dominated by the policy of provision was possible only
at a time when people had not yet learnt to see the interconnection
between economic phenomena. Its true place was in a system of
protection, and it belongs to the discussion of mercantilism as a
monetary system.

The next point is of far greater theoretical and practical importance. It may be seen here, as also in Bodin's statement, that
the connection between the two aspects of exchange was not
always overlooked in earlier times. In other words there existed
a strong mistrust of *importing* goods which were considered useless
and transient stuff, sent into the country by foreigners solely
for the purpose of receiving in exchange the staple products of

"Precursor of Adam Smith", who is far too little known outside Sweden and
Finland.

[27] Bacon, *History of the Reign of King Henry the Seventh* (repr. Works V, Lond.
1803, 63).—*Lettres de Colbert* VII 241.—Petty, *Political Arithmetick*, chap. 10
(Econ. Writings, ed. Hull, I 313).

the country. This view grew quite naturally from the fact that people were loth to see valuable native goods leave the country and to this extent it belonged to the medieval ideas. But it paved the way for the views that were to supersede it. A more striking example of the gradual transition from "hunger for goods" to "fear of goods" could hardly be imagined. At the same time the "fear of goods" was also supported by the aversion from all "luxury", and this again was closely bound up with the whole medieval morality. The aversion persisted for a long time and, together with purely economic factors, led to a dislike of imports.

The trend of thought is clearly expressed in one of the most famous, economic writings of medieval England, the poem, *The Libelle of English Policye*, dated by its editor as 1436/37. Among other things, the author attacks the trade of the Venetian galleys, through which are imported:

> "Nifles, trifles that little have availed
> and things with which they featly blear our eye,
> with things not enduring that we buy;
> for much of this chaffare* that is wastable
> might be forborne for dear and deceivable.
>
> Thus these galleys, for this liking ware
> and eating ware, bear hence our best chaffare,
> cloth, wool and tin, which as I said beforne
> out of this londe werste might be forborne.
> For each other lond of necessité
> have great need to buy some of the thre(e);
> and we receive of (t)hem into this coast
> ware and chaffare that lightly wol be lost."[28]
> * Merchandise

It should be noticed that the author includes cloth, the most important of all English exports, in the list of goods which in his opinion England should keep back. Thus the policy of provision had not disappeared, but was closely bound up with a great aversion to the import of goods regarded as luxuries. In Thomas Starkey's well-known dialogue between Cardinal Pole and Thomas Lupset, written a hundred years later, the same combination recurs: the efforts of the policy of provision to create "abundance" which "maketh everything good cheap" is combined with a great aversion to "all such merchants which carry out things necessary to the use of our people, and bring in again vain trifles and conceits, only for the foolish pastime and pleasure of man".

[28] *Political Poems and Songs*, ed. Th. Wright (Rerum Britannicarum Medii Aevi Scriptores, Rolls Series) II (Lond. 1861) 173 f. (The spelling has been very much modernized in my text.)

The hostility towards luxury imports was connected with a similar hostility towards the import of *non-durable* articles which, according to primitive economic notions, were inferior to any durable goods. It is precisely this "wastable" character of the goods that is explicitly mentioned in *The Libelle of English Policye*. Thus another step is taken away from the policy of provision. The import of wine, for instance, was formerly encouraged in every possible way, while later it was just the lack of durability of this commodity which made its importation seem indefensible. It is altogether very difficult to conceive an anxiety concerning consumption, combined with a simultaneous aversion from consumable objects, of which food-stuffs are the principal. In the *Discourse of the Common Weal*, the idea is expressed as follows:

"I would to God we would follow the example of a poor haven town, that I know did of late, in the merches of Wales, called Carmarthen, (according to another text Carnarvon), when there came a certain vessel out of England, all loaden with apples, which afore time was wont to bring them good corn, the town commanded that none should buy the said apples upon a great pain; and so the boat stood so long at the haven, without sale or vent, until the apples were putrified and lost; and when the owner demanded of the bailiff of the town why he had stayed his sale and vent, the bailiff answered again that the said vessel came thither to fet(ch) the best wares they had in the country, as friezes, broad cloths, and wool; and instead of that he should leave in the country, that which should be spent and wasted in less than a week. And said, bring to us corn and malt, as you were wont to do, whereof the country hath need, and ye shall be welcome at all times, and ye shall have free vent and sale in our port."

"Think ye," continues the doctor, through whom the author himself speaks,

"the great city of London, Southampton, Bristow, Chester, and other, might not learn a good lesson of this poor Welsh town in this doing? . . . If they come for our wools, for our clothes, kerseys, corn, tin, lead, yea our gold, silver, and such substantial and necessary things, let them bring in again flax, tar, oil, fish, and such other; and not to use them as little children, give them an apple for the best jewel they have about them."[29]

In legislation, too, the connection between the dislike for

[29] Th. Starkey, *A Dialogue between Cardinal Pole and Thomas Lupset: England in the Reign of Henry the Eighth* II, ed. J. M. Cowper (Early English Text Soc., Extra S. XII, Lond. 1871) 80, 89 *et passim.—Discourse of the Common Weal* 68, cp. 173. The example obviously refers to a "common bargain" with the officials of the city (cp. Gross, *Gild Merchant* I 136 ff.) and is therefore not so improbable as might appear in modern eyes; *v.s.* I 383.

luxury imports and the aversion from imports in general is manifest at a very early date, in England at least from Edward IV onwards, a reign under which protectionism became predominant. As early as 1463, a statute complained against the "inordinate Array and Apparel to the great Displeasure of God, and impoverishing of this Realm and enriching of other strange Realms and Countries, to the final Destruction of this said Realm". Here religious and protectionist considerations were joined in a higher unity. In the following century and a half, until 1604, the legislature in England was very active against every kind of luxury, and the mercantilist point of view made itself felt more and more. In two ordinances of 1574 and 1588, Cecil referred directly to the balance of trade as the cause for his anti-luxury measures. Nor was this characteristic of England alone. The introduction to the merchants' *cahier* at the meeting of the French Estates General in 1560 complained of the effect of luxury on morals, and then spoke of "the large amount of money which left the country in the form of perfumery, perfumed gloves, embroidery and so on".[30]

In the course of time the mercantilist tendency grew more and more predominant. Ethical considerations disappeared entirely from many parts of the literature and in their place there appeared an amoral, if not immoral, demand for stimulation of native luxury production at any price and the obstruction of foreign sales. This became one aspect of mercantilism as a general conception of society (*v.i.* Part V), and indicates how even the most exaggerated and provocative aspects of mercantilism may, without difficulty, be deduced from the policy of provision.

Finally, there was still another important link between the policy of provision and protectionism: *raw materials and means of production* in general. The connection here was so intimate that many measures can just as well be ascribed to the one as to the other policy; or at least our knowledge of the causes would have to be greater than it usually is before we could pronounce which of the two was the deciding one. If the policy of provision is conceived purely and simply as a "hunger for goods", without any further shades of meaning, it is only natural that it should include things as valuable as raw materials. This was, in fact, the case since the very early Middle Ages. It is equally

---

[30] 3 Ed. IV c. 5.—W. Hooper, "The Tudor Sumptuary Laws" (*English Hist. Review* XXX, 1915) 437.—Cp. Cecil's "Considerations delivered to the Parliament 1559": *Tudor Econ. Docs.* I 327.—France: Hauser, *Ouvriers du temps passé* 258.

well known that the resurrection of the policy of provision during
World War I extended to raw materials. None the less, this
category of goods always had a special position because it was
in no way directly connected with consumption. The attempt
to retain raw materials could therefore not be in the direct
interests of the consumers. At the same time, the measures which
increased the possibilities of production were of a piece with
that striving to encourage production generally and thus became
a part of mercantilism. It might be said that the policy of provision and protectionism met one another at this point, in the
tendency to encumber the owners and producers of raw materials
and other means of production by hindering their sales. The
contrast between the two policies did not then manifest itself until
the aim of the measures was revealed, whether this treatment of
the owners of the means of production intended to call forth an
abundant supply of finished products in the country, or whether
it intended to get rid of these products and keep their total small
in the country. So thorough an analysis of the individual measures,
however, is not always possible with the available material.

Yet at a very early date, the measures for keeping back raw
materials reveal quite clearly a protectionist tendency. This was
the case, for instance, when export prohibitions were placed on
raw materials in the French textile industry, at the instigation
of the producers, e.g. on a petition of the cloth weavers and
finishers of Languedoc at the beginning of the 14th century.
And the same considerations showed through the official motives
for the English policy of export prohibitions under Edward III.
An export prohibition on live rams (1338) was said, for example, to
have been caused by the improvement in the quality of foreign
wool and the consequent damage to the English. A hundred years
later when, under Edward IV, the policy of industrial protection
was in full swing in England, the export prohibitions on raw
materials and other means of production formed an essential
part of the policy.[31]

The "fear of goods" or mercantilism was certainly bound to
come up against insoluble difficulties if it tried to draw the line
between the production which it was desired to encourage in the
country by a system of bounties, and the means of production
which it was desired to render cheap in the interests of this production. This problem, however, belongs to the following chapter.

[31] France: Pigeonneau, I,/311 f., and also in other works on the subject.—
England: export prohibition of 1338 in *Foedera* ed. Rymer (Record Commission) II: II 1034.—Cp. Below's apposite observations, *Probleme der Wirtschaftsgeschichte* 288, 590 ff.—*v.i.* 123.

IV

PROTECTIONISM

1. ITS NATURE AND ITS CONNECTION WITH THE ATTEMPTS TO CREATE EMPLOYMENT

The most incisive criticism of the policy of provision is the same as that directed, with much less justification, by Frederick List in his famous work *Das nationale System der Politischen Oekonomie* (1840) against the classical economic theory—that it has an eye only for the advantage of the moment and not for ultimate results, overlooking, in its eagerness for wealth, the productive forces which create wealth. The foregoing has already shown that the policy of provision attempted to prevent goods from leaving the country because momentarily this decreased the supply of goods. In doing so, it overlooked the fact that in the long run export increased the supply of goods. The policy of provision was therefore a short-term policy and in the long run must also have been a shortsighted policy. It was a consumers' policy in the sense that it took no account of production as the presupposition of consumption.

Long-term policy

In contrast with this, protectionism attempted to direct its attention to the *permanent* foundations of economic life. It therefore signified a keener insight into economic affairs. It was, and in time became more and more, expressive of a more penetrating observation of the interplay of economic forces. None the less, owing to the growing complexity of these forces, mercantilism often arrived at more erroneous conclusions on economic questions than the medieval mind had ever done. Quite apart from this, by its contrast to the policy of provision, protectionism represented a remarkable emancipation from municipal criteria, and thus far constituted something really new, although of course its roots, too, reached far back into the medieval system. The greatest achievement of mercantilism therefore consists in what may be characterized as "long-term" considerations.

Bacon expressed this view of mercantilism most clearly, as has already been exemplified in the second part (*v.s.* II 45). A further example is given in his essay "Of Colonies" (1625). He regarded it as a great danger, leading to the decline of most colonies, that the mother country should try to extract great profits from them during their infancy. "Planting new countries," he said, "is like planting woods." This, which is possibly the most valuable addition to economic knowledge made by the whole of mercantilist thought, was likewise expressed in a passage quoted by Adam Smith from perhaps the best known of all mercantilist writings—Thomas Mun's *England's Treasure by Forraign Trade* (published in 1664, written about 1628). Mun, it is true, is concerned there with the export of precious metals which is not relevant in this context; but his remark is applicable to economic life as a whole. His famous remark, almost monumental in its Jacobean phrasing, is as follows:

"When this weighty business is duly considered in his end, as all our human actions ought well to be weighed, it is found much contrary to that which most men esteem thereof, because they search no further than the beginning of the work, which mis-informs their judgments, and leads them into error: For if we only behold the actions of the husbandman in the seed-time when he casteth away much good corn into the ground, we will rather accompt him a madman than a husbandman: but when we consider his labours in the harvest which is the end of his endeavours, we find the worth and plentiful encrease of his actions."

Thus far mercantilism was in full agreement with every well thought-out conception of economics. Not only List, but even the last exponent of classical political economy, John Stuart Mill, took up precisely the same attitude. In his famous "Infant Industry Argument", Mill advocated "fostering" duties, designed to protect an industry from foreign competition until it was grown sufficiently strong and capable of facing that competition. However much opinions about the practical results of this view may have differed, its truth has never been called in question once it had become customary to think of the economic system, too, within the categories of cause and effect. But it was not without difficulty that such a stage of thought was arrived at. The great importance of mercantilism consists in the fact that it cleared the way for this kind of treatment of economic problems.[1]

The transition from a short-term view of things to a considera-

---

[1] List, *Das nationale System der Politischen Oekonomie*, esp. chap. 12 (ed. H. Waentig, Jena 1904, 220–38).—Bacon, *Essays* (1625) No. 33 (ed. Wright, 139). —Mun, *England's Treasure, etc.*, end of chap. 4 (ed. Ashley, N.Y. and Lond. 1895, 27).—Adam Smith, *Wealth of Nations* (ed. Cannan) I 398.—J. S. Mill, *Principles of Political Economy* (1848) Bk. 5 chap. 10 § 1 (ed. Ashley, Lond. 1909, 922).

tion of permanent effects, however, does not in itself by any means necessarily lead to a "fear of goods". Such a consideration cannot therefore by itself explain the policy that was actually carried out. It explains why mercantilism, in contrast with the policy of provision, might have been expected to advocate greater freedom of foreign trade in the interests of a production which was profitable in the long run—freedom, that is, in the export of finished products, because of the more valuable imports which gradually would have to come to the country. The long-term view could also be given as a reason for temporary import restrictions, or even of export premiums if, that is, it was assumed that by such measures home production could be increased to such an extent that there would finally remain a greater total quantity of goods within the country. The aim in that case was the ultimate increase in the supply of available commodities which, according to Mun, represented the "worth and plentiful encrease" of the husbandman's labour.

"Fear of goods"

However, it is very remarkable that as a rule mercantilism did *not* recognize precisely this criterion for protectionism. It is true that this consequence was eagerly embraced in the case of the precious metals. There the object was an abundant supply. Mun's comparison in fact tried to show that this object could best be reached by first allowing gold and silver to leave the country, so that in the end they could, through trade, indirectly flow back in increased quantities. But as regards other goods, Mun's standpoint, like that of all the other mercantilists, was the direct opposite. It was an attitude which Adam Smith (cf. II 94 above) called the creation of "a constant dearth in the home market". The attitude of mercantilism, therefore, by no means confined itself to taking into consideration long-term effects. In reality it was dominated by a "fear of goods" which was not to be explained by such considerations. This is a factor of essential importance in the history of economic policy, and is therefore worth illustrating in order to demonstrate the various sides of this conception.

The contrast with the policy of provision is, of course, particularly interesting. Plenty, which had been the old ideal, was now considered the gravest danger. Montchrétien, a French author already referred to—who has earned an undeserved reputation because his was the first book with the term "Political Economy" in its title (*Traicté de l'oeconomie politique*, 1615)—took special care to warn people against the danger of plenty. "He who wishes for good order in the arts," he said, "and to maintain their standing, must never decrease profits through abundance. The brightness of the lamp is dimmed if it be too plentifully filled with oil." A later English mercantilist, Nicholas Barbon, who already stands on the threshold of *laissez-faire*, spoke in 1690 of "a dead stock called Plenty". The most common demand of the mercantilist writers was that the import of wine should be completely prohibited, the very thing which had been so eagerly encouraged in the 14th century. No principle of abstinence was involved here: it was the import as such of the commodity that was disliked. Two anonymous writers, separated by 150 years (1530 and 1680), both draw the same charming picture: "Thus do we swallow and p—s out inestimable Treasures."

Native consumption was thus valueless in the eyes of the mercantilists, as will also be shown in the following part from the monetary aspect. A very well-known, if not particularly perspicacious, pamphlet of the Restoration period, *Britannia Languens* (1680)—published anonymously, and often ascribed to a certain William Petyt, and incidentally one of the two writings from which the above quotation concerning wine was drawn—vented its whole hatred against "meer importation", "which is, when the Merchant does Import Consumptive Commodities, which are spent at Home". Charles Davenant, perhaps the last outstanding protagonist of mercantilism among the English pamphleteers, and a writer of quite another calibre, was already influenced by *laissez-faire* ideas to a far greater extent than most writers of the end of the 17th century. His attitude is therefore of greater interest. He said, for example; "It is the Interest of all Trading Nations, whatsoever, that their Home Consumption should be little, of a Cheap and Foreign Growth"—the latter is a peculiarity of Davenant's which can here be ignored—"and that their own Manufactures should be Sold at the highest Markets, and spent Abroad; Since by what is Consumed at Home, one loseth only what another gets, and the Nation in General is not at all the Richer; but all Foreign Consumption is a Clear and Certain Profit" (1697). We need not repeat that this interest in the consumption of other countries did not arise from any altruistic regard for their welfare. Davenant's attitude is all the more instructive because he was not opposed to a surplus of imports *per se*, and in fact even approved of it in certain circumstances. The condition was only that consumption should *not* thereby be increased: "The Gain is so much only as the Nation does not consume of the Importations, but either lays up in Commodities and in Specie or converts into Money or some such adequate Treasure" (1698).

But apart from these rather subtle arguments, people were much more often influenced simply by a naïve fear of buying and an equally naïve eagerness for selling. The most extreme formulation of this attitude is, perhaps, to be found in the writings of Johann Joachim Becher, the most famous of German mercantilist authors. The third of his "mercantilist rules and axioms" was "that it is always better to sell goods to others than to buy goods from others, for the former brings a certain advantage and the latter inevitable damage". It was hardly possible to push the argument any further than that.

This attitude usually became crystallized in a demand for an export surplus, a demand which was expressed in every possible way. Mun, for example, a few pages before the parable of the husbandman, wrote, ". . . we must ever observe this rule: to sell more to strangers yearly than we consume of theirs in value". Somewhat later, in 1660, the demand was made in an instruction to a trading commission that "it may be so ordered, remedied and preparationed that we may have more sellers than buyers in every part abroad". A French dictum, which is often met with, is that "the kingdom" should be "unburdened of its goods" (*"décharger le royaume de ses marchandises"*)—in other words it was of prime importance to get rid of goods. A lengthy discussion contained in the periodical, *The British Merchant*, published by Charles King, is also very characteristic. Its purpose was to attack—and in this it was successful—the proposed commercial treaty of 1713 between England and France. The periodical was later published in book form, and became widely considered a great authority on economic policy. By way of introduction, "General Maxims in Trade", "assented to by everybody" were discussed. The first question that is put is what constitutes the profit of a country, and among the nine points given there is only one which includes manufactured goods for consumption within the country, i.e. the item "indispensable commodities", mostly for military purposes. All the others were surplus natural products which were exported, or raw materials imported as a basis for the export of finished products. The export of finished products was considered "in the highest degree beneficial", the export of surplus natural products "so much clear gain", while the corresponding import was "so much real loss". A practical application of this idea on a huge scale was Napoleon's Continental System. As has been shown, its principles already existed in England, where they had been frankly advocated even before the end of the 17th century (*v.s.* II 99).

In the light of the experience which World War I gave an opportunity of acquiring, with scarcity of goods resulting from an export surplus, it is particularly instructive to see how Sir William Petty and Sir Josiah Child, two of the most clear-sighted and fertile mercantilist writers, regarded the results of such a shortage of goods. Petty believed that Ireland had an export surplus as a result of the interest paid to absentee landlords, and he added the following observation (the italics are mine): "so as Ireland exporting more than it imports doth yet grow poorer *to a paradox*" (1662). According to Petty therefore the natural thing would have been for the country to become richer and richer by always exporting more goods than it received. A few years later (1669), Child, too, took up Petty's arguments, and attempted to establish the circumstances under which "the paradox" could be translated into fact. He is as firmly convinced as Petty that the contrary would be normal, and of course neither of them was led even remotely to realize that the only condition upon which this could be true would be a stock of capital abroad which would ultimately lead to greater imports.[2]

The existence of a "fear of goods" can consequently not be denied. The first thing to do then is to examine its connection with other conceptions. Two obvious factors, which however did *not* play so significant a part, first come to one's mind.

It is particularly important to emphasize that not by any means is the explanation complete simply by showing that all relations between import and export were overlooked. An explanation which goes no further misses the essential nature of the

[2] Montchrétien, *Traicté*, etc. (Rouen 1615) 136.—Barbon, *A Discourse of Trade* 63 (Reprint of Economic Tracts, ed. J. H. Hollander, Baltimore 1905, 32).— Wine imports: [Armstrong], "How to Reforme the Realme", etc.: *Tudor Econ. Docs.* III 124, 128; *Britannia Languens* (Lond. 1680) 184.—*Ib.* 35 cp. 67, 122.—Davenant, *Essay on the East India Trade* (publ. 1698, 31); cp. P. J. Thomas, *Mercantilism and the East India Trade* (Lond. 1926) 82 f. concerning the incidental motives which may have influenced Davenant in making this observation.—Davenant, *Discourses on the Publick Revenues* (Lond. 1698) II 220.— Becher, *Politische Discurs, etc.* Part III chap. 1 (2nd ed., Frankfurt 1673, 261).— Instr. of 1660 Point 7: Cunningham II[3] 914.—"Décharger le royaume", etc.: quoted as a constantly recurring argument for the South Sea trade in E. W. Dahlgren, *Relations entre la France et l'Océan pacifique* I (Paris 1909) 144.—The *British Merchant* (2nd ed., Lond. 1743, I 2–5).—Petty, *Treatise of Taxes* chap. 4 (Econ. Writings, ed. Hull, I 46).—Child, *New Discourse of Trade*, chap. 9 (1698 editn., Lond., 156).

"fear of goods". For the latter also occurred in the by no means infrequent cases where a connection between import and export was very clearly realized. The decisive point was the *attitude* of the interests concerned. The following may be given as one example out of many. An instruction for an English trade commission (1622) points out that attention should be directed to imports—because, be it noted, imports are necessary in order to render export possible. Export remained the guiding policy; people were anxious to get rid of the goods. To attain this end, they saw that they were compelled to purchase goods in return, primarily because the buyers of their own goods would otherwise be dissatisfied and would go elsewhere.

Since there can be no doubt that the pure exchange of goods was regarded in this fashion, it only remains for us to look elsewhere than to an ignorance of the connection between imports and exports if we are to explain the conception. In doing so, we come first to the mercantilist endeavours to increase the stock of precious metals in the country—that is, we enter the sphere of monetary policy. It is also obvious that there was a very intimate connection between the goods aspect and the monetary aspect of mercantilist policy. Most of the examples already given confirm this, and very many more could be cited. None the less, it would be a fundamental mistake to believe that the *whole* explanation is to be found in the monetary aspect. Quite apart from the money or precious metals that an export surplus brought in, such a surplus was considered desirable *per se*. Export was to a very large extent an end in itself.

Selling

We approach still closer to the mercantilist mentality if we amplify the last statement by saying that *selling* was an end in itself. The object was, in fact, to dispose of goods by any possible means. Numerous examples could be given to illustrate this typical attitude but a few will have to suffice.

In a report to Charles II in 1672, Lord Shaftesbury, who was the only really important statesman of the English Restoration period, wrote, "I take it for granted that the strength and glory of Your Majesty and the wealth of Your Kingdoms, depends not so much on anything, on this side of heaven, as on the multitude of your subjects, by whose mouths and backs, the fruits and commodities of your lands may have a liberal consumption." This statement can only be interpreted as meaning that the number of subjects is an advantage to the extent that more goods are used up. The statement is all the more instructive because

Shaftesbury speaks here precisely of native consumption to which very little attention was otherwise paid. In his eyes it was justified by the fact that it helped to dispose of the goods. John Houghton, almost at the same time (1677), made it an argument for calling in foreigners that they "living here consume our corn, cattle, cloth, coals and other things we use". The same standpoint is taken up in *The British Merchant* in its attack on the commercial treaty with France of 1713. It calculated precisely that for every person who emigrated, the country lost £6 sterling through the decrease in the sale of native goods. The loss suffered by France through Huguenot emigration consisted, on that view, in the fact that they bought fewer French products than before.

John Cary, a merchant of Bristol, who incidentally like Shaftesbury was connected with Locke, expressed the same idea in terms which occurred frequently later. People lived and grew rich, he believed, because exchange itself was regarded as the creator of wealth, for this enabled everything to be sold at ever-increasing prices. There is a later variation of the theory in the well-known remark that in certain Scottish islands the inhabitants lived by taking in one another's washing. Cary gives the most complete exposition of this gospel of wealth in connection with his observations on the importance of high wages; that point will be dealt with in a different context (*v.i.* 169 f.). One of his remarks concerning Holland, which was everywhere considered the ideal country economically, may well however be quoted here, and it is certainly very characteristic. "'Tis strange to observe," he said, "how those people buzz up and down among themselves, the vastness of whose numbers causes a vast expense, and that expense must be supplied from abroad, so one man gets by another, and they find by experience that as a multitude of people brings profit to the Government, so it creates employment to each other." The best example of this argument is to be found in one of the most famous, or most notorious, books of the period—Mandeville's *The Fable of the Bees, or Private Vices, Publick Benefits*, even in its original form as published in 1705, under the title *The Grumbling Hive, or Knaves turn'd Honest*. The poetry is incredibly bad from the literary point of view, but the author's mental dexterity—though more particularly his more comprehensive observations in prose—has made the work exceptionally illuminating. From the economic standpoint it expresses the necessity of selling. His principal idea is that human vice is necessary in order that unscrupulous lawyers, venal judges, and parasitic priests, as well as honest citizens dependent upon them

may be enabled to live. Mandeville's numerous critics found it
difficult to deal with this idea of his, which shows how much
it was based upon the general view. The following quotation
from Mandeville purports to show how a country, which he
compares to a beehive, would be ruined if all its citizens were
honest:

> "Now mind the glorious Hive, and see
> How Honesty and Trade agree.
> The Show is gone, it thins apace;
> And looks with quite another Face.
> For 'twas not only that They went
> By whom vast sums were yearly spent;
> But Multitudes that liv'd on them
> Were daily forc'd to do the same.
> In vain to other Trades they'd fly;
> All were o'erstocked accordingly."[3]

From a purely commercial standpoint, this view is only what
must be expected under comparatively modern conditions. It
was particularly tempting to the merchants and friends of .
merchants who contributed so much to the formation of mercantilist thought. In certain circumstances, which were to become
clear in the course of time, it also became the normal view of
circles other than merely the merchants in the narrower sense
of the word. Consequently, generally speaking, explanations
must be sought also outside the sphere of money and precious
metals. For the main part of the idea which I have just illustrated
is still prevalent even to-day in many quarters, in spite of the
comparatively unimportant part played by an eagerness for an
import surplus of precious metals, even where the "fear of goods"
has persisted unchanged. An explanation must therefore be found
which holds good for the popular ideas both of the past and of
the present, and this cannot be found in the sphere of the money
supply. This of course does not exclude the fact that the specific
monetary conception of mercantilism deserves very great attention, and considerable attention is devoted to it in the next part

---

[3] 1622 Instr.: *Foedera* (Rymer) 1st ed. XVII 414 Hague ed. VII: IV 14.—
Shaftesbury: Beer, *The Old Colonial System 1660–1754* I 21.—[J. Houghton]
England's Great Happiness: or a Dialogue Between Content and Complaint (Lond.
1677) 7; cf. below 161.—*British Merchant:* General Maxims in Trade (Lond.
1743, 143–7 *et passim*).—Cary, *An Essay on the State of England, in Relation to
its Trade, its Poor, and its Taxes* (Bristol 1695) 124; for his connection with Locke
vide Thomas (note 2 above) 69.—Mandeville, *The Fable of the Bees* (ed. F. B.
Kaye, Oxf. 1924, I 32—1st ed. I 18). Mandeville's theory, like Keynes',is
quite applicable to depressions when demand is inadequate, but even more than

of this work. But the concern here is with something that has remained predominant over a longer period of time, something which constitutes a strong and decisive break with medieval ideas, but has been adopted in later times without essential alteration.

On closer examination of the matter, it seems appropriate in the first place to dwell upon a phenomenon which was probably more an effect than a cause, but none the less was and still is of vital importance.

Creating employment

The mercantilist "fear of goods" was nourished, among other things, by the idea of creating work at home and of taking measures against unemployment. It is hardly probable that the phenomenon of unemployment appeared suddenly out of the blue just when the new policy began, and that this policy therefore had its cause in the changed character of the labour market. The connection was presumably different. Students who regard increased unemployment as a cause of the rise of protectionism have quoted as proof the dissolution of the monasteries under Henry VIII; if that were so, then things would necessarily have been similar in other countries where the Reformation gained the upper hand. Such an argument, however, is contrary to all the facts. In the first place all investigations show that the monasteries did not play a great role in providing for the needy. It is probable that their irresponsible almsgiving—irresponsible, that is from the point of view of the recipient and of society—created more pauperism than it relieved.[4] In the second place, the new commercial policy went back at least to the middle of the 15th century, and, from its beginning, was connected with the need for employment. And so its rise cannot possibly be explained by the dissolution of the monasteries, which only took place two generations later. Thirdly and lastly, in one of the earliest cases, there was no question at all of the abolition of existing unemployment, but only of the creation of new opportunities for employment, quite irrespective of whether these had previously been too scanty. The most probable explanation is that this policy of creating employment originated precisely in the new attitude towards goods. To believe that unemployment was an effect of the surplus of goods was, then, a natural reaction of this Keynes' *General Theory*, Mandeville's work is intended for general application.

[4] G. Schanz, *Englische Handelspolitik gegen Ende des Mittelalters* (Lpz. 1881) I 469 f.—On the dissolution of the monasteries see Ashley, *Introduction to English Economic History and Theory* II §54; Webb, *English Poor Law History* I ch. 1.

attitude, not the reverse. On the whole there was no question at all of creating work in the way that relief work is to-day provided for the unemployed. It was a matter of subsidizing certain trades suffering from a more or less fictitious lack of orders, or creating entirely new trades, quite independent of whether unemployment existed or not.

Once the new ideas had become established, the unemployment argument found a place of honour in all future proposals and demands that aimed at measures against imports. From the purely theoretical point of view, too, this was perfectly explicable. No doubt it was possible occasionally tó relieve some particular unemployment that happened to exist by excluding foreign goods. It was not to be expected that the usually reverse long-term effects would be noticed. Even in the long run, moreover, employment may be created without a fall in wages if production is directed to branches of industry in which labour cost represents a percentage of the cost of production above the average; and it is conceivable that restrictions on imports can work in this direction. Apart from these economic truths, which probably had very little influence on the policy, it was only natural for people to believe that increased employment could result from embargoes on imports, for at first sight this indeed appears most obvious. When people had once arrived at the view that a surplus of goods was something undesirable, the connection between this and the amount of employment followed almost inevitably.

One of the earliest instances of the application of the unemployment argument as a reason for the prohibition of imports is to be found in Florence in the year 1426. Here there was no reference to any existing unemployment. All that was said was that through a prohibition "many will enter the trades concerned, whereby the poor will gain abundant maintenance". The English legislation on the matter is easier to follow. It goes back to at least 1455. In an Act of Parliament of that year, foreign competition was blamed for having caused the unemployment in the silk industry. Foreigners, it asserted, "destroy the said Mystery, and all such virtuous Occupations of Women". A later Act (1483) even stated that, "All workers in the silk industry, both men and women, are impoverished by the lack of occupations"—and this indeed as a result of imports. There is no doubt that the state's interference in this case was easier because it was a luxury industry, but the importance of the tendency could be shown to be much wider. As early as 1463, the first of these two Acts was extended to a host of other commodities. In 1467 the export of yarn and of unfulled cloth was forbidden on the grounds that the weavers and fullers in the country would thereby have more to do. In other words, export hindrances on semi-manufactured goods served protectionist ends. An almost contemporary French decree of 1466, forming the basis of the silk industry of Lyons, later to become so famous, was less interesting in so far as it was not actually directed against foreign goods. But it, too, mentioned the possibility of giving work to tens of thousands of unemployed men and women. It is seen how very much this argument was in the air at the time.[5]

The first great discussion of this matter, as of nearly all social and economic problems, occurred in England in the middle of the 16th century or rather earlier, during the reigns of Henry VIII and Edward VI. In this connection we cannot but mention a series of writings, written apparently at the latest in the 1530's, two of which at any rate are believed to have been by Clement Armstrong. In one of these works, which however does not appear to be his, there is a demand "that nothing be brought by any of the King's subjects from any strange place beyond the sea, the which may be wrought in any part of the King's dominion". The same demand is constantly repeated by Starkey in the imaginary dialogue between Cardinal Pole and Thomas Lupset, which also appears to date from about 1530. In one of the essays ascribed to Clement Armstrong, too, this argument was put forward with vigour. He formulates it, for example, in the following terms: "By reason of great abundance of strange merchandises and wares brought yearly into England hath not only caused scarcity of money, but hath destroyed all handicrafts, whereby great number of common people should have works to get money to pay for their meat and drink, which of very necessity must live idly and beg and steal."[6]

[5] "Si aliqua inhibitio induceretur, multi se ad ipsas artes administrandas accommodabunt, ex quibus plurimam pauperes homines . . . alimoniam recipient": R. Pöhlmann, *Die Wirtschaftspolitik der Florentiner Renaissance und das Prinzip der Verkehrsfreiheit* (Preisschriften der Jablonowskischen Gesellschaft, Hist.-ök. Section XXI, Lpz. 1878) 103 note 1.—English statutes (in chronological sequence): 33 Hen. VI c. 5; 3 Ed. IV cc. 3 & 4; 7 Ed. IV c. 3; 22 Ed. IV c. 3.—France: Eberstadt, *Das französische Gewerberecht*, etc. (Schmoller's Forschungen XVII: 11) 316 note; cp. Godart, *L'ouvrier en soie* 4 f.

[6] The anonymous writings: "Drei volkswirtschaftliche Denkschriften aus der Zeit Heinrichs VIII von England," ed. R. Pauli (*Abhandl. d. Gesellsch. d. Wissenschaften zu Göttingen* XXIII, Gött. 1878) 56, 67 (the latter also in *Tudor Econ. Docs.* III 120 f.).—Starkey—*vide* prev. chap. note 29—109 *et passim*.

During the period of more conscious mercantilism, there is naturally a constant repetition of this view on unemployment, sometimes with unexpected and interesting variations.

Petty put the decisive argument in favour of this view in unimpeachable terms when he said in 1662 that it would be better to burn the products of the labour of a thousand men than to allow a thousand men to lose their skill by remaining unemployed. This is the same reasoning as List once elaborated, that the power of creating wealth is more important than the wealth itself.

Child's treatment of the problem (1669) went more deeply into economic facts because he linked it up with the question of emigration. His reasoning kept to the same lines as the colonial policy followed in practice. In its general tendencies, it had many counterparts in contemporary literature. In Child's opinion those colonies ought to be encouraged which gave employment to workers in the mother country by buying her products or freighting her ships. In that case, it was not harmful to the wealth of the mother country if people emigrated to the colonies. Conversely, those colonies which took employment away from the workers in the mother country should be restrained in every possible way, or be forced into other activities. According to Child, the English colonies in the Antilles, Jamaica and Barbados were therefore useful to the mother country, because every Englishman there provided work for four Englishmen at home; but "New England is the most prejudicial Plantation to this kingdom" because ten Englishmen there did not give employment to perhaps even a single one at home. Child's view of the problem of population was in general perfectly consistent, and, from the selfish and somewhat narrow point of view of the mother country, was thoroughly justified. Only emigration to colonies with other industrial possibilities than those of the mother country can decrease the supply of the latter's products and raise their prices there, and the reverse applies to the products which the mother country must buy: the supply is increased and the prices fall.[7] The only relevant objection to be made is that,

[7] Petty, *Treatise of Taxes* chap. 6 (Econ. Writings I 60).—Child, chap. 10 (esp. ed. quoted above 190 f., 212–16); Counterparts from the same period: Beer, *Old Colonial System* I ch. 1; on the theory: Heckscher, "The Effect of Foreign Trade on the Distrib. of Income", ch. 13 in *Readings in the Theory of International Trade*, Phila. & Toronto 1949.—A collection of quotations from the preambles to English Acts of Parliament after the Restoration dealing with the creation of employment *vide*: Furniss, *The Position of the Laborer in a System of Nationalism* 51 note 4.

from a dynamic point of view, prosperity in the colonies may be more important to the prosperity of the metropolis than particular trade advantages. The choice of examples made by Child is apt to make this particularly clear to later generations.

Of course consideration for employment was also bound to play a large part in the monetary theory of mercantilism, as may be pointed out already in this connection. It was possible to justify the necessity of importing precious metals, as Malynes did (1601), by showing that it caused prices to rise and created employment. Conversely, the export of money could be opposed on the grounds that it led to unemployment and depopulation, as was done by the author of *Britannia Languens*. Cary placed the creation of employment at the centre of his reasoning, and from it he led up to his demand for high prices (1695). John Law stated in 1705 that it was impossible to set more people to work without creating more money. He believed that there had to be at least sufficient money to pay wages. He regarded this, as others before him had done, as a justification for the mercantilist policy of paper money which was to lead to one of the world's first and greatest inflation crises.[8]

Most interesting are such observations as arrive, through concentrating upon a policy of creating employment, at practical results which are not reconcilable with the usual demands of mercantilism. They demonstrate perhaps most clearly the importance of this point of view.* This is the case, e.g., with Child and Petty, particularly in the latter's pamphlet *Quantulumcunque concerning Money*, written in 1682 and published in 1695. Starting from the need for employing labour, they both came to the conclusion that the export of coin was preferable to the export of uncoined precious metals, because the former led to a native production of coinage. Barbon's position is even more extreme, for he adopted the view throughout that in considering the respective merits of various industries, their capacity to absorb labour was the only important criterion. This led him to the conclusion that the export of precious metals was actually an advantage for the country, for if they remained in the country they only paid little freight and provided little work, but if they

[8] Malynes, "Treatise of the Canker of England's Common Wealth": *Tudor Econ. Docs.* III 399.—*Britannia Languens* chap. 4 (1st ed. 38 ff.).—Cary, *An Essay on the State of England, etc.* 75, 136, 148 ff. *et passim.*—Law, *Considérations sur le commerce et sur l'argent* (French transl., La Haye 1720) esp. chaps. 3, 7, and 8 (58 f., 156, 158, 166, 181, 183 *et passim*); cp. next part.—*Vide* also Furniss, chap. 3.

* See below II 365-6, *Addendum* §7.

were exported they would at least have to pay the cost of transport
The Swedish economist, Anders Bachmanson (Nordencrantz),
writing in the first third of the 18th century, even attacked the
native salt refineries because they prevented the import of salt,
which would encourage shipping. If import provided more work
than native production, then according to him it must be given
preference (1730). And so the idea of creating employment led
certain writers to disapprove of the eagerness for precious metals
and the efforts towards self-sufficiency, which, among others,
were two of the most frequently discussed demands of mercantilism.[9]

The attitude towards technical innovations, labour-saving
machinery and the like, involved the mercantilists in similar and
even greater difficulties, and for obvious reasons led them into
internal contradictions.

From the point of view of a policy aiming at creating employment, the rejection of labour-saving machinery would have been
quite natural. In practice, economic policy during the period of
mercantilism often did have some such effect, as has already
been shown in the first part. This, however, was not because it
deliberately and consciously worked to this end, but because the
gilds and most of the other medieval systems of industrial regulation dragged on even though they did not enjoy much sympathy
among the mercantilist writers and statesmen of the 17th century.
From the practical results it is therefore impossible to determine
the theoretical attitude of mercantilism towards this question;
but there is no lack of utterances showing its character. This
attitude in reality was *not* opposed to technical innovations.

How is this to be explained? Partly by the fear that foreigners
would get hold of the new discoveries, and that new avenues of
employment would disappear still more completely if the discoveries were not exploited within the country. But another
cause lay much deeper. Mercantilists were already possessed of
the spirit of progress, the lust for enterprise and adventure, and
novelty in itself often constituted an irresistible attraction to
them. The 17th and the beginning of the 18th centuries were
the golden age for "projectors". One part of the monopolistic
charters of Charles I was granted for machines of the most
extraordinary kind, among them machines for draining swamps,
sawing wood, enabling ships to sail against the wind, and mills

[9] Child, *New Discourse of Trade* 73.—Petty, *Quantulumcunque*, etc. (Econ.
Writings II 440).—Barbon, *Discourse of Trade* (1st ed. 39 f., 74–6, repr. 23,
36 f.).—Bachmanson, *Arcana oeconomiae et commercii* (Sthlm. 1730) 337 ff.

to turn without wind or water and so on. The same applied to
France, though to a rather lesser degree. Scipion de Gramont
(1620) referred enthusiastically to the fact that "time had been
shortened, work made easier, and trouble decreased", that *one*
man could spin more silk in an hour with the help of a large wheel
than a hundred could previously spin in a whole day, and that the
same applied to "a host of other things which have made human
industry more easy to produce". In Germany, mercantilist
writers were definitely full of projects and schemes. During the
restoration period in England a nobleman, the second Marquis
of Worcester, published an essay in which he enumerated a
hundred of his inventions (1663). Andrew Yarranton brought
out a book entitled *England's Improvement by Sea and Land* (1677),
filling several hundred pages with countless schemes in every
possible field, which were to serve the aim given in the title, to
help "to overcome the Dutch without fighting, to pay debts
without money", etc.* Twenty years later (1697) the famous,
or notorious, Daniel Defoe published an *Essay upon Projects*
reviewing a host of these projects and plans, especially in the
sphere of commerce. The period of speculation towards the end
of the 17th and at the beginning of the 18th century let loose,
as is well known, a flood of schemes for procuring capital from the
gullible public for the most fantastic purposes. Technical innovations, it must be specially stressed, or what passed as such, were
at the time just as enticing as economic advances in other directions. Cary (in 1695) gave a whole series of interesting and
happy examples, and summed up the situation in unusually
characteristic terms when he said, "there is a Cunning
crept into Trades".[10] Clearly, then, it had become psychologically impossible to oppose the new labour-saving methods.
In other words, through its general social outlook mercantilism had already decided in favour of technical innovations.

[10] English patents of monopoly *vide inter alia, Foedera,* ed. Rymer, 1st ed.
XIX 40, 239 ff., Hague ed. VIII: III 27, 153 ff.—France: S. de Gramont,
Le denier royal, traicté curieux de l'or et de l'argent (Paris 1620) 194–97; for other
examples, Boissonnade, *Le socialisme d'État* . . . (*1453–1661*) 178 ff.—Marquis
of Worcester, *A Century of the Names and Scantlings of such Inventions As at present
I can call to mind to have tried and perfected* (Lond. 1663, acc. to the title-page,
written in 1655; repr. with detailed commentaries as a supplement to H.
Dirck's *The Life and Scientific Labours of the Second Marquis of Worcester,* Lond.
1865; the author considers Worcester to have been the inventor of the steam
engine).—I have made use of the first ed. of Defoe, *Essay upon Projects* (Lond.
1697).—Cary 145–8.—Cp. Lipson III 50.—*V.s.* I 284 f.

* See below II 366, *Addendum* §8.

As an economic theory, on the other hand, mercantilism had not made any such decision, and therein lay the dilemma. A *laissez-faire* theory, which considers the function of economic activity to be the catering for needs in the widest sense of the word, encounters no theoretical difficulties on this point, even if it has to admit that the reorganization of production often presents most serious practical difficulties. But mercantilism set out from a directly contrary standpoint, and in addition was preoccupied with a policy of creating employment. Its problem was therefore to bring its own fundamental position into harmony with the progressive attitude towards technical innovations, a problem which was theoretically insoluble. The most that could be achieved was a more or less practical compromise not based on principles.

Such a compromise is noticeable in, among others, Becher. His general attitude was still thoroughly medieval. He was, for example, the sworn foe of the *polypoly*, or unlimited competition, and he demanded that no merchant should be allowed to develop his trade so far as to ruin another. But at the same time, by his very nature and temperament, Becher was an out and out 'projector''. His interest in invention led him to oppose the prohibition of ribbon looms, though he believed that the independent man (*Nebenmann*) competing with the machine should be allowed to exist and work, once the machine had come into use. His contemporary, von Schrötter, on the other hand, appears to have been in favour of the prohibition which Becher opposed (1686).

A further instance illustrated even more clearly the helplessness in the face of this problem. In one of his later works, *A Plan of the English Commerce* (1728), Defoe discussed the problem of creating employment. He mentioned the case of an Englishman who had been ordered out of Russia because he had proposed to reorganize the river traffic by means of a new kind of ship, which required a crew of only 18 to 20 men instead of 120 as heretofore. The Prince had said that it was a scheme for starving his people. Defoe observed that "The Folly of this Conduct makes a kind of Jest upon the People of Moscow". But developing his reasoning further he, too, comes to the conclusion that the population should be kept fully occupied, without making any attempt to resolve the contradiction. In another connection in the same book he even said, "Notwithstanding in general, it is the Advantage of Commerce, to have all Things done as cheap as possible; yet that as it is the grand Support of Wealth and Trade in England, to have our Product consum'd, and in order to it, to have our People and Cattle employ'd; So it is not always the Advantage of England, to lessen the Labour of the said People and Cattle, by the Encrease of River-Navigation." In the end Defoe thus recommended the very thing he had condemned and derided in the Russian example. The same applied in other cases too. The few writers before the middle of the 18th century who deliberately adopted a *laissez-faire* attitude had of course none of these qualms of conscience, but wholeheartedly embraced the labour-saving ideal; they are interesting from a theoretical point of view, though their influence was presumably insignificant. Perhaps the first, and certainly the most surprising of these, Joseph Lee, a "Minister of the Gospel" during the Protectorate (1656), in his *Vindication of A Regulated Enclosure*, wrote, "Let it be granted that our land and business lying nearer together fewer servants will be kept; are any bound to keep more servants than are needful for their business, or may they not cast how to do the same business with least labour: *Frustra fit per plura quod fieri potest per pauciora?*" And almost half a century later (1701), the anonymous *Considerations upon the East-India Trade* began by showing, with a wealth of examples, the absurdity of too great an expenditure of labour, in order to arrive at a conclusion recommending freedom of trade.

In the popular mercantilist literature, of course, not very much was to be seen of the problems in which mercantilism had become embroiled through the employment policy, for that literature existed far more for the purposes of simple and easily understood propaganda. For the practical application of protectionist policy, such propaganda was probably more important than the subtle arguments of the best minds of mercantilism. A good example is Montchrétien's book. The following piece of cheap but effective rhetoric is taken from an appeal directed to Marie de Medici and Louis XIII, who was still a minor—and it is quite typical: "We adjure your Majesties . . ." it runs, "to grant the request made in this most urgent appeal of a large number of your subjects, expressed in the woeful sighs of their womenfolk and the sorrowful cries of their children. Deign to permit them all to represent to you, in all humility, that their trade is the only inheritance of them and their heirs, for apart from their liberty they have nothing besides this income, and foreigners who wish to gain possession of it are no different from him who takes another's property by tyranny", etc. These unfortunates, according to Montchrétien's descriptions, desired nothing more than the "driving out of idleness, the mother of all that is vicious, the root of all that is sinful".[11]

Idleness was indeed one of the most important considerations to the mercantilists. It comes out best, however, in another connection, in the discussion of the mercantilist attitude towards wages, which is reserved for the end of this chapter.

It is precisely the idea of creating employment, and its great importance for mercantilism, which reveals how very much mercantilism regarded *production as an end in itself*. On this point, it was in theoretical agreement with the medieval outlook, however much it differed from it in nature. The great line of demarcation between *laissez-faire*, on the one hand, and all previous, and perhaps even all later, conceptions of society on the other, is very marked here. The next part will indicate how remarkably and how closely this idea of production as an end in itself was also linked up with the mercantilist theory of money.

2. HISTORICAL ANTECEDENTS

Although the "hunger for goods" was normally predominant in antiquity and in the Middle Ages, yet the contrary view also had very early antecedents.

Autarchy

One of its medieval roots was certainly the idea of autarchy or economic self-sufficiency, which is already to be found in Aristotle. But still we must hasten to add that the idea of autarchy is not identical with the mercantilist "fear of goods". The aim of the former is to limit or entirely abolish all trade relations with other communities, and not imports alone. The mercantilist idea of forcing exports and limiting imports is really no more nor less autarchical than the medieval policy of provision, which had precisely contrary aims. But in reality, people were often so vague on these problems both at that time and to-day that they did not realize that exports, just as well as imports, forged links with other countries, even apart from the fact that one presupposed the other. It is significant, for example, to find the Austrian, von Hörnigk, Becher's brother-in-law, making so

---

[11] Becher, *Politische Discurs* part I chap. 4 § 6, part II chap. 4 (1673 ed. 72, 124).—Von Schrötter, chap. 102 (1st ed. 534).—Defoe, *A Plan of the English Commerce* part I chaps. 1 & 7 (new ed. Oxf. 1928, 42 ff., 170 f.).—J. Lee, 'Ευταξία τōυ 'Αγρου, *or, A Vindication of A Regulated Enclosure* (Lond. 1656) 7.— R. H. Tawney, *Religion and the Rise of Capitalism* (Lond. 1926) 259.—*Considerations upon the East India Trade*, esp. chaps. I & VII (1st ed., Lond. 1701) 49–59.— Montchrétien 95 f.—*V.s.* I 271.—Cf. E. A. J. Johnson, *Predecessors of Adam Smith*, ch. 13.

much ado about the "independence" of his country, and yet at the same time demanding that exports should be pushed forward incessantly (1684). Of real autarchy, e.g. in the case of a possible blockade in war-time, comparatively little was said. Becher certainly had it in mind when he suggested that people should not have dealings with their neighbours, for the commerce could not outlast the friendship. Sometimes, as in the *Discourse of the Common Weal*, an attitude directly opposed to the idea of autarchy was taken up. Autarchical tendencies were of practical importance really in one context alone, where they were, it is true, applied only onesidedly, but where they acquired great significance. That was in the relations between the mother country and her colonies. According to the Old Colonial System these two were to supplement one another in such a way that everything possible should be procurable within the unit formed by the mother country and the colonies. But as long as the ultimate goal of mercantilism was to export as much as possible from this economic unit, it was still far removed from any real aspiration towards autarchy. The efforts to produce military supplies within the country may be considered as a partial fulfilment of the idea of autarchy, for there was no desire to develop their export. But it would be quite wrong to say that they played any predominant part at all.[12]

There was, however, also another classical ideal in the economic field, the ambition to sell more than was bought, and this occupied a considerably more prominent place in mercantilist philosophy. Becher's observation recorded above (*v.s.* II 116) expressed this ambition in its extreme form, though he did not refer to any classical precedent. But English works of the 16th and early 17th centuries frequently referred to a statement of Cato major to the effect that the father of a family ought to sell but not to buy (*patrem familias vendacem non emacem esse oportet*).[13]

[12] P. W. von Hörnigk, *Oesterreich über Alles, wann es nur will*, chaps. 8–10, 33 *et passim* (ed. Regensburg 1723 22–41, 187–98).—Becher, *Pol. Discurs* part II (ed. 1673/9).—[Hales], *Discourse of the Common Weal* (ed. Lamond) 61.— Beer bases his whole exposition of the Old Colonial Policy on the principle of self-sufficiency, but he does not appear to realize the limits of its applicability, and Lipson seems to be open to the same criticism (II 463, III 1 f; also 489 f.) The same is true of the collection of examples for France (citing Nowak, *L'idée de l'autarchie économique*, Paris 1925) given in P. Harsin, *Les doctrines monétaires et financières en France du XVIe au XVIIIe siècle* (Paris 1928) 13 ff. and note 3.—*V.s.* II 40 f.—See also: Niehans, *Der Gedanke der Autarkie.*

[13] Cato, *De agri cultura* chap. 2 (ed. Keil, Lpz. 1894, I 15).—Quoted *inter alia* by Cecil: Cunningham II[3] 131 note; Lambarde's marginal observation in *Disc. of the Common Weal* (ed. Lamond 171); Wheeler, *Treatise of*

Taken literally, the dictum makes no sense at all. The psychological truth underlying it is, of course, the fear that an individual or a country could be ruined financially by doing the opposite. Mercantilist literature is therefore full of dirges regarding import surpluses and the outflow of precious metals. To this extent, the new conception is sufficiently explained by a reference to such popular arguments, which seemed to take on an added authority through being fortified by classical quotations. But the principal point still remains unexplained. How was it that this idea happened to attain such prominence just under mercantilism, superseding the hitherto prevailing policy of provision? The reply to this question must be sought in an examination of the beliefs, the policy and the economic world at the birth period of mercantilism.

Municipal policy

Even in the economic policy of the towns, which tended mainly in the opposite direction, there are certain points of contact with this train of thought. It is necessary at this juncture to return to a line of argument broken off in the second chapter of this part. We must investigate, that is, the degree to which the interests of the craftsman led to a protectionist attitude not only towards individuals but also towards goods.

In the first place, such a point of contact may be found in the *Bannmeilenrecht*. This contained hindrances and prohibitions against such crafts outside the town as were carried on within the city itself. These prohibitions appear for a long time to have been confined chiefly to such craftsmen as competed with the municipal craftsmen. But towards the end of the Middle Ages it seems to have become customary to apply them also directly to the goods coming to the city from the *Bannmeile* area around. Thus in 1414, Lübeck forbade the import of harness from villages and dependent rural towns. A famous example is the Low German letter of complaint of the later Middle Ages directed by the small towns of Krempe within the *Bannmeile* of Hamburg against its unscrupulous taskmaster. Hamburg was employing forcible measures to divert corn from Krempe to herself, such as removing ships from Krempe's harbour. At the same time she refused to buy beer from the citizens of Krempe and wanted to compel them to buy beer from Hamburg. The letter declares: "We cannot

Commerce (1601); Malynes, *Lex Mercatoria*, part I chap. 5 (1st ed., Lond. 1622, 60); [E. Misselden], *Free Trade or, The Meanes to Make Trade Florish* (Lond. 1622) 12 f.; but the list is far from complete, this tag being very popular with mercantilist writers.

but think that you intend to remove our corn forcibly from our
store-houses. . . . Our beer you will not admit into your city,
we must drink your beer under compulsion. We should not
much object to this, if you would allow us our trade, so that we
might earn the money with which we could pay for your beer.
But that you decline to do, and destroy instead poor people,
who have furnished you with much good corn." In conclusion,
the latter promises that if Hamburg treats the town well, "it
will send them all its corn and others none". The point is perfectly clear. Hamburg was "a brewery" (as it was called in a
description a hundred years later), but at the same time was
dependent on the supply of corn for domestic consumption and
intermediary trade. It wanted to give its outlying *Bannmeile*
territory the same position as was given by mercantilist states to
their colonies, in other words it wanted to make the dependent
territory the supplement of the "metropolis" as regards both
import and sale.[14]

This constituted a departure from the policy of provision to
the extent that goods were not retained at any price—in the
instance given, not even so important an article of consumption
as beer. People rather concentrated on ensuring the import of
such goods as could not be produced at home. To this extent, the
Bannmeilenrecht of the medieval cities undoubtedly contained an
element which went beyond the bounds of the policy of provision.
But nevertheless this element was apparently very circumscribed,
and did not appear in a more pronounced form until much later.
However important this municipal economic policy may have
been for the colonial policy of mercantilism, it does not take us
much further in the matter of protectionist policy.

Secondly, however, protectionist tendencies were closely connected with the gilds, and particularly with *gild compulsion*, i.e.
the limiting of the right to practise a craft to members of the
handicraft organizations. The earliest sources of gild history
make this quite clear, without going into the debatable questions
of the origins and roots of the craft gilds. Several examples, taken
from the early period, may serve to illustrate the point.

The Rhine toll at Coblenz contained a clause dating from 1104.
No restrictions were placed on bakers, one of the groups of craftsmen mentioned therein, while with regard to another group, shoe-

[14] W. Stieda, "Zwangs- und Bannrechte" (*Handwörterbuch der Staatswissenschaften* VIII[3] 1165 f.).—*Hansisches Urkundenbuch* X No. 663.—In 1369 beer
constituted far more than half of the volume of Hamburg's exports (W. Vogel,
Geschichte der deutschen Seeschiffahrt I, Berl. 1915, 227; cp. 201).

makers, it was laid down explicitly that strangers were not to sell shoes without permission of the toll officials, and that where the right to sell was granted, it implied the payment of a fee to the shoemakers of the city. In the charter of the Magdeburg shoemakers' gild (between 1152 and 1192), strangers or "guests" were prohibited from marketing their wares without the permission of the members of the local gild. A rather later charter of the shoemakers in Halberstadt (1230) similarly made the exercise of the craft within the city by strangers dependent upon the consent of the local craftsmen. Later German examples are of less interest. The clearest expression of this tendency is to be found in England and goes back as far as the second third of the 12th century, being found in the *Libertas Londoniensis*. Without any connection with the gilds it was there laid down that no foreign "mercator"—a term often including craftsmen during the Middle Ages—should be permitted to dye within the city or "execute any work belonging to the burghers". The municipal charter of Montpellier, confirmed in 1204, contained a precisely similar clause.[15]

These examples undoubtedly express a tendency towards the protection of goods far more than is the case with the measures mentioned in the second chapter, directed against the competition of foreign merchants. Nevertheless they too had important points of difference from protectionism proper.

The first point revealed in the German examples is that their fundamental criterion is not whether a person is a stranger or not, but whether or not he is a member of the municipal handicraft organization. Non-citizens were indeed excluded, but in their capacity as non-members, and therefore in precisely the same way as citizens who were not members of the gilds. If strangers became members, the prohibition no longer applied to them, and likewise if the compulsory gild restrictions themselves were lifted. This is supported by many documents. The Cologne gild of bedspread weavers, according to a regulation of 1149, expressly included both natives and strangers. Felt making for hats in Mühlhausen in Thuringia (1131) and cloth finishing in Magdeburg (1183) were prohibited to natives and strangers alike *unless* they became gild members. Non-burgher wool weavers

---

[15] German documents: *Urkunden* (ed. Keutgen) No. 80 and 258 resp. and R. Eberstadt, *Magisterium und Fraternitas* (Schmoller's Forschungen XV: II, Lpz. 1897) 258.—*Libertas Londoniensis: v.s.* chap. 2 note 17.—Montpellier: after "Le petit Thalamus de Montpellier," quoted in Eberstadt, *Das französische Gewerberecht*, etc. 38.—*V.s.* I 376.

were kept out in Halberstadt (1283) *if* they were not members.
When the gild of butchers and bakers of Erfurt was abolished in
1264, all limitations on foreign craftsmen were abandoned, so
that according to a letter of the mayor, the crafts were thrown
open to "every man both native and foreign". The regulations
were thus officially not directed against foreign craftsmen as
such at all, and in practice only to a small degree. They applied
exclusively against the *Bönhasen*, to use a rather later expression,
regardless of whether they lived within or outside the city.[16]

Discrimination against strangers on principle in favour of
burghers occurred in only a surprisingly small number of cases.
Even where it did occur, there remained a *personal factor* in the
protectionist tendency. This is manifest in the English and French
regulations cited above, where there is no connection with any
craft organization, as well as in most of the German examples.
There are only three early German documents known to me
(Coblenz 1104, Magdeburg 1152/92 and Erfurt 1264) that
touch at all on the question of the sale of goods produced outside
the city. Probably in these cases, and almost certainly in all the
others, the prohibition applied exclusively to unauthorized
trading within the city itself. This obviously tallies with the fact
that the prohibitions were not directed primarily against strangers
as such. Still, it is possible to detect in it a rudimentary protection of goods, principally because protectionist policy was
extended in this way to the sphere of *production*. Nothing is more
natural, as the step from ordinary gild regime was apparently
very short indeed. In view of this, the remarkable thing is not
that there was any connection, but that attempts at pure protection of goods were so very rare. The German historian Eberstadt may be right in suggesting that the impossibility of exercising
gild control over the production of "foreign" goods and also
their deviation from the normal types provoked the municipal
craftsmen.[17] But this makes it all the more striking that so little
was done against the import of goods. It indicates that at this
early period of gild history the policy of provision was still predominant, and consequently people were not inclined to take
any measures against the import of goods themselves.

[16] Documents of the years 1149, 1183, and 1264: *Urkunden* (ed. Keutgen)
Nos. 255, 257, 291; the others according to quotations in Keutgen, *Aemter
und Zünfte* (Jena 1903) 202; cp. Below, *Probleme der Wirtschaftsgeschichte* 243
note 1. *Vide* also G. Hazelius, *Om Handtverksämbetena under Medeltiden* (Bidrag
till vår odlings häfder IX, Sthlm. 1906) 39 f., 46, 93, 150 ff.

[17] Eberstadt, *Franz. Gewerberecht* 118.

A general principle

We must therefore seek other causes for the departure from the principles of the policy of provision and the transition to the opposite extreme. In doing so it must be remembered that it is necessary to explain the appearance of a new *general* principle.

This is not to say that the new attitude came into being suddenly, or everywhere with the same force. It first appeared in those branches, and was applied to those goods, which were already extant within the area to be protected. There it already had a certain measure of support in the gilds and the economic policy evolved by the gilds. But even at a very early stage, in fact strictly speaking as far back as the new tendency can be traced, the principle was also applied to goods which were not actually produced within the area but which its inhabitants *desired* to produce there. Even then there was still a touch of municipal economic policy, because the goods people were so anxious to produce fell within the scope of municipal trades and were thus industrial or handicraft products. The example concerning the quarrel between Krempe and Hamburg is an illustration in point. A later example of greater importance is the English contrast, frequently met with, between goods "for the back" and goods "for the belly"; on the one hand food-stuffs, the prices of which were to be kept low, and on the other industrial products, particularly textiles, the prices of which it was desired to keep as high as possible. This contrast persisted obstinately, and in it municipal policy was perpetuated. There was also a lingering idea that different branches of production should be reserved for different countries, as will appear in the fifth part of the present work (*v.i.* 278 f.).

But finally nothing remained of these distinctions. When the encouragement of new industries was no longer applied to one city alone but was extended to the country as a whole, in other words when this tendency reached its zenith, there existed no sort of production that was not considered beneficial to a country, however absurd it might appear from the standpoint of the natural conditions of the country and the character of the people. As we know, it was much more difficult to escape from the rut of municipal policy and to extend the new policy to agricultural products. But finally even this was successfully carried through, and the final stone was laid to the system of "solidarity protectionism" which asserted that all production in a country, potential and existing, should be encouraged. Thus protectionism came to develop the same universality as had characterized the policy of provision.

In examining the causes of this great change, it is tempting—especially to believers in the Marxist thesis that all history is a history of class struggle—to consider the distribution of power between the classes in society and to assume that the interests of merchants and consumers were made subservient to the interests of the producers. It is certainly conceivable that such a change played a part; though as far as I know there is no knowledge of its nature or even any proof of its existence. In any case it appears impossible to put most of the weight on this unknown factor. As far as I have been able to discover, the principal explanation is to be found in the access to popularity of new economic conceptions, not in a new distribution of power.

People are actuated, to a greater extent than one usually tends to admit, by their more or less conscious or instinctive notions of what is right and natural. This does not contradict the view of their being governed by "self-interest", though it may seem to do so; for they partly interpret their own interests in the light of this conception, thinking to gain or lose in accordance with what appears in regard to it as economic gain or loss. On the other hand they often feel hampered in asserting their interests in such a direction as they themselves consider harmful to the general good. They certainly pursue their own advantage with all the strength at their command, but they seek to do it in a way which will harmonize with their own and their fellow-citizens' conception of economic and social good. This can be illustrated by a multitude of examples.

A very good instance is the treatment, under mercantilism, of the products of sheep rearing in a country like England, which was governed by large cattle-owning landlords. The export of these products was prohibited in the interests of the cloth industry and, as Adam Smith remarks, the statutes were written in blood, especially an Act passed during Elizabeth's reign (1565/66). This forbade the export of live sheep on pain of confiscation of property, a year's imprisonment and the cutting off of the left hand, while the death penalty was provided for a recurrence of the offence. The first Restoration Parliament, in which the victorious landed aristocracy had the upper hand, extended the export prohibitions to wool (1660). The reason for this policy, which was after all against the interests of sheep rearers, was that the encouragement of the cloth industry was considered to be in the obvious interests of the country as a whole, and that wool producers did not care to prevent a measure in favour of an industry which was generally regarded as the economic backbone of the country.[18] Again, in the Victorian era the influential industrialists were as great believers in free trade as the rest, though no doubt many of them might have gained something from protection; they lacked both the belief and the courage needed for insisting upon it. Instead, they furthered their interests by pressing for lower tariffs on other products than their own, and resisting legislative interference in the exploitation of women and children; for this attitude harmonized with "the spirit of the age". On the other hand, in protectionist countries to-day, representatives of the export in industries rarely attack tariffs, although these react adversely on their own production. Nowadays it is "good form" for an industrialist, and in fact for any business man, to be a protectionist. In deference to this, the special interests of particular branches of production must stand aside, often because the real position is not clearly appreciated, but just as often too because of the belief that tariffs are beneficial to "industrial life".

In the problems under consideration here, too, we must seek for explanations outside the political and social distribution of power. This is all the more true since the matter under discussion was not a sporadic tendency but a vital reorientation of economic policy. It took place in one country after another and in the course of centuries was applied more and more consistently, regardless of the great variations in the social distribution of power at various times and in individual countries. In these circumstances, it would be absurd to explain the tendency by the incidental balance of social power at a limited period of time and in one particular country. It is not difficult to find, in place of this, an explanation which can claim to be valid for the whole of the subsequent social development of western Europe.

In point of fact, this explanation has already been given in the previous chapter, and can be expressed briefly as the extension of *money economy*. As soon as the result of production, from the producer's standpoint, no longer consists in other goods but in money, then the money yield appears as the only aim of economic activity. Other goods are then considered unwelcome since they are merely competing with one's own products for the monetary

---

[18] Statutes: 8 Eliz. c. 3; 12 Car. II c 32.—Adam Smith, *Wealth of Nations*, Bk. 4 chap. 8 (ed. Cannan II 146); on the 1660 export prohibition on wool (somewhat one-sided) Furniss, *Position of the Laborer*, etc. 33–6.— See also the apposite observations in P. J. Thomas, *Mercantilism and the East India Trade* 58 f., as well as Lipson III 22–34.

equivalent. For a time, *laissez-faire* was able to force back this almost inevitable economic fallacy, owing to the unusual virility of its doctrines, but it was far from being able to eradicate it for all time.

It is of course difficult to relate the rise of protectionist views in time, precisely with the extension of the money economy. A revolution in people's economic views does not occur suddenly. It takes time to complete itself, and in some cases the time required is considerable. Nevertheless, this explanation which we have given fits in also with the temporal development. The first real attempts at a protectionist policy occurred in North Italy in the first part of the 13th century, that is at the end of the Crusades, when money economy was making great progress. Next, the new tendency spread first to the Low Countries, which were in an advanced state of economic development, and to England, later to France and the rest of Europe north of the Alps. It only reached Sweden at the end of the 16th and the beginning of the 17th century; until then natural economy had dominated Swedish economic life.[19] Of course it is not possible to provide a *proof* that this explanation is the right one. The proof must lie in the economic analysis of the situation, and is established if the results arrived at are not contradicted by the known facts and if these do not admit of any other equally plausible interpretation.

3. ITS RISE AND EARLIEST HISTORY

The first definite protectionist measures were taken, as we have already observed, in northern Italy, where economic development was most advanced during the whole of the Middle Ages. The oldest case known to me, significantly enough, is an attempt, by prohibiting imports, to create a native industry of a kind which did not exist there but was already flourishing in another town, that is, not a "protectionist" measure in the literal sense of the term. I refer to Parma, which in 1211 prohibited the import of *pignolati*, as it was called, a special kind of light cotton goods produced in Piacenza. The object was to produce them in Parma itself, and this appears to have been successfully carried

[19] With regard to the special Swedish circumstances, I have treated this matter in my essay "Svensk natura- och penninghushållning i äldre tid" (*Ekonomisk Tidskrift* XXV, 1923, 270 f.). and later in "Natural and Money Economy as illustrated from Swedish History in the Sixteenth Century" (*Journal of Economic and Business History* III, 1930, 21 ff. This article is now available in *Enterprise and Secular Change, Readings in Economic History*, ed. F. C. Lane and J. C. Riemersma (London, 1953) ch. 13.

through about forty years later. A decree of the following year points to the existence of a prohibition against the import of warp yarn, which must have been drawn up by the wool-workers' gild, *arte de lana*, in Florence.[20]

The measures taken in Venice, however, were in every respect more important. The economic development of Venice is generally believed to have started with the salt mines. According to Cassiodorus, they produced "edible money". Towards the end of the 10th century, this domestic production of salt appears to have been used as a commercial weapon for the policy of provision. Istria and the Mark of Verona were forced into subjection by having their supply of salt cut off, causing the death of their cattle. The salt mines were partly under state control, and the fiscal interests of the state must certainly have paved the way for the opposite protectionist tendency, so that in the end efforts were directed to the encouragement of export instead of the rendering of supplies to other places more difficult. In its treaty of 1230 with Venice, which we mentioned before, Ferrara had to be prepared not to obstruct its import of salt from Venice. In 1228 and 1243, prohibitions were enacted against the import of salt into Venice from non-Venetian places on the Adriatic. The policy of hampering imports had thus begun in the case of so important a necessity as salt.[21]

Another measure, which likewise originated in Venice, is even more interesting in the development of protectionism and mercantilism. It consisted in *making export a condition of import*. I only know of one example of this dating from before the 14th century. According to a treaty between Venice and Ancona of 1264, the whole of the money received for goods sold, including the limited number of goods which Ancona was allowed to dispose of in Ferrara, Bologna, and Lombardy, could only be used for purchases in Venice. This stipulation is certainly connected with staple policy, but none the less it is a very typical expression of the belief that was growing up that selling goods was profitable, and importing them was harmful. The contrast with the policy of provision becomes evident when it is compared with the kind of compensation policy carried on in the early Middle Ages and

[20] Affò, *Storia della città di Parma* (Parma 1792 ff.) III 325, in Schaube 768. Santini, *Documenti dell'antica costituzione del comune di Firenze* (Doc. di storia ital. X, Firenze 1895) 376 in A. Doren, *Entwicklung und Organisation der Florentiner Zünfte im 13. u. 14. Jahrh.* (Schmoller's Forsch. XV: III, Lpz. 1897) 9 note 2, and Schaube, *op. cit.*

[21] L. M. Hartmann, "Die wirtschaftlichen Anfänge Venedigs" (*Vierteljahrschr. f. Soz.-u. Wirtschaftsgesch.* II 1904, 434–42).

during World War I, described in the previous chapter (*v.s.* II 85), when licences for export were made dependent upon sufficient imports. It was a complete reversal of this tendency: export being made the condition for import, instead of the reverse.

The Venetian measures were also connected with the North Sea galley expeditions instituted in 1314. At first, non-citizens were allowed to participate in them, but as early as 1321 they were excluded. Towards the end of the same year, they were again accepted, but with the characteristic proviso that the value of their imports to Venice should not exceed the value of the goods which they had exported thence in their galleys. This clause was also applied during the subsequent period, and from 1328 onwards, it became an integral part of the Venetian laws against "merchant strangers" for goods imported from other localities as well. Of the first provision, it was said that it was issued *more solito*, according to custom, although it is not possible to see how far these words refer to the right of outsiders to participate in the expeditions, or whether they only refer to the prescriptions regarding limitation of their right to import. But the expression makes it not altogether improbable that a measure of this sort dates back even further.

In England these regulations were introduced towards the end of the century, in a statute of 1390, the Statute of Employment, which probably followed the Venetian model. The economist, Richard Jones, writing in the 1840's, called it the "Balance of Bargains System", i.e. balancing the import and export transactions of every individual merchant. That a measure corresponding so closely to the principles of primitive mercantilism should later have been taken up elsewhere too is not surprising. It is to be found in Portugal, for example, under the name *aldcaldamentos*, at least from the latter part of the 15th century onwards. [22]

[22] Venice: Schaube, "Die Anfänge der venetianischen Galeerenfahrten nach der Nordsee" (*Hist. Zeitschrift* CI, 1908, 61 ff., 76) acc. to *Arch. ven.* XXIV 94 and (unprinted) *Misti* XI c. 63; the permission of 1328 was given "conditione quod quantum extraxerint de Venetiis possint conducere de Flandria et non plus".—Cp. Simonsfeld (*v.s.* chap. 2 note 2) II 31, 44; the oldest (and incidentally uninformative) source there given, with the corresponding regulation for foreign merchants (No. 799), belongs to the year 1341.—England: 14 Rich. II c. 1; cp. [R. Jones] "Primitive Political Economy of England" (*Edinburgh Review* LXXXV, 1847, 428 ff.) and after him E. v. Heyking, *Zur Geschichte der Handelsbilanztheorie* I(Berl. 1880) 52 ff.—Portugal: Lannoy & Vander Linden (*v.s.* chap 2 note 13) I 138; the date of the law is not given, but its infringement in 1481 is mentioned.

The later extension of protectionism in North Italy is not particularly interesting for our purpose. In Genoa it appeared in the second half of the 14th century. In Florence it was in full bloom before the end of the same century though it lasted only a short while. It was particularly well developed in the second most important city of North Italy, Milan, from the middle of the 15th century onwards. [23]

In the meantime, protectionism had already spread to western Europe. It manifested itself first, perhaps, in the Netherlands. After the middle of the 14th century regulations which, according to Pirenne, originated considerably earlier, had the object of excluding English cloth from trade. In the charters to the Hanseatic merchants in Bruges 1359/60, it was stipulated that they had to send back English cloth, which came into Bruges via the mouth of the Zwijn and that they were not to deal with it in any way, not even to open the bales of cloth. They were permitted to export everywhere "although" as the Bruges text remarks, in typical protectionist fashion, "it is very injurious to the said city of Bruges". In 1434 Philip of Burgundy, the then ruler of the Netherlands, prohibited the import of English woollen cloths and English yarns in all his territories, because these countries, whose backbone was the cloth industry, were "very much injured and obstructed and are still suffering" by the continual imports of the English. [24]

Though it is difficult to establish the date when protection was first introduced into England, the development there is exceptionally interesting. What is apt to confound the issue are the particularly strong tendencies already noted to forbid the export of raw materials, and above all those of the textile industry, on account of their double character as parts of both the policy of provision and protectionism. In the case of the measures of 1271/74, directed against the cloth imports from Flanders into England, there were practically no other motives than those of foreign policy. The researches of Professor Unwin and his followers led them to the same conclusion with regard to Edward III's prohibition against the export of wool and his prohibition against the import and utilization of foreign cloth (1337), only with the addition that fiscal motives were also involved. Professor Unwin

[23] H. Sieveking, *Genueser Finanzwesen mit besonderer Berücksichtigung der Casa di S. Giorgio* I (Freib. i. B. 1898) 147 f.—Schulte (*v.s.* chap. 2 note 2) chap. 50.—Pöhlmann (*v.s.* note 5 of this chap.) 102 note.

[24] "Hoe dat het grooteliic gaet tieghen de draperye van de vorseider stede van Brucghe": printed in *Hansisches Urkundenbuch* I No. 430 § 19, cp. No. 452 § 62, No. 495 § 24.—Pirenne, *Histoire de Belgique* II[3] (Brux. 1922) 197.

assumes that the King's main object in keeping out the competitors of the native cloth industry was to allay the unrest in the
country. But if this is true, public opinion must at the time have
had a certain protectionist bent, or to put it more carefully, the
"love of goods" cannot have been strong enough to prevent
measures against imports. But it is none the less certain that in
Edward III's reign the policy of provision was very much more
predominant, and that the opposite view only asserted itself
much later—in the case of industrial protectionism, only in the
middle of the following century under Henry VI and Edward IV.
It was embodied at the time in statutes which have already
been mentioned above, in connection with the policy of creating
employment and its significance for protectionism (*v.s.* II 122 f.).

But what lends special interest to the development in England
are not these measures, which indeed had many precursors in
other countries, but the sudden change in policy in regard to
the corn trade, where England was unique, though her policy
was the reverse of consistent. As early as 1394, all fixed export
prohibitions on corn were repealed. Instead, the King was given
the right to forbid its export, if and when circumstances
demanded. It is true that this did not signify a real change in
policy; it was no more than the extension of the King's power to
this field. But still people's new attitude to imports and exports
was important, for it showed the reversal of the old ideas. It was
said of the export prohibitions, which in effect were still valid,
that as a result "Farmers and other Men which use Manurement
of their Land, may not sell their Corn but of low price, to the great
Damage of all the Realm". That is perhaps the first time in
modern history that a low price for corn is characterized as
injurious to society. This quotation is taken from the preamble
to an Act of 1437, which permitted the export of corn as soon as
the price fell below a certain level. This much, however, remained
of the policy of provision, that export to an enemy was always
and invariably excepted. It was thus believed that he would
benefit from the import of corn. This Act was originally intended
to remain in force for a short time only, but some years later it
was given permanent validity.

People had already gone so far along the new road that in
1463 a prohibition could be imposed on the import of corn.
This was to be enforced if the price did not rise above a certain
level, roughly the same level as that fixed by earlier Acts as a
maximum for the right of free export. In the preamble to the
Act of 1463, it is further stated that farmers suffered considerable

injury, resulting from the import of corn from other countries when domestic prices of corn were low. Under the earlier Tudors, this attitude was once again largely abandoned, imports were again permitted and export prohibitions were renewed, though of course subject to the granting of licences. From the middle of the 16th century onwards, however, the protectionist policy of the previous century was again adopted, and price limits for the right to export were successively increased, although the King usually retained the right to forbid exports altogether. But it was only after the Restoration (1673) and finally after the Revolution of 1688 that the step towards complete protection in the sphere of corn duties was definitely taken (1689), as was briefly mentioned in the previous chapter.

Professor N. S. B. Gras, it is true, has proved on the whole convincingly that protectionist and mercantilist policy, especially that of the Tudors, in many ways had an existence only on paper. In practice, he shows, it was of no account, because the price limits fixed by law were usually so high as to render export impossible, and even then the Government, in addition, frequently prohibited export when prices were lower. This certainly shows the tenacity of the policy of provision even in England. But the main point of interest for our purpose is the theoretical attitude, and with regard to this, an attitude such as that expressed in the freedom given to corn exports in 1437 and the 1463 prohibition against imports was something quite unique at the time. And even if the export prohibition in practice was only rarely applied, it is significant enough that it occurred at all. Professor Gras's interpretation is that the rapidly growing food requirements of London were the decisive factor in economic policy. Illuminating as this interpretation may be in many respects, it is calculated to disguise what is, from the general historical point of view, the fundamental fact, i.e., that the country with the most rapidly growing capital, and therefore the one that might be expected to encourage imports of food-stuffs, was more interested than any other country in the encouragement of agriculture by the maintenance of high prices and the facilitation of exports; in other words, that protectionist tendencies in this vital field gained ground there, while in most continental countries these tendencies failed to assert themselves even in the subsequent three or four centuries.[25]

[25] The Acts mentioned in chronological order: 17 Rich. II c. 7; 15 Hen. VI c. 2; 3 Ed. IV c. 2.—Gras, *Evolution of the English Corn Market*, esp. chap. 4; cp. his later works, esp. *An Introduction to Economic History* (N.Y. & Lond. 1922) and my criticism of the same: "Den ekonomiska historiens aspekter" (*Hist. Tidskr.* L, 1930, 21 f.).

The progress of protection in the sphere of industry in these continental countries is of less interest. The development in France—in industry alone be it noted—was approximately similar to that of England and Belgium, though at the outset rather less striking. The final irruption of protectionism appears to have coincided in all three countries and to have succeeded in the middle of the 15th century. In France, a charter of 1443 for the cloth weavers of Bourges contained prohibitions against the purchase and use of cloth from Normandy because that province, it stated, was "in the power of our hereditary enemies and adversaries, the English". The well-known decree of 1466, which led to the rise of the Lyons silk industry, refers to a great loss of gold and silver which the country experienced through the import of gold and silk materials. To speak of a loss of gold through the import of gold materials is typical of protectionism.[26]

To describe the advance of protectionism in other countries would hardly add anything essential to the picture. The data regarding protectionism in Europe are so abundant that any such description would require several volumes. But this would involve endless reiteration. These phenomena have their proper place in the economic histories of individual countries and not in a unified exposition of mercantilism as a system of protection. None the less several important theoretical problems remain to be dealt with.

4. THE ATTITUDE TO THE FACTORS OF PRODUCTION: RAW MATERIALS AND LABOUR

If the proposition that the "fear of goods" must be considered a fundamental tendency of protectionism be accepted, we are faced with the question of whether there were any exceptions to the policy of hindering imports and encouraging exports. In fact a number of exceptions did occur.

The simplest instance was that of money and the precious metals. They provided so clearly a case of the reversal of the relationship towards other goods that the efforts to retain them or to attract them are self-evident. As shown above (*v.s.* II 125), several mercantilist writers certainly recommended the export of coins in preference to the export of uncoined precious metal, but this does not affect the principle as such. One of the very rare deviations from orthodox doctrine is to be found in Barbon. His

---

[26] Quotation following various collections of documents inaccessible to me: Eberstadt, *Franz. Gewerberecht, etc.* 311 f., 316 note 5; Godart, *L'ouvrier en soie* 4 f.—*Supra* II 122 f.—Cp. *infra* 214 f.

point of view, also mentioned above, was that precious metals might very well leave the country so long as employment was thereby increased. But this attitude was altogether exceptional.

Raw materials, machinery

The question of the actual factors of production, raw materials, semi-manufactured goods, machinery and labour did, however, present a serious problem. Adam Smith himself pointed out that mercantilism reversed its usual practice of obstructing imports and encouraging exports when dealing with the factors of production.[27] He explained it by saying that mercantilism was preoccupied with the balance of trade. It is obvious that this factor played an important part; but equally important was the regard for employment. With a view to this, attempts were made to put into practice an idea which has always lain at the root of protectionist policy both at the time and later. I refer to the grading of goods, either according to their stage of manufacture or to their character as factors of production. Fewer restrictions were then imposed on their import and more on their export, the earlier the stage of manufacture and the more marked their character as factors of production. Colbert expressed this standpoint in brief when he said, "The whole business of commerce consists in facilitating the import of those goods which serve the country's manufactures, and placing embargoes on those which enter in a manufactured state."[28] Where raw materials were concerned, this principle must have led to a premium on import and the discouraging of export, and the object, which was to retain these goods, stood out very clearly.

But none the less there was an insoluble contradiction in this attitude. Considering the question superficially, it may indeed appear as though products of an earlier stage of manufacture always serve to produce those of a higher stage. But of course this is by no means always true. A means of production may be

[27] Adam Smith, *Wealth of Nations*, Bk. 4 chap. 8: Conclusion of the Mercantile System (ed. Cannan, II 141–50). This chapter, which first appeared in the third edition of the work, was the outcome of Adam Smith's intimate experience of customs conditions, which he gained through his appointment in 1778 as Commissioner of Customs in Scotland. It contains a detailed description of the treatment of the factors of production by English mercantilism. Where no other source is given in the remarks that follow, the statutes in question may be found quoted in that chapter.

[28] "Tout le commerce consiste: A décharger les entrées des marchandises qui servent aux manufactures au dedans du royaume; Charger celles qui entrent manufacturées," in addition he gave two further points regarding "drawbacks" and freedom from export duties—the whole being a dream of the future: (undated): pr. in *Lettres de Colbert* VII 284 note 2.

of a much more advanced stage of manufacture, that is, may contain much more labour, than the object for whose production it is employed. When that is so, the contradiction cannot be resolved.

At the present day machinery is the most important example of this. Protectionism to-day applies to machinery the criterion of their stage of manufacture and not of their character as means of production. That is to say, efforts are made to hinder the import and encourage the export of machinery. In the mercantilist period, machines were of so little importance that neither of these two alternatives had yet been clearly decided upon. In any event machines, as mentioned before, were rather suspect, because they rendered labour superfluous. But when commercial policy began seriously to adopt a definite attitude towards the problem, it first took up a line which to-day has been entirely abandoned. The export of machines was prohibited, because it was feared that this would help a competing industry in another country. One of the first examples of this was the export prohibition, mentioned in another context (I 264 f.), against stocking frames in England (1695/96), followed by a similar measure in France in 1724. About this time there was also a considerable fine in France on the export of textile implements in general. In various other ways, too, every possible obstacle was placed in the way of this export. At the beginning of the 1720's, Jonas Alströmer, the most enthusiastic protagonist of manufactures in Sweden in the 18th century, experienced the greatest of difficulties in smuggling from France and Holland the equipment which he needed for the formation of the Alingsås textile works. In England it was not until a somewhat later date (1750 and 1774) that the export of various textile machines and instruments was forbidden and there soon followed similar prohibitions against the export of iron-producing machinery (1781). Once this policy had been set going it was elaborated on all sides and pursued for a considerable time. In England, the country where an independent machine industry originated, the prohibition against its export was not abandoned in effect before 1825, while officially it persisted until 1843.

This mercantilist policy cannot be called either more or less consistent than the policy of modern protectionism, directed against the import of machinery. Where a principle admits of two mutually irreconcilable points of view, it is impossible to say which of them is the right consequence of the principle. All that can be said is that protectionism to-day is even more consistently dominated by the literal "fear of goods" in this respect than was mercantilism in its time.[29]

However, during the greater part of the mercantilist period other factors of production than machines played a far larger part. An equally hopeless inconsistency was manifested with regard to them.

From the time of Edward IV, i.e. from the end of the Middle Ages onwards, the import of wool cards into England was prohibited. They constituted an important means of production in the textile industry, which normally enjoyed greater favour than any other. A decree of 1630 went so far as to proscribe the sale of cards produced within the country from worn-out patterns. The maintenance of employment was given as the official motive for the measures, but in fact, at least as regards the latter prohibition, the object was to assist one of the oldest industrial joint-stock companies, the Mineral and Battery Works. Similarly in France (1599–1601) the import of indigo was forbidden in order to protect the manufacture of woad, the native dye for colouring blue. The textile manufacturers were naturally highly incensed at this, for they could hardly dispense with the best dyes. In both these cases native production of the means of production was protected to the detriment of the production of the finished product.

In the large majority of cases on the other hand, the export of factors of production was forbidden in the interests of the production of the products, as for instance the export of wool and of woollen and worsted yarn, hides and horns. The treatment of leather export in England is particularly instructive. It was first prohibited by an Act of 1662. The preamble to a new Act of 1667/68 stated that as a result of the strict prohibition against the export of leather "the Prices thereof and consequently of Raw Hides are very much abated to the great discouragement of the Breed and feeding of Cattle and fall of the Rents and Value of Land", while shoemakers and other leather workers had nevertheless kept the price of their goods fairly high. The policy

---

[29] Acts: 23 Geo. II c. 13 (1750); 14 Geo. III c. 71 (1774); 21 Geo. III c. 67 (1781); 6 Geo. IV c. 107 (1825); 3 & 4 Will. IV c. 52 (1833); 6 & 7 Vic. c. 84 (1843).—For the rest, see Adam Smith and also: G. R. Porter, *Progress of the Nation* Part II chap. 5 (Lond. 1847 ed., 263–8); Smart, *Economic Annals of the Nineteenth Century, 1801–1820* 738 f., do. do. *1821–1830* (Lond. 1917) 377 ff.; Clapham, *Economic History of Modern Britain* I 485 f.—French edict of 1724: pr. in *Recueil des règlemens* IV 63 ff.; cp. Levasseur, *Hist. d. cl. ouvr. avant 1789* II 584 *et passim*.—Alströmer: G. H. Stråle, *Alingsås manufakturverk* (Sthlm. 1884) 53–7.

of preventing exports, with its reactions on the production of producers' goods, thus resulted in a typical dilemma. Prohibiting the export of a semi-manufactured commodity might result in not being able to export the commodity at all. In England, in this connection, the particular care was undyed and unfinished cloth; the desire was not to allow it out of the country in non-processed form. On the continent, people would indeed have welcomed the excellent English cloth, but were not at all satisfied with English dyeing. James I endeavoured to emphasize and enforce the old law against the export of undyed cloth. One of his best known lawyers, with the curious name of Sir Julius Caesar, thereupon asked in Council (1616) whether in order to give work to 10,000 dyers and finishers, 100,000 spinners and weavers were not being thrown out of work.[30]

The great problem of mercantilist policy regarding means of production was its relation to agriculture. The instruction of the English commission for trade in 1622 summarized the dilemma in the following terms: the commission was to consider what means to employ "so as our own Dominions may be supplied in Time of Want, and yet in Time of Plenty the Husbandry and Tillage not to be discouraged".[31] Indeed, the position in the case of sheep and cattle breeding has already been mentioned. But even in England, corn-growing was still by far the most important branch of agriculture, and until the middle of the 18th century the indifference with regard to the growth of fodder-plants was considerable. In corn policy, however, the important dividing line was between the new system, as it gradually developed in England, and the old system of regulation, based on town economy and maintained on the continent, particularly in France. As in the cases discussed above, it is impossible to say which of the two corresponded more closely with mercantilist principles. Food-stuffs could be considered a factor of production, in fact

[30] Wool cards: laws—3 Ed. IV c. 4 (1463); 39 Eliz. c. 14 (1596/97); 14 Car. II c. 19 (1662); proclamation of 1630: pr. *Foedera* (ed. Rymer) 1st ed. XIX 163 ff., Hague ed. VIII: III 102 f.; cp. Scott, *Joint-Stock Companies to 1720* II 424 f. It must be added that 14 Car. II c. 19 § 2 again repealed the prohibition on the sale of repaired wool cards.—French import prohibition on indigo: Boissonnade, *Soc. d'État* 257.—The laws quoted concerning the export of leather: 14 Car. II c. 7; 19 & 20 Car. II c. 10.—On the export of undyed and unfinished cloth in England, see particularly Friis, *Alderman Cockayne's Project and the Cloth Trade* (index under "Cloth, undyed and undressed, export of"), which is largely devoted to this question, and also for the later development Lipson III 384 ff.; Sir J. Caesar's statement: see his "Notes from Privy Council Meetings," pr. Friis 471.

[31] Pr. *Foedera*, 1st ed. XVII 414, Hague ed. VII: IV 14.

the most important of all, as a basis for the supply of human labour-power. In that case, just as with other factors of production, their prices should be kept low. But on the other hand it could also be said that if agriculture were to be maintained, it must be encouraged by high prices; in that case the same methods ought to be applied as in the promoting of other industries.

If a means of production was itself produced, then the methods employed on the continent in the case of food-stuffs, and in England in the case of most of the other means of production as well, were bound to decrease its supply. Precisely the same disadvantage urged by the mercantilists against the policy of provision must appear if such methods were used to create a plentiful supply of industrial means of production. Only purely natural products could escape this effect, so long as the cost of working them and the profits were covered by the prices; in other words, the policy of forcing down prices could be innocuous only in so far as it was confined to affecting the value of the non-processed natural factors of production, the "indestructible powers of the soil", to employ Ricardo's expression. With very few exceptions, however, natural values at that period were so low that they would have offered very little scope for a policy of provision. And when that limit was passed, every forced lowering of price reacted on the supply. It follows that the policy pursued on the continent, obstructive as it was to the development of agriculture, has undoubtedly been an important cause of the stagnation of continental farming. How far the lowering of prices in the case of other factors of production influenced their supply is much less clear. Adam Smith agrees with other 18th-century writers that the prohibition on the export of wool depressed the price of English wool in England itself. Although this assumption seems tempting, it cannot easily be substantiated from the available statistical material. Even Adam Smith assumed that the effect of the lower prices on the quality and quantity of wool was compensated by the demand for mutton.[32] How far the policy of obstructing exports affected the production of machinery is even more difficult to say, because it was compensated in other ways, principally by means of privileges of the

---

[32] Adam Smith, *Wealth of Nations* I 230, II 150 ff., with reference *i.a.* to John Smith, *Chronicon Rusticum-Commerciale, or Memoirs of Wool* (Lond. 1767) II 418 note; cp. Th. Rogers, *A History of Agriculture and Prices in England* V (Oxf. 1887) 407: "I am indeed disposed to infer that on the whole the price of wool was almost stationary in England during the seventeenth century, and indeed for some time afterwards."

most varied kind. But it is probable that to some extent technical development was thereby held in check.

Whatever the methods of application, mercantilism by its treatment of the factors of production was led into impossible and unresolvable contradictions. The consequences were unusually interesting. At a very early stage in the development of English mercantilist ideology, it consisted in the idea of subsidizing all industries equally and indiscriminately, a system which to-day goes by the name of "all round protection" (*Solidaritäts-system*). It was precisely this which the specifically English form of mercantilist protectionism had in mind, the principle that industry and agriculture should be equally promoted by protective tariffs. In effect, this form of mercantilism has become the prototype of modern protectionism. Now a consistent application of such principles is, first and foremost, almost an economic impossibility, because it is utterly hopeless to make the stimuli which work upon different parts of economic life balance one another nicely. Moreover, if this were achieved, nothing would be gained except a reversal, by a most cumbersome and roundabout way, to the starting-point, one industry paying what another receives. Clear as this is, it is besides the point in this connection. For our concern here is not with economic realities but with the world of economic ideas, and the argument is interesting here only in so far as it led to the growth of the English system. Modern parallels abound, but the argument came out most clearly in the victory of agrarian protectionism in Germany under Bismarck.

In spite of these contradictions, the system of "all-round protection" has a natural appearance of justice on its side, which in those times as to-day contributed to its popularity. This can be seen in the reasons put forward in support of it both in the 16th and in the 19th centuries. The mercantilist position is stated, for example, in the *Discourse of the Common Weal* (1549). The author, speaking through the Doctor, imagines the Husbandman addressing the rest of producers on the following lines: "What reason is it that you should be at large, and I to be restrained? Either let us all be restrained together, or else let us all be at like liberty. Ye may sell [your wool] over the sea, your fells, your tallow, your cheese, your butter, your leather, which riseth all by grazing, at your pleasure, and that for the dearest penny ye can get for them. And I shall not send out my corn, except it be at xd. the bushel or under." In true mercantilist style, the "Doctor" comes to the conclusion that the desired end could be reached by lowering the price of both groups of commodities, but that an increase in the price of both would be the better method. Approximately the same argument was used in Bismarck's "December letter" of 1878, as it was called. "But protective tariffs for individual industries," he said, "have the effect . . . of a privilege and meet with the disapproval of the representatives of the non-protected industries like every other privilege. This disapproval will not be shown towards a system of tariffs which . . . gives all home production an advantage over the foreign in the home market."

And so even in its modern form, "all round protection" is an attempt to raise the prices of all commodities, not to lower them.[33]

Labour

Apart from raw materials and machinery, there was another and the most important factor of production in regard to which mercantilism had to formulate its attitude, i.e. labour. The attitude of mercantilism towards labour is therefore of special interest. In the main, it is the position of labour in the mercantilistic system of protection, and not the attitude towards labour as a whole, with which we are here concerned. The brilliant treatise of the American economist, Furniss, on the later English mercantilists' conception of the worker is one of the few really well-thought-out contributions to the study of mercantilist ideology and its import, because it takes into account the economic significance of the ideas. It is not my intention to recapitulate his work.[34] The points which we must deal with here, however, hardly come within the scope of Furniss's treatment, since he approaches the question from another angle. We are engaged in a parallel treatment and not with an elaboration or a repetition of his.

Strange as it may seem, labour could, theoretically, be dealt with much more easily than the other factors of production, because it was not *produced* in the sense that the latter were produced, or at any rate did not appear to be. The choice between a curtailment and increase in the supply, between high and low prices, did not therefore involve difficulties of principle in the case of labour. As the object was to prepare as large a volume of production

[33] [Hales], *A Discourse of the Common Weal* 56, 62.—Bismarck's December letter pr. *i.a. Textbücher zu Studien über Wirtschaft und Staat*: I: *Handelspolitik* (ed. J. Jastrow, Berl. 1912) 60.

[34] From the point of view particularly of the present work, the material given in Furniss suffers from the defect that it is largely drawn from the middle and latter half of the 18th century, a period in which mercantilist notions had already become thoroughly confused with other ideas.

as possible for sale abroad, it was difficult to reach any conclusion regarding the question of workers and wages other than that the cost of labour must be kept as low as possible, and in fact, that it must be calculated to "strengthen the country's position on the world market", as it is popularly termed to-day. It is no doubt true that the lasting export surplus which was aimed at would, in all probability, not have been reached as a result of such a policy—even, of course, ignoring the fact that if the same policy was pursued by all the countries taking part in the exchange, all its effects must have cancelled out. But this is a conclusion from the theory of international trade which mercantilists were unable to draw, and which they could therefore not take into account. And it is, besides, no very serious objection to their argument. For, even if the total exports of a country in proportion to the total imports could not be increased by forcing down wages, there was still some justification in the mercantilist idea. By forcing down wages, at any rate the export of such products as contained relatively more human labour could be increased, and such a policy could at the same time restrict the import of the same group of products. To this extent the mercantilist theory on this point was quite sound. The conclusion drawn followed logically from the eagerness to create a great export surplus of "labour products" whose price, and hence whose cost of labour, would therefore have to be kept low. The corollary was that efforts had to be made to maintain as abundant a supply of labour as possible at as low a price as possible. This was, in effect, attempted in many cases.

But in reality, even from purely mercantilist standpoints, the matter was by no means as simple as that. This was because the mercantilists held other economic tenets apart from the doctrine of an export surplus. And so it came about that the attitude towards labour, too, entangled mercantilists in theoretical problems which they attempted to resolve in various ways. Even such a basic principle of protectionism as the gospel of high prices could lead here to other results. The most fundamental contradiction in the whole attitude of course was a different one, i.e. wealth for the "country", based on the poverty of the majority of its subjects. This inevitably upset the fine economic edifice built upon it, and, as will be seen, it was pointed out at the time too, though it was mostly left to the earlier *laissez-faire* theorists to expose its flaws.

If the problem of labour is approached from the point of view of the cost of production, the supply price for the application of labour must be a result of its *quantity*. This quantity, to put it simply, was determined by two factors: the number of workers and the effectiveness of the individual worker. If the problem was still more simplified—ignoring the workers' capacity and considering only their willingness to work—then broadly speaking there remained the two factors: the size of the population and the industriousness of the people. The mercantilists had therefore to aim at the largest and most industrious population possible. On the whole, this was in fact usually the case. There were, indeed, many differences of opinion, but on this ideal people were in the main agreed. None the less it must be added that this ideal was not just the effect of the desire for an export surplus, but had other grounds as well.

Idleness

With regard to the mercantilists' conception of industriousness and sloth, it must be said that there was hardly any point on which opinion was so unanimous as in the condemnation of idleness. References to this are so numerous that it would be absurd to enumerate them. Even during the intensive discussions which took place in England before the middle of the 16th century, there were constant complaints against idleness and beggary, which were described as twin brothers. In Starkey's dialogue of the 1530's, for instance, Cardinal Pole is made to say, "This body (i.e. the body politic) is replenished and overfulfilled with many ill humours, which I call idle and unprofitable persons, of whom you shall find a great number, if you will a little consider all states, orders, and degrees, here in our country." About fifty years later Robert Hitchcock, the author of a pamphlet entitled *Politique Platt*, referred to "that loathsome monster Idleness" (1580). Another fifty years later Malynes called it "the root of all evil". Child, who nursed a particular hatred against the high rate of interest, said that it suffered "Idleness to suck the Breasts of Industry", and later still Cary called idleness "the Foundation of all those Vices which prevail amongst us", and so on and so forth.[35]

It might be assumed that this attitude was simply a result of puritanism. Since Max Weber's famous essays made their appearance shortly after the beginning of this century, historians have usually given the puritan ideal of labour first place in the treatment of the spiritual revolution in the economic sphere. But

---

[35] Starkey (see above, chap. 3 note 29) 76 f., 89 *et passim*.—Hitchcock, "Politique Platt"; pr. in part in *Tudor Econ. Docs.* III 240.—Malynes, *Lex Mercatoria* Part I chap. 45 (1st ed. 229).—Child 21.—Cary 165.

in any case it is a fact that the aversion to idleness and the
denunciation of it on principle were even stronger in Catholic
France than in Protestant England. A remark of Montchrétien's
with the same purport has already been quoted. In an even more
picturesque expression, the same author called idleness "the
grave of living man". Colbert exceeded all others in his condemnation of idleness. It is no exaggeration to say that his letters
are filled, from beginning to end, with the fight against sloth
(la fainéantise) both in his own particular spheres of interest, as
well as in the French provinces in general or in the French colonies.
Idleness was the unforgivable sin. When one of his brothers
became bishop of Auxerre, in which for various reasons he was
personally interested, he expressed the hope that the idleness
prevalent in the district would be strenuously attacked. This
attitude also accounts for his dislike of alms-giving and of church
activities in general. No doubt this was, to some extent, a reaction
against medieval tendencies, but the real explanation is probably
to be found in mercantilism itself. Mercantilism was indeed a
new religion, and in deifying the state it opposed the medieval
religion, which had worshipped at quite other shrines.[36]

Child Labour

To the modern observer, the ideal of economic activity was
nowhere expressed so peculiarly as in the question of child labour.
The belief that child labour, whether in fact or as an ideal, was
a creation of the Industrial Revolution is a gross fallacy.

In the mercantilist view, no child was too young to go into
industry. Whereas from the beginning of the 19th century
onwards, after tentative beginnings, stronger and stronger
measures were taken to limit child labour by law, under mercantilism the power of the state was exerted in precisely the opposite
direction. Here again Colbert is particularly typical of the
general attitude. He remarked on one occasion (1665), in words
which would hardly after all be endorsed by modern psycho-
analysts, "Experience has always certainly shown that idleness in
the first years of a child's life is the real source of all the disorders
in later life." In a decree of 1668 affecting the lace-making
industry in Auxerre, which was particularly dear to him, he

[36] On Puritanism, see Tawney, *Religion and the Rise of Capitalism*, 229 ff.,
260.—Montchrétien, *Traicté de l'oeconomie politique* 53; cf. above, note 2.—
A wealth of examples from the English literature of mercantilism is found
in E. A. J. Johnson, *Predecessors of Adam Smith*, 281–89.—*Lettres de Colbert*
II 209, 680, 714 and note 1, 785, III : 11 395, 406 note, VII 232, etc., cf. E.
Levasseur, *Histoire des classes ouvrières et de l'industrie en France avant 1789*,
II 236 f.

commanded, in order to remedy such disorders, that all the inhabitants of the town should send their children into this industry at the age of six, on pain of a penalty of 30 *sous* per child. About the same time the Intendant of Alençon called the lace industry in his district a "manna", because it employed children of seven and grey-haired old men. With regard to England it was enthusiastically pointed out that the children there entered industry at an even earlier age. In a popular poem about a great cloth manufacturer of the second half of the 16th century, John Winchcomb (called Jack of Newbury), probably published for the first time in 1597, we find a lyrical picture of 150 children sitting and cleaning wool in return for a wage "wondrous" in their eyes, while others "with mickle joy" attended to other processes of cloth manufacture. A German memorandum of about the same period (1581) asserted it as a recognized fact that boys and girls were employed in the English cloth industry from the ages of four and five onwards. The French mercantilist, Laffemas, in his description of the various plans which were being discussed on the occasion of a great conference during Henry IV's reign (1604), sung a hymn of praise to the various inventions because they enabled "small children" or "children of seven years old and onwards" to earn their living.

In this respect, the observations made later by Defoe (in the 1720's) are particularly interesting, and what has now been said will show that it was not the outcome of post-mercantilist "capitalism". They show clearly that in Defoe's opinion such conditions led to the greatest possible happiness of the population. In his description of England in the years 1724 to 1726, he mentions Norfolk, Taunton and the West Riding of Yorkshire, where children of four and five could all earn their own livelihood. In his *Plan of the English Commerce* (1728) he compared the prosperity of the industrial districts with the "unemployed counties", whose only means of support was agriculture: "How many Millions of People," he asked, "are kept in constant Motion, Men, Women, and Children employ'd, Infants (so they may properly be called) of five, six and seven Years of Age, made capable of getting their own Bread, and subsisting by the Labour of their own Hands, and a prodigious Wealth, accumulated among the common People?" It goes without saying that the manufacturers then considered themselves benefactors when they created such employment. Several of them, for example, wrote in this strain in a petition of 1696, that, thanks to them, "the poor People take in their Children from the Highways, and their Infant Idleness;

and bring them to the Wool, and the Wheel; whereat One of Five Years of Age will earn 4d. a Day, and prove the better Worker by having had so early an Experience thereof."[37]

Population

The population of the country was thus to be kept in industry as far as was physically possible. But the further problem arose of the optimum size of the population. On this point people were not so unanimous, though the differences of opinions referred less to the ideal to be striven after than to the presuppositions and the means for its attainment.

Authors and politicians are to be found who took up a sceptical attitude regarding the desirability of an increase in population, and even spoke of over-population; in fact, some went so far as to doubt whether it was worth striving for the largest possible population. Bacon is an outstanding example. His attitude can be clearly seen in the statement of his quoted at the end of the second part (*v.s.* II 45). But he stood almost entirely alone in his insistence upon quality, as against quantity, of population. Malynes hardly went as far, but even with him we find an almost Malthusian dread of over-population. "For unless the three Impostumes of the world, namely, Wars, Famine, and Pestilence, do purge that great Body; all Kingdoms and Countries become very populous, and men can hardly live in quiet, or without danger." Even a century earlier, Starkey had made Cardinal Pole speak of the two-fold danger of scarcity of people and over-

---

[37] *Lettres de Colbert* III : II 395.—Proclamation of 1668 : in P.-M. Bondois, "Colbert et l'industrie de la dentelle" (*Mémoires et documents pour servir à l'histoire du commerce et de l'industrie en France* ed. J. Hayem, VI, Paris 1921) 267 f., cp. 233.—See also *Correspondance administrative sous Louis XIV* (ed. Depping) II 813.—Statement of 1696 : *Journals of the House of Commons* XI 496 f. ; cp. Thomas, *Mercantilism and the East India Trade* 99 f.—Other examples : Kulischer, *Allgemeine Wirtschaftsgeschichte* II 187–90.—The usual view is that child labour is of much greater antiquity in England than in France. This is certainly very likely, but children of four years and upward were employed in the domestic industry of coarse woollen manufactures in Gévaudan, for example, according to a description of 1698 (Levasseur, *op. cit.* II 323). The valuable statistics on the Lyons silk industry (pr. Godart, *l'ouvrier en soie* 26) show a large number of children even for the year 1660, in addition, be it noted, to the apprentices. —"The Pleasant History of John Winchcomb": long extract in Ashley II 255 f.—German example: quot. Ehrenberg, *Hamburg und England in Zeitalter der Königin Elisabeth* (Jena 1896) 160 f.—B. de Laffemas, "Recveil presénté av Roy, de ce qvi se passe en l'assemblee du Commerce": pr. *Archives curieuses de l'histoire de France*, ed. M. L. Cimber & F. Danjou, I Série XIV (Paris 1837) 226, 237.—Intendant in Alençon: Levasseur II 250.—Defoe, *Tour Through the Whole Island of Great Britain* (Everyman's Library I 62, 166, II 195).—Defoe, *Plan of the English Commerce* (repr. Oxf. 1928, 56, 69).

population, though the former, it is true, was considered the more important of the two. It was, in fact, at the beginning of the 17th century, when Bacon and Malynes were writing, that it was customary to speak of the over-crowding of population. This led statesmen and writers to look with equanimity on colonization simply as a means of getting rid of people who could not maintain themselves and would otherwise take to vagrancy, theft and murder and end their days on the gallows.

The second half of the 17th century was dominated by another ideal, but it provides the best economic analysis before Malthus of the problem of population. This is to be found—likewise in connection with a discussion on colonial policy—in Child. In his view, the size of the population was entirely a function of potential employment. "Such as our employment is for People, so many will our People be," he said, "and if we should imagine we have in England employment but for one hundred People, and we have born and bred amongst us one hundred and fifty People; I say the fifty must away from us, or starve, or be hanged to prevent it." The reverse obtains according to him, if too many people leave the country, "For much want of People would procure greater Wages, and greater Wages, if our Laws gave encouragement, would procure us a supply of People without the charge of breeding them."[38]

Broadly speaking, an almost fanatical desire to increase population prevailed in all countries during the period when mercantilism was at its height, i.e. in the latter part of the 17th century; and as will easily be seen, the clearly thought-out argument of Child was not opposed to it. This partial change of outlook must certainly be related to the fact that people were more confident of the possibilities of increasing production, and that the belief in the necessity of low wages had come to stay. But though less unanimous, the desire for an increase in population at all costs had certainly existed at earlier dates, too,

[38] On the history of theories of population cp. C. E. Stangeland, *Pre-Malthusian Doctrines of Population* (Columbia Univ. Studies in History, etc. XXI: III, N.Y. 1904), which is an accurate and useful, although a rather mechanical, compilation; and particularly both of Beer's works already quoted: *Origins of the British Colonial System* ch. 2 and *Old Colonial System* I ch. 1, likewise Furniss ch. 2.—The quotations in the text: Bacon, *Essays*: No. 29 in the 1625 edition (ed. Wright 122),—Malynes, *Lex Mercatoria*, Part I ch. 46 (1st ed. 234). —Starkey 46 f., 72 *et passim*; that he did not regard over-population as a great danger is seen in the fact that in his book Pole even proposes bounties on marriage (148, cp. 74 f.).—Child ch. 10, esp. 186 ff. in the previously mentioned edition.

notably in connection with the aspirations towards a pure policy of power. To quote two different authors of the middle of the 16th century, "In the multitude of people is the state of a King," said the one; and the other: "The King's honour (as some men say) standeth in the great multitude of people."[39] It is equally obvious that it was precisely this view which Bacon attacked. From the second half of the 17th century onwards, this idea became stereotyped, so to speak, and on occasions forced all other considerations into the background.

In this connection, the unambiguous statement is frequently to be found that wealth itself consists in the largest possible population. Child, for example, wrote, "The Riches of a City, as of a Nation, consisting in the multitude of Inhabitants . . ." Roger Coke, normally one of the most independent of mercantilist thinkers, stated "Greater numbers of people increase strength"; and again, "Greater numbers of people improve Trade." The author of *Britannia Languens* puts the point even more emphatically: "People are therefore in truth the chiefest, most fundamental, and precious commodity." Davenant always reverted to the same gospel of the wealth of a country, expressing it, for instance, as follows: "People are the real Strength and Riches of a Country"; "we see," he continues, "how Impotent Spain is for want of Inhabitants, with their Mines of Gold and Silver and the best Ports and Soil in the World."

The idea, with the examples given in illustration of it, was not peculiar to England. Among the Germans it was Becher who expatiated at length upon the necessity of populousness (*Populosität*). The actual starting-point in his chief work, the *Politische Discurs*, was "a populous, rich commonweal", and he followed up this definition, which he emphasized in large type, with a sixteen-page commentary. "The most exalted maxim for a state, a city or a country should be a populous productiveness"; ". . . the purpose of civil society (which should consist in a large number of people)"; ". . . the foundations of a country consist in *a large number of common people and much money*"—a true mercantilist combination. Becher's view of the relationship between the wealth of a country and industry may be seen from the following statement, which may be considered the antithesis of the Malthusian theory: "Sustenance, say I, is a fishing rod or a hook for enticing people." His chief objection to monopoly, too, was that it led to depopulation, because it allowed a single

[39] "Polices", etc.: pr. *Tudor Econ. Docs.* III 314.—Latimer, *Seven Sermons before Edward VI* (Eng. Reprints, ed. E. Arber, Birmingham 1869, 40).

individual to amass enough to provide for a large number of people. In the same way his brother-in-law, Hörnigk, considered the primary function of the state to be the creation of as large a population as it could possibly maintain ; and so on and so forth.[40]

French economic literature is fairly meagre in the 17th century, and so few observations are to be found there on this point. But in actual practice, France surpassed all other countries in its efforts to stimulate the increase in population by all conceivable means. Utterances of statesmen and their colleagues to that effect are nowhere so prolific as in that country.

Thus in 1666, an Act sponsored by Colbert prescribed that young men who married before the age of twenty were to be exempt from the *taille* until the age of twenty-five, while those marrying before twenty-one were to enjoy the same privilege until the age of twenty-four. The same law granted various considerable tax-exemptions to the father of a family of the taxable classes with ten or twelve children, of whom none were to be priest, monk or nun. With regard to the non-taxable classes, the father of a family was, under the same conditions, allowed an annual pension of 1000 to 2000 *livres* in the case of a nobleman and half that amount if he were a *bourgeois*. In the previous year, Colbert had already attempted to regulate the dowry system, so that parents should no longer be induced to send their daughters into convents, but should marry them off. A decree of 1669 applying to Canada prescribed essentially the same rules as the original law of 1666, except that it gave preference, on certain considerations, to those who had most children, and imposed fines on fathers who did not marry off their sons before the age of twenty and their daughters before the age of sixteen. The correspondence of Colbert and his successors with the colonial officials reveals the well-nigh fanatical fervour of the attempts to force up the numbers of the population. "An Intendant must not believe that he has done his duty unless he has made sure of a yearly increase of at least 200 families," wrote Colbert to the Intendant in Canada and enjoined him to take care that boys marry between the ages of eighteen and nineteen and

[40] Child: Preface, chaps. 2 and 10 (prev. cited ed., unpag. 88, 179).—Coke, *Treatise* I 2, 10.—*Britannia Languens* ch. 14 (1st ed. 238).—Davenant, *An Essay upon Ways and Means of Supplying the War* (1701 ed. Lond. 140 ff.); cp. *Discourses upon the Publick Revenues* II 196, *Essay upon . . . the Ballance of Trade* 79 *et passim.*—Becher, *Politische Discurs, passim* (1673 ed. 2, 110–13, 305–21, 584—my italics).—Hörnigk, *Oesterreich über Alles, wann es nur will*, ch. 9, Rule 3 (1723 ed. Regensb., 30).

girls between fourteen and fifteen (1668). "You must find ways and means of making all the inhabitants marry who are in a position to do so" was the injunction to the Governor-General of Cayenne in 1671. Whole boatloads of young girls were shipped across to increase the marriage frequency. Soldiers who refused to marry these girls were punished. In the same spirit, an official in France, too, wrote to the minister of finance at the beginning of the 18th century that it was reprehensible to allow a number of children to die who might later populate the country. Another proposed a payment of 30 *livres* for each marriage concluded, for which he gave the exquisite reason: "since this assistance will be given only to young people, it is not entirely useless to the state, for it will supply *subjects at a cheap price*" (*fournit des sujets à bon marché*, 1711; italics mine).[41]

Measures such as were taken in France were also demanded in other countries, but they were somewhat alien to the general spirit of English and Dutch statecraft. For this reason they were not put into effect. But instead, these and other Protestant countries vied with one another in attracting foreign workers, particularly Huguenots, after the repeal of the Edict of Nantes, as well as, for example, Jews. English authors of the latter part of the 17th century frequently and vigorously asserted that England should become a "general Azilum" (Davenant), and should concentrate on naturalizing the foreigners. The foreigners often met with opposition from craftsmen and traders organized in gilds, and this was one of the reasons why economic reformers so distrusted the old system of internal industrial regulation. Even the import of negro slaves was sometimes regarded from the same standpoint. It will easily be seen how this eagerness to attract foreigners was based upon the absence of nationalism, in the proper sense of the term, and the concentration upon the state as the object of economic policy, as was pointed out at the beginning of this volume. The changed attitude upon this point explains the contrast with the present treatment of aliens. At the same time, all countries alike tried by every possible means to prevent the emigration of their own subjects. There is no doubt that in the second half of the 17th century, they all held essentially

[41] Edict of 1666 pr. *Rec. d. anc. lois franç.*, ed. Isambert (see above, Part I ch. 5 note 13) XVIII 90–3.—Dowries etc.: *Lettres de Colbert* VI 13 f.—1669 ordinance pr. *ib.* III: II 657.—Colonial correspondence: *ib.* III: II 405, 408 f., 412, 446, 449, 451, 513, 526, etc., etc.; on the period after Colbert, e.g. *Corr. administr.* (ed. Depping) II 593 ff., 694, *etc.*—Statement of 1711: pr. *Correspondance des contrôleurs généraux* (ed. Boislisle & Brotonne) III Nos. 974 and 1178.

the same views on population. These views were typical, more-over, both in the subsequent period and partly also in the previous, although there they had not been so unanimous.[42]

It is natural to wonder how the notion that there could never be too great a population could ever be reconciled with the anxiety concerning the insufficiency of employment. In actual fact, this contradiction was never resolved.

Mandeville, in his *Fable of the Bees* (1705, 1714, 1723 and 1729), was especially inconsistent on this point. On the one hand he demanded a larger population. "We have hardly Poor enough," he said, "to do what is necessary to make us subsist." He believed, quite rightly, that a large number of improvements, canal works and draining, could be carried out, so that more hundreds of thousands of poor people could be employed than actually existed in England and, in fact, for more than three or four hundred years. On the other hand, however, his provocative essay on the indispensability of human vice for the existence of society was based on the idea that without such vice there could not be sufficient employment. Why could not the people, in his opinion, be used for improvements instead of vices? It is im-possible to say: the first-named idea had simply been lost sight of. He repeated the second idea in a later addition to his book: "Such is the calamitous Condition of Human Affairs that we stand in need of the Plagues and Monsters I named . . . in order to procure an honest Livelihood to the vast Multitudes of working poor."

The contradiction was less clearly expressed in the majority of authors. They may probably be considered to have meant that any number of people could be employed in a country so peculiarly blessed by nature as, in their opinion, their own particular mother country was, if only economic policy were properly administered and above all, of course, if their own favourite ideas were put into practice. For the most part their solution of the unemployment problem was workhouses and poorhouses, which, on the one hand, were to provide the employ-ment required by the people and, on the other, to maintain their

[42] Examples for all this, esp. Child (ch. 7 and *passim*), Coke, *Treatise* I *passim*, partly Davenant, e.g. *Discourses*, etc. II 202, likewise—on the negroes —[J. Pollexfen], *A Discourse of Trade, Coyn, and Paper Credit* (Lond. 1697) 87, and [W. Wood], *A Survey of Trade* (Lond. 1718) 191; further, the material given by Beer; on the practical policy esp. Cunningham, *Alien Immigrants to England* (Lond. 1897) ch. 6 and his prev. mentioned work II[3] § 199 and also the wider literature on the immigration of the Huguenots; cp. also below 303 ff.

diligence, the absence of which was considered the chief cause of unemployment.

In any case, the difficulty of procuring employment never led the authors of the end of the 17th century to revise their ideas on the suitability of the largest possible population. When advocating an increase in population, it is true, they always referred to the fact that the population must also be maintained, that society, to use one of Becher's expressions, must be "nourished" (*nahrhaft*), but beyond this they did not trouble themselves. At the most they believed that *other* countries must, for this reason, be careful about increases in their population. Thus Davenant, for example, comes to the following typical conclusions: "There are indeed Countries, to whom their full Complement of Inhabitants would be dangerous, and subject them to frequent Famines in bad and unseasonable Years for Corn. As for Example, if France had as many People as the Land will feed in times of common Plenty, half of 'em must have perish'd during their late Dearths for want of Bread" [this was written in 1699] . . . ; "but England (with any moderate Care) is not liable to such a Fear, tho' its present Numbers should even be doubled." The fact that he argues that the hated enemy country cannot increase its population any further proves how important such an increase was considered. As we have just seen, the efforts to increase the population in that country, which Davenant regarded as particularly unsuitable for such a policy, happened to be especially determined.[43]

The connection with low wages

If, then, during the heyday of mercantilism the demand for as large a population as possible and at the same time for the maximum possible supply of labour never abated, the question arises whether the protagonists of this policy were clear in their minds that it would inevitably lead to a decrease in wages. Even without proof it might be safely assumed that they did see this point, for it was a piece of economic reasoning of the kind which progressive minds, even at that time, could easily grasp. But in fact there are a number of explicit statements to this effect. Even if they are not very numerous, they indicate none the less that the point was perceived.

[43] Mandeville, *Fable of the Bees*: "An Essay on Charity and Charity Schools" and "A Search into the Nature of Society" respectively (ed. Kaye, I 301 f., 318, 355; 1st ed. I 345, 364, 410 f.).—Workhouses and Poorhouses: Webb, *English Poor Law History* I ch. 4 and Furniss ch. 4 & 5.—Davenant, *Essay upon . . . the Ballance of Tr.* 79 f.

Child's statement, quoted above, to the effect that "much want of People would procure greater Wages" proves that this was so. And writers other than so clear-minded a person as Child also recognized it. The author of *Britannia Languens* was not endowed with too much perspicacity, but he too had the same idea, and it was on this that he based his advocacy of low wages. "The odds in Populacy must also produce the like odds in Manufacture," he wrote; "plenty of people must also cause cheapness of wages; which will cause the cheapness of Manufacture; in a scarcity of people wages must be dearer, which must cause the dearness of Manufacture." In an author who saw the principal wealth of the country in the size of its population the argument is quite clear. Pollexfen some years later (1697) reckoned that every worker represented a profit of £5 sterling for the nation and that the want of such people, "as it hath made Servants scarce for Labour, so it hath advanced their Wages, which doth fall heavy upon Land and Trade, and the advance of Wages hath proved an inducement to Idleness". Mandeville, as usual, puts the matter the most provocatively. One of his many observations on this point is of particular interest because it places labour on a par with the other factors of production, which is the point from which I set out in my discussion on this question. "Would not a Wise Legislature," he says, "cultivate the Breed of them (the workers and poor) with all imaginable Care, and provide against their Scarcity as he would prevent the Scarcity of Provision it self? . . . From what has been said it is manifest that in a free Nation where Slaves are not allow'd of, the surest Wealth consists in a Multitude of laborious Poor." He thus asserted the necessity of a plentiful supply of labour. He made it equally clear that this went hand in hand with an utmost limitation in wages, when he stated, "as they (i.e. the working population) ought to be kept from starving, so they should receive nothing worth saving. . . . It is the Interest of all rich [*sic*] Nations, that the greatest part of the Poor should almost never be idle, and yet continually spend what they get." "The Poor should be kept strictly to Work, and that it was Prudence to relieve their wants, but Folly to cure them."[44] As was always the case with Mandeville, he stated here what most people of his time were thinking, but in a way that made them wince. That was the secret both of the indignation he aroused and the difficulty of refuting him.

---

[44] *Britannia Languens* ch. 7 (1st ed. 153 f.).—Pollexfen (see above, note 42) 47.—Mandeville, *op. cit.*: Remarks Q & Y, "Essay on Charity", etc. (ed. Kaye, I 193 f., 248 f., 287; 1st ed. I 212. 280, 327 f,).   See below II 366-7, *Addendum* §9.

The demand for a dense population was thus established and low wages were regarded as its result. But at the same time we may observe the existence of *another* view of the relationship between the level of wages and the supply of labour. This view takes account not of the size of the population but its willingness to work. According to it, in contrast to the previous, the wage level was not an effect, but a cause, of the size of the labour supply. The idea is not unknown in modern theory; for it is often reckoned to-day that higher wages produce greater willingness or greater skill. On certain conditions, we have then what may be called, to use a somewhat abused cliché, an economy of high wages. But strange as it may seem, the mercantilists sought the connection between the wage level and the willingness to work in precisely the contrary direction. To reduce the doctrine to a brief formula, we may say that it was an *economy of low wages*. The underlying idea was that high wages had no other effect than to drive the workers into sloth, drunkenness and other vices. For this reason, according to the statements of many mercantilist writers, the more people were paid, the less they worked. Furniss calls this "the doctrine of the utility of poverty". This covers the situation, if—to turn aside from the main point for a moment— it is only remembered that this utility of poverty is something quite different from its utility in medieval asceticism, where poverty opened the door to everlasting salvation. Of the many examples, which are nearly all given in Furniss, only one need be repeated here. Sir William Petty, who had no private interests to bias him in favour of employers, and who had a better scientific culture than most writers of the Restoration period, elaborated a project for the storing of corn by the state in years of good harvest. He gave the following reason for his proposal. He had heard from cloth manufacturers that in years in which the supply of corn was great, labour was dear. The increase in wages obtained by the workers under such conditions was to be prevented, according to Petty, by raising the price of corn in the way which he suggested. This example is really sufficiently characteristic.[45]

Connecting the two points of view, we see that they could easily lead to the goal of mercantilism—increased export of the products of labour. In both cases the effect would have been on the one hand, increased labour services and on the other, lower labour costs. One could then justifiably expect the in-

[45] Petty, *Political Arithmetick* ch. 2 (Econ. Writings I 274 f.).—For the rest, Furniss ch. 6.

creased supply of products to find foreign buyers. To this extent the argument therefore held good.

There is, however, another point. The very aim of increased wealth, pursued by mercantilists with such ardour, necessarily led to effects which, in their view, would cancel this result, for wealth was considered the mother of all idleness. Colbert remarked on one occasion on "the idleness of the Spaniards, an effect of their riches". Mun said "As plenty and power do make a nation vicious and improvident, so penury and want do make a people wise and industrious." They must have considered it very important therefore to prevent such a state of affairs. If wages could be kept low, there was some prospect of avoiding the undesirable effects of riches.[46]

The conclusion at which they arrived was therefore this: wealth for the nation, but wealth from which the majority of the people must be excluded. Possibly, even probably, they thought, in all good faith, to provide riches in this way for the state or the monarch, for common military and other political purposes. Interpreting it less sympathetically but probably no less adequately, we may deduce at the same time some other purpose than this. It approximates suspiciously closely to the tendency to keep down the mass of the people by poverty, in order to make them better beasts of burden for the few; not only *de facto* but, as we see here, deliberately and with set purpose.

That this was so is already evidenced by the fact that the claims of private peoples' servants for higher wages were almost always condemned. So independent an author as Roger Coke, for instance, attacked the whole Poor Law legislation of Elizabeth because it "encourages wilful and evil-disposed persons to impose what wages they please upon their Labours"—"excessive wages of servants as well as labourers". Mandeville was indignant at the demand of servants for wages and was of the opinion that they required no money remuneration at all—"but what does them hurt as Servants", for they after all received their keep. The same motive recurs in the dislike for all measures tending to lead to the education of the masses. Pollexfen, for example, wrote, "How much the breeding up the Children of poor people to Learning and Scholarship hath conduced to their avoiding of Labouring Employs may well be considered; for few that have once learnt to Write and Read, but either their Parents, or themselves, are apt to think that they are fit

[46] *Lettres de Colbert* VII 232.—Mun, *England's Treasure*, etc. ch. 19 (ed. Ashley 100).

for some preferment, and in order to it, despise all Labouring Employments."

In the 1723 edition of his book, Mandeville added an Essay on Charity and Charity Schools (from which some of the previous quotations have been drawn) and with even less ambiguity he expressed the same point: "the People of the meanest Rank know too much to be serviceable to us [sic]"; and then again, "To make the Society happy and People easy under the meanest Circumstances, it is requisite that great Numbers of them should be Ignorant as well as Poor."[47]

This attitude towards labour was related both to the past and to the future. Looking backward, it was bound up with the idea of a suitable subsistence and the inferiority of the masses to the privileged classes—both medieval ideas. With practically insignificant exceptions, all official wage-fixing therefore prescribed maximum wages. Out of every ten interferences with the relationship between employers and employed, at least nine were in the interests of the employers. The authorities penalized workers' associations and strikes, but closed their eyes to corresponding action on the part of the employers. This was true particularly of the French administration, whereas in England, the tendency at that time was to some extent different—as we have shown in the sixth chapter of the first part—and even later was never quite as one-sided as in France. But there is no doubt at all that the state everywhere exerted its influence on the side of low wages and unfavourable conditions of work. Mercantilism inherited from the past the tendency towards low wages and abundant supply in the labour market.

In addition, this tendency encountered corresponding effort on the part of the new, politically and socially influential, capitalist employers, and was to that extent in alliance with the forces that were daily gaining in strength. The quotations cited above, from the writings of mercantilists and the remarks of statesmen, belong in the main to the 17th century and in no case go beyond the year 1730. It appears that the point of view just described gained ground in the course of the 18th century, especially among so-called practical people. A host of illustrations could be quoted; but as this view is much better known than the connection with old ideas, one very characteristic instance may suffice. It consists of a long extract from a memorandum of 1786 to the silk manufacturers of Lyons, written by a co-manufacturer named Mayet.

    [47] Coke, *Treatise* I 75.—Pollexfen 47.—Mandeville, *op. cit.*: "Essay on Charity", etc. (ed. Kaye I 288, 302, 305, 1st. ed. I 328, 345, 350).

Through him, we see that, in spite of his deliberately challenging and paradoxical way of stating the matter, Mandeville was merely expressing what was at the back of many people's minds. Mayet wrote:

"In order to assure the prosperity of our manufactures it is necessary that the worker should never become well-to-do (*ne s'enrichisse jamais*), and he should have no more than he actually needs to feed and clothe himself properly. In a certain class of people, too much well-being lessens industriousness, and encourages idleness with all its attendant evils. As soon as the worker acquires a measure of well-being, he becomes particular in his choice of work and in the matter of wages. . . . If necessity ceases to compel the worker to rest content with the wages offered to him for his employment, if he is able to free himself from this kind of slavery, if his earnings exceed his needs to the extent that he can maintain himself for some time without the labour of his hands, then he employs this time to form an association. . . . It is therefore very important that the manufacturers of Lyons keep so strict a hold on the worker that he must always work; they should never forget that the low price of labour is useful not only in itself, but even more because it makes the worker more active, more industrious and more effectively subject to their will."[48]

High wages

The tendencies outlined above were not, however, the only ones during the period of mercantilism. Here and there high wages were also advocated, and some of these cases show that the fundamental tenets of mercantilism could be used for that purpose also. It is true that many statements to this effect are too aphoristic to afford any insight into the arguments on which

[48] Lengthy extract in Godart, *L'ouvrier en soie* 266 f.—On the French policy, see the literature quoted in Part I ch. 5 above, esp. Hauser, *Ouvriers du temps passé* and *Travailleurs et marchands de l'ancienne France*, also Martin, *La grande industrie sous Louis XV*. In a letter of 1715 (pr. *Corresp. d. contr. gén.*, ed. Boislisle & Brotonne, III No. 1866) the Intendant at Berry reports on what to him were unwarrantable wage demands which the day labourers were able to make, because the great mortality during the war had lowered the supply of labour. They asserted "*avec arrogance*" that the masters had had their chance, and that now their turn had come. The servants demanded "*des conditions ridicules*," e.g. they wanted white bread. French writers who took up a contrary attitude, however, are not entirely lacking, particularly among those with pro-reform tendencies in the French administration of the 18th century (examples: Levasseur, *Hist. d. cl. ouvr. av. 1789* II 834 ff.; Martin, *op. cit.* 325). —Furniss, esp. ch. 7, should be consulted for the English literature of the end of the 18th century. An essay of 1770 which he quotes frequently, *An Essay on Trade and Commerce* (ascribed to one W. Temple), shows a high degree of similarity to the argument of Mayet; see, e.g., Furniss 147.

they are based. They are therefore interesting only to show that such variations also occurred. One of the recreants was Child. An opponent of his on the question of lowering the legal rate of interest had proposed to introduce a law designed "to retrench the Hire of Poor Men's Labour". Child attacked him with the comment that it was "an honest charitable Project, and well becoming a Userer". Child then declared that the Dutch paid higher wages than the English and for this reason Holland was able to attract people: "Where ever Wages are high universally throughout the whole World, it is an infallible evidence of the Riches of that Country," and *vice versa*. Even more summary was Davenant's declaration that in a poor country, interest is high, land is cheap, and the price of labour and food likewise low.[49]

Apart from these more occasional utterances, two further arguments of great theoretical interest were put forward. The first concerned the very fundamentals of the protectionist system. The "gospel of high prices" was even extended to labour as a productive factor, thus illustrating the tendency of immanent principles to assert themselves. Concern for *sales* made the worker's purchasing power, *ergo* high wages, appear desirable—the same principle, that is, as has become decisive in modern economic policy. This notion is naturally to be found chiefly among those who saw a kind of *perpetuum mobile* in sale itself or in exchange. It can hardly be denied that this view followed more logically from the basic idea than the conclusion which advocated "luxury" as the reflection of the welfare of society, but at the same time endeavoured to keep the masses as badly supplied as possible. Mandeville took the greatest trouble to refute the criticism levelled against him that his objective must really be luxury for the poor, too. The main representative of the opposite, and in itself more consistent, view was his contemporary John Cary, the Bristol merchant, whose book appeared rather earlier (1695). It may be noticed in passing, as a reminder to the believers in the Marxist interpretation of history, that there could be no reason, from their point of view, why a Bristol merchant should be more favourable to the English working classes than a Dutch medical man like Mandeville; but in this case he was, and the reason must be sought in another quarter than that in which Marx and his followers have been accustomed to look.

Cary delivered himself of the proposition that "Both our Product and Manufactures may be carried on to advantage

[49] Child, Preface (unpag.).—Davenant, *Discourses*, etc. II 21.

without running down the labour of the Poor", and marshalled two reasons in particular in support. First he cited the labour-saving, technical innovations of which, as we have seen above, he was a convinced advocate. To him they were a solution of the problem as to how high wages could be paid without adversely affecting sales. The scope of his argument would have been even wider if he had recognized a causal connection here with high wages. The second of his reasons was of a theoretical character: he demanded the application of the "gospel of high prices" all along the line. "Nor am I of opinion," he said, "with those People who think the running down the Prices of our Growth and Product . . . is an advantage to the Inland Trade of this Kingdom, but on the contrary I think 'twould be better for it if they were sold higher than they are. . . . To prove this, let us begin with the Shop-keeper or Buyer and Seller, who is the Wheel whereon the Inland Trade turns." Cary then assumed that the price of goods dealt with by the retailer, particularly food-stuffs, was increased between the buying and the selling by about £25 to £30 *per annum*. "But the Consequence thereof in the Profits of his Trade will be much more; for by this Means the Farmer may give a better Rent to his Landlord, who will be enabled to keep a more Plentiful Table . . . and carry on a greater Splendour in every thing. The Farmer according to his condition may do the same and give higher Wages to the Labourers employed in Husbandry, who might then live more plentifully, and buy new Clothes oftener . . .; by this means the Manufacturer would be encouraged to give a better price for Wool, when he should find a Vent as fast as he could make; and a Flux of Wealth causing variety of fashions would add Wings to Men's Inventions . . . this likewise would encourage the Merchant to increase his Exports . . . by which regular Circulation Payments would be short, and *all would grow rich*."[50] The notion that general wealth arises through everyone paying something more to everyone else is as typically mercantilist as one could wish, and it demonstrates how in this way people could come to oppose the demand for low wages. Low wages were not only unnecessary because everybody could be well off, but they were directly obstructive from the selling standpoint, because *nothing* ought to be cheap.

Interesting as this is—economists following the events and reasonings of the past few years would probably call the view "reflationist"—Daniel Defoe may be said to have made some

---

[50] Mandeville, *op. cit.*: Remark Y.—Cary, *Essay on the State of England*, etc., 143-50.—My italics.—cp. above II 119.

observations very like those of liberalism. He was, without exaggeration, a precursor of the notion of the economy of high wages, which, incidentally, was excellently suited to his almost "American" optimism and his chauvinistic self-satisfaction in economic matters. In *A Plan of the English Commerce* (1728) he declared that English people enjoyed higher wages than others, and yet produced more work, because they lived better and could thus work with greater pleasure. This he regarded as the fundamental reason for the superiority of English industry, whose eulogies he sang from the first to the last page of his book. His optimistic belief in higher wages, however, also had another and more important aspect. He went so far as to deny categorically the fundamental mercantilist idea that a country might become rich through the poverty of its people. This is all the more astonishing since otherwise Defoe is not far removed in his outlook from that of Cary, as, for example, when he says that "one Hand washes t'other Hand, and both the Hands the Face". It is possible that his criticism of mercantilism was felt, though not uttered, by other opponents of the economy of low prices, but to my knowledge it was never before expressed nearly as lucidly as by Defoe.

Defoe first spoke of China, India and the other Far-Eastern countries with their incredibly cheap manufactures and their resultant greater sales. But the result in his opinion is that "the People who make all these fine Works are to the last Degree miserable, their Labour of no Value, their Wages would fright us to talk of it, and their way of Living raise a Horror in us to think of it". He then applies the argument: "If then these Gentlemen," he says, "who are for forcing the Consumption of our Manufacture in England, (or in any of those Countries in Europe where they work cheapest,) by their mere Cheapness, are content to reduce the wages of the People that make them, to the rate of those in China or India, there is no doubt they might increase the Consumption and sell off the Quantity; *but what would be the Advantage? They would sell their Goods and ruin their People*; the Benefit of which in the Gross, I confess I do not understand."[51]

Defoe thus really revealed the vital contradiction in the mercantilist ideals concerning wages. If he has not plagiarized some author unknown to me, then, fresh and vigorous, though decidedly superficial, a writer that he was, he exposed the inconsistency of the view which so many people had held before him

[51] Defoe, *Plan*, etc. ch. 1 (repr. 1928, 47, 49 f.; italics mine). This is not

and were to hold after him. With the eyes of the unprejudiced child he recognized here the essentials; he saw, like the child in Hans Andersen's fairy tale, that the emperor was not wearing any clothes. But apart from the question as to whether the criticism really originates with Defoe or with some earlier writer, it none the less attacked what was, in practice, one of the most important doctrines of mercantilism.

It is a strange accident that the criticism of the economy of low wages assumed two so very different theoretical forms at the same time. On the one side, the typical mercantilist ideas were followed through to their logical end and it was found that wages must be high with a view to sales. Of course an increase in wages based on these motives would have been completely illusory. On the other hand, it was denied that selling was the final goal of economic activity and instead, the material welfare of the people was put forward for consideration. The latter outlook had its eyes on economic realities and finally led to Adam Smith.

to maintain that Defoe always expressed himself in this way; it is very possible that he had considerable assistance with his voluminous productions. P. W. Buck, *The Politics of Mercantilism* (N.Y. 1942) 92, quotes one of Defoe's works which is unknown to me, *The Great Law of Subordination Consider'd* (Lond. 1724) as follows: "The advance of Wages . . . is the support of all the Insolence of Servants, as their ruin'd manners is the Spring of it."

PART IV

MERCANTILISM AS A MONETARY SYSTEM

I

THE CONNECTION BETWEEN MONETARY POLICY AND COMMODITY POLICY

That the dictum "wealth consists in money, or in gold and silver" was the real core of mercantilist theory was certainly Adam Smith's view when he placed it at the head of the fourth book of his *Wealth of Nations*, even though his detailed criticism of mercantilism in the pages that follow also attacked many other aspects of that theory. For a long time, Adam Smith's was the generally accepted interpretation, but the research of the last three-quarters of a century has led to a revision of judgment especially in this respect.

This much, however, was true in the descriptions of the earlier critics of mercantilism, that money and the precious metals occupied a central position in the mercantilist ideology and economic policy. There are few mercantilist writings that are not mainly preoccupied with what is usually known in English works as *"treasure"*, which was without exception synonymous with money or precious metals. Thomas Mun's second and posthumously published work *England's Treasure by Forraign Trade* (1664) has been regarded by later generations as the chief exposition of these theories. Consideration for precious metals was the constantly recurring motive of economic legislation and administration. It also influenced, more or less openly, the three closely allied fields of foreign policy, colonial policy and voyages of discovery. In fact, the hope of discovering gold and silver mines became one of the chief driving forces in the expansion of European peoples to other parts of the world. When it was seen that Spain alone had discovered the philosopher's stone, so to speak, trade with the Spanish mainland and her colonies became the chief factor in economic policy, while attacks on Spain's silver fleets by piracy and on her stocks of silver by diplomacy, bribery, and smuggling became a primary interest. If trade in other directions offered greater possibilities, these were regarded merely as a means of indirectly acquiring control over the flow of silver from Mexico and Peru and so letting the countries without mines of their own "abound with gold and silver". For this reason, too, the theme was always "The life of commerce and trade is money". This is far too obvious to require further alluding to.[1] The question

---

[1] The following references may suffice:
In view of the statement of Miss Lamond, the editor of the modern edition

that should be investigated is, rather, why "treasure" occupied so central a place in mercantilist theory, and what this signified.

A tight hold on money and the precious metals and the fear of losing them was thus one of the main aspects of mercantilism. But it does not follow that mercantilism differed in *principle* from the outlook of earlier times. It is certainly true that these factors occupied the thoughts of the mercantilists and influenced their economic policy to a greater degree than ever before (or after); but the medieval policy of provision, together with its measures against the export of the precious metals, demonstrates that even before the period of mercantilism, these were regarded in just the same way. If, then, the underlying attitude towards money and the material from which money was created did not alter in the period between the Crusades and the 18th century, it follows that we are dealing with deep-rooted notions. Perhaps the same

of [Hales'] *Discourse of the Common Weal of this Realm of England* (1549) that the book contains no sign that exaggerated importance is placed on "treasure", and that such exaggerations were altogether less common than is assumed (170), it is interesting to point out that the word "treasure" occurs more than fifty times in this book of 130 small pages of text, sometimes four or five times on the same page (cp. the—incomplete—list in the index under "Treasure").

On the conception of trade with Spain, Colbert's instruction of 1679 to the Ambassador in Madrid is particularly significant (pr. *Lettres de Colbert* II 700–703), but the whole of the rest of his correspondence, too, demonstrates a like interest (e.g. *ib.* II 421 and note 3, 488, 519, 659, 690, etc.).—A. Serra, *Breve trattato delle cause che possono fare abbondare li regni d'oro e d'argento dove non sono miniere* (1613).—"The Life of Commerce and Trade is Money", e.g. in the Instruction to the English commission of trade of 1622 (pr. *Foedera*, ed. Rymer, 1st ed. XVII 414).

There is a great danger, in giving an historical presentation of theories and doctrines, of basing it on quotations torn from their contexts. This has led me in this part to keep more strictly than usual to those writings to which I have had access in the original. They are, in the first place, such as can be found in Swedish libraries; but I have been able to supplement them through visits to the British Museum, the Goldsmiths' Library, and the Bibliothèque nationale. It may be said that the outstanding features of the mercantilist doctrines are blurred, rather than distinguished, through taking note of every crank who was able to put his views into print. If my method has led to any arbitrariness in the choice of authors quoted, I hope, at least, that no aspect of importance to my presentation has suffered from it.—For the modern literature on the subject, I refer the reader to an appendix at the end of this part.—Since the authorship of the less outstanding anonymous writings is not a major consideration, I have thought it better not to enter into closer investigation on such points; in general, I have employed the names accepted in modern treatises, even when I was not convinced of their accuracy. With anonymous works, the names are placed in square brackets.

notions have persisted even beyond the 500 years included in that period, even though not nearly to the same degree as the "fear of goods". The fact that during World War I most belligerent countries were loth to part with their stocks of gold in exchange for the most indispensable commodities is clear evidence that the leading politicians still clung to the notion that precious metals far outweigh everything else, or at any rate that they ascribed such a notion to their countrymen. With the exception of the period of *laissez-faire*, no age has been free from these ideas. It was only the unique intellectual tenacity of *laissez-faire* that for a time overcame the beliefs of the "natural man" on this point. Mercantilism thus meant primarily that, under the pressure of the new intellectual enlightenment in various spheres, people were, for the first time, directing their deliberate attention to aims which they had long cherished unreflectingly, and which the new intellectual ferment invested with a hitherto undreamt-of significance.

For the same reasons we must exercise the utmost caution in attempting to interpret mercantilism in the light of certain specific monetary conditions and circumstances obtaining in the 16th and 17th centuries. As we have already indicated in passing, in the first part, the circumstances of the time were not decisive. The monetary system and the position of the precious metals underwent a complete change in this period; it was, at least in many countries, the period of transition from a predominantly natural to a predominantly money economy, and at the same time, from an insignificant to an extremely abundant silver production. But the basic conception of money and of the role of the precious metals was not altered by this. An illuminating example to the point is to be found in a polemic around the Saxon coinage system of the period about 1530. The argument of one party is in the last degree "mercantilist" and at the same time it unconsciously fixes its own origin as dating from the period preceding the great changes, since it includes Spain among those countries with no silver mines of their own.[2]

One part of these great changes in economic life, the transition to a definite money economy, influenced the treatment of goods, as we observed in the foregoing part. To this extent protectionism was a more decisive novelty in mercantilism than was the monetary policy.

[2] *Die drei Flugschriften über den Münzstreit der sächsischen Albertiner und Ernestiner um 1530*, ed. W. Lotz (Samml. älterer u. neuerer staatsw. Schriften des In- u. Auslandes, ed. L. Brentano & E. Leser, II, Lpz. 1893) 71 73.

The connection between the attitude towards goods and towards money must have been very peculiar, if the two opposing programmes regarding goods could be reconciled with one and the same monetary programme. The explanation is that economic relationships were only examined and discussed as a whole with the advent of mercantilism. The mercantilist treatment of the problem led definitely to greater clarity to the extent that an increased amount of money almost necessarily, and an increased amount of precious metal most probably, led to an increase in prices, both processes thus being natural instruments of a policy of high prices. We shall show that the mercantilists often realized the connection, although it did not occupy a central position in their system.

They were *primarily* concerned with another relationship between goods and money. The fear of a surplus of goods led to endeavours to obstruct imports and stimulate exports, and these efforts were meant to lead to an additional value of exported goods relatively to imported goods, or in other words to an "excess of exports". The balance then had to be imported in the form of precious metals, which were not generally reckoned as goods, and so two birds were killed with one stone. On the one hand the country was rid of an unwelcome surplus of goods, which was believed to result in unemployment, while on the other the total stock of money in the country was increased. This of course was infinitely more consistent than the medieval argument, which was out to prevent the export both of the precious metals and of goods. If the latter had led to a surplus of imports, an outflow of precious metals to other countries would have had to take place. Medieval economic policy was dominated, as the foregoing part shows, by an unreflective bias towards "surplus" in general, and this it wanted in money and goods alike. The mercantilists recognized that they had to decide between the two and, for a two-fold reason, they fanatically adopted the first alternative. The synthesis between the "fear of goods" and the "hunger for money" is here so complete that the mercantilist view may equally well be deduced from either. The argument sustained a practical rebirth on a gigantic scale in Napoleon's Continental System. English writers during the French wars in the 1690's had just the same attitude as Napoleon was later to take up, that the enemy could be ruined by supplying him with goods which he would have to pay for in money.

This however did not mean that the mercantilist policy could be certain of maintaining intact the relationship between its monetary and its goods policy.

If the mercantilists were able to ensure an export surplus, then a decrease in the circulation of goods and an increase in the circulation of money, together with higher internal prices, would be the necessary result; while the reverse would obtain in those countries into which the *export* surplus of goods was sent, and from which the *import* surplus of money came. Thus far everything coincided with their theories. But if this result was arrived at by manipulations which did not lead to a new equilibrium in foreign trade, reactions must inevitably have set in. Higher prices would stimulate imports and discourage exports and the dreaded surplus of *imports* would follow close on the heels of the previous inflow of money. If it were possible in such circumstances to prevent the outflow of precious metals in payment for the import surplus, the result would be a definite dislocation of the exchange —a rise in the value of the foreign currency, in other words, a fall in the foreign valuation of the native currency. More native money units would be obtainable for one foreign unit, and on this basis a new equilibrium would be reached. But even apart from the fact that such a development was usually regarded with great suspicion, the mercantilists themselves were firmly convinced that it was useless to retain the precious metals in the country during an "unfavourable balance of trade." And so there only remained the first alternative—a surplus in the import of goods as a result of the preceding surplus in the import of money. To the extent that the mercantilists had an insight into the arguments just put forward, they found themselves in a dilemma. The inflow of precious metals which they desired more than anything else set forces in motion which led to its own destruction—first an increase in domestic prices, and secondly a resultant import surplus. We shall see later on how they attempted to resolve this problem.

All this held good only on the assumption posited above: equilibrium in foreign trade remaining unchanged. Now there were certain limited possibilities of creating a *new* equilibrium in foreign trade, i.e. by restricting imports and encouraging exports. By such measures one could avoid the consequences outlined above. Import restrictions and export premiums result in increased prices and attract money into the country even with the exchange remaining unaltered. To this extent the monetary theory of the mercantilists harmonized well enough with their protectionism, although this argument was not clearly grasped until much later—and even to-day there are theorists of great fame to whom it is still obscure.[3] For this reason, the mercantilists were faced here, too, with an insoluble problem, although in most cases they failed to realize it.

Mercantilism as a monetary system is therefore highly inter-esting, because it shows how economic thought in its infancy grappled with some of the most important problems of economic policy. On the other hand it would be false to consider this aspect of mercantilism as significant from the point of view of the develop-ment along the lines intended. The very fact that all countries put the same ideas into practice nullifies the wide-spread, but as a rule quite undemonstrable, assumption that the increased supply of money or precious metals was the effect of mercantilist policy. It was well-nigh impossible for all the mercantilist countries together to have been affected, since this was a question of an increase in the total production of precious metals and not merely one of dividing a given quantity among all the countries.

Spain was the practical example which the later mercantilists always quoted against the earlier, medieval policy concerning precious metals. It was maintained that Spain sought to prevent the export of precious metals by directly forbidding it, while a successful policy necessitated the fostering of an export surplus by general economic measures so that an import surplus of the precious metals would follow automatically. This was a criticism of the older bullionist policy by the proponents of the new mer-cantilism in the stricter meaning of the term. They could point to Spain's futile attempts to retain her precious metals through prohibition of exports, her gold and silver flowing out meanwhile "like rain off a roof" despite the fact that practically all the new production came from her own colonies. This, they thought, was proof of the fallacy of the policy.[4] It is clear that their reasoning was also incorrect. Gold and silver were Spain's natural exports, and would have flowed out regardless of any policy designed to

---

[3] On the theory, let me refer to my exposition in *Bidrag till Sveriges ekono-miska och sociala historia under och efter världskriget* (Sthlm. 1926) II 25–36 (Ameri-can edition: *Sweden, Norway, Denmark and Iceland in the World War*, New Haven 1930, 150–63); further, below 258 f. The correct theory originates primarily with Ricardo (*Principles of Political Economy and Taxation*, 1817, ch. 7). The wrong notion, refuted by him, which to-day has been resuscitated under the name of the "Theory of Purchasing Power Parity", even in its more developed form disregards this relationship.

[4] The simile belongs to the Venetian, Vendramino (1595; see M. Ansiaux, "Histoire économique de la prospérité et de la décadence de l'Espagne aux XVIe et XVIIe siècles" (*Revue d'économie politique* VII, 1893, 1031).This concep-

retain them. Even on the assumption that they could have been held for a time, the result would have been a rapid rise in the country's prices, a powerful impulse to an excess of imports and a resulting outflow of bullion.

Even if the reasoning against the effectiveness of the bullionist policy had been better, it is obvious that its substitute, the policy of mercantilism in the narrower sense, had not proved its capacity to draw precious metals into a country. It was commonly believed that the Netherlands was exceptionally well supplied with precious metals, but this ought instead to have constituted a refutation of the argument, since the Netherlands did less than most other countries towards adopting a mercantilist monetary policy.[5] While this mercantilist conception is interesting *per se*, there is little reason to accept it as accurate. It is wiser to adopt a sceptical attitude towards these theories, based as they frequently were on trade had distributed the precious metals among the countries essentially according to the amount of business transacted and the growth of a money economy in every individual case. At any rate, an assumption such as this can be more easily justified than conclusions based on assertions regarding conditions which "the man in the street" even to-day cannot discern, or correctly interpret, and which baffled even the most experienced and learned observers, on account of the lack of economic statistics at that time.[6] Such conclusions are challenged by the most elementary laws of historical criticism.

tion of the Spanish development and its causes is to be found throughout the whole mercantilist literature, from Mun (*England's Treasure by Forraign Trade*, ch. 6) onwards; cf. above Part I, ch. 7, note 21.

[5] On plentiful money in the Netherlands, see especially one of the best observers of that time, Sir W. Temple (*Observations upon the United Provinces of the Netherlands*, 1672, ch. 6; 2nd edn., Lond. 1673, 233 f.): "More *Silver* is seen in Holland among the common Hands and Purses, than *Brass* either in Spain or in France, though one be so rich in the best Native Commodities, and the other drain all the Treasures of the West Indies" (my italics).— Child, *A Discourse concerning Trade* 1668 (in *A New Discourse of Trade*, Lond. 1698, 9), attacks the easy notion that the low rate of interest in Holland "proceeds only from their abundance of (money)". A modern author, van Brakel (*Handelscompagnieën* xiv), assumes a great stock of silver to have existed there.— On Dutch policy: E. Laspeyres, *Geschichte der volkswirtschaftlichen Anschauungen der Niederländer und ihrer Litteratur zur Zeit der Republik*, 282 ff.

[6] Davenant complains frequently about the secrecy on the part of public authorities (*Discourses on the Publick Revenues and on the Trade of England*, Lond. 1698, I 266, II 330, 434; *An Essay on the Probable Methods of Making a People Gainers in the Ballance of Trade*, Lond. 1699, 6). The whole tendency of the political arithmetic, originating with Sir William Petty, led often to freely invented statistics and was denounced, e.g., by Defoe with great scorn (*A Plan*

The present part of this work is thus an analysis of mercantilist arguments in the sphere of monetary policy. Where appropriate and where possible, these are compared with what actually happened, but about the effects of economic policy on the provision of money and the monetary system hardly anything can be said.

Even if such results may have been insignificant or altogether unavailable, mercantilism as a money system has by no means been unimportant in the development of economic life. Its effects led to results lying in opposite directions. Through its connection with protectionism and the policy of power, this aspect of mercantilism became what was perhaps the most highly valued and most frequently employed argument for a policy of economic rivalry between nations, the commercial and colonial wars considered as struggles for the precious metals. Mercantilism as a money system was therefore largely responsible for this result; such was its most important direct political effect. Through the intensive discussions of the connection between foreign trade and the monetary system in the long run, however, these mercantilist ideas exercised at the same time a revolutionary influence which already pointed more or less to *laissez-faire*. The intensity of the mercantilist discussions on money led to a more profound understanding of the factors which the 18th-century economists found indispensable as the premises for their often contrary conclusions.

In this and in the following part my exposition will be confined more strictly than usual to the period before 1715. The last decade of the 17th century brought forth some very intense and fruitful economic discussions in England. Several writings taken from the first fifteen years of the following century form as appropriate a natural boundary line for a treatment of mercantilist thought as can be found. Standing out more prominently among these late contributions are John Law's arguments in favour of paper money mercantilism. Mandeville's poem, *The Fable of the Bees: or Private Vices, Publick Benefits*, with his much more important prose commentaries, and the discussions following on the proposal of an Anglo-French trading agreement in connection with the

of the English Commerce, 1728, Part I, ch. 5, repr. Oxf. 1928, 128 f.). See my detailed comparison of England's Baltic trade as presented by Roger Coke (*Treatise* III 54, IV 98) with the figures from the records of the Sound duties: "Samhällshistoria och statistik" in *Historieuppfattning, materialistisk och annan* (Sthlm. 1944) 55–59. See below 344.

Peace of Utrecht. The remainder of the 18th century has, on the whole, been omitted, and it is not clear at the present moment whether it made any important contribution to mercantilist thought. It is probable that its chief interest, from this point of view, consists in its blending of mercantilist ideas with those of *laissez-faire*, which before 1715 had only appeared sporadically. The interplay of old and new in the ideas of the period that followed would prove a fruitful and important study, but it will have to remain for somebody else to undertake this task.

Following the usual practice in the present work, here too I confine myself as a rule to those writings which exerted some influence in their own time or for other reasons can be regarded as the expression of a widespread belief. Where for special reasons other sources are used, the fact will be duly noted. To make the exposition readable, the quotations must be kept within comparatively narrow bounds and this is not difficult, as the fundamental conceptions are decidedly uniform. The practical demands certainly showed large variations and the pamphleteers "usually esteem the immediate Interests of their own to be the common Measure of Good and Evil", as was realized even at the time. But the very fact that opposing practical standpoints were derived from the same principles or interpretations of economic phenomena is evidence of the fundamental uniformity of outlook. This may be seen, for instance, at an early stage of development, in the struggle between the upholders and opponents of coinage depreciation in Saxony around 1530, as well as in the arguments between the supporters and opponents of the East India Company and of abolishing the restrictions on the export of precious metals at the beginning and at the end of the 17th century—Malynes against Misselden and Mun, Pollexfen and Cary against Child and Davenant. No less characteristic of the times is the profound theoretical agreement between so determined a business man, preoccupied only with his own interests, as Sir Josiah Child, the governor of the East India Company, on the one hand, and Sir William Petty on the other, one of the few economists of the period who was actuated primarily by scientific interest.[7]

[7] For verification of what has been stated here, I must refer to the whole presentation in this part. Sir W. Ashley has associated the development of economic ideas with the differences of party politics ("The Tory Origin of Free Trade Policy", in *Surveys, Historic and Economic*, Lond. 1900, 268–303). For a criticism of this approach, see P. J. Thomas, *Mercantilism and the East India Trade* (Lond. 1926) 96 f., 142, 173.—The quotation is taken from Sir Dudley North, *Discourses upon Trade* (Lond. 1691) xii (Reprint of Economic Tracts, ed. J. H. Hollander, Baltimore 1907, 12); cf. N. Barbon, *A Discourse*

of Trade (Lond. 1690), in the same collection (Baltimore 1905) 7.—On the social criticism which developed in France towards the end of the 17th and at the beginning of the 18th centuries, see appendix to this part (below 263). —Just before the publication of the first Swedish edition of this work Jacob Viner published his extremely well documented essay, "English Theories of Foreign Trade before Adam Smith", *Jour. of Polit. Econ.* XXXVIII, 1930, re-printed in his *Studies in the Theory of International Trade* (Lond. 1937; this edition cited here). When I had had the opportunity to study his treatment of the subject, I was happy to find a high degree of agreement between our presentations, so high in fact, that I did not find it necessary to alter greatly the later editions of my work on the basis of his. Those changes which have been incorporated in the present edition have been noted in their respective places.—On the other hand, I take quite a different view from that taken by Sombart on the monetary theory of mercantilism, and indeed on mercantilist theory in general. My reasons are chiefly the same as those presented by F. H. Knight in his essay, "Historical and Theoretical Issues in the Problem of Modern Capitalism" (*Jour. of Econ. and Business History* I, 1928, 119 ff.). But in accordance with my general plan, I must content myself with references to positive evidence supporting my standpoint, and refrain from polemics against other interpretations.—I shall, however, return to Keynes' treatment of mercantilism in a special supplementary chapter.

II

THE IMPORTANCE OF THE PRECIOUS METALS OUTSIDE THE MECHANISM OF EXCHANGE

1. INTRODUCTION

It might appear to be fairly easy to analyse the mercantilist ideas on money, for the contemporary pamphleteers were by no means reticent in expressing their views. But the difficulty experienced even to-day of discovering adequate terms for expressing economic phenomena verbally was naturally much greater in the early stages of economic thought, especially for writers who were not theorists at all and not always accustomed to render their thoughts in writing. Even at the time people complained of this. For instance, the anonymous author of one of the better mercantilist pamphlets (later found to bear the name Simon Clement), *A Discourse of the General Notions of Money, Trade and Exchanges* (1695), which reveals Locke's influence, points out in this essay, in agreement with an earlier writer, that it was unfortunate that learned people paid so little attention to commercial problems. "And though I have addicted myself to Search after the True Notions of these Matters," he said, "beyond many other Merchants, who have their Heads continually filled with Business; yet I see my self so Defective in these Respects, that I can rather Wish, than ever Hope to be Master of those Accomplishments, that might Render me Capable of Expressing my Thoughts with less Difficulty to myself, and more Clearness to others." It is at times really pathetic to see how these untrained minds attempted to handle intricate economic arguments.

It was not long, however, before people generally came to realize the truth of the remark of Dr. Samuel Johnson, the literary oracle of the waning 18th century. His faithful biographer, Boswell, had expressed astonishment that Adam Smith (for whom Johnson had little esteem) had written on trade, although he was personally unfamiliar with business life; to which the great man replied: ". . . there is nothing which requires more to be illustrated by philosophy than trade does".[1] Until then, economic literature had been written mainly by politicians and merchants. Before the beginning of the 18th century, Sir William Petty

---

[1] [Clement], book quoted in the text 27.—J. Boswell, *Life of Dr. Samuel Johnson, sub anno* 1776 (ed. G. Birkbeck Hill, Oxf. 1887, II 430).

and John Locke were the only writers on economic questions who belonged to philosophic and scientific circles. At the most, we could add Jean Bodin, Thomas Hobbes, Samuel Pufendorf, and Wilhelm Leibniz, who interested themselves in economic problems as the occasion offered. It is therefore misleading to apply the same rules of criticism to mercantilist expositions as to the works of people of academic training who are accustomed to express their thoughts on paper. Above all we are liable to go astray if we pick out isolated statements. On the other hand, the fact that the ideas in the mercantilist writings are not properly worked out theoretically sometimes makes it difficult to reconstruct the arguments. This difficulty is increased by the fact that many things are often taken for granted which we should definitely have expected to be explicitly stated.

In these circumstances one must employ every possible means to achieve clarity. One way of doing this is to divide mercantilism as a monetary system into two parts: the first dealing with the function of money and the precious metals as a means of exchange, i.e. in connection with the actual exchange mechanism, and the second with its importance in other directions. The position of the precious metals in international exchange may be included in the first group of problems. It is beside the point to criticize or defend mercantilism unless this distinction is kept in view. It must therefore be applied as far as possible, although as a rule it was not recognized by the mercantilists themselves, and although there are important links connecting the two aspects. In this chapter only the second of the two parts will be investigated.

2. IDENTIFICATION OF WEALTH AND MONEY

The function which the mercantilists assigned to money and the precious metals outside the exchange mechanism was characterized, by its critics, by the expression mentioned above, the identification of wealth and money. This must really have meant that in the mercantilist view there could be no other object of economic value apart from money. Expressed in this way, the statement is so obviously absurd that it may be taken for granted that no mercantilist ever actually held this view. On the other hand many statements are to be found—and not merely in the earliest period of mercantilism—which suggested that money and wealth are equal or something very similar. It may be well to illustrate this immediately, although it does not lead us far in our discussion.

Several of the most categorical of the statements identifying money and wealth are contained in one of the two Saxon pamphlets of about 1530, advocating coinage depreciation (*Die Müntz Belangende*). Such remarks as "wealth, it is money"; "wealth as money"; "what usually goes in general by the name of wealth is, in common knowledge, this: money, as the true watch-word; for where there is much money, there is wealth, as it is truly said". Even more characteristic than the remarks in this rather unintelligent pamphlet are the views put forward by the other side. They are considerably better thought-out and present a sharp rejoinder (*Apologia und Vorantwortung*), but its author refrains from making any protest against the argument of the identification between wealth and money brought forward by the coinage depreciators. The same outlook, expressed rather more carefully, is to be found in the two roughly contemporary English essays (1519/36), similarly quoted above, attributed to Clement Armstrong. In what is probably the older of the two, for example, we read, "The whole wealth of the realm is for all our rich commodities to get out of all other realms therefore ready money, and after the money is brought in to the whole realm, so shall all people in the realm be made rich therewith." The second essay asserts, "better to have plenty of gold and silver in the realm than plenty of merchants and merchandizes".

Jean Bodin, one of the few philosophers among the mercantilists, declared in his famous essay on money (1568), "the surplus of gold and silver, which is the wealth of a country, must justify to some degree the rise in prices". Three quarters of a century later (1647), another French book, ascribed to the priest Mathias de Saint-Jean (whose former name was Jean Éon), called *Le commerce honorable ov considérations politiques*, described gold and silver as "*la pure substance du peuple*". Montchrétien had said before that (1615): "We live not so much from trade in raw materials (*élémens*) as from gold and silver." At the very end of the period to which we are limiting ourselves, the very influential collection of articles known as *The British Merchant*, edited by Charles King (1713), stated, in opposing the projected commercial treaty with France, that all countries with whom England traded "contribute to the Prosperity and Happiness of this Nation " in proportion as England's trade with them yielded a balance of gold and silver.[2]

---

[2] *Drei Flugschriften* (note 2 prev. ch.) 47, 71, 73, 75, cp. 113.—[Armstrong], "A Treatise concerninge the Staple" and "How to Reforme the Realme" (pr. "Drei volkswirtschaftl. Denkschr. aus. d. Zeit Heinrichs VIII von Engl."

It is not my intention to prolong these quotations endlessly; they could fill many pages. It may be said that the discussions concerning national wealth which took place in England towards the end of the 17th century among less intelligent, but none the less characteristic, writers led to a pure Midas-like view of the precious metals, i.e. that all economic value consisted in precious metal. The anonymous *Britannia Languens*, for example, stated (1680) that "our present Stores of Merchandize" were *not* a part of "the National Wealth"; they were only a potential "treasure". It was only when they really led to an increase in the "treasure" that they could be reckoned a national asset. In accordance with this idea the author declared epigrammatically that "Poverty is but the privation of treasure". In the whole of this book of 300 pages, "treasure" is almost the only subject of discussion, though in one passage population is described as "the chiefest, most fundamental and precious commodity". The meaning of this apparent exception is seen from the sentence immediately preceding: "Sufficient stores of Treasure cannot otherwise be gotten, than by the industry of the people." This idea of the function of population, as the increasing of the stock of precious metals in the country, runs through the whole exposition. The author emphasizes, for instance, that a large population would lead to low wages, which in turn would mean cheap manufactures and would thus facilitate exports. The views expressed in these examples, though drawn from one work in particular, are entirely typical of a large part of mercantilist literature. The American historian, Furniss, has already developed this idea in his previously mentioned study on the conception among mercantilist writers of the function of labour in society.[3]

In all these cases the point that something is implied which in a present-day discussion of similar subjects would invariably be stated explicitly, must be taken into consideration. The mercantilists would naturally not deny that people must eat, clothe themselves, and have a roof over their heads. In the same

in *Abhandl. der Gesellsch. d. Wissenschaften zu Göttingen* XXIII Gött. 1878, ed. R. Pauli 32, 72; repr. *Tudor Econ. Docs.* III 105, 124).—Bodin, *Discours sur le rehaussement et diminution des monnoyes* (Paris ed. 1578) unpag.—[Saint-Jean], *Le commerce honorable ou considérations politiques* (Nantes 1647, incorrectly given on the title-page as 1646) 101 f.—Montchrétien, *Traicté de l'oeconomie politique*, Book 2, 1st ed. [II] 14.—*The British Merchant: General Maxims in Trade* 2nd ed. (Lond. 1743) I 20.

[3] *Britannia Languens*, sections 7, 13, 14, 1st ed. (Lond. 1680) 153, 222, 234 f., 238.—E. S. Furniss, *The Position of the Laborer in a System of Nationalism, passim.* —See above II 153.

way they certainly did not imagine that food, clothing and houses could be made from the precious metals. It is true that the fact that they did not state this explicitly was far from being unimportant, for their silence had powerful psychological cause and effect; but it would be grotesque to interpret their silence as though what remained unsaid did not exist for them. Many statements can be found referring to other objects of wealth and other revenues or means of satisfying needs than money, in fact passages which talk of real wealth and real income, even though all this was generally put on one side.

With regard to commodities, the result of the tenacious policy of provision was that food-stuffs were treated according to these principles longer than any other commodities. Armstrong's characteristic dictum that agriculture increases the wealth of food supplies and trade the wealth of money has already been mentioned (*v.s.* II 94). That trade too had the function of providing commodities obviously did not occur to him, although of course he could not possibly have denied it. As time went on, it became more widely realized that it was impossible for everything to consist of money. Montchrétien, in his bitterness regarding the damage done to his countrymen by foreign traders, and convinced that his native country was capable of standing alone, laid special emphasis on the importance of commodities (1615). For example, he declared, "It is by no means the surplus of gold and silver, the store of pearls and diamonds, that make men rich and wealthy; it is the supply of articles necessary for maintaining life and clothing; he who has more of these has more wealth"—how he could make this tally with his other statement cited above, he himself would probably have been embarrassed to explain. Mun was of the opinion (in *England's Treasure by Forraign Trade*) that a prince must lay up a war treasure, but he added that if a prince lacks goods which he can buy with his money when he needs them, he is just as poor as though he lacked the money with which to buy the goods. Mun also asked, therefore, what was the use of money without goods. Wilhelm von Schrötter (Schröder), who was, in general, strongly influenced by Mun, remarked in his book *Fürstliche Schatz- und Rent-Cammer* (1686), probably with this argument in mind, that war treasure could also be laid up in kind.[4]

[4] [Armstrong], ed. Pauli 75, ed. *Tudor Econ. Docs.* III 127.—Montchrétien Bk. 2, 1st ed. [II] 153, cp. 150.—Mun, *Engl. Tr.* ch. 18 (ed. Ashley 95) cp. ch. 19 (*ib.* 104 f.).—W. v. S[chrötter], *Fürstliche Schatz- und Rent-Cammer* ch. 109 (1st ed. Lpz. 1686, 552).

Moreover the discussions on national wealth and similar topics often led to other things than money. Thus Mun in his earlier work, *A Discourse of Trade from England unto the East Indies* (1621), declared that "riches or sufficiency consisteth in the possession of those things which are needful for a civil life. This sufficiency is of two sorts: the one is natural, and proceedeth of the Territory itself: the other is artificial and dependeth on the industry of the Inhabitants." Roger Coke evinced an exceptionally keen interest in the provision of goods. In one of his books, it is true, his first thesis is "Money is Treasure", but his forty-third is "Goods are Riches", although the relationship between treasure and riches is nowhere explained. Schrötter presumably meant the same thing when he stated, using a different but quite typical terminology, that domestic trade makes for happiness but not for riches. The latter was the preserve of foreign trade, which was able to bring in "treasure".

Quite naturally the literature concerning what came to be called Political Arithmetic manifested the furthest departure from the identification of money with wealth. Through attempting to compute every possible social phenomenon in terms of figures, it aimed at a scientific or theoretical result, and therefore helped to direct attention to matters which had been lost sight of by the advocates of the thousand and one practical projects. Petty, the actual father of the Political Arithmetic and the inventor of the term, made calculations concerning the value of the fixed and mobile property of the country, which he called its wealth, and even added to this the separate "value" of the population. He points out explicitly that according to his reckoning, the amount of money was less than *one* per cent of this total (*Verbum Sapienti*, written about 1665, published 1691). In a later work he declared that the result of trade was not "Wealth at large but particularly abundance of Silver, Gold, and Jewels" (*Political Arithmetick*, written about 1676, published in 1690). A generation later Charles Davenant, who belonged to the same school of thought in spite of having adopted more of the argument of *laissez-faire* than any other influential mercantilist, embarked on lengthy and detailed discussions of national wealth in his *Discourses on the Publick Revenues* (1698). He included not only all kinds of real capital, but even such imponderables as political power. Like Petty, he went so far as to say that, as its commerce and industry grew, so a country, like an individual, transformed the precious metals into "Stock of another kind", i.e. ships, buildings, furniture, foreign goods, silverware, etc. It is true that the actual factors of production in the national wealth were altogether subordinated in this branch of mercantilist literature, too, in favour of the durable objects of consumption; but to some extent this presumably corresponded to the economic facts; and what these examples show is that other objects of wealth than the precious metals could sometimes loom important in the eyes of the Political Arithmeticians.

One of the best discussions of the relations between wealth and money, finally, occurs in a pamphlet called *The East-India Trade a Most Profitable Trade to This Kingdom*, ascribed to the well-known East India director and City merchant, Thomas Papillon, or at least said to be written at his instance and in his house (1677). The following extracts are characteristic of its approach: "It is true that usually the measure of Stock or Riches is accounted by Money, but that is rather in imagination than in reality: A man is said to be worth Ten thousand pounds, when possibly he hath not One hundred pounds in ready Money; but his Estate, if he be a Farmer, consists in Land, Corn, or Cattle, and Husbandry Implements. . . . Suppose the person possessing and managing the Farm to have attained to a Stock of Money over and above what is necessary for the carrying on the Concern of his Farm, Who would not count him a ridiculous fool, to let his Money lie in his Chest idle. . . . He might with his money have bought Goods in one Market where they were cheap, and carried them to another Market, where they were dearer, and so together with the benefit of the Carriage, have added so much more to his Stock". Reading this at the present day, one might think that at last a perfectly sane and practical view of the actual conditions had been hit upon, and incidentally also a keen criticism of what is generally believed to be the usual mercantilist approach; but this would be a mistaken conclusion.[5]*

3. DISREGARD OF CONSUMPTION

It is impossible to obtain a clear understanding of the prevailing ideas from a comparison of dicta such as these. For if the treatment

[5] Mun, *A Discovrse of Trade from England vnto the East Indies* 1st ed. 49 f.—Coke, *Treatise* III: *England's Improvements* (Lond. 1675) unpag. Intro.—[Schrötter] ch. 29 § 3 (1st ed. 163 f.).—Petty, *Verbum Sapienti* ch. 1, 2, 5, 6; *Political Arithmetick* ch. 1; *Quantulumcunque concerning Money*, Q. 23 (Econ. Writings, ed. Hull, I 105–14, 259, II 446).—Davenant, *Discourses* (note 6 prev. ch.) II 59 ff., 358 f., cp. (for the next paragraph in the text) I 12, 221, II 96, 101, 163.—[Papillon] *op. cit.*; for the authorship cp. Macaulay, *History of England*, ch. 18 (orig. edn., IV, Lond. 1855, 140 note).

* See below II 367, *Addendum* §10.

by these writers is considered as a whole, it is seen almost invariably that they aim at something other than what appears to follow logically from their general observations.

This is particularly true of Mun and his friends and successors. Let us take, for instance, the last and apparently most convincing of the quotations given above, the one from the pamphlet ascribed to Papillon. The conclusion he arrives at is: "Suppose a Foreign-place where Commodities cannot be purchased but with Money or Bullion, and that 100 thousand pounds in Bullion laid out there, should purchase such quantities of Goods as would yield on sale in some other Foreign-parts *200, to 250 thousand pounds, to be returned to England*; were it not the Kingdom's interest to embrace so gainful a Trade?" (my italics). It is thus clear that in this case, too, the final gain of the country is considered to be the additional amount of "treasure", and that the previous argument was put forward simply to fortify the ordinary position of the East India merchant, i.e. that bullion should be allowed to go out of the country in order to bring in more of it in exchange.

Davenant's writings are of special interest, both because he is certainly governed by a scientific spirit to a larger degree than the mass of pamphleteers and, even more, because he, the typical eclectic, tries to blend the old and the new, more so perhaps than anyone else. Thus, though he took into account, as has just been shown, all kinds of material and non-material objects of wealth, this did not prevent him from remarking, for instance, that if money is taken out of the country, " 'tis not the Substance of such particular Persons . . . but 'tis the Riches of the whole People, consider'd in a Body together, that goes away". And this enlightened mercantilist, standing on the threshold of *laissez-faire*, went so far as to emphasize that it was more profitable to have a war inside than outside the country, because if carried on abroad it drew money out of the country. Only when the mercantilist arguments are thus followed up is it possible to piece together the picture of economic relationships which they represent, leaving aside the choice of isolated observations. These relationships are by no means so simple that the mercantilist views of them become inexplicable; though this of course does not necessarily mean that they were right in any sense of the word.

In the third part (*v.s.* 118 ff.) it has been shown how very much the sale of commodities was considered an end in itself. Of course this also acquired the greatest importance in the treatment of money. The consequence was that consumption, or the satisfaction of demand as such, was not regarded as of any importance.

Contrariwise, the disposition of the productive forces in the country was not considered an economic element of cost at all. It was thought that nothing was to be gained from the economic point of view by increased home consumption and that in no case was any cost involved in the use of domestic factors of production. For example, so late and enlightened a writer as Simon Clement (1695), who came under the influence of Locke, stated explicitly that he did not count as expenditure what was used at home. As a result, exchange within the country or domestic trade was believed to be incapable of producing wealth, for one person's profit was counter-balanced by another person's loss, and the transaction was nothing more than a "commutation" or a transference from one pocket to another. At the most one could have said, with Schrötter, as in the passage quoted, that such trading made people happy but not rich, or, with Mathias de Saint-Jean, that foreign trade "fattens" the natives while domestic trade only provides them with sustenance. But while exchange, in so far as it catered for human wants, was thus considered unimportant, or at any rate not conducive to wealth, it was believed that wealth could always be acquired by going beyond the boundaries of one's own country. Everything gained in this way by native production was regarded as net profit for the country, without allowing for the sacrifice in the form of application of the productive forces within the country. On the other hand it was always preferable to produce a commodity at home, be it procurable never so cheaply from abroad.

One mercantilist writer after another calculated the country's profit in such a way that only the purchasing price of the foreign raw materials (or commodities in general) was reckoned as outlay, while the costs arising from freighting in native ships or from trading expenditure in general were calculated as part of the country's profits. This profit consequently grew bigger and bigger the more distant and expensive the actual trade. Mun and his disciples excelled in computations of this nature. Clement, for example, averred that if the requirements of a country's troops abroad were satisfied with native commodities, which cost 20 per cent more than they would have done if bought on the spot, the gain in any case amounted to 80 per cent over that of the other method. Writers in a silver-producing country like Austria (particularly von Hörnigk and von Schrötter) estimated that an amount of silver corresponding exactly in value to its cost of production was as profitable to the state as a 100 per cent profit to a private person and that a return equivalent to only half the cost of production must therefore mean a 50 per cent profit. It was then easy for mercantilist authors to quote numerous cases which, in their opinion, involved profit for the state though loss for merchants and producers. Von Hörnigk, for example, who was essentially a man of the world, made no secret (in his *Oesterreich über Alles, wann es nur will*, 1684) of the fact that the silver mine recommended by him was no business for a private person, "whom a business of that kind would speedily and effectively bring into bankruptcy".

The central part of this argument was admissible even if the connection between import and export were not overlooked. All import could not indeed be rejected; for as has already been shown in the third part, imports were often regarded as a means for making other countries willing to accept one's exports. This was emphasized for example by Mun, as well as in an instruction to an official committee of inquiry (1622) of the same period, and later also in Davenant and Cary. On occasions, foreign trade was even conceived as an exchange of goods. This was so in the writings of such varied celebrities as Jean Bodin, in his monetary tract of 1568, John Law, in the book in which as a young man (1705) he laid the basis of his "system", and likewise his contemporary Bernard Mandeville, in the prose commentary to one of the most widely discussed writings of the 18th century, the *Fable of the Bees* (1714), which has already been frequently mentioned in these pages. But so long as import was not considered a means for the provision of goods, but an indirect method for the disposal of them, the underlying attitude remained unchanged.

If we attempt to pursue this argument to its logical conclusion, it is obvious that the outcome could be nothing other than "treasure". For in the first place any amount of native productive power could be used up without any cost to the country, and secondly, it was believed that riches were not increased if this "cost-free" power led to a greater supply of goods from abroad. Consequently all that remained was to direct the productive powers to the acquisition of money and precious metals. This could be done either directly (in silver-producing countries) by mining, without regard to the small return in relation to the capital and labour invested; or the same result could be effected indirectly by export—whether or not occasioned in that case by import, though if so, the import would have to be of smaller value than the export; in any case, it would have to yield a balance of precious metals. If the premises were once accepted or, rather, were not considered demonstrably mistaken, there was nothing remarkable in the conclusions. For there was, then, practically no alternative than to consider the acquisition of precious metals desirable, irrespective entirely of whether they would later have a function to fulfil or not. This may appear paradoxical; but the logical consequence of so facile a notion was, in fact, paradoxical.

For two centuries, writers on economics were unanimous in the belief that the argument here outlined was sound. To quote them all would only be to repeat the same thesis *ad nauseam.*

Among the writers of the early 16th century, we find the notion either formulated in general terms or implied, as a necessary basis for the argument as applying to concrete cases: thus in Clement Armstrong and the probably later Thomas Starkey, in his imaginary dialogue between Cardinal Pole and Thomas Lupset, as well as in Hales in *A Discourse of the Common Weal* (1549). In the 17th century we find it, in England, in both works of Mun, and even in Sir William Petty—in whom, however, it was not so prominent as in most of the others, as well as, of course, in *Britannia Languens.* Among the French supporters of the view there was Mathias de Saint-Jean, and among the Austrian, Hörnigk and Schrötter, to mention but a few. I know of no mercantilist analysis which opposed this argument or attempted to replace it by another. A partial exception must, perhaps, be made in the case of Davenant, when, following his usual reasoning, he tried apparently to show that the building up of capital was as much an end in itself as money. He thus asserted, on the one hand, like all his predecessors, that with regard to domestic consumption the profit of the one was the loss of the other, and that freights were pure profit even if the freight costs were higher than the freight revenues, while all *foreign* consumption he considered an equally clear and assured profit. On the other hand, he considered the national gain to be that part of the imports which the nation does not consume, "but either lays up in Commodities, or some such adequate Treasure". The fundamental orthodoxy of this would-be heretic is significant.

Adam Smith, therefore, was not by any means tilting at windmills when he wrote: "Consumption is the sole end and purpose of all production . . . But . . . the mercantile system . . . seems to consider production, and not consumption as the ultimate end and object of all industry and commerce." [6]

[6] On the outlook as a whole: [Armstrong], ed. Pauli 32, ed. *Tudor Econ. Docs.* III 105.—Starkey, *A Dialogue between Cardinal Pole and Thomas Lupset*

4. THE IDEA OF SURPLUS

The mercantilists had, however, another and more fundamental argument which brought them to the notion of
"treasure", still without regard to the use to which it might be
put. This argument, moreover, was much more plausible in their
time than it is to-day. It could be called the idea of surplus. It
was clear to them that just as an individual, a country must take
care that expenditure does not exceed income, in fact if possible
must aim at the opposite. The surplus would then be the nation's
profit or increase in wealth, while a deficit would be the reverse.
It is obvious that such a notion presupposed some theoretical
interest, and therefore could only arise when economic life was
no longer taken for granted, but was considered a matter for
reflection and possible improvement. The vital point on which

(pr. England in the Reign of King Henry the Eighth, II, ed. J. M. Cowper,
Early English Text Society, Extra Series XII, Lond. 1871, 96).—[Hales],
Discourse of the Common Weal, ed. Lamond 65, 84.—Mun, *Discourse* 23 ff.;
Engl. Tr. ch. 4, 7, 14 (ed. Ashley, 21 f., 36 f., 70).—Petty, *Verbum Sap.* ch. 9,
Pol. Arithm. ch. 10 (Econ. Writings I 117, 313).—Davenant, *Discourses*, II 138 f.,
213, 220 ff., 384 f., 419 *et passim*; "An Essay on the East-India-Trade" (as
appendix to the foregoing work) 31 ff.—[M. de Saint-Jean] 151 f. A condensed
statement of the conception occurs, too, in a pamphlet by the rather over-rated
B. de Laffemas (*Les tresors et richesses pour mettre l'Estat en splendeur*, Paris 1598,
21 f.).—[S. Clement], *Disc. of the General Notions of Money, Trade, and Exchanges*
18, 35.—P. W. v. Hörnigk, *Oesterreich über Alles, wann es nur will* ch. 9, 9th
rule (Regensb. ed. 1723, 31 f.).—S[chrötter] ch. 29 § 3, 66 § 2, 67 § 7 (1st
ed. 163 f., 262, 292).—Modern parallels: see, e.g., *Festskrift till Pontus Fahlbeck
den 15. Okt. 1915* (Lund. 1915) 114: "Sweden pays nothing for Swedish sugar,
protected by customs duties, if Swedish raw material, Swedish labour, and
Swedish capital are employed in the making thereof. For foreign commodities,
both raw materials, capital and labour must be paid."

On the relation between imports and exports, see Bodin's work, quoted
in note 2, unpag.: "ce qui entre en lieu de ce qui sort cause le bon marché
de ce qui defailloit."—Mun, *Engl. Tr.* ch. 15 (ed. Ashley, 81).—Instruction
of 1622 to a commission on the cloth trade pr. *Foedera*, ed. Rymer, 1st edn.
XVII 414.—Coke, *Treatise* I: Wherein is demonstrated that the Church and
State of England are in Equal Danger with the Trade of It (Lond. 1671)
54, 60, 62 f.; *Treatise* III unpag. Introduction: Petitions No. 31, 44, etc.—
Cary, *An Essay on the State of England* (Bristol 1695) 52 f., 126.—Davenant,
*An Essay upon the Probable Methods of Making a People Gainers in the Ballance of
Trade* (Lond. 1699) 46, 127 f.—[J.] Law, *Considérations sur le commerce et sur
l'argent* ch. 4, 7 (La Haye 1720, 91 ff., 165 f.): "Le commerce entre deux
nations différentes n'est que l'échange des denrées."—Mandeville, *The Fable
of the Bees: or, Private Vices, Publick Benefits*, Remark (ed. F. B. Kaye, Oxf.
1924, I 109 ff.): "buying is bartering."—Adam Smith, *Wealth of Nations*,
Bk. 4 ch. 8 (ed. Cannan II 159).

this argument stood or fell was clearly the question of the tangible form in which the surplus or deficit was realized. And the most natural thing was to consider this as changes in the amount of money. We might almost say that this was a necessary link in economic thought under conditions of money economy. In this case, too, the conclusion was obviously "treasure".

This idea, stated explicitly, recurs continually in the literature of mercantilism, and if one includes its implicit form as the unstated assumption behind mercantilist reasoning, it was probably ubiquitous. Some examples from as widely separated periods as possible within the mercantilist epoch may serve to illustrate the point.

In an extraordinarily lucid and intelligent memorandum of the time of Queen Elizabeth, the usual question of the causes of an outflow of precious metal was being discussed. The author, who remains unknown, gradually leads up to the *causa causarum*, the fundamental basis on which all the others rest, namely, "If England would spend less of foreign commodities, than the same [native] commodities will pay for, then the remain must of necessity be returned of silver or gold; but if otherwise, then it will fare in England in short time, as it doth with a man of great yearly living, that spendeth more yearly than his own revenue and spendeth of the stock besides."

Mun developed the idea at the beginning of his two essays, giving figures, in accordance with his excellent business habits. An individual with an annual income of £1000, and with £2000 ready money in his safe will have lost, he asserts, all his money in four years if he spends £1500 a year, but he can double his wealth in the same time if he only spends £500 a year; "which rule never faileth likewise in the Commonwealth, but in some cases (of no great moment)". John Locke, the only philosopher among the leading economic writers of the period and one of the greatest among the philosophers, imagined society in the form of the island of Portland, administered on the lines of a public estate (*Some Considerations of the Consequences of the Lowering of Interest, and Raising the Value of Money*, 1691). In his example, the first proprietor of the island has a surplus of a £100 a year, if he sells and receives the balance in money; but his spendthrift son does the reverse. The former grows rich and the latter poor; *ergo*: "We have seen how Riches and Money are got, kept or lost, in any Country; and that is by consuming less of Foreign Commodities than what, by Commodities or Labour is paid for." As we see here, the argument remained unchanged from the time of a Tudor politician to the founder of 18th-century philosophy.[7]

To-day no comparatively educated person would imagine that the normal way of effecting an increase in one's wealth or capital was to place ready money into a safe, or of effecting a decrease to take money out of it. To-day he would reckon on the amount paid into his banking account or taken from it. Quite a number of people even know that the savings find their way from the banks into real capital investments in industry and other commercial activities. Now it would be a mistake to believe that capital invested in the form of the furnishing of credit never occurred in Tudor times. On the contrary, it obviously played an important part in England even at that time, precisely in industry and trade, and there is no doubt that it constantly grew in importance later. But it took a long time for people to rid themselves of the feeling that interest was something reprehensible; and the hoarding of money clearly went on for a very long time. Direct capital investment without the mediation of credit naturally occurred side by side with credit, and the mercantilist writers took passing note of it when it occurred in agriculture in the form of land improvements. But it is doubtful whether they all realized that this constituted real capital development, though it appears from the passage previously quoted that the author of the pamphlet ascribed to Papillon did so (v.s. II 191.)[8] If, then, it is explicable that they frequently pictured an increase or a decrease in wealth as a change in "treasure", then it is also equally clear how they took the *salto mortale*—which is quite evident in the quotation from Locke—from the increase in capital to surplus in foreign trade. For what was conceived to be the only admissible form of surplus, i.e. "treasure", could

[7] Memorandum of the time of Elizabeth: pr. Schanz, *Engl. Handelspolitik* II 649.—Mun, *Discourse* 1 f.; *Engl. Tr.* ch. 2 (ed. Ashley, 8).—Locke, the essay quoted in the text (in *Several Papers relating to Money, Interest and Trade*, etc., Lond. 1696, [I] 26 f.).—Cp. Adam Smith, *Wealth of Nations*, Bk. 4 ch. 3, who comes to the conclusion that there is a distinction between the balance of trade and "the balance of annual produce and consumption" (ed. Cannan L461).

[8] On the granting of credit in the Tudor period: R. H. Tawney's introduction to Th. Wilson, *A Discourse upon Usury* (Lond. 1925) 19, 43–60; for a later standpoint cp. Child, *A Discourse conc. Trade* (note 4 in ch. 1) 19: "most of our Trade being carried on by young men that take up money at interest."—On the hoarding of money, e.g. Macaulay, *History of England*, ch. 19, 20 (1st ed. IV, Lond. 1855, 320, 490 ff.).—On land improvements (in connection with the rate of interest), e.g. [Sir Th. Culpeper], *A Tract against Usurie* (1621), repr. in Child, *op. cit.* 222 ff., and Child himself, *op. cit.* 49.

be achieved in a country without silver or gold mines only by this kind of trade.

On the other hand, as the following will demonstrate, the mercantilists were very doubtful as to the utility of an amassed treasure. But precisely for this reason, a surplus of precious metals was considered more valuable for society than it would have been if it came to private individuals; for society could dispose of the metals in other ways than by hoarding them: it could allow them to circulate. And so a solution, the treatment of which belongs to the next chapter, was reached.

It is now clear that the insistence on the part of the mercantilists upon an increase in circulation need not in the least have been rooted in any insufficient supply of the circulating medium. Conversely, that insistence cannot demonstrate the actual existence of any insufficiency. Increased circulation was required in order to dispose of the desired influx of money and precious metals, and that influx was considered the only way of increasing the wealth of the country. There was an undeniable, if somewhat fantastic, logic in this argument. Once this is clarified, we need no longer suppose that some peculiar state of affairs existed, corresponding to the mercantilists' theoretical outlook.

5. MONEY AS CAPITAL AND REVENUE

The notions outlined here show that *money was identified with capital*. This moreover is very natural. Even to-day we have "the money market", "dear money", and "cheap money" as reminders of these notions which recur again and again in various forms. The explanation is primarily that provision of capital and credit in a money economy nearly always takes place in the form of general purchasing power, i.e. of money, and is not measured in quantities of other material objects. A more profound analysis would also consider the strong and manifold connection between money and capital, which consists in the fact that changes in the value of money on the one hand, and variations in the rate of interest from the equilibrium rate of interest on the other, are closely linked up: the effect of supernormal and subnormal rates of interest on the value of money, and on the other hand the possibility of lowering the rate of interest through an increase in the quantity of money. No other branch of economics has been more beset with confusion and misunderstanding, and it would indeed have been remarkable if the new economic thought had found the correct solution from the start. We could not really expect anything else than that money and capital should be identified with one another, and it is moreover easy to realize that this identification differed little from that of money and wealth. The latter identification requires, for this reason, a further explanation.

The position of the more perspicacious mercantilists was in this respect, as in many others, perfectly clear within certain limits. For them, money was—to use the terminology of to-day— a factor of production, on the same footing as land, sometimes regarded as "artificial" wealth as distinct from the "natural" wealth; interest on capital was the payment for the renting of money similar to rent for land. In so far as mercantilists sought to discover objective reasons for the height of the rate of interest —and they did so more and more during the period—they found such reasons in the total quantity of money. Many of the quotations brought hitherto illustrate this; and it is of paramount importance for the subject matter of this chapter. From the abundant material available, only the most typical examples will be selected, so as to demonstrate first and foremost how lasting this notion was, how deep-rooted and independent of practical considerations. To separate the two constituent parts of the notion—money as a factor of production and interest as determined by the amount of money—is an unnecessary labour.

Both of the protagonists in the struggle over monetary policy and the East India trade in the early 1620's in England were in entire agreement on this point. Gerard Malynes stated, giving detailed reason for his assertion, that "Plenty of money decreaseth usury in price or rate" (*Lex Mercatoria* and *Maintenance of Free Trade*, 1622). His truculent and rather unscrupulous adversary, Edward Misselden, replied that "The remedy for Usury may be plenty of money" (*Free Trade, or the Meanes to make Trade Florish*, same year). Of two leading writers of half a century later, Child, the omnipotent leader of the East India Company and its most skilful advocate, discussed (1668) the question of how far the legal maximum rate of interest, which he emphatically demanded, would result in drawing "the money" of the Dutch away from England. He found a remedy for this dreaded disadvantage in the easier transference of bills of debt, if these were used as currency, for this, he said, "will certainly supply the defect of at least one-half of all the ready money we have in use in the nation". Petty, the other writer, who was entirely unaffected by the clash of interests, was in agreement with the rest when he explained the "natural" fall in the rate of interest from 10 per cent to 6 per cent by the increase in the amount of money (*Politi-*

cal Arithmetick, 1676), and advised lending at interest as an appropriate remedy for a country with too much "Coin" (*Quantulumcunque concerning Money*, 1682). Still later, towards the end of the
century, Davenant spoke at length of the "Radical Moisture",
which was presumably equivalent to capital, in the modern sense
of the term—it occurs, too, in Malynes—and at the same time he
was obviously interested in real national wealth. But, like Petty,
this did not prevent him from explaining the decrease in the
rate of interest as due to "a greater quantity of money got some
way or other into the Kingdom" (1698).

This reasoning, naturally enough, was by no means confined
to England. Several years later (1701 and 1706), for example,
French merchants and statesmen complained of the prevailing
scarcity of coin (*disette des espèces*) as the cause of the high interest
rates, and they were anxious to lower the rate of usury by increasing the circulation of money.

In the 1690's inflationist aims were given a most powerful
fillip, as will be examined more closely in the following chapter.
The relation between these aims and the identification of money
and capital is obvious. From the theoretical point of view, a
much admired little pamphlet by John Asgill, entitled *Several
Assertions Proved in Order to Create Another Species of Money than
Gold and Silver* (1696), is particularly interesting in this connection. Its reasoning is, indeed, quite impossible, but none the less
it provided, on the whole, an accurate picture of the consequences
of a fall in the rate of interest; and by combining this with the
notion that the rate of interest was dependent on the quantity
of money, it arrived at its extremely characteristic conclusion.
The argument was as follows. Like several of the "projectors"
of that time, Asgill had made what he called the invention of
issuing paper money against security in the form of land—the
most famous instance of which occurred a century later, during the
French Revolution, in the form of the assignats. Now Asgill, in
accordance with almost all mercantilist writers, wanted to make
the value of land as high as possible, and he found his "invention"
of invaluable assistance because it would lower the rate of
interest and, if it achieved its theoretical object, would abolish
interest completely. This would make land "inestimable", i.e.
give it infinite value. So as not to arouse exaggerated hopes,
Asgill added prudently, "But this is the Invention perfected, which
we must not promise ourselves to see. I only mention it, to show
that the falling of interest by this invention, will be a growing
improvement to lands, even to an infinity." Such arguments

as these should surely give pause to those who look upon the tenets of mercantilism as expressions of the actual conditions of the time; for in fact, they are something quite different: they are bold conclusions drawn from theoretical notions. The admiration aroused by the writings of Asgill and the many who thought like him proves sufficiently that they represented widely held views.

Another train of thought, rooted in the same fundamental economic outlook, is adequately represented by the Austrian von Schrötter. He was one of those who, throughout, used the term "capital" in referring to what properly belonged to money and money alone, as for instance when he said "and thus a prince can use the whole capital of the country, and even more than what the whole capital is worth [sic], if only he uses it up again and puts it into circulation among the people". While this may be true of money as used in exchange for different goods and services each time, Schrötter apparently believed that the same material objects might be consumed several times, rather like Eber Särimner in the Nordic saga, who rose again every time he had been devoured by the gods. The idea is very difficult to uproot. In the Dutch literature, for example, it occurred in the belief that a war could support itself for an unlimited period if only money remained in the country—a belief which recurred in literally the same form among prominent German economists during World War I, and in both cases was due to the confusion of real capital objects with money. For if money itself is "consumed", this simply means that it passes into someone else's possession, and this process may continue indefinitely. No elaborate explanation is required to show that things do not work out so favourably in the case of material objects which are employed in the upkeep of a prince's court, for the maintenance of soldiers, or for the manufacture of munitions.[9]

[9] Malynes, *Consvetudo, vel Lex Mercatoria*, Part II ch. 11 (1st ed. Lond. 1622, 335), cp. Part I ch. 5 and Part II ch. 2 (1st ed. 64, 266), and *Maintenance of Free Trade* (Lond. 1622) 98.—Misselden, *op. cit.* 116 f.—Child, *A New Discourse of Trade*, Preface (unpag.) and *A Discourse conc. Trade*, repr. in the previous work 15.—Petty, *Pol. Arithm.* ch. 6; *Quantulumcunque* Ques. 27 (Econ. Writings I 304, II 446).—Davenant, *Discourses on the Publick Revenues*, II 12, 23, 57, 96, 316.—Des Casaux du Hallay, merchant of Nantes, to the *contrôleur général* 1701 ("la disette présente des espèces et . . . le prix excessif qu'en retirent pour intérêt ceux qui le donnent dans le commerce"); the *contr. gén.* to the Intendant in Champagne 1706 ("chercher toutes sortes de voies pour rendre l'espèce plus commune dans le public, afin que, si l'on ne peut pas empêcher tout à fait ces usures, ou en diminue au moins le prix")—pr. *Correspondance des contrôleurs généraux*, ed. Boislisle II No. 332, 984.—Asgill, esp. Themes 10 & 12 (Reprints of Econ. Tracts, Balt. 1905, 19 ff.); cp. Defoe's enthusiastic

From the point of view of the relationship between money and capital there is no mercantilist author more interesting than John Locke. What places him in so unique a position is the fact that his philosophic training enabled him at times to attain a clarity of argument unparalleled among other mercantilist writers. At the same time, since his general outlook was mercantilist in every respect, one may obtain from him a clearer picture of this outlook than from any other writer, at least in those matters with which he deals. The contrast between Locke and his younger contemporary, Davenant, is, in this respect, particularly marked. The latter was confused and inconsistent, partly perhaps just because he was far more open to post-mercantilist ideas than Locke. One of the two points which Locke discusses, with a lucidity unexcelled in mercantilist illustration, is precisely the relation of money to capital. He was a devastating critic of the demand for a maximum rate of interest, which had its most talented advocate in his contemporary Child. This illustrates afresh the fundamental agreement in outlook, even where there were great differences in practical demands. The same situation reappears in the case of John Law; for in spite of the temperamental differences between Law and Locke, between the daring speculator and the staid scholar, and in spite of the criticism levelled by Law against the famous philosopher, he was yet powerfully influenced by Locke, and not least, on this particular point, by Locke's ideas on money.

The point of departure in Locke's argument was the identity of capital and money, and this conception persists throughout Locke's book from the first page to the last. "The natural Value of Money," he wrote, "as it is apt to yield such an yearly Income by *Interest*, depends on the whole quantity of the then passing Money of the Kingdom, in proportion to the whole Trade of the

judgment (*An Essay upon Projects*, Lond. 1697, 67), which does not by any means stand alone: "Mr. John Asgill . . . in a small tract entitled . . . has so distinctly handled this very Case [a bank founded upon land as security] with such strength of Argument, such clearness of Reason, such a Judgment, and such a Style, as all the Ingenious part of the World must acknowledge themselves extremely Oblig'd to him for that Piece." For the sake of completeness, I might add that Asgill did *not* mean what a modern economist would tend to read into his argument, i.e. that the rate of capitalization (the inverted rate of interest) becomes infinitely high if the rate of interest falls to zero.—S[chrötter] ch. 7 § 7 (1st ed. 68).—Comparisons between natural and artificial wealth in the above sense to be found, e.g., in *A Discourse of Money* (Lond. 1696) 21, ascribed on very dubious grounds to J. Briscoe.—Laspeyres, *Gesch. d. volksw. Anschauungen der Niederländer* 138.—For modern parallels, see my book *Världskrigets ekonomi* (Sthlm. 1915) 153.

Kingdom, (i.e.) the general Vent of all the Commodities." The rate of interest, in other words, is determined by the amount of money which, according to Locke, determined the value of money or the level of prices. "In Money there is a double Value," he says at another point, ". . . as it is capable [first] by its Interest to yield us such an yearly Income; and in this it has the Nature of Land, the Income of one being called Rent, of the other, Use"; secondly, "Money has a Value, as it is capable by Exchange to procure us the Necessities or Conveniences of Life; and in this it has the Nature of a Commodity". Here there is no possible ambiguity that money is considered *partly*, to use modern terminology, a factor of production, on the same footing as land and, like land, capable of yielding an annual profit, and *partly* a general means of exchange. With perfect consistency, Locke concluded his refutation of the arguments in favour of a maximum rate of interest in the following terms: "All the imaginable ways of increasing Money in any Country are these two: Either to dig it in Mines of our own, or to get it from our Neighbours. That 4 per cent is not of the nature of the *Devising-rod* [divining-rod], or *Virgula Divina*, able to discover Mines of Gold and Silver, I believe will easily be granted me. The way of getting from Foreigners, is either by force, borrowing, or Trade"—and since 4 per cent did not possess this power either, he considered his thesis proved. Locke's argument would be irrefutable if capital really were synonymous with money, and interest with the price for the loan of money; as this is not so, it is entirely irrelevant.[10]

On its own assumptions, the mercantilist argument was thus applied with perfect clarity, so far as it went, and the reasons for the increase in the stock of money satisfactorily given. If a greater quantity of money was to have the same importance for the economic life of a country as an increased amount of land or other natural materials, then obviously no further proof was required as to its desirability. The wealth of society obviously grew, in that case, with the quantity of money. But if further proof of his conception was nevertheless required, a very powerful proof was to be found in the belief that in this way the high rate of interest, which was universally attacked, could be lowered, even though interest as such had already proved ineradicable. Of course, if asked point-blank, the mercantilists would certainly not have said that money could produce commodities in the same way as land could. They merely omitted to carry their ideas to their logical conclusion and thus acquired what

[10] Locke (see above, note 7) 49, 52, 71 f., 128.—On Law, see below esp. 251.

was in their eyes an unshakable support for their monetary policy.

By considering the matter from a point of view opposite to that of most mercantilist writers, and further illustrating this mercantilist ideology in the sphere of money, it is possible to obtain an even clearer impression of how deeply rooted these notions were. An opportunity for doing this is provided by Johann Joachim Becher, the most original thinker among German mercantilists and the most remarkable personality in the whole of the economic literature of that time. In striking contrast with the best known among the English writers, who were sober men of business, Becher was a surgeon, chemist, and alchemist, inexhaustible in his supply of invective against his adversaries, a projector, a dreamer and a fanatic all combined. He would sometimes let fly at princes, whose good favour he nevertheless curried, and at other times would even direct scathing attacks on the practical aims of the mercantilist system itself, employing arguments that were surprisingly revolutionary for the 17th century. In 1668 he brought out his most famous work, which later went through a number of editions, the *Politische Discurs von den eigentlichen Ursachen des Auff- und Abnehmens der Städt, Länder und Republicken*, setting forth, in the main, orthodox mercantilist views. A short while later, in 1669, he published an extremeiy peculiar little book of an entirely different nature called *Moral Discurs von den eigentlichen Ursachen des Glücks und Unglücks*, which was completely overlooked by his contemporaries. There followed in 1678 his *Psychosophia oder Seelen-Weisheit*, a book similar in character, but somewhat wider in scope. In both the latter, Becher put forward ideals of a semi-Rousseauesque, and at the same time communist complexion, long before Rousseau was born. In them he broke a lance with the problems of practical mercantilism, not only as regards the princes' craving for money revenues, but also as regards their endeavours to increase the quantity of money. From our point of view, the important thing is that these very heresies concerning practical policy prove quite clearly that even Becher regarded economic affairs in no way different from his contemporaries. He reproduced the universally held beliefs, but in a so to speak inverted form.

Like many another Utopian, Becher regarded money itself as the primary evil. "Thus it is money's father who tyrannises the world and it happens that he becomes great and owns slaves; many thousands of unfortunate people must suffer under the spectre of money. For if there were no money it could not but

follow that we should all be equal and happy." "Money is the
cause of all idleness and slavery. He who has money will not work,
but pays for work. . . . Contrariwise he who has no money,
therefore becomes a slave. . . . Thus is money the mainspring
and source of all sloth, slavery and many other attendant evils."
If money (or its currency) were abolished, "all would then become
equal, and no one would any longer wish to serve another but
all would have to work". Labour would take the place of money,
a thing which everyone could possess and he who had not such
money might well be despised. What Becher calls money in these
passages quoted from the *Moral Discurs* was clearly capital. Any
possible doubt may be allayed by the interesting comparison of
this passage with an idea taken from his conception of a Utopia
(elaborated in detail in his *Psychosophia*). "A stock of money,"
he says, "must be accumulated to make a start during one or two
years."

What he evidently means by this is that his Utopian society
would have to live during its early years from an accumulated
stock, before communistic production had gathered steam. Money
as a means of exchange was no more necessary at the beginning
than later. It is likewise evident that the nature, and even the
existence, of means of exchange must have been altogether irrelevant with regard to the possibility of living without work, which
was precisely the state of affairs which Becher wanted to abolish;
this is most easily seen from the fact that slavery was anything but
a creation of an economy of exchange. What Becher intended was
to do away with capital and thus remove any possibility of
unearned income, and this he meant to bring about by abolishing
money. His bitter criticism of society, therefore, contains precisely
the same theoretical conception as that to be found in the
respectable bourgeois mercantilists, who were in complete
harmony with those social principles of the 17th century that
Becher turned against. The contrast in social ideals thus did
not prevent complete agreement in theoretical outlook.[11]

The identification of money and capital is very closely related
to the identification of money and income, that is the belief that

[11] Becher, *Moral Discurs* (Frankf. a. M. 1669) 150 f., 157–60; *Psychosophia*,
Ques. 116 (2nd ed. undated, 111 f.). Of the former, which is said to be very
rare, one copy is to be found in the Royal Library at Stockholm, unfortunately
without the name of its former possessor. It must be emphasized that these
books do not at all owe their importance to their influence upon contemporary thought, for that was probably nil, but to the light they throw upon the
workings of the mind of one of the foremost mercantilist writers.

income consists in money because it is expressed in money. This belief was only to be expected, but it was pregnant with consequences.

Less of it is to be found, perhaps, in Petty's writings than in those of any other mercantilist. That he was able to steer clear of the belief was undoubtedly due to the methods of his political arithmetic. They led him to emphasize, in the earlier of his two treatises on Ireland (*Political Anatomy of Ireland*, written about 1671–73, published 1691), that money, in England just as in Ireland, was no more than a tenth part of the annual "expense", or what to-day would be called the annual revenue of the country. From this fact Petty drew two conclusions, firstly, that a doubling of "cash", by destroying half of the "wealth", was obviously bad economy; secondly, that both must increase in the same proportion. In this diagnosis only the substitution of wealth for "expense" (income) is unwarranted—otherwise it is quite consistent. But at least a few years earlier (in *Verbum Sapienti*, written in 1665, though published in the same year as the previous work) even Petty had shown a fairly strong inclination to identify money and income. For among the various and manifold virtues of money, he naïvely includes the following: "It beautifies the whole, although more especially the particular persons that have it in plenty." Since Petty could not possibly have meant that these fortunate beings adorned their persons with gold or silver coins like gypsies, he must obviously have been thinking of their money income; but that did not prevent the argument from being part of the discussion on the quantity of money in the country. The majority of mercantilists, however, obscured the facts to a much larger extent.

In evidence of this are the quotations from Becher, given above, as also Schrötter's conception of "capital"; for what Schrötter called capital was in fact more in the nature of income. Becher manifested the same confusion in another connection. In the latter part of his lifetime he attacked alchemy—though he still believed in its practicability—with the argument that nobody would make shoes or bake bread any longer if he were able to manufacture gold. A good parallel may be drawn in this connection to a later author, who was also preoccupied with the economic fundamentals of society but had totally different practical attitude. I refer to Mandeville, who, in explaining his charming notion that it was dangerous to give working people an opportunity for saving, said, "It would be easier . . . to live without money than without Poor, for who would do the work?"

That even money would not provide anything for the poor man to live on if all people abstained from working was a consideration which he, just as much as Becher, overlooked.

Of greater practical importance was the effect of this confusion, treated in Part II, on the principles of public finance, particularly with regard to the amount of money sufficient for the payment of taxes. Discussions on the point usually set out from the idea that in. drawing its revenues the crown distrained on a corresponding part of the quantity of money in the country. For this reason Clement Armstrong in the 1530's believed that just as much precious metal must be imported from abroad as the king wished to raise from the people. For the same reason Colbert in 1670 entered upon his lengthy disquisitions upon the relationship of the total amount of taxation to the quantity of money in circulation. And for the same reason, too, Davenant in 1698 considered it necessary to impose less heavy taxation on outlying English counties, because money in his opinion was accumulating in London. It is not difficult to see how the perpetually impecunious governments during the period of mercantilism must have been led by such notions into directing their policy to the gaining of as large as possible a store of the precious metals as a necessary condition for an increase in revenue; Colbert's endeavours in that direction have been noticed in the second part.

These views of the politicians had some reality behind them, more particularly because of the difficulty in some countries of collecting taxes in money instead of in kind. To the extent that this was the case, the problem belongs to the next chapter.

The conception is illustrated still further from a new and theoretically very instructive angle by the mercantilists' belief that whenever money changes hands it creates *new* income. Schrötter was expressing a generally accepted mercantilist idea in particularly clear terms when he wrote: "The more a manufacture causes money to pass from one hand to another (which we call exchange) the more useful it is to the country, for so many people does it maintain", or in another passage: "Through the exchange of money the sustenance of so many people is multiplied." Schrötter thus believed that, because every time money changed its owner it represented one income after another, it itself was what provided sustenance in proportion to the number of hands through which it passed. In this he expressed one aspect of the deep-rooted belief in the "utility of luxury" and the evil of thrift. Thrift, in fact, was regarded as the cause of unemployment, and for two reasons: in the first place, because real income was believed to diminish by the amount of money which did not enter into exchange, and secondly, because saving was believed to withdraw money from circulation—this latter point of view is not discussed here. It was thus perfectly consistent of Schrötter to head his sixth chapter *"How a prince should limit his thrift"*. In 1695 the same argument was put forward by Cary with even greater clarity, if that were possible. He stated that if everybody spent more, all would obtain larger incomes "and might then live more plentifully". There then arose, in his opinion, a "flux of wealth", "causing variety of Fashions, which add Wings to Men's Inventions".[12]

What this shows is what would naturally be expected, although it is not in general emphasized. The root of the customary mercantilist outlook was not grounded specifically in the identification of money and capital, but *throughout* in an entirely explicable, though no less fateful difficulty of distinguishing between Juno and the cloud, between money and what money represented.

6. THE ACCUMULATION OF TREASURE[13]

Apart from the many possibilities, treated above, of confusing money with what it represented—apart, too, from its function as a means of exchange, treated in the next chapter—a third reason for the interest in money and precious metals may be considered, namely their use as treasure in the literal sense of a stock of valuable,

[12] Petty, *Pol. Anat. of Irel.* ch. 11; *Verbum Sapienti* ch. 5 (Econ. Writings I 192 f., 113).—Becher, *Psychosophia*, Ques. 118 (p. 126).—Mandeville, Remark Q (I 193 f.).—[Armstrong], ed. Pauli 61, 67, ed. *Tudor Econ. Docs.* III 115, 120.—Colbert: see above 47 f.—Davenant, *Discourses* I 52 f., 59, 238.—S[chrötter] ch. 6 and 17 §§ 6, 11 (1st ed. 58, 111, 115).—Cary, *An Essay on the State of England, in relation to Its Trade*, etc. (Lond. 1695) 148 ff.—It would be tempting to take up in this connection the distinction between "investment" and "saving", so much discussed during the great depression of 1929/33. But this would take me too far afield, and it does not appear to be necessary. Even if the explanations given along these lines have been correct with regard to present-day difficulties, I do not think that they would cover any important part of mercantilist views and facts. That "panics" and credit dislocations may have had something to do with the way of looking at money in the 17th century is pointed out in the next chapter (*v.i.* 222 f.); but the fundamental unity in mercantilist doctrine during a long period clearly points to an explanation unconnected with occasional occurrences.

[13] This section has been re-arranged and partially revised from the first edition. In general, reference should be made to Viner, *op. cit.*, 22–25, and 45–51, which includes many quotations which, for reasons of space, cannot be given here. There appears to be no fundamental difference between our interpretations.

easily saleable objects, primarily kept with the intention of using them in exchange for indispensable commodities in times of crisis. It might be expected that this idea represented an important motive in mercantilist monetary policy, but in fact this was not so, not, at least, as a basic principle. The relationship is not entirely simple, and complete consistency is to be found neither in the realm of practical policy nor in theoretical discussion. The general tendency among the more discerning of the seventeenth century mercantilists seems fairly clear, however, and can best be seen by examining their general conception of money. If we do this the subject takes on a new and a somewhat unexpected appearance.

At the outset it might be wondered whether states showed any interest in the accumulation of treasure, with the prime objective of preparedness in case of war. When it is remembered that at the beginning of World War I the German *Reich* had accumulated a war-chest of 205 million marks in Spandau, and that the gold reserves of the central banks of both France and Russia were looked upon primarily as war-chests, it would seem natural to expect that great importance would have been given to such accumulations in the warlike seventeenth century.

If one examines the policy actually pursued, however, it appears that this consideration was either insignificant or entirely non-existent during the heyday of mercantilism. It was found at the end of the Middle Ages and only sporadically during the 16th and early 17th centuries, even in economically well-developed countries, in particular in Italy. Pope Sixtus V, for example, accumulated a great war treasure in the Papal States, which disappeared nevertheless within a year of his death—a common fate for such accumulations. At the beginning of the next century, traces of such a policy make their appearance in France under Henry IV and Sully. During the following period, however, no such accumulation of state treasure existed in either France or England. The countries where such accumulation did take place were of no significance in the development of the main doctrines of mercantilism, and their methods of national finance were medieval rather than mercantilist in character. Examples of such countries are Sweden under Charles XI, whose treasure met the same fate as that of Sixtus V, and more particularly, Prussia under Frederick William I, though in this case after the period here considered. Thus, whatever may have been the extent of the mercantilists' interest in war treasure, clearly this interest led to no results worthy of mention.

It might also be expected that precious metals fulfilled another function in the hands of the state, namely, to provide reserves in the modern sense, without any regard for the purposes of war. In the mercantilist period, the most obvious use for such accumulations might well have been to provide for needs arising out of crop failure, other occasional import needs, or to cover a temporary decline in exports. This possibility is mentioned in the literature, as will be seen, but I do not know of any practical application of this idea.

There is thus but little to be said about the actual practice of accumulating treasure. The treatment of the subject in the literature is considerably more interesting, although it should be noted that it figures more prominently there than ever it did in reality.

The Renaissance exponents of the art of statecraft, like the Scholastics before them, looked upon the accumulation of treasure by a prince as a sign of financial strength. The German political theorists of the 16th and early 17th centuries—Bornitz, Besold, Faust, Klock, Obrecht, and others—devoted a major part of their interest to a "treasure chamber" (*aerarium*). The German Cameralists were appropriately named; their interests lay primarily in the strengthening of the prince's *camera*, but as far as I know, this interest was not in treasure in precisely the meaning used here. Even if it had been, it was not an interest which greatly affected developments in western Europe which are my chief concern here.

One of the first expressions of these ideas is found in the work ascribed to Hales, *A Discourse of the Common Weal*. A marginal sub-heading summarizes his views: "A prince ought to have great treasure, or else his subjects, against all events". The text then continues as follows: "for if we should have wars or dearth, as we have had, and should need either artillery (munitions) or other aid of strangers, it is not the coin we have now could provide us that. And so likewise, if we should have great scarcity of corn within the realm.... Then our commodities were not able in a notable scarcity to contervalue it, sithe now in plenteous years it doth bring in but scant enough of things necessary. Then if both war and dearth should come together, as it hath ere this, how should we do? Surely we should be in a very hard case, and much in danger of strangers. On the other side, if there were some store of treasures within the Realm, though there should happen to be both wars and dearth, yet we should be able to abide them for a year or ij or iij; for I had as lief a thousand men had in a dear year £100,000 among them in good coin as a thousand barns full of corn worth a hundred pounds a piece; for the money would fetch as much corn as all the barns would come to. And money is, as it were, a storehouse of any commodity you would have." Here was a clear reference to a cash reserve for unforeseen needs—peaceful needs.

During the 17th century, however, writers who took this attitude were few and far between. Apart from one French writer, there are in fact only two deserving of our close attention, both of them leading mercantilist authors—Mun and Petty.

Several short chapters were devoted to the question of state treasure by Thomas Mun in his second and most famous work, in which he dwelt upon the evils that lay in store for a prince who neglected his duty in this respect. In Mun's opinion £700,000 ought to be set aside annually "to make the Kingdom exceedingly rich and powerful in short time". At the same time, his main view was that the increase of treasure should never exceed the amount of precious metal which flowed into the country as a result of an excess of commodity exports. In his discussion thereof, he refers with considerable realism to the material resources a prince might use to serve the ends of war—and to some extent—of peace as well. His discussion deserves to be quoted *in extenso* on this point:

"Neither are all the advances of Princes strictly tied to be massed up in treasure, for they have other no less necessary and profitable wayes to make them rich and powerfull, by issuing out continually a great part of the mony of their yearly Incomes to their Subjects from whom it was first taken; namely, by employing them to make Ships of War, with all the provisions thereunto belonging, to build and repair Forts, to buy and store up Corn in the Granaries of each Province for a years use (at least) aforehand, to serve in occasion of Dearth, which cannot be neglected by a State but with great danger, to erect Banks with their money for the encrease of their subjects trade, to maintain in their pay, Collonels, Captains, Souldiers, Commanders, Mariners, and others, both by Sea and Land, with good discipline, to fill their Store-houses (in sundry strong places) and to abound in Gunpowder, Brimstone, Saltpeter, Shot, Ordnance, Musquets, Swords, Pikes, Armours, Horses, and in many other such like Provisions fitting War;...".

On the following page Mun continues in the same vein: "for although *Treasure is said to be the sinews of the War*, yet this is so because it doth provide, unite and move the power of men, victuals, and munition where and when the cause doth require; but if these things be wanting in due time, what shall we then do with our mony?" This is far from being a defence of war treasure, and it may be asked why such preparations for defence ought first to be emphasized when treasure would otherwise exceed the inflow of precious metals.

Petty explained the need for precious metals for purposes of protection in general with an argument he never tired of repeating, that ordinary goods were wealth merely *"pro hinc et nunc"*, since their value was entirely limited to the time and place in which they existed. Money, on the other hand, was "universal wealth". Another point of view was of greater importance for him, however, namely that a country could just as well have too much as too little money. Since he held fast to his demand for an excess of imports of precious metals, the question was where this excess should go if it were not to go into circulation. Accumulation by the state was thus a remedy, although the small significance Petty allotted this method is seen from his advice at another point that the heaviest coins be melted down and made into plate and gold and silver vessels. This advice did not spring from any real interest in the building up of reserves in the form of precious metals. It must be stressed that here, as so often elsewhere, the mercantilist authors were governed by purely theoretical considerations; they felt the necessity of following their reasoning to its logical conclusion, rather than of accounting for existing practices which they observed. This was the case with Petty in particular, for whom personal interest clearly played no part; it can hardly be maintained that his standpoint was based on the observation that there existed insufficient gold and silver plate.

There were, of course, writers who with greater or lesser reservation condemned the idea of accumulating treasure. A French contemporary of Mun, Scipion de Gramont, who certainly attracted no attention in his own time, discussed the reasons for the disappearance of gold and silver in *Le denier royal* (1620). He pointed to the accumulation of treasure by princes, which he maintained "marvelously impoverishes a kingdom", but he was able to favour—for some unstated reason—the accumulation of a state treasure by France. Among the Austrian authors, Hörnigk and Schrötter dealt explicitly with the question, though to some extent in a purely negative fashion. Schrötter, for example, employed the usual mercantilist arguments in drawing a lurid picture of how the country's monetary circulation would be depleted of all its money through a greatly increased state treasure —which strictly speaking is a correct assertion *if* one could assume that the fall in prices thus occasioned would not have repercussions on the international movement of precious metals; but we return to this in Chapter IV. Schrötter also drew a perfectly logical parallel between the accumulation of treasure by the monasteries and the export surplus of precious metals, which was indeed the worst eventuality he could imagine. Davenant explained the extreme poverty of many Eastern nations—which were believed to have more gold and silver than any other countries in the world—by the fact that treasure "was suffered to stagnate in the Princes' Coffers".

If the accumulation of treasure by the state was viewed with more suspicion than sympathy, it goes almost without saying that private hoarding was to be shunned like the plague. There were some exceptions, however. The anonymous pamphlet contemporary with that of Hales', called *Policies to Reduce this Realme of Englande vnto a Prosperus Wealthe and Estate* (1549) states that the silver plate owned by the "very Riche" made a good reserve for wartime, in that it might provide a "Subsidie for the mentenaunce of the warres" without "eney grouchinge" of parliament. It was more common to view this kind of accumulation as a means of preventing precious metals from flowing out of the country, but this was only the lesser of two evils. So wrote the defender of the East India Company, Misselden (1622), noting that too much silver plate would necessarily create a shortage of money, but that this was better, nevertheless, than an outflow of coins from the country.

Ordinarily there was no question about condemning such dissipation of money. Laffemas, Henry IV's tailor and economic advisor, considered gold and silver ornaments, along with imports of foreign goods, as the reason for the country's ruin, and deprecated the misers who "shut in their treasures" (1598). In one of his proposals for legislation can be found a paragraph prohibiting gold and silver ornaments "in order to enhance the quantity of *coined* gold and silver" (1601). During the alleged "scarcity of money" in England after the failure of the new Merchant Adventurers Company under James I (1620-23), the House of Commons vented its wrath on those whom it thought responsible through excessive use of silver plate. It was said that even "gentlefolk of ordinary fashion" had begun to use these articles. The alleged dearth of money and coin was offered by the government as an excuse for granting a monopoly for the production of silver and gold thread. It is significant that so eager an advocate of the utility of luxury as Fortrey (*England's Interest and Improvement,* 1663) made an exception with respect to commodities containing much gold, silver or silk, "whereby the public treasure is wasted and lost". The same intention lay behind Colbert's contemporary measures against the melting down of coins into silver plate. Thus the overwhelming desire for an import surplus of precious metals was obviously not occasioned by a desire for silver ornaments, gold and silver thread, or the like. When the conversion of coin into plate was recommended in exceptional cases, there was some specific reason for it, as has been shown in the examples of Misselden and Petty.

In the main, then, it would be following a false scent to seek any fundamental explanation for the mercantilists' eagerness for an import surplus in the desire for accumulation of state treasure. Indeed, such accumulation was not generally even considered desirable. As has been shown here, expressed by the conscious motives of the mercantilists, the primary explanation consists of their eagerness for *circulation of money*. According to Schrötter, the prince should refrain from "attacking the country's capital and seizing a part of it for his treasure". Among the educated in western Europe, the notion that anything was to be gained by sitting like some surly dragon glowering over one's treasure was losing favour. In all probability this was the most important of the more or less conscious motives lying behind the phraseology of the day. The ideals of the time were life and movement, trade and shipping; the precious metals would come as a result, but at the same time would serve these ideals. There was no place in such a *Weltanschauung* for the accumulation of treasure. It was well put by Hugh Chamberlen (1696), as quoted by Viner: "Money is living riches, plate but dead; that being capable of turning and improving trade when this is not." It was not accumulated treasure the mercantilists had in mind when they made their innumerable references to "the sinews of war", or when Hobbes (1651) called it the means whereby states stretch their arms into foreign lands, although at times it is tempting to believe so. The opinion undoubtedly was that an abundant circulation would serve to make payments necessitated by war or other unforeseen occurrences, but I am not aware of any analysis of this relationship. Neither am I cognizant of any interest in the practical use of money or precious metal for definitive export—that is, for an export which was not expected to increase the quantity of money in the country in the final reckoning. Had the mercantilists been faced by the same situation as that confronting the belligerent continental states in 1914, it is quite certain that they also would have tried to prevent the export of precious metals as long as possible.

Thus inevitably one is referred to the function of money and precious metals *within* the mechanism of exchange as the decisive, conscious motive for the mercantilists' eagerness to increase the quantity in the country. The relationships between the monetary systems of different countries, that is, rates of exchange, are also a part of this consideration. In the sphere of exchanges, however, there is a further connection with that which has been discussed here: the role of precious metals in international payments. All of this belongs to the two chapters which follow.[14]

[14] War treasure: Ehrenberg, *Zeitalter der Fugger* I 15; my essay "De europeiska staternas finanser på Karl XII:s tid" in *Ekonomi och historia* (Sthlm. 1922) 105 ff.; Papal States: L. von Ranke, *Die römischen Päpste in den letzten vier Jahrhunderten*, 8th ed., I 302–6, II 134, 149; France: [V. de Forbonnais] *Recherches et considérations sur les finances de France depuis 1595 jusqu'en 1721* (Liège 1758) I 169–75 (on the years 1609/10), cf. G. Martin & M. Bezancon, *L'histoire du crédit en France sous la règne de Louis XIV* I (Paris 1913) 6; Prussia: Schmoller, *Umrisse und Untersuchungen* 174 ff.; see also A. Oncken, *Geschichte der Nationalökonomie* I (Lpz. 1902) 128.—Statements on war treasure, etc: K. Zielenziger, *Die alten deutschen Kameralisten* (Beitr. Z. Gesch. d. Nat. ökon., ed. K. Diehl, II, Jena 1914) 116 f., 124, 126, 128, 176 ff. *et passim*; [Hales], *Discourse of the Common Weal* (ed. Lamond) 113 f., cf. 72.—Mun, *Eng. Tr.* (ed. Ashley) 90 ff. *et passim*, quotations from 94 f.—Petty, *Econ. Writings* (ed. C. H. Hull) I 35 f., 119, 193, 259 f., 269, II 446.—S. de Gramont, *Le denier royal* (Paris 1620) 155–65.—[Schrötter] ch. 3 §§ 7–9, ch. 6 § 2, ch. 50 § 3 (1st ed.) 43–47, 60, 246 f.—Davenant, *Discourses* II 64.—*Policies* (*Tudor Econ. Docs.* III 324).—Misselden, *Free Trade or The Meanes to Make Trade Florish* (Lond. 1622) 11.—Laffemas, *Les trésors et richesses pour mettre l'Estat en splendeur* (Paris 1598) 5 f., 21; *La commission, édit et partie des memoires . . .* (Paris 1601) II 15.—Debates in the House of Commons, 1621: *Parliamentary History* I 1188 f., 1195 f.—English Proclamation of 1622: *Foedera* (ed. Rymer, 1st ed. XVII) 376 f.—Patent of the gold-wire drawers 1623: *Select Charters of Trading Companies* (ed. Carr) 122.—Fortrey, *England's Interest and Improvement* 26 (Repr. of Econ. Tracts 27).—*Lettres de Colbert* VI 14.—Hobbes, *Leviathan*, Part 2 ch. 24 (1st ed. 1651) 130; (ed. A. R. Waller, Cambr. 1904) 180.—See also the quotation from Hörnigk at the beginning of the next chapter.

III

THE MECHANISM OF EXCHANGE

1. THE IMPORTANCE OF CIRCULATION. NATURAL AND MONEY ECONOMY

"Gold and silver, once they are in the country, whether of native origin or whether brought from abroad by industry, is in no manner of ways to be taken out again, be it for what it will and be there as much as possible, nor should it be buried in chests and coffers, but *always to remain in circulation*; neither should it pass much into such manufacture where it is immediately destroyed and not brought back into use. For in such a case it is impossible that a country, once provided with a considerable ready money (Barschaft), least of all if it does possess gold and silver mines of its own, should become poor; indeed, as regards the latter, impossible that it should not continually wax in wealth and property."

This "fourth rule" (1684) of von Hörnigk provides a concentrated expression of the practical monetary programme of mercantilism, with the circulation aspect (my italics) at the heart of the whole conception. One cannot possibly overrate the importance of the circulation of money in the ideology of the mercantilists; it would be easy to fill many pages with illustrations of the point. It may be sufficient, however, merely to give some particularly typical quotations.

The comparison of money with blood was current even long before the circulation of blood was discovered and before Hobbes (1651) had made the comparison popular. It occurred in the 16th century; thereafter Malynes, for instance, with his traditional nature symbolism, compared money with the soul, which he localized in the blood: "For if Money be wanting," he observed, "Traffic doth decrease, although commodities be abundant and good cheap." In one of his famous essays ("Of Seditions and Troubles", written 1607-12, published 1625), Bacon made use of another and less poetic simile: "Money is like Muck, not good except it be spread." By money he meant here chiefly capital, which ought not to accumulate in the hands of a few people, but of course made no distinction between this and the means of payment. A practical application of this view, which Bacon would presumably not have sanctioned, is to be found in the suggestion of a French intendant a century later (1709). He recommended that Jews be favoured, giving as his reason that "since they possess neither [bought] offices, estates, houses or state bonds, it must necessarily happen that their money circulates in trade."

In a host of other observations, there was more direct reference to the means of payment. In the normal way, the discussion was dominated by the idea that money was inadequate for the number of transactions which had to be carried out, and that consequently unemployment and money scarcity resulted. Pamphlets of the *Britannia Languens* (1680) type were, of course, particularly full of complaints of this kind, but they were also to be found in pamphlets and essays of a superior kind. In an English instruction to a commission of trade of 1626, it was stated, for example, with regard to the import of money that it was "the principle thing whereof our kingdoms need", "for the ready balancing of commodities in Commerce between man and man". Petty, in 1662, emphasized that it would be a pity to have too small a quantity of money, for "the mischief thereof would be the doing of less work, which is the same as lessening the people, or their Art or Industry; for a hundred pound passing a hundred hands for Wages, causes a 10,000 pounds worth of Commodities to be produced, which hands would have been idle and useless, had there not been this continual motive to their employment". Many others after him were of the same mind, particularly John Law, who in this respect made history. Finally the notion was given its most balanced expression in one of the many attempts of Davenant to define the national wealth: "Numbers of Men, Industry, advantageous Situation, good Ports, Skill in Maritime Affairs, with a good annual Income from the Earth", he observed, "are true and lasting Riches to a Country; But to put a Value upon all this, and to put Life and Motion to the whole, there must be *a quick Stock running among the people*; and always where that Stock increases, the Nation grows Strong and Powerful" (1698).[1]

It is now our task to discover the motives behind this eager desire for money for purposes of circulation.

[1] Hörnigk, *Oesterreich über Alles* ch. 9 (Regensb. ed. 1723, 30). Hobbes, *Leviathan* 179 f.—(Regarding the comparison of money with the blood, see also, e.g., Harsin, *Doctrines monét. et fin. en France*—see above, Part 3, ch. 4, note 12—18, 54 and note 2).—Bacon, *Essays*, ed. Wright, 60.—Malynes, *Lex Mercatoria* Part 2, Introduction (1st ed. 253).—Intendant Saint-Contest to the contrôleur général (pr. *Corresp. d. contr. gén.*, ed. Boislisle, III, No. 539 note).— *Britannia Languens* Sect. 13 (1st ed. 224-30).—Instruction of 1626: pr. Cunningham II[3] App. C, 903.—Petty, *Treatise of Taxes* ch. 3 (Econ. Writings I 36).— Law, *Considérations* (see above, note 6 in ch. 2), ch. 2, 17 f., 23 f., *et passim.*— Davenant, *Discourses* (see above, note 5 in ch. 1) II 170; my italics.

In this connection, the fact that a greater diffusion of exchange (both between countries, by means of foreign trade, as well as within countries by means of the greater differentiation of production) meant a larger employment of means of exchange in general may have played a part. To my knowledge this argument never was brought forward, but unconsciously it may possibly have contributed.

Next, it is conceivable to find an explanation not in an extension of trade as such, but in an extension of that part of trade that made use of the definite kind of payment or means of exchange called money, i.e. that there ensued a quickening of the transition from natural to money economy. This has long been regarded as the chief explanation for the mercantilists' endeavours to increase the quantity of money in circulation, and from the theoretical point of view it is obviously a welcome interpretation. For to the extent that the increased quantity of money required was meant for a larger number of transactions, the transition to a more intensified money economy would be possible, theoretically speaking, without causing any undesirable decline in prices, and inversely an increase in the quantity of money was possible without raising prices. The same applied obviously to the explanation given in the previous paragraph, the increased number of transactions in general.

Although the theory is thus arranged in its most attractive form, it is rather more difficult to apply it to the relevant facts. The transition to a money economy never occurs at once, and can hardly be assigned to any definite period whatsoever. From the time when money came to be used at all until the present day, money economy and natural economy have existed side by side. In the most advanced of European countries, however, that is, Germany, France and England, the most important part of the change appears to have taken place in the latter part of the Middle Ages. For instance, barter is spoken of in the *Discourse of the Common Weal* (1549) as something prehistoric, and reference is made to Homer. Much of the transition to a money economy was thus considerably older than mercantilism, in the sense of a deliberate insistence upon increased circulation, though money economy paved the way for mercantilism as a system of protection, as shown in Part III. This is enough to show that the transition to money economy does not provide a major motive for the desire to increase the means of circulation. The fact that the need, in any case, was only seldom consciously felt may be seen in the fact that the idea played a very subordinate part in mercantilist literature and in mercantilist official state documents. At the most, one may perceive in this desire a "cunning of reason", serving ends which were hidden to the persons concerned.

Still, this motive was not entirely lacking, even in definite utterances. I refer primarily, in this connection, to the sphere of public finance. The princes were anxious to collect their taxes in money since they had to pay their debts in money, too; but it was difficult for the peasants to pay in money. The desire of Colbert and other mercantilist statesmen for a quantity of money which would facilitate the payment of taxes in money could, with some good will, be interpreted as though it were influenced implicitly by such considerations. But apart from this, there are convincing utterances in the same direction in at least *one* leading mercantilist, namely Becher.

Becher's views, in all his writings, revolved round the "turning into cash" (Versilbern) of the income of the inhabitants, to use a favourite expression of his own. This expression meant, partly, that sales in general were made easier, but partly, too, that taxes were raised in money. As in other connections, Becher's loyal writings were here distinguished from his revolutionary really only in their aims, not in the underlying theoretical construction. In his orthodox *Politische Discurs* (1667), he directed his criticism against the fact that the farmer was not enabled to "turn into cash" the little that he had, so that he could pay his burdensome taxes in money. Here these were taken for granted, and Becher's practical proposal was intended to facilitate their payment as well as money payments in general, by "a universal magazine and storehouse" in which the sales were to take place. In his revolutionary *Psychosophia* (1678), on the other hand, he attacked the heavy burden of monetary taxation and the lack of inclination on the part of great lords to accept payments in kind. And he gave this as the chief reason for abolishing the tyranny of money in general. The importance of facilitating the "turning into cash" must have made the old alchemist a trifle dubious about his own statement that work which produced something useful for one's fellow man is to be preferred to the same effort in alchemy, when he remembered what properties gold had: "It would turn out differently, if one were to estimate so highly the turnover and the turning into cash which is saved in the making of gold, for gold is immediately money."

It is therefore probable that the difficulty of money payments made itself strongly felt in Becher's world. Peculiarly enough, there is a witness to this of roughly the same period in Petty, although he belonged to an almost entirely different sphere, when he stated in his first book (1662) "the paying in kind . . . would lessen a considerable grievance to the poor people". Petty had just returned from nearly seven years in Ireland when he wrote this; it is very likely, therefore, that what he had in mind were Irish rather than English conditions. But various utterances point to the fact that some link did exist between mercantilism as a monetary system and the difficulties of the transition to a money economy, although it was apparently only very slender.[2]

It is certain that this is partly due to the fact that the link even in the prevailing economic conditions was different from what could be constructed theoretically. For the construction to have been based on the actual conditions of the mercantilist period, the increase in the quantity of money would have had to be sufficient precisely for a diffusion of the money economy without any increase in prices. But the influx of precious metals from the new world effected a great increase in the prices of most European countries, at the latest from the second half of the 16th century onwards. It is thus putting the cart before the horse to say that the development of money economy in the 16th century would have made it necessary to increase the quantity of money. On the contrary, a much greater development of money economy would have been necessary than actually took place if, having regard to the available quantity of money, an increase in prices was to have been prevented. Conditions changed in the 17th century and prices became relatively stable for the first time, and towards the end of the century a small fall in prices was presumably widespread. If at that time natural economy went back further, the situation may possibly have contributed to such observations as those of Becher and Petty. But for this very reason, the explanation has a very limited significance, because, as remarked above, the fundamentals of mercantilist doctrine were the same before, during, and after the great rise in prices.

2. SCARCITY OF MONEY

Apart from the need for money to ensure a transition to money economy without a resultant fall in prices, there was a sufficiency

[2] [Hales], *Discourse of the Common Weal*, ed. Lamond, 47 f., 72.—Becher, *Politische Discurs* Part 2 ch. 1, 18, 25 (2nd ed., 99 f., 108, 173, 238 ff., *et passim*); *Psychosophia* Questions 112, 119 (2nd ed. 97 f., 132).—Petty, *Treatise of Taxes* ch. 3 (Econ. Writings I 35).

of other phenomena which found expression in the form of a *scarcity of money*.

Many of the phenomena characterized as a money scarcity were far too vague, so that one cannot discern what reality if any there was in them. For example it was stated, time and again, that the strength of a country did not lie in armies and fleets, for these could make no move without money, which made the wheels go round. Such observations were at the most the result of observing that the state had to control the means for the provision of troops and the equipment of ships, without considering to what extent there arose thereby a need for money. A whole host of other phenomena characterized as need for money may be regarded as dealt with already, because in fact it was not money but capital that the writers had in mind; they can therefore be left entirely out of consideration here. An example of these is the constantly recurring case in which money scarcity was given as a cause of the high rate of interest.

The supply of capital in the form of credits could, however, exercise great repercussions on the monetary system in the true sense of the term, i.e. on the quantity and application of the means of payment, for the credits served as a means of payment or, if you will, determined the velocity of circulation or effectiveness of the current means of payment. This is by no means merely a modern phenomenon. During upheavals in economic life, in times of crises or panic, a sudden lack of confidence resulted in fewer credits, and thus led to difficulties which can be termed acute scarcity of money. In modern times Walter Bagehot, with his happy combination of practical experience and theoretical insight, has given what is perhaps the best description of these phenomena. He pointed out, moreover, that the only remedy once a crisis had set in was to grant unlimited credit, on sufficiently strict conditions, to all sound creditors, i.e. incidentally, to abolish eventually the restrictions on the quantity of means of payment. "A panic," he said, "is a species of neuralgia, and according to the rules of science you must not starve it" (1873). And in fact such upheavals and crises as took place in the period that followed this utterance, down to the outbreak of the Great War in 1914, were treated in this way. In the mercantilist period, especially in the 17th century, with its highly speculative trade and its unstable credit relations, there were sufficient of such crises in economic life, and so far it was only natural that complaints were heard regarding scarcity of money. It is by no means remarkable that this feeling of a lack of means of payment gave rise to a fear regarding the inadequacy of the stock of precious metals or metallic coins in a period when paper money and bank-notes were common in very few countries. To this extent theories were not far removed from the facts. But as regards the analysis of the causes of the actual state of affairs this was not so.

The best instance to my knowledge of a typically mercantilist discussion of a state of affairs of this kind is the debates in the English House of Commons concerning the scarcity of money, which occurred in 1621, when a serious depression had set in particularly in the cloth export. The conditions were described very clearly by one of the most influential members of parliament, Sir Edwin Sandys. He stated that the farmer and the artificer had to suffer almost everywhere, that looms were standing idle for want of money in the country, and that peasants were forced to repudiate their contracts, "not (thanks be to God) for want of fruits of the earth, but for want of money". The situation led to detailed enquiries into where the money could have got to, the want of which was felt so bitterly. Numerous attacks were directed against all persons who were supposed to have contributed either to an export (export surplus) of precious metals, or to their disappearance on account of corresponding activities within the country —the latter has already been touched upon in the previous chapter.

Still another factor contributed to the actual scarcity of money, namely the upheavals of the monetary system. It had always been difficult to discover the right amount of token coins to be circulated and created, and at times this resulted in an acute shortage of such coins. Moreover, bimetallism drove sometimes gold and sometimes silver coins out of the country. It is possible that the last named factor also contributed to the English crisis of 1620/21. Finally, we must add the almost insuperable difficulties arising out of the clipping and deterioration of the coins and the provision of means of payment for commerce during coinage changes. It is obvious that all this must have given rise to searching discussions. But it is remarkable that really only in the early period were they connected with a claim for an increase in precious metals, and even then they were frequently led to a demand for coinage depreciation or to other measures regarding coinage policy, rather than to real mercantilist proposals.

On the whole, it is a source of surprise that the scarcity of money in the material sense played so small a part in the principal mercantilist doctrines. Mun, who indeed was one of the chief exponents of these doctrines, published his pamphlet on the East Indian trade simultaneously with the above-mentioned deliberations of 1621 concerning the scarcity of money, and his reaction to them was to throw cold water on the whole idea. "Concerning the Evil or want of Silver," he said, "I think it hath been, and is a general disease of all Nations, and so will continue until the end of the world; for poor and rich complain, they never have enough. . . . Well, I hope it is but imagination maketh us sick, when all our hearts be sound and strong." It is true that Mun evidently wrote this passage with the direct intention of defending the East India Company against the charge that it had caused damage by its export of precious metal; and the same may be said to apply to Child when he expressed himself a half-century later in an equally superior manner in the matter of the scarcity of money. But if connected with the fact that mercantilist literature rarely referred to concrete events of the above kind when putting forward claims for an increased circulation, the utterances of Mun and Child, both protagonists of the mercantilist doctrines, together with what has been said above, indicate that these events played no essential motivating part in mercantilism as a monetary system, though their influence was not altogether absent.[3*]

3. THE QUANTITY THEORY. RISING PRICES

The most important explanation of the desire of the mercantilist to increase the quantity of money in circulation must be sought elsewhere. Apart from the more or less instinctive motives, three trains of thought may be distinguished which lead to the ultimate goal of the mercantilists: first, an identification of the quantity of money in circulation with money income, secondly, an interest in rising prices, and thirdly, preoccupation with the prices of other countries, i.e. with international exchange relationships. Of these three points of view, the first has already been treated in the immediately preceding chapter, and it only remains to deal with two others, primarily with rising prices.

Before investigating whether the mercantilists' desire to increase

[3] W. Bagehot, *Lombard Street*, esp. ch. 2, 7 (repr. in Works and Life, ed. R. Barrington, Lond. 1915, VI 41).—On the English "crises" of the 16th and 17th centuries esp. Scott, *Joint Stock Companies to 1720* I.—Debate of 1621 pr. in *Parliamentary History* I 1188 f., 1194–98 (Sandys' statement 1194); cf. Br. Suviranta, *The Theory of the Balance of Trade in England* (Helsinki 1923) 93.— Mun. *Discourse* 45.—Child (note 5 in ch. 1) Preface (unpag.), 167.—Cf. Adam Smith, *Wealth of Nations*, Bk. 4 ch.1 (ed. Cannan I 404).—See above II 214.
* See below II 367, Addendum §11.

the quantity of money was linked to the relationship between this quantity and price development, we must ask whether they saw any connection at all between the quantity of money and the price level. There is no doubt that they did. The quantity theory in its primitive form—i.e. prices determined by demand for goods on the part of the holders of money—is so simple an idea that it occurred at a very early date; the Roman jurist Paulus and later Copernicus are among the many who have been named as its originator. No more than the statesmen were the mercantilist authors in doubt as to the connection, even though, of course, they did not quite see its general significance nor recognize its implications.

Even as early as the Saxon coinage controversy around 1530, the opponents of depreciation put forward arguments reminiscent of the quantity theory. They refuted the assertion that a scarcity of money could exist simultaneously with an increase in the price of all other things (1530). They made, in fact, the drastic observation, "If there were no money in the country, goods would have to be cheap, for he who has no money seldom buys dear. And if there were no money in the country, nobody would seek to have goods." At a later date, after the middle of the 16th century, Bodin engaged in his famous polemic with Malestroit concerning the causes of the great rise in prices. He asserted "the chiefest and almost sole [cause] which no one has yet touched upon is the surplus of gold and silver" (1568). He soon had an English successor (1581) in the editor of the then thirty-year-old *Discourse of the Common Weal*.

In the 17th century, this outlook appears to have become universal. Malynes, for example, mentioned as the first characteristic of money the fact that a plentiful supply of it makes everything dear, and on the other hand, a scarcity of it brings about a fall in all prices. If all prices had risen, that in his opinion was due to the "Oceans of Monies" which had come from the West Indies; this "caused the measure to be made lesser, whereby the number did increase to make up the tale" (*A Treatise of the Canker of England's Common Wealth*, 1601, *Lex Mercatoria*, 1622). There is no need to prolong the list of instances, and we may therefore pass on directly to the last decade of the century.

Starting from the axiom that supply and demand determine price, Locke was led to assert that the value of money was determined solely by its quantity, because the demand for it is constant. He drew moreover the same conclusion as is drawn to-day in the saying that one penny would suffice to carry on the trade of

the world, when he stated, for example, " Any quantity of that
Money (if it were but so much that everybody might have some)
would serve to drive any proportion of Trade, whether more or
less, there being Counters enough to reckon by" (*Some Considerations of the Consequences of the Lowering of Interest*, 1691).[4]

It would therefore have been remarkable if mercantilists had
not recognized the connection between the increase in the quantity of money, which they desired to bring about, and the rise in
the price of goods.

This, of course, is not to say that they had necessarily an
accurate general conception of the factors determining the value
of money. In this respect the mercantilists displayed considerable
uncertainty and a lack of agreement among themselves. It was particularly common to overlook the significance of the velocity of
circulation. Occasionally, the identification of money and income,
as described in the previous chapter, led to the belief that every
piece of money represented an equally large income, thus making
national revenue and quantity of money synonymous terms.[5] Other
writers, and Petty in particular, were however perfectly clear in
their minds as to the unimportance of the quantity of money compared with income and property. But while in this case Petty's
political arithmetic came to his assistance, in another way it led
him sadly astray. It led him, in fact, to the notion expressed in the
quotation given above (218), that a fixed quantity of money
was necessary to give employment to the whole population.
Here was an error which must be regarded as typical of a purely
statistical approach without a sufficient background of economic
theory. The result was the same wherever the need for currency
was conceived quantitatively. This point of view obviously really
meant that the implications of the quantity theory were overlooked;
for if not, it would have been noticed that a smaller quantity of
money necessarily led to a lower level of prices all round, and
not to a complete shortage of money in one part of trade and
unaltered prices in all the rest. But on the other hand, a remark
such as Locke's, for instance, shows that some mercantilists

---

[4] *Drei Flugschriften* (note 2 in ch. 1) 99.—Bodin, *Discours* (note 2 in ch. 2)
unpag.—*Discourse of the Common Weal* 187.—Malynes, *Canker* (repr. *Tudor Econ.
Docs.* III 387); *Lex Mercatoria* Part 2 Introduction (1st ed. 253 f.).—Locke,
Considerations (see above, note 7 in ch. 2) 71, 75.—The question of *which* connection between the quantity of money and prices should represent a complete
quantity theory may be left out of account; it is purely a matter of definition.

[5] An unusually outspoken application of this attitude can be found in *A
Discourse of Money*, probably erroneously ascribed to J. Briscoe (Lond. 1696)
48–59.

were perfectly clear on this point. It is possible to obtain a clearer and more profound insight into their outlook by keeping to those who did think clearly on this point, or at least if we overlook the vagueness. In this way attention can be directed to the attitude of the mercantilists towards rising prices.

As pointed out above, the acceptance of the gospel of high prices without further refinement could not have been an easy task. The medieval ideal of plenty was tenacious, and implied that commodities should be "good cheap". Thus general price rises opened the flood gates to all manner of complaints. In the animated discussion on economic and social questions which took place in England toward the end of the reign of Henry VIII, and even more during the minority of his son, it was not easy to spread such a gospel. Nevertheless, the call for protection was strongly heard, and protectionist authors made desperate attempts to show that their demands for excluding foreign goods would lead to abundance, and above all, bring down the high prices. Among such writers were Armstrong (1535-36?), Thomas Starkey (*Dialogue between Cardinal Pole and Thomas Lupset*, 1538?) and the unknown author of *Policies to Reduce this Realme of Englande vnto a Prosperus Wealthe and Estate* (1549).[6]

Generally speaking, the first work to present a moderate mercantilist programme was one from the same year, ascribed to John Hales, *Discourse of the Common Weal of this Realm of England* (1549). Here the rise in prices was viewed, characteristically for this school, with unmistakable sympathy. It could even be maintained that the rise in prices was recommended; actually the mere tolerance of such a phenomenon was a *volte face* in view of the opposition general at the time. In such circumstances, it is in fact noteworthy that the suggestion that prices should fall was turned down. The same was the case with Bodin in his comment cited above (1568), and with the publisher of Hales' pamphlet (1581).[7]

The discussion of the 1620's between the defenders and the opponents of the East India Company is also of interest here. Gerard Malynes, who led the attack, had formulated his concise statement favouring the rise of prices in one of his earlier works, *Treatise of the Canker of England's Common Wealth* (1601): "the more ready money, either in specie or by exchange, that our merchants should make their return by, the more employment would they make upon our home commodities, advancing the price thereof,

[6] [Armstrong] (see above, note 2 in ch. 2) ed. Pauli 67–73, ed. *Tudor Econ. Docs.* III 120–25.—Starkey (see above, note 6 in ch. 2) 172–75 *et passim.*— *Polices*, ed. *Tudor Econ. Docs.* III 311-45, esp. 314, 331 ff. See above 153, 187 and below 238 and 243 ff.

which price would augment the quantity by setting more people on work." This was perhaps the first time that the claim that rising prices increase employment was ever clearly expressed.

In his *magnum opus*, *Lex Mercatoria* (1622), Malynes returned to the discussion of similar considerations in detail. He distinguished between two groups of commodities, those for "the back" and those for "the belly", and naturally it was the former which interested him most since they were proudly regarded as England's staple wares. "It is better," he wrote, "to pay somewhat more for commodities, than to have them altogether over cheap, especially for commodities serving the back, and not for the belly." Looking more closely at this distinction, one can say that a minor reservation was made for the medieval ideal of cheapness in the case of foodstuffs, while the gospel of high prices was accepted for English industrial products. Malynes continued: "For those countries where things are good cheap are destitute of trade, and want Monies; and although things for the belly are good cheap, there is less benefit to be made by Merchants", and thus brought the interests of the latter to the forefront. "Strive not to undersell others to the hurt of the Common-wealth, under the colour to increase trade: for trade doth not increase when commodities are good cheap, because the cheapness proceedeth of the small request and scarcity of money, which maketh things cheap: so that the contrary augmenteth trade, when there is plenty of money, and commodities become dearer being in request." For a writer as confused as Malynes usually was, this reasoning was uncommonly clear and consistent. More striking is the indication he gives that he could distinguish between a change in the general price level due to a change in the quantity of money, and changes in the price of a single commodity due to variations in supply and demand. It was the advantages in an increase in the general price level which he wanted to show, with only a minor reservation for the prices of foodstuffs.

These views certainly did not prevent him from pointing out the dangers of increasing prices when on other occasions there came a proposal he did not favour. Thus he wrote that depreciation of the currency "was to reform things by a Remedy worse than the disease; the inhauncing of our Moneys will increase the prices of all things". But here his foremost adversary, Misselden, did not fear the consequences and went a step further in this new direction by declaring: "all will be abundantly recompensed unto all in the Plenty of Money, and quickening of Trade in every man's hand. And that which is equal to all, when he that buys dear shall sell dear, cannot be said to be injurious to any." The essence of the new programme had thus become the harmlessness and the positive good in the rise in the general level of prices.[8]

From the following half-century comes what is probably the most concise expression of the gospel of high prices either at that time or later. It is found in the work of the then much-admired Samuel Fortrey, *England's Interest and Improvement* (1663): "And as for the raising of price and value of our lands, or of anything else that is our own; it is of so great an advantage, that *it might be wished, nothing were cheap amongst us but only money*" (my italics). By this reservation Fortrey presumably meant merely that the rate of interest should be low; if he had meant a low value of money, the consistency of his reasoning would have been so much the greater.

Five years later Child expressed himself in a similar vein, although less tersely: "Where-ever Provisions are for continuance of years *dear* in any Country, the People are *rich*; and where they are *most* cheap throughout the World, for the most part the people are very *poor*" (my italics). This view was the antithesis of the medieval conception on the essential topic of foodstuffs, and here Malynes' reservation had been given up entirely. A few years later (1671), an obscure but perhaps fairly typical little pamphlet, *The Use and Abuses of Money*, made a proposal which appeared frequently even after it was opposed by writers like Malynes. It proposed depreciation, and put forth the following argument: "If money be scarce, all things are the cheaper; if money be plenty, all things will afford the better price; or if they bear not a better price, there is a quicker return, which is answerable." That had been Misselden's argument fifty years earlier. A new and characteristic view followed: "Where Money is plenty, Workmen will be more plenty, and every one more industrious in applying himself to work; if so, it must needs follow a plenty of Workmen will cause a fall of their Prices." According to this, increasing commodity prices went together with decreasing money wages, and real wages would fall for two reasons: the rise in the price of commodities, and a greater supply of labour—and greater industriousness—which would directly force down money

[8] Malynes, *Canker* (*Tudor Econ. Docs.*) III 387, 399; *Lex Mercatoria*, Part I, ch. 8, 42, Part 2, Intro. (1st ed. 84, 89, 213, 253; distinction between changes in the general price level and changes in the price of particular commodities: "plenty of Money maketh generally *all things* dear, and scarcity of Money maketh generally things good cheap; whereas *particularly* commodities are also dear or good cheap, according to plenty or scarcity of the commodities themselves, and the use of them." (Italics mine); *The Center of the Circle of Commerce* (Lond. 1623) Dedication (unpag.).—Misselden, *Free Trade* (Lond. 1623) 106 f.—On the Dutch literature, Laspeyres 87.

wages. Even if this result was not the primary one intended, it is clear that the interest of employers in rising prices was well complemented.

The upward march of prices in England ceased during the latter part of the 17th century, but this called forth proposals and measures to work in the opposite direction. In the first place there was the demand just mentioned, "to raise the value of the coin", (as giving metal a higher value as coin was called) in short, depreciation. In England this demand was left unfulfilled, but the tendency to intensify protectionism became so much the stronger. The policy of tariff protection shifted largely to outright import prohibition; political tensions between France on one side, and England and the Netherlands on the other, played an important part in this. In England, where, unlike the continent, resort had not been made to depreciation, an almost complete break was made with the medieval policy of provision with respect to foodstuffs from abroad. After a short-lived attempt to subsidize the export of corn, the export premiums became a definite policy in the famous Corn Bounty Act in connection with the revolution of 1688/89. The change in domestic policy with regard to corn was not so abrupt, but it must nevertheless be maintained that England—quite by herself—had arrived at the opposite pole from the medieval policy of provision, and was to remain there. Support for the new policy, while presumably not unanimous, was certainly dominant.[9]

Becher's later, anti-money attitude (1669) throws a paradoxical light on even this aspect of mercantilist doctrine. He demonstrates how a social ideal completely opposed to that voiced by this English pamphlet of 1671, quoted above, could be reconciled with the same basic conception of money as was found there and in mercantilist literature generally. Becher frantically attacked money as such for its extreme, and allegedly inescapable, *rarity*. "They, then, who have not gold and silver are poor. I say they are poor, they suffer want and death, indeed, they lose heaven, because they cannot have a thing of which nature itself has given so little and yet the world wants so much." If a tyrant came and commanded that diamonds of a given weight, rarer yet than precious metals, should be used as money, "think you not that many thousands of people would die of hunger?" Even if one went

---

[9] Fortrey 13 (Repr. 19); for opinion on this pamphlet, see introduction to the modern edition.—Child 16.—*Use and Abuses of Money* (Lond. 1671) 4, 25 f.—See also Cary's statement, above 169 f.—Statutes: 25 Car. II c. 1 § 31 (1673), 1 W. & M. sess. 1, c. 12 (1689).—Gras, *Evolution of the English Corn Market* 144 f., 253 f.—Cf. above 94.

to the other extreme and made money of leather, shells, or the like, it would have to bear an impression, which would then be the source of the value; i.e., the scarcity would remain. *Ergo*: abolish money entirely, because in the prevailing degenerate state of society poverty resulted from lack of money, not lack of goods.[10]

4. INFLATION. PAPER MONEY MERCANTILISM

This aspect of mercantilism attained its zenith and then its demise in the eventful years between the revolution of 1688 and 1720, the year of Law's French Mississippi Fraud and the English South Sea Bubble. These events ushered in a new era. In Chapter VII of Part I we have shown the reaction on the development of joint stock companies. In the monetary sphere, the effects in France were so deterrent that it was not until the paper money system of the French Revolution that any change was made, for fear of risking a repetition of the same events. For mercantilism as a monetary system, the period 1689–1720 had a two-fold and very curious significance. On the one hand, it brought about both a theoretical and a practical application of the mercantilist thesis of the blessings of an increase in circulation. On the other hand, it also severed the connection between the two phenomena which mercantilists previously had never in practice distinguished : between the quantity of money and the quantity of the precious metals. Most of the practical conclusions of mercantilism had to be changed when an increase in the quantity of money was capable of being carried out *without* an import surplus of precious metals. But if, instead, such an attempt led to failure, this could only serve to strengthen the conviction regarding the necessity of a plentiful stock of precious metals at a time when the belief in the advantages of an increase in circulation remained unshaken, and money without a metallic basis had proved itself deceptive. Whether or not this contributed to the inner transformation and the ultimate death of mercantilism in the 18th century cannot now be determined; in any case that question does not belong to our present purpose. What is relevant here is to see the course of events in the light of previous developments.

The idea of covering the need for money without precious metals was by no means foreign to the mercantilists of the early 17th century. Both the Italian and the Dutch, and to a lesser degree the Hamburg, experience with bank money, played a role in this connection. General account appears to have been taken

[10] Becher, *Moral Discurs* 149 ff. In his unbounded hate for money, Becher was a product of the same spirit as the money-worshipping mercantilists.

of the fact that the banks of deposit or giro undertook credits of larger amounts than were accounted for by the silver deposited in them. Mun, who had spent some time in Italy and had been very impressed by what went on there, had already attacked the axiom that money is the soul of trade, in his most famous book (written presumably in the 1620's, but first published in 1664). In his opinion, the Italians had shown that they required but little money for their domestic transactions, "more than for their ordinary expenses". Mun described trade as financed there—by means of exchange transactions and banks in the form of "credits from one to another daily for very great sums with ease and satisfaction by writings only". Somewhat later (1641), Henry Robinson, too, referred to the banking system of Tuscany, and used it as a model for the bank he wanted to create, in addition to a currency of private bills, which would "add livelihood unto Trade, and encrease the stock of the Kingdom" (*England's Safety in Trades Encrease*). Still later (1650) a typical monetary crank, William Potter, proposed unlimited increase in bills or notes of a similar character, and argued elaborately that they would "perpetually" create a corresponding increase in every sort of resources as well as commodities and even, for some obscure reasons, an enormous *fall* in prices (*The Key of Wealth*).

For the time being, projects like those of Potter were of small importance. But writers of quite a different stamp carried on the discussions in the direction of non-metallic currency. Thus a previously quoted passage of Child's expressed the same view as that of Mun. A third authority of the time, Petty, also pointed out—this time following the Dutch practice—that it was possible to increase the quantity of money through the banks, who, in the view which he expressed on numerous occasions, were capable almost of doubling the efficiency of the coinage. He suggested a 50 per cent covering for bank notes, and thus wanted to maintain the quantity of money which he regarded as necessary for the country's requirements. On the continent, there was a general move towards banks. Schrötter, for example, had an extensive project for a so-called exchange bank, whereby the "capital" of a country was to be quadrupled; but none of these numerous writers came to the conclusion that the precious metals would thus be superfluous. More often, like Mun, they drew the inference that silver and gold could be reserved for foreign trade.[11]

[11] Mun, *Engl. Tr.* ch. 4 (ed. Ashley 23).—Robinson 34–37.—Potter 7 ff., 18 ff. *et passim.*—Child, see above 200.—Petty, *Treatise of Taxes* ch. 3; *Pol. Arith.* ch. 1; *Quantulumcunque* Qu. 26 (Econ. Writings I 36, 265, II 446).— S[chrötter], proposal as an appendix to ch. 81 (1st ed. 360–404).

In connection with the foundation and earliest development of the Bank of England (1694), there arose that school of fervent and indefatigable writers who wanted to bring about the wished-for increase in the quantity of money without being tied down to the precious metals, i.e. against security of lands. To them belonged the advocates of the notorious "land banks", Chamberlen, Asgill, Briscoe, and others. A close parallel to this was found in the other schemes for "mobilizing" property; that is to say, creating credit means of payment against the security of physical property of various kinds. The financing of trading companies through loans to the state of what the shareholders had subscribed as capital was the best example of this tendency. While their sporadic forerunners had only been symptomatic of the new approach, these views now attained significance.

The repercussions of these events on mercantilism as such provided the writers with plenty of food for thought, and in expressing their views they represented the most diversified standpoints. Several authors maintained unshaken their belief that gold and silver was the only key to happiness, and they feared that the money substitutes would drive the precious metals out of the country. The prolific Sir Francis Brewster may be quoted as representative of this conception (*New Essays on Trade*, 1702). Others, indeed, admitted that, for the time being, paper money could replace metallic money, but maintained that the latter was the only possible ultimate means of payment, especially during war-time. They discovered in this an argument against the permanent export of the precious metals as carried on by the East India Company. John Pollexfen, the pertinacious opponent of the company, for example, expressed himself in this direction (*A Discourse of Trade, Coyn, and Paper Credit*, 1697). But the result of this was not that the supporters of the company became, without further ado, agreeable to the idea of paper money. Davenant is of particular interest in this connection, as the chief author after Child from the camp of the company's supporters. As pointed out on several occasions above, he had the capacity of grasping fertile considerations of various origin, but was incapable of welding them into a consistent whole. It is therefore not surprising that he gives the strongest impression of mercantilism at the parting of the ways, between the belief in the precious metals and the belief in paper money. For this reason, the most important of his observations may be quoted (1698).

"Paper credit," Davenant wrote *inter alia*, "did not only supply the place of running Cash, but greatly multiplied the Kingdom's Stock. For Tallies and Bank Bills did to many uses serve as well, and to some better than Gold and Silver; and this Artificial Wealth . . . did make us less feel the Want of that real Treasure the War . . . had drawn out of the Nation." But, continued Davenant, the country did *not* grow richer as a consequence; it was only a pawning of its assets whereby their transformation into a "running Stock" came about. This mobility on the other hand, "did quicken" all trade and industry. Paper money was thus not wealth—which was what Davenant, for the moment, assumed of metallic money—but on the other hand it provided, at least as ably as the latter, the stimulating function which was the basic motive for the increase in circulation. However, Davenant was not quite certain even of the latter, for he proceeds immediately to say "Whether or no this was a right Condition of Health is hard to determine: Perhaps a Body-Politic, with this florid Complexion, might yet have lurking in it Apoplectic Symptoms." No better picture of inflation can be desired than is conjured up by the words "florid complexion" and "apoplectic symptoms", and the possible connection between inflation and paper circulation had thus become clear to Davenant even before the end of the 17th century. But with regard to the practical consequences of this, as he honestly recognized, he was uncertain. That it could have been the increase in circulation itself and not its paper money character which created this high complexion of the body politic, was obviously far from his mind. While he never broke with the fundamental conception of mercantilism with regard to money, at the same time he was very doubtful as to the possibility of a changed application of principles which the appearances of paper money opened up.

The man who took the decisive stride.towards paper money mercantilism, and was destined, after many unfortunate attempts, to apply his ideal in practice on a gigantic scale, was John Law. This is not to say that Law's approach was essentially different from that which the earlier representatives of paper money had said and desired. All he did was to express the doctrines of the new school with particular clarity, and he becomes of special interest because he later was able to translate his ideas into action.

It is not easy to give an accurate picture of the argument put forward by Law in his earliest work which, as a young man, he laid before the Scottish Parliament and also published in book form (*Considerations on Trade and Money*, 1705); much of it does not belong here at all. But Law's fundamental mercantilism and the breach which he constituted with the former mercantilist practice are clearly manifested therein.

The point of departure in Law's argument was an explicit and complete mercantilist recognition of money circulation as the animating principle of commerce. The circulation of money was decisive as regards employment and the growth of industry. Law asserted, for example, in close connection with what Brewster had said a few years previous, that England had never had sufficient money to employ the whole of its population. On the basis of this, he then erected his whole credit structure. He showed, in the first place, that only a shortage of money could destroy credit—what he said in this connection regarding the effect on the foreign exchanges must be postponed. He then said that it would be so much the better if the desired result could be obtained without increased use of metallic coin. The next step in his argument—and in this I do not keep to Law's own train of thought— was to refute the old mercantilist solutions. In doing so, Law attacked mercantilist commercial policy which, indeed, wanted to attain the end by the old method, that is, by an import surplus of precious metal. It is true that Law's criticism was not directed at this point, but merely wanted to demonstrate the impracticability of import prohibitions; but in any case, the point is significant of his breach with the old mercantilism. As a major factor in his argument there followed a detailed criticism of metallic coinage and credit money against the security of precious metals. As proof of the unsuitability of metallic coins he cited, among others, the fact that the demand for them had obviously fallen, since the rate of interest, the price for money, had fallen from 10 to 6 and further to 3 or 4 per cent! He thereupon put forward his plan for a paper currency against security of land. Such paper money was to be superior to the metallic coinage in every respect. The latter, according to the plan, was so far dethroned that the new notes were to represent in value *varying* quantities of gold and silver. Law declared that this was just as comprehensible as the fact that money, under the prevailing conditions, corresponded to varying quantites of all other goods, e.g. wine, and in this he was of course quite consistent. The new money, he said, could never fall in value, but the reasons he gave for this were not very clear and, for the rest, are irrelevant in this context. The point under consideration here is primarily that Law's work constituted, on the one side, a breach with the mercantilist attitude towards the precious metals, while starting, on the other side, from an almost fanatical belief in the fundamental mercantilist conception of money: that the size of the circulation was the predominating motive force of economic life.

The mercantilist idea of the stimulating effect on economic life of an increased quantity of money was, for the most part, correct, and incidentally a very important deduction. As pure deduction, the notion has only one weakness, though a very serious one: it did not distinguish between an increase in the quantity of money—which usually had the effects conceived—and the absolute quantity of money, which played no part whatsoever. Law's assertion that England had never had enough money for the whole of its population is an illustration of this. In the long run, the defect consisted in the fact that no question was asked whether and to what degree such stimulation of economic life was desirable, and, over a long period of time, possible.

David Hume, one of the most important of those who overthrew theoretical mercantilism, displays on this point a profound comprehension of the mercantilist outlook with regard to the effect of money circulation. His work, it is true, takes us considerably beyond the period which this part otherwise deals with. But one observation of his may be brought in as a conclusion of our description of this important and fascinating aspect of mercantilism as a monetary system. At least as a description, it epitomizes the best aspects of this in an incomparable manner. How far Hume's theoretical explanation is also relevant is not so clear. "In every kingdom," wrote Hume in his famous essay on money (*Essays, Moral, Political, Literary*: "Of Money", 1752), "into which money begins to flow in greater abundance than formerly, everything takes a new face: labour and industry gain life; the merchant becomes more enterprising the manufacturer more diligent and skilful and even the farmer follows his plough with greater alacrity and attention." Hume found the explanation in the fact that some time elapsed before the new money began to affect prices. The conclusion which he drew from this was that, "It is only in this interval or intermediate situation, between the acquisition of money and a rise of prices, that the increasing quantity of gold and silver is favourable to industry." On this Hume erected his conclusion, "It is of no manner of consequence, with regard to the domestic happiness of a state, whether money be in a greater or less quantity. The good policy of the magistrate consists only in keeping it, if possible still increasing; because by that means, he keeps alive a spirit of industry in the nation, and increases the stock of labour in which consists all real power and riches.

A nation, whose money decreases, is actually, at that time, weaker and more miserable than another nation, which possesses no more money, but is on the encreasing hand."[12]

By referring to "the *domestic* happiness of a state", Hume possibly wanted to point out that the problem was different in commercial relationships with other countries. At any rate, this was the opinion of the mercantilists. Further exposition of the point belongs to the next chapter.

[12] Brewster, 21, 38.—[Pollexfen] 66–78.—Davenant, *Discourses* II 162–71. —Law (note 6 in ch. 2) esp. ch. 2–5, 7–8 (French ed. 17 ff., 58 f., 66ff., 91–95, 105 f., 117, 156, 158, 166, 181, 183).—Hume *Essays* (ed. T. H. Green and T. H. Grose, Lond. 1875, New Impr., Lond. 1898, I 313 ff.; date given 285).—Viner (see above ch. 1 note 7) 292 refers to a precursor of Hume of 1697, J[ames] H[odges], one of the many advocates of depreciation ("raising the value of the coin"). In his fairly comprehensive book *The Present State of England, as to Coin and Publick Charges* (Lond. 1697) he carries on, in fact, in this strain, as, for example, in the following passages: "The raising of the Value of Money doth never immediately or suddenly occasion the raising of the Price of Commodities, but that always followeth at some distance and cometh on gradually" (126), "Dearness of Commodities on this account is a sign of the thriving and increase of Riches in any place where it is" (127). But I do not know that this work excited any interest amongst its contemporaries.—A peculiar inter-play of the various aspects of mercantilism was manifested in the treatment, on the part of the mother country, of the provision of money to the English colonies, as well as in the monetary policy of the colonies themselves. This is too specialized a point to be considered here, but the reader is referred to C. Nettels, "British Policy and Colonial Money Supply" (*Economic History Review* III, 1931, 219–45).

IV

THE EXCHANGE RELATIONSHIP WITH OTHER COUNTRIES

1. "SELLING CHEAP AND BUYING DEAR"

The mercantilists conception of the importance of the quantity of money with regard to the exchange relationship with other countries was a major cause for their desire for an abundant stock of the precious metals.

In the course of a century and a half this standpoint was formulated again and again in this way, that a country with relatively less money than other countries must "sell cheap and buy dear". Both from the theoretical and the practical point of view, this is of so much importance that it requires careful illustration.

Even in the original edition of the *Discourse of the Common Weal*, that is in the middle of the 16th century, this attitude was already manifested. Hales said, in fact, "And yet if strangers should be content to take but our wares for theirs, what should let them to advance the price of other things (meaning: among others, such as we buy from them), though ours were good cheap unto them? And then shall we be still losers, and they at the winning hand with us, while they sell dear and yet buy ours good cheap, and consequently enrich themselves and impoverish us. Yet had I rather advance our wares in price, as they advance theirs, as we now do; though some be losers thereby, and yet not so many as should be the other way." On this point he had the unqualified approval of his editor several decades later (1581). In the 17th century, this attitude recurred again without any fundamental change in significance. Thus, Malynes believed this unfortunate position to be the result of what he dreaded above all things, i.e. a foreign under-valuation of the English exchange. At other occasions the greatest stress was laid directly on the distribution of the quantity of money among countries as the cause for it. Malynes thus regarded it as dangerous if other countries obtained a more than proportionate share of the world's quantity of money in comparison with England, and considered this point of vital importance, in contrast to the absolute increase in the quantity of money. The same conception then recurred continually. In his *Verbum Sapienti* (written 1665, published 1691),

Petty believed that the violent efforts to increase the quantity of money could only cease "when we have certainly more money than any of our Neighbour States (though never so little), both in Arithmetical and Geometrical proportion". During the period between the writing and the publication of this work, Coke declared, "If our Treasure were more than our Neighbouring Nations, I did not care whether we had one fifth part of the Treasure we now have" (1675).[1] Most interesting of all, however, is Locke, for, as with the identification of money and capital, here too he reproduced the mercantilist point of view with peculiar clarity.

As quoted above (226), Locke arrived at the conclusion that any amount of money, be it of the smallest, would suffice for even the largest amount of trade. It might then have been expected that he had drawn one of these two conclusions: *either* that it was unnecessary to worry at all about obtaining enough money, *or* that a large quantity of money was desirable to bring about a rise in prices. Now the inflationist idea was absent in Locke, and so it appeared as though nothing else remained for him than to decide in favour of the first alternative, and thus to throw overboard entirely the whole mercantilist conception with regard to money. But Locke arrived at an entirely different result. The reason is that he took into consideration the prices of other countries. In fact, Locke declared that the above had only been a theoretical construction, for it applied only to an isolated country; to-day, however, countries were no longer isolated, but entered into commercial relations with one another. In these circumstances, the whole situation, in Locke's opinion, assumed a fundamentally different complexion. Locke was not alone in taking this stand; Pufendorf, for example, believed the same. But the peculiar thing about Locke is that he attempted a comprehensive theoretical explanation. His trend of argument was as follows.

The prices of the same things, expressed in gold and silver, must necessarily be the same in different countries. This would not occur if one country had a smaller stock of money than another. A country with a small stock of money was therefore faced, according to Locke, with an unwelcome choice: either to sell its

---

[1] [Hales], *Discourse of the Common Weal*, ed. Lamond, 47, 188.—Malynes, *Maintenance of Free Trade* 76, *Center of the Circle of Commerce* 49, *Canker* (in *Tudor Econ. Docs.* III 388); *Lex Mercatoria* Part 2 Introduction (1st ed. 254).— Petty, *Verbum Sap.* ch. 10 (Econ. Writings I 119).—Coke, *Treatise* III (note 6 in ch. 2) 45.—See above 22 f.

goods at lower prices or to lay up a large portion of its commerce; and not only that, but in addition to buy foreign goods at high prices. A small stock of money would thus lead to a two-fold loss in foreign trade, low export prices and high import prices. On the assumption that England had half the quantity of money that other places had, Locke summed up his conclusions as follows: "Such a state of poverty as this" (i.e. of money) "though it will make no scarcity of our Native Commodities amongst us, yet it will have these ill consequences, 1. It will make our Native Commodities vent very cheap. 2. It will make all Foreign Commodities very dear, both which will keep us Poor: for the Merchant making Silver and Gold his measure, and considering what the Foreign Commodity costs him (i.e. how many Ounces of Silver) in the country where Money is more Plenty, i.e. Cheaper . . . will not part with it here, but for the same quantity of Silver . . . so that . . . we shall pay double the Value that any other Country does, where Money is in greater Plenty." With this were bound up other lesser disadvantages. Locke thus created a foundation upon which he was able to erect the whole mercantilist programme and to put forward a complete catalogue of dangers which arose inevitably if this programme were not carried out. Thus it would be to the detriment of agriculture if the decay of commerce led to the export of half the quantity of money. The rents drawn from agriculture would fall, until a general prosperity "shall restore to the Kingdom the Riches and Wealth it had formerly". In many places Locke says that a country would become very much poorer through an import surplus, and very much richer through an export surplus. He thus omits no tenet of the entire mercantilist creed.

One should assume that this argument could easily have been met with the following question: if prices in other countries were in general twice as high as those in England, as a result of the larger quantity of money, why should that not apply also to the English export goods, making these sell just as dear abroad as the native goods of the foreign country? and why could not the foreign goods be sold just as cheap in England as the native English commodities? At least the first part of this objection was so obvious that it did not escape mercantilists of far less sagacity than Locke. But they all found some dark reason for refraining from following it to its logical conclusion. Malynes (1601) looked at the matter in this way, that an export of money from England to other countries would result in a fall in the price of English commodities, and a rise in the price of foreign goods; "And so might it fare with the price of our home commodities being transported to those places." This latter, however, would not in his opinion occur and his reason is couched in incomprehensible terms: foreign coins, he said, might have a higher value—presumably on account of the seigniorage—than was represented by their metal content. In a later, insignificant pamphlet, called *Great Britains Remembrancer*, written by Sir Ralphe Maddison (1640, new edition with the title as given, 1655), it was also admitted that foreign countries had really to pay just as much for English goods as for their own, but the idea was later shelved, the explanation given being that the English merchants were forced to sell abroad because of their foreign indebtednesses and that the foreigners were not prepared to pay more when they knew that the goods were worth less in England, and so on.

Locke's own reply would obviously have been, as may be seen from the above quotation, that the same quantity of silver had to correspond to an equal quantity of goods in various countries. He would then have had to follow up this step in the argument by saying that the quantity of silver, which expressed the value of the commodities in any particular producing country, would have to determine the prices of the commodities both at home and abroad; thus French prices for French commodities and English prices for English commodities. It is obvious that such a conception, if followed to its logical conclusion, was irreconcilable with Locke's quantity theory approach, for the quantity theory necessarily led to the conclusion that the quantity of money in one country influenced *all* prices in the country, and, consequently, the prices of imported goods also. It is difficult to explain how this consequence could have been overlooked.

It is even more difficult to explain why the purely practical conclusions were not put to the test. For no one could have failed to notice that commodities competing with one another, e.g. French and English cloth, exercised a reciprocal influence on each other's prices. Expressed more generally, this means that a price bridge between native and foreign commodities which entered into international trade raised the demand for cheap goods and lowered the demand for dear goods, so that a state of equilibrium was reached in which the prices of the former were necessarily raised and the prices of the latter lowered. If the mechanism of this equilibrium was not clear to the mercantilists, that is not to be wondered at, for it is not simple. But it is difficult to explain why they hardly ever gave a thought to the consequences of so well known a phenomenon as the stimulation of

English cloth export resulting from a low price for English cloth, and vice versa. Had they been alive to the consequences of this elementary fact of everyday life, nothing would have remained of the foundation of their favourite idea that an increase of money was necessary in consideration of the prices of foreign countries. That they closed their eyes to something as simple as that points to the conclusion that they had a preconceived opinion with regard to the result, namely the notion of the paramount importance of the need for money.

Independent of such views, a high level of native prices could not have been regarded as a good thing from the point of view of international exchange, because it would necessarily favour imports and hinder exports. If the connection between the quantity of money and the price level had been recognized in these circumstances, the mercantilists must immediately have been disturbed about the consequences to the balance of trade of an increase in the quantity of money. At least one of the foremost mercantilists caught a glimpse of these facts in a moment of inspiration, although he was incapable of drawing any broad practical conclusions from them.

The writer in question was Mun. He reported in detail on the decline of the English cloth exports and the development of production in the competing countries resulting from the excessive price of English cloth. He then posed the question how far the fact that there was then more money in the country than previously would cause foreigners to buy more than before and so bring about an expansion of trade. He attacked this supposition with vigour on the following grounds : "For all men," he said, "do consent that plenty of money in a kingdom doth make the native commodities dearer, which as it is to the profit of some private men in their revenues, so is it directly against the benefit of the Public in the quantity of the trade; for as plenty of money makes wares dearer, so dear wares decline their use and consumption, as hath already been plainly shewed in the last Chapter upon that particular of our cloth." In this Mun undoubtedly displayed greater powers of observation than were manifested by most other mercantilists, and in particular Locke.

Mun thus appears to have been very near, on this point, to correcting the basic mercantilist outlook with regard to the precious metals. This was also the case to the extent that his indifference towards the increase in circulation is to be explained by his conception of its effects on foreign trade. Had Mun followed his argument through to its conclusion, only one possible application of the precious metals could have remained, the accumulation of a treasure. Strictly speaking, Mun was not particularly interested in this either, although he gave it his approval on principle. From the purely logical point of view, he was thus near to causing a vital readjustment of mercantilism as a monetary system. But from the psychological point of view, few people obviously could be farther from this than the author of *England's Treasure by Forraign Trade*. His own conclusions with regard to the effect of the circulation of money on exports were expressed simply in the usual demand of the East Indian trade for free export of precious metals. Silver, in his opinion, had its specific function in serving foreign trade. With regard to its final use, on the other hand, he says nothing. He does not explain what should happen to it if the export of precious metals resulted in an export surplus of commodities and an import surplus of money and silver, which was the objective of all the endeavours.[2]

Yet this description of the mercantilist viewpoint of the connection between the quantity of money and international exchange contains one great flaw, the fact that the foreign exchanges are left out of consideration. This defect must now be remedied.

2. THE FOREIGN EXCHANGES

If comparisons of prices expressed in the monetary units of different countries are to have any meaning they must obviously take into account the reciprocal value ratio of the monetary units, this ratio being usually characterized as the foreign exchanges, although it does not presuppose exchange in the technical sense of the term as the form of adjustment of transactions. The theoretical and practical mysteries of the foreign exchanges were naturally even more troublesome in times of disorganized monetary

[2] Locke, *Some Considerations* (note 7 in ch. 2) 19 f., 76–79, 88; *Further Considerations Concerning Raising the Value of Money* (same ed.) 15 ff., 66 ff. *et passim.*— Malynes, *Canker* (*Tudor Econ. Docs.* III 392 f.)—Maddison 20 f.; also Clement, who was generally dependent upon Locke (see above 185), expressed the same thought with rather similar vagueness (31 f.).—Mun, *Engl. Tr.* ch. 3, 4, 5 (ed. Ashley 10 f., 24, 30). In the last place referred to, Mun conceives of the purchase of estates as an outlet for money, without making clear whether he thought in good earnest that this would withdraw the money from circulation.—An occasional heretic on this point was Henry Robinson, when he said (*England's Safety in Trades Encrease* 57): "It is our benefit that monies be plentiful also in such Countries where we carry our commodities to sell, and shall otherwise have little encouragement to continue it." But the very first principle laid down in his *Briefe Considerations concerning advancement of Trade and Navigation* (Lond. 1649) represented the ordinary view.

conditions than in the 19th century, with its gradually consolidating monetary systems; in earlier times they were so striking that they could not fail to attract attention. Least of all would such an indifference have been expected under mercantilism, which displayed an overmastering interest in both the monetary system and foreign trade.

The controversies centreing around the foreign exchanges really belong to the period before 1630. Apart from the Netherlands, which are normally left out of account in this part, they were brought to a head by the controversy between Malynes on the one hand and Misselden and Mun on the other. The former wanted to control the exchanges through direct interference, and therefore demanded the restoration of the office of Royal Exchanger, the latter maintained the conception of an immutable economic inter-relationship in foreign trade, namely the balance of trade theory, which they made to serve the interests of the East India Company. Through the victory of the latter tendency, the balance of trade occupied the field of attention to so large an extent that the exchanges thereafter were very much lost sight of. Possibly this tendency was also connected with the changes in actual conditions. At least with regard to England, the greater order attained in the monetary system ensured the fact that convulsions of the foreign exchanges resulting from monetary causes occurred far less frequently than formerly. Even before that, the taking up of loans by the English government abroad had ceased. The problem of the foreign exchanges had therefore lost the ear of English politicians which it had gained in the Tudor period, when Sir Thomas Gresham had preached untiringly of the great dangers the foreign exchanges threatened to the position of the Prince (and of his own preternatural skill in overcoming these dangers); and as mercantilist literature before the 18th century was primarily English, the result was that this literature paid only passing attention to the problem of the foreign exchanges during the heyday of mercantilism.

Nevertheless the questions consciously occupying the minds of mercantilists in the 17th century were not to be dissociated from the foreign exchanges; and for this reason the concept of the exchanges must imperceptibly have acquired great influence on the whole system, especially on the balance of trade theory, which could not possibly be elaborated comprehensibly without explicit or tacit assumptions with regard to the foreign exchanges.

The notion of the foreign exchanges had two aspects, their equilibrium and their deviations from the equilibrium. It was at least tempting to treat these as two separate problems; but by another method various misunderstandings might perhaps have been avoided.

Of the two problems, the deviations from equilibrium were of course of the greater interest, if only because equilibrium as such appeared to be taken for granted *a priori* where there was a metallic standard; in other words it was considered to be determined by the mint par, the relationship of the silver content of the different coins. This norm, it is true, was not applicable in comparing the coins of different metals, but it was made to suffice for the most important cases. The "true value" of the foreign exchanges was the "intrinsic value" of the coins. This was what Malynes never tired of calling the *par pro pari* of the foreign exchanges, like for like, a definition which also contained a moral evaluation. All this was common to the earlier discussion whose conclusions Malynes embodied in his books. Interwoven with this was the struggle against interest in general, still frequently determined by ethical or religious considerations, as may best be seen in Thomas Wilson's *Discourse upon Usury* (1572), which is, for the rest, rather barren from the economic point of view. In the period after Malynes the ethical considerations faded out. The problem lost its great significance, but the conception of the right or normal exchange remained the same. This may already be seen in the fact that the otherwise so unsparing critics of Malynes agreed with him on this point. Misselden thus said, "The fineness of monies is that Cynosure or Center, whereunto all Exchanges have their natural propension." Later on Locke concluded his discussions of the changes of the foreign exchanges by referring to the way in which the parity should be reckoned on the basis of the "intrinsic value", and his description was supplemented several years later (1695) by Simon Clement, who obviously had had practical experience. To this extent full agreement prevailed. When the mercantilists instituted international price comparisons they accounted for price on the basis of the mint par.[3]

On the question of the deviation of the foreign exchanges from

[3] Valuable data: pr. Schanz, *Englische Handelspolitik* II 614–49 and *Tudor Econ. Docs.* III 305–404 (Memorandum of 1564 346–59).—On Gresham: J. W. Burgon, *Life and Times of Sir Thomas Gresham* (Lond. 1839) *passim*, esp. letters 1553 and 1558 pr. in I 97, 463 ff., 483 ff.—Malynes, esp. *Lex Mercatoria, passim* (the third and last part is devoted exclusively to the foreign exchanges).—Wilson, *A Discourse upon Usury* (note 8 in ch. 2) *passim*, esp. 270 f.—Locke 83.—[Clement], *Discourse* (see above 185) ch. 4 & 5. These references also apply in part to what follows.—Misselden, *The Circle of Commerce or the Ballance of Trade* (Lond. 1623) 97.

parity there was far more difference of opinion. The two opposing schools of thought, however, here, too, looked at the theoretical points through the same spectacles. Their difference consisted rather in this, that they emphasized different factors and omitted to draw several conclusions which naturally arose out of their common standpoint.

Malynes' conception of the movements of the foreign exchanges may best be seen in the following passage: "So that the matter of Exchange being made a merchandise, requireth this consideration for the reducing thereof to his first principle and foundation, which is the intrinsic value of coins of country and countries according to weight and fineness, albeit the price thereof in Exchange doth rise and fall according to scarcity or plenty of money, proceeding of the few or many deliverers and takers thereof in the course of traffic, not by commodities only, but also by Exchange devised upon monies, in nature of merchandise." Starting from the coinage parity as the decisive norm, Malynes thus reckoned with the movements of the exchanges as an effect of supply and demand of bills of exchange, which did not all depend on commercial operations, but were also partly drawn up speculatively or, inversely, withdrawn from the exchange market. On this point Malynes had no other conception than the best informed contemporary and earlier public opinion. This may be seen with particular clarity from a detailed report on the foreign exchanges which had been drawn up a half-century earlier for an English Royal Commission (1564). But Malynes went much further than others with his fantastic notions of the "Feats of Bankers performed by Exchanges", i.e. exchange manipulations. This, his chief practical idea, led him also to the project he advocated throughout his lifetime, the reintroduction of the office of Royal Exchanger, through whom all exchange operations and all trade in precious metals were to take place— an official whose appointment dated from the Middle Ages and was revived fitfully down to the reign of Charles I (1628). The only thing that could, in Malynes' opinion, lead to an export of bullion, a corresponding import surplus of goods and, worst of all, a scarcity of money, was a deviation of the foreign exchanges from the *par pro pari*. He therefore vigorously opposed the widespread belief that the "raising of the value of the coin", i.e. coinage depreciation, would be able to counteract silver exports. In his opinion it could only cause an alteration in the parity.

Granting Malynes' premise that English money was undervalued abroad when compared with the silver content of the respective coins—or, more correctly, undervalued to a greater extent than their cost of carriage—his whole argument was water-tight and often much sounder than that of his rather overbearing opponents, especially Misselden. What nevertheless made Malynes' reasoning altogether unreal was that he supposed the situation to be permanent. Actually, of course, the rush of money out of the country, in order to have it made into silver at a higher value without even the risk of a loss—Malynes at one time estimated the gain to be 11 per cent in the month and 132 per cent in the year, later reduced somewhat more modestly to $6\frac{1}{9}$ and above 73 per cent, respectively—would have redressed the exchange in a very short time. That Malynes' belief in habitual undervaluation had much to do with actual conditions also appears distinctly improbable. The chaotic state of the currency in most countries made correct estimates of the parity very difficult, and when in doubt, people of course normally concluded that they had been over-reached by the foreigner. An author who distinguished himself from most of these writers by having no axe to grind, Rice Vaughan, said, some years later, that he had heard some merchants express belief in a deviation from parity, but "so I heard others of as great worth and experience to deny them, affirming that they knew none other valuation of our Money with foreign but according to the Intrinsical value of either of them" (*A Discourse of Coin and Coinage*, published posthumously in 1675, probably written around 1630).[4]

Of greater interest than this criticism of the expressed beliefs of Malynes, however, was their background and, even more, what they left out of account. With an occasional exception, to him the foreign exchanges were the beginning of all things. The chain of events began in the foreign exchanges, the latter dominating commodities and money, not vice versa—this was the ever-recurring idea. As he tersely summarizes in his *Maintenance of Free Trade*: "All the said causes of the decay of Trade are almost all of them comprised in one, which is the want of money; whereof we find the abuse of exchange to be the efficient Cause." Now, however, the passage quoted in a previous page shows that he did not regard manipulations as the sole cause of move-

---

[4] Quotations from Malynes: *Lex Mercatoria*, Part 3, ch. 10 (1st ed. 413, cf. also, on what follows, 291, 382, 415, 418 f., 422, 485 *et passim*), *Maintenance of Free Trade* 76, 104, *Center of the Circle of Commerce* 28 f., 48 f.—Royal Exchanger: Tawney's Introduction to Wilson (prev. note) 137–54; documents pr. in Schanz and *Tudor Econ. Docs.* III.—Vaughan, ch. 21 (orig. edn., Lond. 1675, 204).

ments in the exchanges. He also included the actual effects of trade, which consisted in the claims on one country often being greater than the claims of that country on others, and vice versa. So that the foreign exchanges could deviate from the parity even without the "Feats of Bankers". Quite irrespective of whether Malynes was right in ascribing much influence to the latter, his diagnosis could therefore not have covered all the facts. Had Malynes pursued his reasoning to its conclusion, he would obviously have been forced to face the question of how the claims of one country happened to be sometimes larger and sometimes smaller than its debts, and the foreign exchanges therefore departed from parity and the precious metals set in motion.

It was this that Malynes' opponents did. They went beyond the foreign exchanges and declared the *balance of trade* to be the decisive factor in the influx and outflow of silver; and in doing so they created the mercantilist monetary and commercial doctrine in its narrower sense. This argument however was not so late that it was a creation of the direct opponents of Malynes; it only happened that it was expressed more clearly by Mun than by others before him and in the later period was taken over from Mun's description. Following the matter up the conception has been traced back to the end of the 14th century (1381), and it had already been clearly stated before the middle of the 16th century. What was kept in mind was the manifest fact that if exports were greater than imports, or vice versa, the difference had to be paid somewhere or other, and this payment had to be made in precious metal. Fundamentally this could not, of course, be an alternative explanation to that of Malynes. It merely took his explanation one step further. The two camps, however, did not recognize this and Mun, for example, put the contrast in the form of an either/or. "It is not the undervaluing of our money in exchange," he said, "but the over-balancing of our trade that carrieth away our treasure." Only with regard to the exchange manipulations did there exist real difference of opinion. The new school regarded them as insignificant in comparison with the overwhelming influence of the balance of trade.

It was peculiar that Misselden and Mun were able to present their balance of trade theory as a contrast with the foreign exchange theory of Malynes, for no possible doubt should have existed that the balance of trade exercised its influence on the movements of the precious metals precisely via the foreign exchanges. Almost in the identical words as those used by Malynes and others before him, Mun, too, said, "As plenty or scarcity of money do make the price of the exchange high or low, so the over or under balance of our trade doth effectually cause the plenty or scarcity of money." In spite of apparent contrasts, the younger school thus really adopted the standpoint of the older and carried it further—more or less incidentally—by making the deviations of the foreign exchanges from parity dependent upon the balance of trade, and—emphatically—by making the movements of silver, as an effect of these deviations, likewise dependent upon the balance of trade.[5]

One cardinal problem, however, yet remained. What determined the balance of trade itself? This was never made clear. The mercantilists, it is true, discovered innumerable ways of stimulating exports and hindering imports, but that the balance of trade was linked up with the relative prices in different countries in one way or another and thus with the relative quantity of money, this idea was never elucidated. It was hinted at in passing by Mun, but was never fitted organically into the general plan. Had it been possible to weld the various fragments together properly, it would have become clear that (1) relative quantities of money, (2) relative prices in different countries, (3) balance of trade, and (4) the foreign exchanges, represented a comprehensive system of mutually dependent factors. It would have been possible to set out at any point and yet always return to the

[5] Statements of the officials of the Mint, Aylesbury and Crantren, 1381/82 *Rotuli Parlamentorum* III 127.—Early detailed discussions of the balance of trade: "Policies", etc. 1549 (*Tudor Econ. Docs.* III 316 ff., 321 ff.); a briefer discussion in [Hales], *Discourse* 63, 171. Thereafter, various works in *Tudor Econ. Docs.* III.—Quotations from Mun, *England's Treasure*, ch. 10 (ed. Ashley 48), and ch. 12 (Ashley 54 f.); the former also to be found in Misselden, *Circle of Commerce* 117.—In general see Mun, *passim*.—Locke, quoted in text below, 254; (*Considerations* 82).—It is hardly worth while to follow in detail the reasoning of the balance-of-trade school, and this applies in particular to Misselden, whose great strength lay in literary adroitness and invective, rather than in logical stringency.—The conception that the foreign exchanges mirror the balance of trade for each country was very common, and was held, for example, by Locke in the quotation given here. This idea recurred during the first World War; see above, ch. 1, note 3, 180 (*op. cit.*, Swed. ed. II 20; Amer. ed. I 144 f.). This reasoning is correct only on the assumption that there is no arbitrage. That arbitrage was a normal phenomenon during the 17th century—and much earlier, for that matter—is beyond doubt. Another problem, to some extent related to this, was the need for a "favourable" balance with *each* country rather than such a balance with *all* countries. For a more recent discussion of this issue, see Charles Wilson, "Treasure and Trade Balances: the Mercantilist Problem"; Heckscher, "Multilateralism, Baltic Trade, and the Mercantilists"; and Wilson, "Treasure and Trade Balances: Further Evidence", in *Economic History Review* (2nd Ser.; II, 1949, 152 ff.; III, 1950, 219 ff.; and IV, 1951, 231 ff., respectively).

starting-point, so that, to take one example, an increase, as compared with other countries, in the quantity of money necessary to the equilibrium would necessarily neutralize itself along these lines: rise in prices—import surplus—a larger total of foreign claims on the country than the country had abroad—an outflow of precious metals. The citadel of mercantilist monetary policy would thus have collapsed. An attempt to increase the quantity of money in circulation would then appear as an attempt to fill with precious metals the cask of·the Danaides. The connection between any one pair of these factors was clear to the mercantilists. With perfect apperception, they recognized the link between the quantity of money and prices; in certain clear moments they also saw the connection between prices and foreign trade; and they always understood the bond between foreign trade and (the foreign exchanges and) the movements of silver. It was only the whole chain of interconnectedness which was hidden to them.

Such a state of affairs may appear peculiar. But we should not forget that foreign trade is a complicated matter. The situation, in fact, is very significant of what in general clarifies or clouds economic phenomena. For what very often, if not normally, decides the issue is not the knowledge or ignorance of the individual factors, but whether elementary ideas, each individually clear and recognized as correct, are integrated into a consistent system.

In fact, not only was such a synoptic view absent in this case, but even a precisely *opposite* conception of the effect of the quantity of money on the foreign exchanges is to be found in two of the, in theory and practice, most influential mercantilists. They believed, that is to say, that a larger quantity of money would *increase* the foreign valuation of the domestic currency or would make "a favourable exchange". This presumed effect upon the foreign exchanges became immediately a new argument in favour of the claim for an increase in the quantity of money. Given the correctness of such an argument, the increase in the quantity of money would obviously continue automatically unto infinity. For if this were granted, each increase would continually have to call forth a new stream of precious metals. The representatives of the theory can hardly have thought of this, for if they had, they themselves would presumably have doubted the validity of their standpoint.

The two authors in question were Locke and Law. Locke did not think of laying chief stress on the presumed effect of the quantity of money on the foreign exchanges; but the importance of his exposition to the bolder construction of Law is quite clear.

In Locke one can, perhaps, find an explanation for his attitude, for like most other mercantilists, he explicitly put "money" and bills of exchange on the same footing. This led him to draw a parallel between the obvious rise in the foreign valuation of the currency of a country, resulting from greater foreign claims, and on the other hand, such results as depended upon a great native quantity of money, so that both the large foreign claims as well as the large quantity of money would enhance the foreign valuation of the currency of the country. Locke, in fact, expressed himself in the following terms, "These two together regulate the Commerce of the World, and in both the higher rate of exchange depends" (like all English authors even at that time, Locke understood by a higher foreign exchange a more "favourable" foreign exchange, higher foreign valuation, i.e. a larger number of foreign money units for one native money unit) "upon one and the same thing, *viz.* the greater plenty of Money in one Country than in the other; Only with this difference, that where the over balance of Trade raises the exchange above the *Par*, there it is the plenty of Money, which private Merchants have in one Country which they desire to remove into another: But where the Riches of the Country raises the exchange above the *Par*, there it is the plenty of the Money in the whole Country."

In Law this argument, to which Locke consciously ascribes a subordinate position, became a major point. He discovered in it a principal proof for the fact that it was necessary to have an increased quantity of money, and that there could be no objection to cover this requirement with paper money. "If trade," said Law, "can be carried on with a 100,000 *lib.* and a Balance then due by Foreigners; The same measures, and a greater Quantity of Money, would make the Balance greater." "Most people think scarcity of Money is only the Consequence of a Balance due; but 'tis Cause as well as the Consequence, and the *effectual way to bring the Balance to our side, is to add to the Money*" (my italics). Thus this reversed connection between the quantity of money and the exchanges became a support for mercantilist paper money policy.[6]

---

*[6] Locke 80.—Law ch. 3, 8, *et passim* (quotations from the Scottish edn. of 1705, 42, 115).—Viner (see above, ch. 1 note 7) 423 f. draws attention to a little-known anonymous work (ascribed to one Samuel Prat), through which, in his opinion, a view of the *whole* picture is obtained. The book, *The Regulating Silver Coin, Made Practicable and Easy to the Government and Subject* (Lond. 1696) is certainly ingenious, but I do not think this interpretation tenable. For it assumes that by silver value the author meant the purchasing power of silver in terms of goods, although he was exclusively preoccupied, in fact, with the silver value of the coins of different countries.   See below II 368, *Addendum* §12.

3. PROHIBITION OF THE EXPORT OF SILVER AND THE BALANCE OF TRADE THEORY

By keeping to the actual point of departure of the mercantilists we thus arrive at the conclusion that the coinage parity determined the state of equilibrium of the foreign exchanges. This conception has even been extended somewhat in the foregoing description by postulating that at an exchange rate corresponding to the coinage parity, silver would necessarily have the same purchasing power in different countries. The foreign exchange problem is not, however, quite so simple as that, and a glance at the policy which was actually pursued brings to light other possibilities. It is seen also that the mercantilist objective of an increased circulation of money might have been attained, in spite of everything, without disturbing the exchanges, though on other premises than those from which the mercantilists, at least consciously, set out.

In the first place, we come up here against the question of whether the goal could have been attained simply by obstructing the outflow of precious metals by the aid of *export prohibitions*. This had been the medieval policy and was continued everywhere, with greater or less tenacity, beyond the middle of the 17th century. In earlier times people held the view that payments abroad meant an outflow of precious metal and believed, in particular, that silver would never return if the payments were made *ab initio* in this manner. The writings ascribed to Armstrong in the period down to 1535 took up this stand. Even clearer did the conception manifest itself in the notes which have been handed down for a speech in the House of Commons in 1523, delivered presumably by Thomas Cromwell. The speaker warned the country against military enterprises in France under the personal leadership of the king. He said that the war would cost just as much as the whole of the circulating money in the country. This in his opinion would force England to adopt a leather currency. He personally had nothing against this, but it could become awkward if, say, the king were taken prisoner and ransom had to be paid. The French in fact would probably refuse to return the English king on payment of leather, as they refused even to sell their wine except on payment of silver.[7]

---

[7] [Armstrong] (note 2 in ch. 2) ed. Pauli 18–21, ed. *Tudor Econ. Docs.* III 93 ff.—Speech 1523: pr. *Letters and Papers, Foreign and Domestic, of the Reign of Henry VIII*, ed. J. S. Brewer, III: II (Lond. 1867) 1248. It appears incredible but is nevertheless true that a very conscientious scholar who deservedly enjoys a great reputation has taken this argument seriously (Schanz I 485).

The aversion to the export of silver then became a major argument in the 17th century in the attacks on the East Indian trade, which had to pay for its Indian goods with precious metals. This criticism persisted and was to be found here and there even at the end of the century.

Against the whole of this approach was directed the new tendency, the balance of trade theory, represented with particular vigour by the spokesmen of the East India Company, but regarded in wider and wider circles as the only tenable standpoint. At a comparatively early date, in 1663, this new school carried the day, in that England abolished the export prohibition on bullion and foreign coin, maintaining it only for English coin (by 15 Car. II, c. 7, § 9). This was done by referring to "several considerable and advantageous Trades"—i.e. primarily the East Indian trade—which "cannot be conveniently driven and carried on without the Species of Money and Bullion". In France, progress along this line was slower. It is true that Barthélémy de Laffemas, court tailor and adviser to Henry IV, wrote a short statement in favour of the free export of precious metals in the early years of the 17th century; but this did not achieve any practical significance. Much more important was the fact that Colbert's sympathies with regard to such a policy were unmistakable, although he was unable to proclaim them at all so frankly as was done in England. The prohibition was thus retained longer in France, occasionally even on pain of death if no licence were obtained. But hints were always dropped about not going to extremes, only avoiding excessive export. In one case (1679) Colbert even prevented a distraint from being put into effect.[8] Gradually among the

[8] An interesting expression of the new firmness of faith: Pepys' Diary for the 27 Jan. 1665 (*Diary*, ed. H. B. Wheatley IV, repr. Lond. 1923, 342).— *Lettres de Colbert* II 450 (Year 1669), 695 ff. (Year 1679); *Corresp. administr. sous Louis XIV*, ed. Depping, III 519 (Year 1682), 618 (Year 1681).—According to Harsin 75, Sully, the great minister of Henry IV and an opponent of Laffemas, is said to have definitely made himself familiar with the later mercantilist programme in a pamphlet whose tendency is evident in its title: *Comme l'on doibt permettre la liberté du transport de l'or et de l'argent hors du Royaume*, etc. (Paris 1602). I could not discover such a pamphlet in the *Bibliothèque nationale*, and since every particular given by Harsin corresponds with a paper written by Laffemas, which is apparently the one meant. In itself, this short, eight-page pamphlet is quite superficial.—I have no closer knowledge of the conditions in Italy. But it is asserted (e.g. by G. Arias, "Les idées économiques d'Antonio Serra", *Journal des Économistes* LXXXI, 1922, 284) that Venice allowed the free export of its coins as early as the beginning of the 17th century. It is, moreover, apparent that Mun in particular was deeply influenced by Italian conditions, and as has already been noticed in the previous chapter, an investigation of this connection would probably be worth while.

economically leading countries, it became almost axiomatic that the export of the precious metals should not be prevented through prohibitions, but through the workings of the balance of trade. The terrifying example of Spain, where the prohibition was maintained on paper, was continually and with tiresome monotony marshalled in illustration.

The arguments of the new and victorious tendency were primarily two in number and were repeated again and again.

In the first place it was believed that it was impossible to enforce compliance with the prohibitions. Bodin had already declared this in 1568, and roughly a hundred years later Petty (1662) and Fortrey (1663), said the same thing in practically the same words. Locke (1691) believed that prohibiting exports was like "hedging in the cuckoo", and even so vigorous an opponent of export of bullion as Pollexfen (1697) admitted that the export prohibitions on coin in England had probably had little effect, considering that in Spain and Portugal the export went on undisturbed as if no prohibitions existed, even though the penalty was death.[9] In satisfying this consideration the new English legislation of 1663 was not very satisfactory; for it was no easier to safeguard coin than bullion against being smuggled out of the country. Pollexfen's observation therefore rightly applied precisely to the new and milder prescription.

The English statute of 1663 took note of the other consideration, which Mun tried to illustrate with his analogy of the husbandman who scatters good seed on the land that he may in due course reap fourfold in golden harvests. "It is found by experience," runs the preamble to this section of the 1663 Act, "that they are carried in greatest abundance (as to a Common Market) to such places as give free liberty for exporting the same." It became an axiom of mercantilist doctrine that the country would in no circumstances be able to keep more or less than the balance of trade permitted, and that the only possible point of attack was the balance of trade itself.

The importance of this changed attitude of mind towards increased freedom of trade is obvious and cannot be over-emphasized. Under the corrupt and ineffective administration of the *ancien régime*, the states obviously lacked the necessary weapons for preventing movements in the precious metals, in the

---

[9] Bodin (note 2 in ch. 2) unpag.—Petty, *Treatise of Taxes* ch. 6 (Econ. Writings I 57).—Fortrey 33 (repr. 31).—Locke 24.—[Pollexfen], *Disc. of Trade, Coyn and Paper Credit* (see above 233) 9.

way, for example, that this was effected successfully during the first World War and is quite possible even in peace time today.

From the purely theoretical point of view, however, things were different. The theoretical advance achieved by the later mercantilists—the greater comprehension of economic phenomena —was, in this case, at least doubtful. It is not at all certain that an export prohibition of bullion, of course supposing it to be effective, is unable to increase permanently the stock of precious metals within a country. When denying it, the younger mercantilists clung primarily to the fact that the balance of trade had to be equalized somewhere or other. From this they concluded that the import or export surplus necessarily led to a transference of as much precious metals as corresponded to the balance. "After all," as Locke said, "if we are over balanc'd in Trade, it [the precious metals] must go." The possibility of an adjustment by means of credit operations was left aside here, though occasionally noticed at the time; it was expressed most clearly by Locke himself. But apart from this, the fundamental weakness of this argument was the fact that it did not pay attention to the repercussions on the *equilibrium of the foreign exchanges* and thus indirectly on the balance of trade itself which might result from effective hindrances to the movements of the precious metals. If the argument is taken a step further, the unhappy consequences of clinging to the conception that the coinage parity represented the equilibrium of the foreign exchanges, even with effective export prohibitions on gold and silver, become manifest. Apart from movements of capital, an import surplus of commodities in a country results in a surplus of the country's debts abroad in excess of its claims on other countries. It thus causes a dislocation of the foreign exchanges which decreases the foreign value of the domestic currency. If, now, this state of affairs cannot be brought back into equilibrium by the outflow of precious metals, the foreign valuation of the domestic currency remains below the par of exchange. In consequence, the export of goods is stimulated and the import of goods discouraged. The exporters, in other words, receive more native units of money for every foreign unit, but the importers have to pay more native units for every foreign unit. By this adjustment between imports and exports, the balance of trade is corrected *without* the transference of precious metals. If the conditions persist, then the foreign exchanges, i.e. the foreign valuation of domestic currency, also keep so much below the par of exchange that this adjustment remains.

In principle, this is the same system as prevails in the absence of restrictions on the movements of precious metals, though with one very important practical difference. Where the precious metals are free to move, the adjustment takes place through the outflow of gold and silver from a country with an import surplus. There follows a fall in prices in this country, which leads to a stimulation of exports and a falling off of imports. Where prohibitions on the export of precious metals are in force, the price level in the country on the other hand remains unaffected, but the same adjustment takes place ultimately through a movement in the foreign exchanges. This movement in the foreign exchanges leads to domestic goods being cheaper abroad, where the domestic prices are unchanged, and contrariwise the prices of foreign commodities rise in the country, where the prices abroad remain unchanged. The goal can be arrived at therefore through an adjustment in the foreign exchanges, i.e. more precious metals can be kept in circulation than were otherwise possible. In *this* respect, the criticism of export prohibitions through the later mercantilists was decidedly false—though it should not by any means be assumed that the earlier mercantilists either had a clear conception of these phenomena.

Where hindrances were placed on the movements of the precious metals, the foreign exchanges had no necessary connection at all with the metallic content of the coins. This may already be seen in the fact that foreign claims on a certain number of native units of money do not, in such a case, give the foreign creditor a chance of receiving precious metals in return. It only gives him as much purchasing power as is represented by the monetary units in the country. But it is easily seen that this truth was difficult to recognize. The best illustration of this is, perhaps, the fact that it was not clear even to such critics of mercantilism as Hume and Adam Smith. Adam Smith, in fact, regarded the matter in this way, that if an increased quantity of the precious metals were retained in the country, a rise in prices would ensue and consequently the exports of the country would be discouraged and foreign goods would be enabled to prevail in the domestic market. He did not understand that the foreign exchanges would, as a result, bring about a lasting adjustment and once again bring about a state of equilibrium between imports and exports.[10]

[10] See above, note 5.—Hume *Essays* (note 12 in ch. 3): "Of money" (ed. Green & Grose I 311).—Adam Smith, *Wealth of Nations*, Bk. 4 ch. 5 (ed. Cannan II 12 f.).—Ricardo's criticism, *Principles of Political Economy and Taxation*, ch. 16 (*Works and Correspondence*, ed. P. Sraffa, Cambr. 1951, I 229 f.).

And so if Hume and Adam Smith, the much abler theorists, went astray on this point, it is not surprising that the mercantilists did likewise.

The conception of the par of exchange as a norm for the foreign exchanges could be mistaken, precisely in the monetary system of that time, even if the international movements of the precious metals between countries were not obstructed. Such a situation would arise if the purchasing power of the coins was made higher than the purchasing power of the precious metals contained in them. This idea was of little importance to contemporary theory. It is only mentioned in passing at this juncture in order not to omit any factor of theoretical interest which had some influence on the actual monetary policy in spite of its insignificance with regard to the economic outlook.

A rise in the purchasing power of the coins above the purchasing power of their metal content is possible when a policy of restricted minting is pursued as, for example, with silver in the bi-metallist system of the Latin Coinage Union after 1878, and in Sweden with regard to gold in World War I. In principle this is no different from the use of paper money since, in effect, coins virtually become notes printed on metal. The conditions for this were undoubtedly provided under mercantilism, since the right of individuals to coin precious metals, the condition which would prevent a rise in the value of coins above that of their metal content, was at least not guaranteed. Thus it was possible for rulers to create for themselves a coinage with a purchasing power above that of its metallic content. This would have kept down the domestic price level and in the long run would have led *ceteris paribus* to an increase in the foreign valuation of the domestic currency over the par of exchange. But no silver would have been brought into the country as a result, for the higher purchasing power held not for silver but for silver coins, which could not be had for the amount of silver contained in them. How far the governments of the time appreciated the possibility given here is difficult to determine in the confused circumstances of the coinage. But there can be no doubt that Gustav Vasa did something of this kind during the latter part of his reign.

Another measure which had a similar effect was the charging of *seigniorage*. If the seigniorage exceeded the actual cost of minting, those who had delivered the silver received a quantity of coin with a silver content less than that of the silver which they had given up. The resulting coin had clearly a higher value than its silver content. But even if this measure was of little practical significance, it demonstrates that the explanation of the mercantilists' conception of money cannot primarily be found in the actual monetary conditions of the time, but in quite other causes.[11]

The primary interest to mercantilism of what has been discussed here is that, if the writers of the time had rightly understood it, they would have seen the uselessness of aiming at a *par pro pari*, when the actual equilibrium for the foreign exchanges was other than the par of exchange. But after Malynes, the whole of this consideration lost any interest that it had had. The points explained here were, moreover, useless to the mercantilists, for what they wanted, an increase in the quantity of money in the country, could not be achieved in that way. However, it *could* be attained through something quite different, and that, on the other hand, is important, at least in theory.

Even without hindrances on the export of the precious metals, it was possible to increase the native circulation of money, at least to a limited extent, and to raise home prices; what is more, this possibility was completely in line with mercantilist economic policy, though not with its monetary policy. That the policy which we have in mind had also a monetary essence was, as far I know, quite hidden to the mercantilists. It was the *commercial policy*—hindrances on the import and the stimulation of the export of commodities—which must have contributed to raising home prices. This must have raised the quantity of precious metal in circulation within a country under a purely metallic currency and under conditions of mobility of the precious metals. The chain of cause and effect is as follows.

One-sided hindrances in international trade—in this case hindrances on imports—effect a dislocation in the equilibrium of the foreign exchanges. With hindrances on imports it becomes no longer so profitable to use foreign goods as it was before, while the demand of other countries for the native goods in general remains unchanged. Under a purely metallic standard this leads to an influx of precious metals into the country with a consequent rise in prices. As a result imports are stimulated afresh and (or)

[11] On Gustav Vasa: see Heckscher, *Sveriges ekon. hist.* I : 1 210 ff.—A theoretical error in the first edition of *Mercantilism* has been corrected in this edition. Cf. Viner's review in *Economic History Review* VI, 1935, 101.—On the monetary system in general, see, for example, the compilation by E. Nübling, *Zur Währungsgeschichte des Merkantilzeitalters* (Ulm 1903); G. Schmoller, *Grundriss der Allgemeinen Volkswirtschaftslehre* II (Lpz. 1904) 74, 83; sources in Schanz (see above, note 3), etc.

exports are restricted, until the imports and the exports are once again equilibrated. But this result—equilibrium of the foreign exchanges—is attained on the basis of a larger quantity of money and a higher domestic price level in the protected country in comparison with the previous situation and in contrast with other countries. The foreign exchanges thus remain unaltered although the price level has risen and the quantity of money is, as a result of the import hindrances (or export premiums, or both), increased. This is due to the fact that as a consequence of these measures it is less worth the while of merchants in the country to buy goods from abroad or, conversely, it is more profitable for foreigners to buy native goods than it was before. For this reason, the former have less use for claims on other countries, and the latter greater use for claims in the country in question than is indicated on the basis of the domestic purchasing power in both countries.[12]

This state of affairs represents the "cunning of reason", or if you will, of absurdity; for it shows that without being aware of it, the mercantilists worked towards a goal by the aid of their *commercial policy* which their monetary policy was intended, but unable, to attain. However, as pointed out in the introductory chapter of this part, this procedure was almost certainly of very limited practical scope, not because it is difficult to influence money and prices in this way, but because all countries acted in a like manner, and the quantity of money could not be increased for all of them together so long as a purely metallic standard was maintained. If paper money mercantilism had been triumphant, this result might have become important. But in any case the situation does not diminish in interest with regard to mercantilism, for, on the whole, the importance of mercantilism lay more in its self-imposed tasks than in its accomplishments. Mercantilism's desires harmonized better with the goal it set itself, the increase in the quantity of money in the country, than free trade theorists have generally admitted and than the mercantilists themselves recognized. Whether their striving after an increase in the quantity of money had any point at all is a totally different question.

4. THE CONVENTIONAL NATURE OF MONEY

The real essence of mercantilism as a monetary system may thus be taken as clarified. The conception of the mercantilists may be explained without any great difficulty as an attempt to find a way through the general tangle of monetary policy.

[12] See above 178 f., and ch. 1, note 3.

In conclusion, however, we must point out that the mercantilists themselves were in no way aware that they idolized money and the precious metals. On the contrary they often explicitly emphasized their consciousness of the conventional nature of money and its limited function, even to such a degree that it must be regarded as their general opinion. Almost everything that they stated on the matter had age-old roots reaching back to Aristotle and the schoolmen, but what is important is that they held fast to it. Several examples finally may serve to illustrate this aspect of their outlook.

In the above-mentioned speech made in the English House of Commons in 1523 it was stated, indeed, that in itself there was nothing against a leather currency to supply requirements within the country. Shortly after, the advocates of coinage depreciation in Saxony pointed out that it was much easier to discover a remedy for a surplus of money than for the prevailing money scarcity; in this they did not want to prejudice the issue so as to suggest that there could not be too much money. Once again, a few decades later, Hales, through the mouth of one of the characters in his dialogue, repeated that it was a matter of indifference what kind of money was current in the country, even if it were leather. The person through whom the author himself speaks did, it is true, deny this without further reason given, but he admitted that "Men commonly say so".

In the 17th century the view assumed more definite shape. Montchrétien's emphatic stress on the importance of goods has already been illustrated, and similar English utterances on the point have been reproduced (v.s. 189 f.). Petty also reckoned with the possibility of too much money. He identified himself with the conception that the proper measure of value should be the two "natural" elements, land and labour (1662). The fundamental anti-money attitude of Becher has been illustrated above in detail. Even mercantilists who manifested complete approval of the existing social order expressed similar sentiments on this point. Thus the author of *The Use and Abuses of Money* (1671), a contemporary of Becher's with inflationist tendencies, declared that so far from money being the *summum bonum*, the greed for it was in fact the *summum malum*. Davenant ascribed the decline of the human race to commerce. As usual one finds in him a recapitulation of all that had been said on this matter previously: the conventional nature of money simply as "counters"—the same picture as Locke used a few years before (v.s. 225 f.); the possibility of having too large a quantity of precious metals—Petty's view;

and the great importance of other objects of wealth besides money. Schrötter, the Austrian mercantilist, though he took his stand on the formula that the wealth of a country was to be judged by its quantity of money, gave as his only reason for this simply that gold and silver by general consent were "the universal price of all things", and not that they were valuable in themselves. The examples could be supplemented and prolonged further.[13]

Mercantilism as a monetary system is thus not to be explained as a conscious idolatry of money. The vital point in it in the field of the rational was the concept of the function of money and the precious metals in society and for the development of economic life which it intended, i.e. (1) as capital and income, (2) in circulation and (3) in international exchange. How this arose we have endeavoured to demonstrate in the foregoing exposition. At the same time it is not to be denied that unconscious ideas contributed to this view with regard to money and the precious metals and their function, and that such unconscious elements provided a halo of significance to the terms gold, silver, and money, which is not exhausted by the functions consciously ascribed to them.

[13] *Drei Flugschriften* (note 2 in ch. 1) 63.—[Hales], *Discourse of the Common Weal* 33.—Petty, *Treatise of Taxes*, ch. 4 (Econ. Writings I 44).—*Use and Abuses of Money* 5.—Davenant, *Discourses* II 16, 62, 210 f., etc.—Schrötter, ch. 29 § 3, 31 § 1 (1st ed. 164, 168 f.).—Harsin, 60, quotes particularly well-formulated expressions of this argument, after S. de Gramont, *Le denier royal* (Paris 1620), a pamphlet noticed before in these pages. It is also evident that Gramont is an unusually clear advocate of the subjective value theory, e.g. from the following passages: "L'or n'est que le signe et l'instrument usuel pour la [= la valeur] mettre en pratique, mais la vraie estime d'icelles [choses] tire sa source du jugement humain et de cette faculté qu'on nomme estimative . . . je dis que les hommes estiment les choses ou pour l'utilité, ou pour le plaisir, ou pour la rarité d'icelles" (47 f.).—Cf. E. A. J. Johnson, "The Mercantilist Concept of 'Art' and 'Ingenious Labour'" (*Economic History*, Supplement to the *Economic Journal* II 1931, 240).

APPENDIX

MERCANTILIST LITERATURE IN MODERN WORKS

The treatment of mercantilist literature has not been the strong point of modern works on mercantilism. The reason for this is that economists with a theoretical training have paid little attention to the history of mercantilism. Nevertheless, in so rich a literary output as that on mercantilism, there are naturally treatises illustrating points within the literature; moreover, numerous works give long, connected extracts from different parts of the contemporary literature. In the following, however, I omit both those works dealing with economic history or mercantilism as a whole, as well as treatises on the history of economic thought or economics as a whole. With the exception perhaps of the great work of Sombart, none of these authors has, to my knowledge, anything vital to offer for our purpose.

Considering its importance, *English* mercantilist literature has been given comparatively scant treatment. Until fairly recently, there has been no single work on its general development which is of more than historiographic interest. From that point of view, however, Wilhelm Roscher's short essay written as early as 1851-52 must be mentioned: *Zur Geschichte der englischen Volkswirtschaftslehre im sechzehnten und siebzehnten Jahrhundert* (Abhandl. d. Sächsischen Gesellschaft der Wissenschaften III). A later, but also very summary, piece of writing is Hjalmar Schacht's thesis: *Der theoretische Gehalt des englischen Merkantilismus* (Kiel 1900). The situation has recently improved somewhat and E. A. J. Johnson's *Predecessors of Adam Smith* (N.Y. 1937) ought to be mentioned. This work gives an incisive treatment of ten authors, each handled separately, and a discussion of some common problems. M. Beer, *Early British Economics* (Lond. 1938) does not impress me as being equally valuable. It is, to be sure, rich in original ideas although his viewpoint is normally that of the materialistic interpretation of history; and gives evidence of a wide reading and learning, his views impress me, however, as having been developed with inadequate care.

In comparison, *German* mercantilist literature has been subjected to a much more comprehensive treatment. For open-mindedness and thoroughness, no work can compare with Roscher's *Geschichte der National-Oekonomik in Deutschland* (Geschichte der Wissenschaften in Deutschland, Neuere Zeit, XIV, Munich, 1874), though both in systematic arrangement and in consistency the author leaves much to be desired. In the present century considerable interest has been reawakened in the German Cameralists, the authors of those compendious works devoted to the art of government, above all to the art of increasing the revenues of the prince. It was precisely the fact that the Cameralists did not isolate economic phenomena that led an American sociologist, Albion W. Small, to take particular interest in them. The title of his book indicates the point of view from which he regarded them: *The Cameralists, The Pioneers of German Social Polity* (Chicago 1909). Shortly afterward, a Danish author, Axel Nielsen, published *Die Entstehung der deutschen Kameralwissenschaft im 17. Jahrhundert* (Jena 1911). This work undertakes the particular task of demonstrating the dependence of the Cameralists on Aristotle. There follow two detailed German works with copious quotations from relevant writings: Kurt Zielenziger, *Die alten deutschen Kameralisten* (Beiträge zur Geschichte der National-ökonomie, ed. Karl Diehl II, Jena 1914), and Louise Sommer, *Die österreichischen Kameralisten in dogmengeschichtlicher Darstellung* (Studien zur Sozial-, Wirtschafts- und Verwaltungsgeschichte, ed. Carl Grünberg XII-XIII, Vienna 1920, 1925). These two works also discuss in detail the real meaning of the term mercantilist or Cameralist. It seems to me impossible to give a single answer to the question, for it must surely be clear from the outset that such expressions are simply instrumental concepts with which one attempts to obtain a better grasp of the facts, and they can be differently delimited according to the purpose in question. Finally, for one Cameralist there is also a modern monograph: Heinrich Ritter von Srbik, *Wilhelm von Schröder,* (in the Sitzungsberichte der Akad. d. Wiss. in Wien, CLXIV: 1, 1910). With the exception of Schrötter (or Schröder) and his two immediate forerunners, Becher and Hörnigk (Hornigk, Horneck), the German Cameralists, however, were imbued with a spirit of their own. In general character, they had little in common with the writers of western Europe, who lived in a world of private commerce, shipping and credit and were immersed in it, however much they may have failed to grasp its more profound significance. To force these two groups of authors into the same category is to obscure the facts. Further, it must be said from the point of view of general European history of ideas, that Cameralism went underground, only to reappear to some extent in the reaction against *laissez-faire* toward the end of the 19th century, and even more strongly later on. On the development before *laissez-faire*, the Cameralists had no great influence, and their influence on the development of economic thought was perhaps even less. From the point of view of the present work, therefore, there has been little reason to deal with them to any great extent. Had the interest been in studying the historical roots of National Socialism, for example, the situation would have been different.

For another reason, the literature of the Netherlands takes a subordinate position in the treatment of mercantilism. The ideas contained in what we have called mercantilism played a minor part in that Utopia of economic politicians and authors of the 17th century. It may be presumed that this was due to the lack of consolidation of state power compared to most other states, but perhaps the country's merchants were all too successful to have felt a need for the support offered by mercantilist policy. Among modern treatises, I shall therefore confine myself to the most accessible of them, a well-documented work with apt and pointed conclusions: Etienne Laspeyres, *Geschichte der volkswirthschaftlichen Anschauungen der Niederländer und ihrer Literatur zur Zeit der Republik* (Preisschriften der Jablonowskischen Gesellschaft XI, Lpz. 1863). With regard to the Italian literature, there is a series of monographs, but they are highly specialized and in general have not been available to me.

From the middle of the 18th century onward, in addition to the English writings there appeared certain *French* works which exercised an equally important influence on the development of ideas. As a result, attention was also directed to the earlier French authors. But until the end of the 17th or the beginning of the 18th century, economic discussion occurred only sporadically in French writings; works which have recently been brought forward as literary contributions to economic discussions of the 17th century in France consist mostly of memoranda on limited questions the influence of which could hardly have been great. The economic content of this contemporary French literature is usually meagre. By comparison, the utterances of statesmen in general and Colbert in particular are infinitely more important, and from the point of view of the development of ideas, more significant than those of any other practical politician. It is true that in the latter part of the reign of Louis XIV economic necessity and difficulties evoked a series of noteworthy pamphlets, primarily those of Boisguillebert and Vauban. The former, however, should clearly be grouped with the precursors of the Physiocrats; the latter was concerned primarily with taxation problems which gave him little opportunity to go into ordinary mercantilist questions. On the other hand, in the first half of the 18th century, there arose in France a discussion which has with good reason been described as "reform-mercantilist". It is true that it contains no essentially new features, and it was not until the Physiocrats that economic thought received any really original contributions from France. I shall therefore be content to mention here only two modern treatises on French mercantilist literature: Fritz Karl Mann, *Der Marschall Vauban und die Volkswirtschaftslehre des Merkantilismus* (Munich & Lpz. 1914), which is extreme in denying to mercantilism the character of a theory or system; and Paul Harsin, *Les doctrines monétaires et financières en France du XVIe au XVIIIe siècle* (Paris 1928), of particular value because of its rich documentation, but suffering from a tendency to draw far too broad conclusions from the occasional utterances of authors who were considered unimportant both by their contemporaries and by earlier modern writers as well. (Strictly speaking this book relates to the following section.)

So far we have considered works on the mercantilist literature of individual countries, but in addition there are studies of another type: those which aim to show how particular economic problems were treated by contemporary authors. The more important contributions are often to be found in works of this kind. Here the work of American scholars, stimulated by the American interest in economic theory has been prominent, above all the book by Edgar S. Furniss, *The Position of the Laborer in a System of Nationalism, A Study of the Labor Theories of the Later English Mercantilists* (Hart, Schaffner and Marx Prize Essays, XXX, Boston & N.Y. 1920). Although this book draws its material from mercantilist literature and is confined to one particular aspect, the author shows so keen an eye for what is vital, and is so little inclined to be either apologetic or contentious, that it must be regarded as one of the best works published so far on a special aspect of mercantilism.

The remaining works in this group may be enumerated quite briefly:

From the point of view of economic theory, the connection between the monetary system and foreign trade must receive primary mention. It is precisely this connection which is the subject of a more recently published treatise: James W. Angell, *The Theory of International Prices; History, Criticism, and Restatement* (Harvard Economic Studies, XXVIII, Cambr. Mass. 1926). The brief observations made in the treatise with regard to mercantilist doctrine do not, however, penetrate to the core of the problem. As for the sphere of the actual monetary system, there is also a somewhat earlier treatise: Arthur Eli Monroe, *Monetary Theory before Adam Smith* (same collection, XXV, Cambr. Mass. 1923). Great attention is paid there to mercantilist literature, but the mechanical division of the subject does not bring out properly what is specifically mercantilist in the main part of the exposition. Perhaps that was not at all the intention of the author. Also the brief survey of mercantilist monetary theory which is given in the conclusion cannot compensate for this defect.—An important element in the mercantilist doctrine of monetary policy is treated by J. V. Tallqvist in a work called *Merkantilistiska banksedelteorier* (Acta Academiae Aboensis, Helsingfors 1920). To my knowledge, this is the first place in which the inflationism of that period is directly connected with the monetary ideas of mercantilism; and that is a great advance. On the other hand its analysis and criticism suffer by reason of the fact that the problem is not treated economically from the point of view of monetary theory. The author limits himself to the problem of whether bank notes can circulate without cover or the obligation to redeem them. The effect of the output of paper money on the value of money and on the economic system in general on the other hand is not dealt with or, at least, not given prominence. As a result the strength and weakness of the mercantilist discussions are not brought out as well as they could have been. Another central part of the mercantilist theory, the theory of the balance of trade, was made the subject of a special piece of research at quite an early date, namely in a small book, not without merit for its time although unfinished: Edmund Freiherr von Heyking, *Zur Geschichte der Handelsbilanztheorie* (Berlin

1880); the subject was taken up later by a Finnish economist, Bruno Suviranta: *The Theory of the Balance of Trade in England; a Study in Mercantilism* (Helsinki 1923). The treatment in this latter work contains much that is stimulating, but if it attempts to rehabilitate mercantilism by referring to the specific monetary conditions of the 17th century, the attempt is doomed to founder on the chronology. The fundamental conception of mercantilism was, in fact, already present in the Middle Ages, and its evolution into a balance of trade theory dates back at least to the middle of the 16th century, that is to the time before the great increase in the world's quantity of money, the cessation of which is used by the author to explain the endeavours to increase the nation's stock of precious metals. I hardly need to repeat here how valuable I consider Viner's work on the mercantilist theory of international trade to be; see ch. 1 note 7, 184 above. Finally, it should be mentioned that E. A. J. Johnson, *op. cit.*, part 3, presents what he calls a primitive theory of production before Adam Smith. (Incidentally, it seems to me that in doing so he denies his own statement that the use of the term mercantilism or any other common designation for the economic doctrines of the time is unsuitable. It would not be difficult to present an equally unified formulation for many other aspects of economic thought as well as the one he has chosen.)

I must confine myself to these brief references; many of the works cited here contain further references in adequate measure.

PART V

MERCANTILISM AS A CONCEPTION OF SOCIETY

THE CONCORD BETWEEN MERCANTILISM AND *LAISSEZ-FAIRE*

The doctrine of mercantilism is not exhausted in a description of its economic content in the narrower sense of the term, such as was attempted in the two foregoing parts of the present work. In other words in its conception of the proper economic policy to be pursued, mercantilism was also dominated by certain typical social ideas: by the conception of how society as a whole or man as a social animal was created, and how therefore he must be treated. This aspect also should therefore be investigated if we are to understand why mercantilism became what it did. This is the last task of our exposition of mercantilism. Even this preliminary definition of our task shows that no attempt will be made at a treatment of the philosophy of the state or conception of society prevalent at that time. Only as much of this outlook of the time must be treated as is necessary to deduce from it an explanation with regard to economic policy and the conception of it.

The specific economic doctrine and the general sociological theory harmonized in this point, that by way of contrast with the concepts of earlier ages they represented something new and, moreover, they were largely conceived to be so. The mercantilists always aligned themselves with the reformers; conscious conservatism was foreign to them, however much in practice they capitulated to the hardy vitality of medieval municipal policy. An author so entirely lacking in modern characteristics as Malynes was able to assert proudly that his favourite doctrine, that the foreign exchanges dominate gold and commodities, had never been clearly perceived by the great classical forerunners, Aristotle, Seneca and Cicero, "who were but in the infancy of Trade". His opponent Mun, who took his stand on the formula that the export of precious metals was a means for increasing the "treasure" of a country, asserted that that was "so contrary to the common opinion, that it will require many and strong arguments to prove it before it can be accepted of the Multitude, who bitterly exclaim when they see any monies carried out of the Realm". Similar utterances on the part of Petty, Davenant and others are to be found in sufficient number. Theoretical mercantilism really attempted to break new ground all along the line and moreover it was conscious of the fact.[1]

Nevertheless there was an essential distinction between the economic and the general social doctrines in mercantilism, which becomes apparent precisely when the question arises of its relations to the foregoing and subsequent phases of development.

In many respects the economic doctrine of mercantilism was merely a first attempt to bring logical order into the confused jumble of phenomena. There are few spheres in which the ancients contributed so little significant thought as the economic; and as for the Middle Ages, in the main they lay in the shadow of Aristotle. It could not therefore be expected that mercantilist economic beliefs should be anything but primitive. It followed, again, that they necessarily stood opposed on vital points with a later more penetrating conception. And in fact this was so. In purely economic matters the contrast between mercantilism and *laissez-faire* was fundamental. If this contrast had many causes, one of them, if not the most important of them, was the fact that only gradually did men learn to penetrate the dark arcana of economic relationships. The literature of the end of the 17th and the beginning of the 18th century, as we have learnt in the foregoing, demonstrates quite clearly the progressive metamorphosis in the fundamental outlook of mercantilism, consequent quite simply on the fact that only gradually did the human intellect master its economic problems, and thus in many respects the development was determined from within, by a devolution of the ideas as such. In the immediately following period came the final irruption of this metamorphosis, namely the rise of a science of economics.

In modern treatments of this problem the cause of this change is usually sought in other spheres, that is in external circumstances and their reaction on the economic ideals and the aims of human beings. That this also played a great part almost goes without saying; here as throughout we are dealing with an extremely complicated interplay of the most varied intellectual and material forces. Nevertheless, it may certainly be said that the so to speak autonomous development of the purely economic doctrines, the struggle of the mercantilists with the logical consequences of their premises, has usually been underestimated in modern treatises. The proof of this lies largely in the general

[1] Malynes, *Lex Mercatoria*, Part 1 ch. 10 (1st ed. 416).—Mun, *England's Treasure by Forraign Trade* ch. 4 (ed. Ashley 19).—Davenant, *Essay upon . . . Methods of Making . . . Gainers in the Ballance of Trade* (1st ed. 90).—Petty, *Pol. Arithm.* ch. 10 (Econ. Writings, ed. Hull, I 313).

conception of society on the part of mercantilists. For had the change come from without, in all probability it would have reached economic doctrine via a corresponding change in the general intellectual climate or *Weltanschauung*. However, a study of the social starting-points of economic ideas shows that the change from mercantilism to liberalism was *not* primarily a change in the general conception of society.

In fact it shows that the mercantilist conception of society was not of the same primitive nature as the economic theory specific to it. The explanation is obvious: the mercantilist conception of society was able to build on the intellectual achievement of several thousand years. It follows, further, that mercantilism as a conception of society was by no means so different from *laissez-faire* in the same regard as was the case within the economic sphere; in the first-named field they had a much longer common history to build upon than in the second. It is even possible to go farther and affirm that on many points both mercantilism and *laissez-faire* were based on *one and the same* conception with regard to man as a social animal, and that both had the same view of what the proper method of treatment of this animal must be. As for the general conception of society, a sharp division obtains between the Middle Ages and the following period, and another division not so sharp between *laissez-faire* and the conservative or historico-romantic conception of society; on the other hand there is no real dividing line between mercantilism and *laissez-faire* in this field. That this was so in the actual philosophy or theory of the state can hardly ever have been doubtful. The doctrine of *natural right*, the main lines of which were laid down in the last few centuries of the Middle Ages, and which came to full flower in the 16th century, dominated speculative sentiment until the advent of the historical spirit at the beginning of the 19th century. And this generalization applies not only to this limited sphere, but also to the general social orientation. The concept of man in society remained the same in many vital points. This gave mercantilism and *laissez-faire* common features even in connections other than, specifically, the philosophy of the state. Particularly typical and well known are the threads binding Hobbes, the most acute philosopher of the school of natural rights, but the theorist of absolute government, on the one hand, to the English utilitarians, Bentham, James Mill, and John Austin on the other.[2]

[2] See, e.g., J. Bonar, *Philosophy and Political Economy in Some of Their Historical Relations* (Lond. 1893) 85; L. Stephen, *The English Utilitarians* (Lond. 1900) I 302 f., II 76 ff., III 321, 325; F. Meinecke, *Die Idee der Staatsräson in der neueren Geschichte* (Münch. & Berl., 1924) 267 ff.

What cries out for explanation in this situation is not the agreement itself, for that is to be expected. What is contradictory is merely the fact of the identity of the general conception of society in mercantilism and in *laissez-faire* existing side by side with vital differences in the economic doctrines. How could a social philosophy common to mercantilism and *laissez-faire* go together with an economic system which in mercantilism was as far apart from that in *laissez-faire* as are the antipodes? It is this question which we shall endeavour to elucidate in this part, after the mercantilist conception of society has been adumbrated in its most typical features.

II

THE NATURE OF THE MERCANTILIST CONCEPTION OF SOCIETY

1. FREEDOM AND TRADE

Peculiar as it may appear, mercantilism in fact, and even more in the eyes of its representatives, was directed towards liberty, and on account of its general economic tendency primarily toward economic liberty.

In the first place this made itself felt in the purely practical sphere. It was a natural corollary of mercantilism in its capacity of a unifying agent. Since we are concerned here with the tasks which mercantilism imposed on itself, we may overlook the fact that it had little success in its work as an agent of unification. It is obvious that the endeavours to attain economic unity within the state would, if effective, have resulted in greater freedom of economic life within the state. Domestic tolls, local privileges, and inequalities in the system of coinage, weights and measures, the absence of unity in legislation, administration and taxation, it was against these that the mercantilist statesmen struggled. They therefore opposed everything that bound down economic life to a particular place and obstructed trade within the boundaries of the state. Here again, they defended a revolutionary principle; the revolution would, if it had been successful, have abolished a host of hindrances to economic liberty. On this point, the description of the industrial code and its development in England (in the 6th chapter of the first part) has, in particular, given many illustrations.

At the same time, our concern here is with efforts which did not postulate economic freedom as their theoretical starting-point, but which did indirectly tend in the same direction, in so far as they had any effect at all. The aim was the superiority of the state over all other forces within a country. But in actual fact, the theoretical striving after liberty on the part of the mercantilists went ever so much further. It was consciously grounded in a theoretical conception of the utility of freedom, and was therefore made, at least in principle, to apply even beyond the boundaries of the state. A great host of illustrations may be adduced in proof of this. The actual notions of the mercantilists do not tally with the idea usually held with regard to them, and their ideas are even so contradictory among themselves that it appears suitable to document them in detail before entering upon explanations.

If the fact was altogether too obvious to overlook that the mercantilists arrayed themselves on the side of liberty, this has usually been explained as an effect of Dutch influence. The explanation was obvious in so far as Holland was on the whole the model country to which the mercantilists referred at every turn, but precisely for this reason the explanation is unsatisfactory; for if it held, mercantilism would have consisted throughout in an imitation of the Dutch, which was very far from being the case. The best evidence for the central position of the belief in liberty in mercantilist ideology is to be found in its most prominent practical representative and statesman, who did not by any means choose the Dutch in particular for his schoolmaster.

There are very few slogans of such frequent recurrence in the voluminous correspondence of Colbert as the phrase "Liberty is the soul of trade" (*la liberté est l'âme du commerce*) ; and it is to be found also under many variations. Sometimes he said that trade had to be "utterly free" (*extrêmement libre*), that it was "the result of the free will of man", that "commerce consists universally in the liberty of all men to buy and sell". In another place he wrote "His Majesty has long been aware on account of his great experience that liberty is the soul of trade and desires that merchants should have complete freedom to do as they wish, that they may be induced to bring hither their food-stuffs and merchandise which they believe they can sell in the most rapid and most secure manner". This was by no means merely a phrase. In fact Colbert never tired of reminding his intendants within the country and his governors in the colonies, or even of threatening them with force, if they seemed to him to be placing obstacles in the way of trade. A typical example is one of his letters of the year 1671 to an itinerant intendant. The latter had drawn up and forwarded two ordinances. Colbert replied and wrote that if he sent him such ordinances again, the King (i.e. Colbert) would be compelled to dismiss him: "For ten long years His Majesty has worked to create complete freedom of trade in his realm, has opened his ports to all peoples that trade may be increased, and in these ordinances (of the intendant) there is not a word that is not calculated to fetter this liberty of trade which is the soul of commerce and without which it could not exist. The object of your mission is to increase this liberty."[1]

On this point, Colbert distinguished himself from other mercan-

[1] *Lettres de Colbert* II 473, 477, 632, 681, III : II 584.

tilists only in his tendency to formulate his views in more theoretical terms. Similar examples are to be found in almost all others. Laffemas, one of the oldest mercantilist writers in France, called one of his pamphlets Les discours d'une liberté générale (1601). In connection with the assembly of the French Estates General in the year 1614—the last one before 1789—the third estate declared, starting from colonial trade, that with reference to all branches of economic life, "Commerce, trade and manufacturers, ought to be made free for all things and for all places." In England Sir Edward Coke, the "Father of the Common Law", observed at roughly the same time (1621), "Freedom of trade is the life of trade." Axel Oxenstierna, the Swedish Chancellor, who became the virtual ruler of his country after the death of Gustavus Adolphus, wrote in 1633 that "trade has been diminished, as it always loves freedom". Five years later (1638), the Swedish Government wrote to the city magistrates at Riga, "Since commerce is of such a character and faculty that where it shall be made to flourish and take its proper course, this must occur through liberty and the prevention of everything that might obstruct its course." Two Danish customs laws of the end of the century (1683, 1686) state that they were drawn up "with particular regard to the free and untrammelled course of trade". Becher said, "So should one also allow commerce its free course" (1667). In other words, liberty as a condition of trade was an axiom which belonged to the international phraseology of mercantilism.

If it happened that a mercantilist differed from this opinion, his observations usually show that he was aware of his contravention of the generally prevailing view. Thus for example, de Villeneuve, the French Ambassador at the Supreme Porte (1728/41), expressed himself against "this phantom which is called the liberty of trade"—nowadays one would hardly expect to find the phantom at all in mercantilism. Kammerdirektor Hille, an influential co-worker of Frederick William I of Prussia and the instructor of Frederick the Great in matters of economic policy, declared that, in contrast with his monarch, who repeated the Colbertian phrases, he held the "usual tale" that trade must be free to be incorrect, or at least not correct in all circumstances (universellement).[2]

---

[2] États généraux de 1614: extract in G. Picot, Histoire des états généraux IV (Paris 1872) 128.—Sir Edw. Coke: Proceedings and Debates 1621: quot. Campbell, Lives of the Chief Justices of England I 313.—Swedish instances: Axel Oxenstiernas skrifter och brefvexling first part I 484; Register of outgoing

It goes without saying that the conception of freedom of trade should not be taken in its modern context; but just as false as this assumption would be is the idea that it was pointless. The slogan of freedom of trade was employed—and not only by Colbert— as an argument for or against definite measures. The fact that it could occupy such a position in economic discussions shows that certain weight was placed upon it.

Freedom of commerce included as a rule also freedom in the exercise of any other trade, according to verbal usage "commerce" (just as "trade") being taken quite generally as a collective definition of all industrial activity. In the sphere of industrial production there was in addition the attitude to monopolies, which has been treated in sufficient detail above in connection with the English industrial code. Even on the continent the free exercise of a trade was, in principle, regarded as theoretically correct. But it could hardly have any practical application on account of the impossibility of abolishing the medieval regulation of trade, and also as a consequence of *other* new ideals besides that of liberty. The situation here was reminiscent of that resolution of the French national convention during the Revolution which aimed at abolishing the death penalty, but was made, so to speak, in the shadow of the guillotine, in other words on the assumption that an entirely new situation would arise to make the realization of this decision possible. But in Colbert's case, his theoretical attitude was not entirely without effect on the actual situation in which he found himself. A well-known utterance of his demonstrates sufficiently what principles guided him in the matter (1679). "You may be convinced," he said, "that I shall never hesitate to withdraw all privileges if I see in it a greater or even just as great an advantage." And again, "It will cause great difficulty to obtain exclusive privileges for all manufactures already in existence in the country, and they (the privileges) will only be maintained for such as are entirely unknown."[3] Here Colbert adopted the same attitude as was expressed, in its best known terms, in the English Statute of Monopolies (1623/24), which is still the basis of modern patent legislation.

To this attitude several different factors contributed.

letters, 17 April 1638 (Swedish Royal Archives), respectively.—Denmark: after Birck, *Told og Accise* 50.—Becher, *Politische Discurs*, Part 3 ch. 1 (1673 ed. 263).—Villeneuve: quot. Masson, *Hist. du comm. franç. dans le Levant au 18ᵉ siècle* 15.—Hille, etc.: quot. W. Naudé, "Die merkantilist. Wirtschaftspolitik Friedrich Wilhelms I.," etc. (*Hist. Zeitschr.* XC, 1902, 15, 29, cf. 34–40).

   [3] *Lettres de Colbert* II 694 f.

On the one hand it should not be overlooked what was pointed out in connection with the anti-monopoly attitude in England, that even the medieval tradition was sympathetic to a certain sort of freedom. The medieval influence was thus not without importance to the notion of economic liberty under mercantilism, thus, for example, the previously quoted *Discourse of Corporations* with its extreme anti-monopolist tendency preserves clear traces of its intellectual medieval origin even towards the end of the 1580's. Its tendency was purely that of the policy of provision; it regarded the primary disadvantage of monopoly as "a cause of all dearth and scarcity in the Common wealth" and as being opposed to the nature of society and its development in cities, whose aim was "to live in plenty and cheapness".[4] Here one may perceive a tendency towards economic liberty that was never entirely broken off and therefore connected medieval and *laissez-faire* ideals. In as far as in mercantilism we are only dealing with the background of opinion which expressed itself in traditional formulae, the heritage of the Middle Ages is certainly a partial explanation of the strivings towards economic liberty.

On the other hand this does not provide an essential explanation for that enthusiasm for liberty which influenced economic realities; and for this other origins must be sought.

An important cause lay undoubtedly in the general intellectual development which has usually been derived from the Renaissance —a conclusion that is not affected by the lively discussions to-day on the nature and the first beginnings of the Renaissance. In philosophy we may refer first and foremost to Spinoza and Hobbes, both of whom tried to characterize absolutism as a means for the realization of the intellectual freedom of the individual.[5] But it cannot be over-emphasized that these factors had only a very indirect bearing on mercantilism and on the mercantilists. The most immediate urge for them was still of an economic nature, and it is not difficult to establish in this case wherein their motive consisted.

The decisive factor was the belief in the blessings of *trade*, and the importance of trade for all the objectives which mercantilism pursued, not least the interest in power. This side of mercantilism

[4] Pr. in *Tudor Econ. Docs.* III 266.—Cf. above, I 274 f., II 94 f.

[5] See, e.g., Meinecke, *Idee der Staatsräson* 277, cf. 264, 268.—The new conception of the Renaissance is represented in Germany by Burdach and others, and has obtained a gifted, though somewhat one-sided, representative in Sweden who has marshalled many new points in its favour, in a book of which a French edition has now appeared, J. Nordström, *Moyen-âge et renaissance* (Paris 1933).

moreover has often been overlooked in directing attention primarily to its industrial protectionism; and, to the extent that the "fear of goods" is most prominent, with justification. But for the mercantilists, the desire to rid oneself of goods was bound up quite closely with trade and more particularly foreign trade; and so the literal sense of the name mercantilism is not altogether misapplied. Partly, there were in this respect traditional conceptions, for which Seneca and Aristotle have been given as authorities, with regard to inter-state exchange as being a weapon in the wise hands of providence. Partly, too, and much more important, this belief was linked to the whole new tendency evoked by the influence of the merchants and the state's striving after power. In many respects this attitude presents a profound contrast with the medieval conceptions, for it was of considerable difficulty to justify pure trade, without the technical manufacture of goods, by the canonical social ethics and theory of value. But it is none the less possible to establish in this case, too, a certain connection with medieval ideas.

The descriptions particularly common in the 16th century of the economic interdependence of various countries on account of the differentiated allotment of the material gifts of nature, occasionally include a really lucid idea of the economic function of international division of labour, and are probably, at least to some extent, to be derived from the religious and ethical heritage of the Middle Ages.

It was in this sense that the English authors of about the middle of the 16th century pursued their arguments. The pamphlet ascribed to Clement Armstrong, called *Howe to Reforme the Realme etc.* (1535/36), was decidedly narrow in its outlook, but with regard to import goods it states that they are "needful for the common weal of the realm which God hath ordained in other countries and not in England". William Cholmeley wrote a few decades later (1553), "As God hath enriched us with wool, lead, leather and tin, so hath he enriched other countries with other commodities which we may in no wise lack." It was the "Doctor", as usual, in the *Discourse of the Common Weal* (1549), who summed up the argument best. "Surely," he said, "common reason would that one region should help another when it lacketh. And therefore God hath ordained that no country should have all commodities; but that, that one lacketh, another bringeth forth and that, that one country lacketh this year, another hath plenty thereof the same year, to the extent that one may know they have need of another's help, and thereby Love and society to grow amongst all the more"—a pretty little sermon on the religious sanctity of international trade.[6]

The English conception was not distinguished on this point from the continental. One of the most detailed formulations of the idea is to be found in a French statute of the same period (1557). In connection with a resolution of an assembly of the nobles, extensive export freedom was commanded. The reasons given are so verbose as to compel a certain amount of abbreviation: "Experience has always shown," it runs, "that the chief means of making the nation and the subjects of the kingdoms, counties and provinces wealthy, rich and prosperous has been and still is the freedom of trade and commerce, as it is exercised with neighbours and strangers to whom they sell and with whom they exchange food-stuffs, manufactures and commodities, which they carry forth from the places and countries that they find themselves in, so as to bring back others which are lacking there, with gold, silver and other useful things. . . . Otherwise the commodities and fruits which grow in the countries aforesaid . . . as also the specialities (*singularitez*) and manufactures which are made there, would necessarily have to be consumed by the inhabitants on the same spot . . . whereby the aforesaid fruits would therefore . . . largely become almost useless." Roughly ten years later (1568) Bodin wrote in entirely the same spirit in his famous pamphlet on money, on the subject of the mutual interdependence of countries because of the apportionment of divine gifts among them—he believed that they could not wage war among themselves for this reason—and of the religious duty to allow others to participate in what the native country was blessed with.

Utterances of this kind were not limited to the 16th century. The continual reference to the blessings of trade is to be found, too, in the following century and later. For the beginning of the 17th century we have, among others, a good example in the so-called contract of the Swedish General Trading Company of 1625. But Colbert and his colleagues also employed this argument industriously in their directions of policy, when addressing themselves to foreigners. In the French bye-laws for the East India and Northern Companies it was played upon at great length. The bye-laws of the Northern Company, for example, were introduced in the following pretty terms (1669), "Whereas

---

[6] The references to Seneca and Aristotle: Misselden, *Free Trade* 25.—The first two quotations pr. *Tudor Econ. Docs.* III 129, 131, the last, *Disc. of the Common Weal*, ed. Lamond, 61.

trade is the most fitting means for reconciling different nations and for maintaining a good mutual understanding between opposing spirits, whereas it (further) . . . diffuses surplus in the most harmless manner, makes nations happy and states prosperous," etc. A similar paean of praise was sung to trade in the introduction to the famous manual for merchants *Le parfait négociant*, issued a few years later (1675) by Jacques Savary, Colbert's assistant in the field of commercial legislation. It is therefore entirely misleading that a similar utterance in the French chamber of commerce in the year 1701 (by the deputy for Bordeaux) has been interpreted as an expression of the growing *laissez-faire* ideas. In reading mercantilist observations on trade, it is in fact surprising to note the extent to which not only ideas but even expressions are in accord with those of the more eloquent and flowery advocates of *laissez-faire*. To give one example among hundreds, the remarks just quoted might be compared with those of a Swedish representative of the old *laissez-faire* school, J. A. Gripenstedt. On the occasion of a joint meeting of the four estates of the Swedish parliament of the time, he, as minister of finance, in the year 1857, made two speeches in which he lauded trade to such a decree that both were later called his "flower paintings". "I believe," he said, "that trade in its great world-embracing diffusion is the mightiest weapon in the hands of Providence for the edification of the human race; indeed, that it is the great and deep and yet quietly flowing river, gently but surely carrying the fate of the human race towards a higher culture, a higher radiance and a more universal brotherhood. And therefore I repeat once again: honour trade and its magnificent work, the blessing of mankind!"[7]

This religious and ethical complexion apart, mercantilism contained two further elements with regard to which intentions were probably more sincere; first, the direct interest of the merchant and—peculiar as it may appear—partly also the tendency to commercial warfare, which Colbert, as we have seen, had carefully kept at a distance from *these* manifestations. For the rest, the distinction between this and what has already

[7] Statute of 1557: pr. *Recueil des anciennes lois françaises* (ed. Isambert, etc.) XIII 506 f.—Bodin, *Discours sur le rehavssement et diminvtion des monnoyes* (1578 ed., unpag.).—"Contract" of the General Trading Company: pr. *Samling utaf K. Bref . . . ang. Sweriges Rikes Commerce . . .* (ed. Stiernman) I 914.— Bye-laws of the two French companies: pr. *Lettres de Colbert* II 785, 800.— Savary, *Le parfait négociant* Bk. 1 ch. 1.— Deputy for Bordeaux 1701: pr. Martin, *La grande industrie sous Louis XIV* 376.—J. A. Gripenstedt, *Tal, anföranden och uppsatser* I (Sthlm. 1871) 264.

been illustrated was not great; a small number of further quotations from some of the best English pamphleteers is therefore all that is necessary.

Thomas Mun concluded his famous pamphlet, *England's Treasure by Forraign Trade*, with the following grandiose eulogy of commerce, "Behold then, the true form and work of foreign Trade, which is, The great Revenue of the King, the honour of the Kingdom, The Noble profession of the Merchant, The school of our Arts, The supply of our wants, The employment of our poor, The improvement of our Lands, the Nursery of our Mariners, The walls (=ships) of the Kingdom, The means of our Treasure, The Sinews of our Wars, The terror of our Enemies. For all which great and weighty reasons, do so many well governed States highly countenance the profession, and carefully cherish the action, not only with Policy to increase it, but also with power to protect it from all foreign injuries: because they know it is a Principle in Reason of State to maintain and defend that which doth Support them and their estates." Roger Coke bridges the gulf between mercantilism and *laissez-faire* in an even more typical manner. On the one hand, the whole of his literary work is permeated with bitterness and envy on account of the commercial superiority of the Dutch, and to this extent, his outlook was firmaments removed from the cosmopolitan tendency to economic harmony of Hume and Adam Smith; but on the other hand, his economic arguments contained more liberal doctrines than do most others among mercantilists of note. The second of his four collected pamphlets, which incidentally was directed specifically against the Dutch (1671), eulogizes trade in its preface in the following terms, "And this is so well understood, that Trade is now become the Lady, which in this present Age is more Courted and Celebrated than in any former, by all the Princes and Potentates of the World, and that deservedly too: For she acquires not her Dominion by the horrid and rueful face of War, whose footsteps leave ever behind them deep impressions of misery, devastation, and poverty; but with the pleasant aspect of Wealth and Plenty of all things conducing to the benefit of human Life and Society, accompanied with strength to defend her, in case any shall attempt to Ravish or Invade her."[8]

Mun's passage quoted above indeed contains mention of the "Noble profession of the Merchant". The growing importance of middle-class ideals, expressed in the admiration for the rich,

[8] Mun, ch. 21 (ed. Ashley 119).—Coke, *Treatise* II: *Reasons of the Increase of the Dutch Trade*, Preface to the Reader (unpag.).

industrious and thrifty Dutch—illustrated in northern literature perhaps most clearly by Ludvig Holberg, the most important dramatist of Denmark—naturally furnished a major reason why trade enjoyed such a continually growing appreciation, while it had been suspect in the eyes of the church and despised by medieval nobles. Although not himself a merchant, Davenant went even further than the merchant Mun when, towards the turn of the century, he wrote of "The Merchant, who deserves all Favour as being the best, and most profitable member of the Common-Wealth". It is equally typical that a French Catholic priest, Father Mathias de Saint-Jean, wrote a whole book on the "Honourable Commerce" (*Le commerce honorable*, 1647), the second part of which praised trade and shipping and ascribed to it all possible benefits, in language that sounds almost ironical to modern ears, but is actually used in all sincerity. In a chapter on the utility of trade to all subjects, he said first that priests gained by it through the alms and endowments of merchants. He then treated of the advantages of trade to the *noblesse de robe*, who thereby received high prices for its services, thanks to the many law-suits engendered by trade. He then continued, "It is the consummation of marriages with the daughters of burghers, who have often gained their estates in trades", which brought the members of this *noblesse* to their offices. If the priesthood had gone so far in one of its representatives, though truly a shallow-minded one, it is easy to see that more bourgeois circles entertained not the slightest doubt about the blessings of trade.[9]

The high esteem in which the merchant's activity was held is manifested, too, in another feature of mercantilism which hitherto has not been given sufficient attention. Although they idealized the state, the mercantilists were by no means as a rule supporters of state enterprise in the economic field. In Sweden it was Axel Oxenstierna who struggled consistently and with deep conviction against tendencies of this kind. His most significant literary contribution in the economic sphere is a memorandum on the copper trade, which, from the point of view of the government, was the most important branch of Swedish economic life (1630). In this memorandum he was at pains to advocate the transference of the trade to private hands. Commenting upon the opposite method which had been attempted in the previous

---

[9] L. Holberg, esp. *Jean de France* (1722) Act 1 Scene 1, and *Den 11. Junii* (1723) Act 1 Scene 1.—Davenant, *An Essay upon Ways and Means of Supplying the War* (1695; 3rd ed., Lond. 1701, 57).—[M. de Saint-Jean] Part 2, esp. ch. 6, quot. 179.

years, he said, "It (the copper trade) has gradually gone downhill, which is not to be feared as long as private persons pursue the trade and his Royal Majesty dominates the *consilia* of all with his customs duties." He adopted a similar attitude towards a later proposal (1639) with regard to a new organization for trade with France. The Minutes of the State Council on the matter records, "*Ex incidenti* there arose the question of whether the Crown was to engage in the said trade with advantage, which the Chancellor decided in the negative. The Crown ought only to direct the activity and encourage that commerce may grow and increase, and then impose and wisely moderate the customs duties upon it."

In truth mercantilism, at least in the countries of Western and Northern Europe, did not favour state enterprise at all. According to modern and even according to old liberal standards, in many cases it even went surprisingly far in precisely the opposite direction. I have already shown (at the end of the 7th chapter of the first part, *v.s.* I 453 f.) that the criticism directed by Adam Smith against the trading companies was mainly directed against the fact that these private business concerns acquired functions which could only be exercised properly by the state itself in the interests of its subjects; that, in fact, the mercantilist system allowed legitimate state functions to pass into the hands of private merchant corporations. This was true in almost every sphere of activity. The English and Dutch merchant companies were each in themselves a kind of *imperium in imperio*, a state within a state. In many cases they even wielded a world-wide power. In social matters, too, in England things were preferably left to private enterprise, and that, indeed, in a manner which would no longer be dreamt of to-day (*v.s.* I 255 f.). All this is an expression of the firm belief of mercantilists in the propriety of free commercial activity, and thus furnishes an illustration of the portion of the mercantilist conception of society which is being considered here.

It must certainly be admitted that conditions in this respect varied in different countries. Of the out-and-out mercantilist countries, only England displayed these features in their extreme form. But Sweden was not far behind, in spite of a Civil Service that was one of the best of the time. Not only Oxenstierna, one of the principal creators of Swedish administrative organization, but all his successors in the 17th century, worked in the same direction by word and deed and not least among them the founder of the short-lived Swedish absolutism, Charles XI, the father of Charles XII. It was especially important that the iron industry, with its steadily increasing domination of Swedish economic life, was systematically brought into private hands; but it was the same with almost all other branches of industrial life, including the eagerly encouraged, though rather artificial, textile manufactures.

Several of the German states, by way of contrast, instituted the regular state business enterprises which their mercantilist authors had demanded. In the German mercantilist literature, the merchant was in general regarded with much greater distrust than in the English. But Germany was by no means looked up to as a model in economic matters at that time. France was, of course, of much greater importance. Colbert, too, believed that a merchant required perpetual admonishing and stimulating. The French trading companies were thinly disguised state enterprises, as is shown in the chapter on the development of company organization (*v.s.* I 345 ff.). But even in so "paternal" a country as France there is nevertheless a powerful tendency in favour of private trade. Attempts were made to give even the French companies the form of private enterprises. If that failed it was largely due to the mistrust on the part of capitalists and merchants, although admittedly also to the fact that when it came to the point, the minister could not refrain from interference. That in France, too, private enterprise was regarded as a desirable, if not an attainable, goal allows no room for doubt. To this extent French policy illustrates the same tendency which reached full flower in the two maritime powers, England and Holland, and dominated Sweden, too.[10]

[10] Oxenstierna: *Skrifter och brefvexling*, first part I (Sthlm. 1888) 350; cf. 491; *Svenska riksrådets protokoll* VII (Sthlm. 1895) 504.—For the rest I must refer, with regard to Sweden, to the first volume of my study, *Sveriges ekon. hist.* I : 2 680–83. Of the German and Austrian mercantilists, it was primarily Becher who never tired of demanding state undertakings, among them a "magazine" with a monopoly of import and perhaps also export, the former to leave the raw materials to the merchants, who would then have them worked up by the craftsmen. Becher declared this to be entirely reconcilable with the principle of trading freedom, for "free commerce consists in this, that things are bought without hindrance according to what is good and cheap" (*Politische Discurs* Part 3 ch. 1 point 2; Frankfurt ed. 1673, 277–88, quot. 286). Concerning his projects and those of the other German mercantilists there is a copious literature; see e.g., H. v. Srbik, *Wilhelm von Schröder* (Sitzungsberichte der Akademie der Wissenschaften in Wien, philosophy and history section CLXIV: I, Vienna 1910, 131 ff.).— On the mistrust of merchants, see below 320 f., Von Schrötter made of chapter 106 of his *Fürstliche Schatz- und Rent-Cammer* "a general caveat of the merchants concerning advice-giving", partly for political reasons; but he also had in mind their aversion to domestic manufactures—a rather unusual attitude for the time, because the merchants, indeed, were as a rule the financiers of the manufactures.

Their belief in trade and the merchant goes a long way towards explaining why the mercantilists made economic "liberty" their lodestar. If the chain of motives is traced back further, one arrives at a universal intellectual reorientation and its special application to economic activity. In spite of the mercantilists' static outlook on economic affairs and the economic system of the world as a whole, they tried with a fanatic zeal to secure, each for his native country, as large as possible a share in the activities of this system, which was regarded as an unchangeable total. In its psychological tendency mercantilism may therefore, to this extent, be regarded as dynamic. The mentality of the most powerful spirits among its statesmen, navigators, merchants, and writers was poles apart from the medieval ideal. In addition, their ideal was that of acquisitive trade. And so it is perfectly explicable that this ideal itself and the individuals who practised it must have appeared to the mercantilists in a sublime light, and that "liberty" must have appeared to them as the principle proper for the attainment of their ideal. All in all, there was manifest that universal emancipation of the mind which was growing at that period, rooted in the changes in economic life and yet reacting upon them.

What the actual significance of the abstract idolizing of "freedom of trade" was, is a question of a different order. It touches upon the relation between the conception of society and economic doctrine. This problem will be carried a step further after other aspects of the mercantilist conception of society have received consideration.

2. ETHICS AND RELIGION

The point in which the breach between mercantilism and the medieval outlook was widest and most decisive was certainly in the domain of the ethical. We may say that the mercantilists were amoral in a two-fold sense, both in their aims as also in the means for the attainment of their ends. This two-fold amorality arose from their widespread indifference towards mankind, both in its capacity as a reasoning animal, as also in its attitude towards the eternal. Hobbes' Leviathan or "Mortal God", the state, dominated the arguments of the mercantilists to such a degree that in the place of an interest in human beings came the interest in the state. This certainly explains a part, but not the whole, of their lack of moral consideration, as will now appear.

Amoral ends

Firstly, the welfare of society or, in actual fact, the welfare of the state was substituted in place of the amelioration of the individual. This was a perfectly simple corollary of the *raison d'état*, or pure machiavellism. But the amorality of the new policy was not exhausted in this rearrangement. In addition, the welfare of the state itself or the *raison d'état* was conceived emphatically as materialistic or economic (in the popular sense of the term). To this there was no counterpart in ordinary machiavellism. The breach herein manifested with the religious and ethical attitude of the Middle Ages in the sphere of political ideas was profound.

With regard to the ethical conception of economic matters, the treatment of the inexhaustible problem of *interest* or usury was typical. The change in the mercantilist doctrine, when compared with the canonical medieval conception prevalent formerly, with its opposition to interest on moral and religious grounds, did not consist simply in a clearer insight into the economic factors leading to the taking of interest. That, in the main, was a post-mercantilist development. What was decisive was that the attitude towards the problem of interest was determined by an entirely new set of motives, fairly independent of whether and in what form interest was approved of at all. These new motives were of an economic nature, connected with the effects of interest and of the prohibition against interest on economic life; they no longer had anything to do with divine precepts. The canonical authorities had certainly tried, with adroitness and skill, to formulate the prohibition against interest in such a manner as not to collide more than necessary with economic activity, which indeed was inescapable. But they did this without abandoning the principle of the absolute nature of the prohibition, which among the canonical authorities was grounded in a religious decree unaffected by temporal considerations. In many fields real interest-taking was permitted, because it involved the taking of a certain amount of risk. Where no risk was considered to be involved interest-taking was forbidden. The novelty then was that precisely a temporal and economic foundation was adopted. The change occurred primarily in the reasons given rather than in the practical conclusions drawn. In the course of time, however, changes took place in the latter, too. The problem is dealt with at length in the literature on the subject, in a way which I think perfectly correct, and the considerations pointed out here are brought out there with proper emphasis. The facts may therefore be described in all brevity.[11]

That the earlier conception still flourished at a comparatively late period may be seen clearly in Thomas Wilson's *Discourse upon Usury* (1572), which, indeed, was by no means profound, but was highly esteemed at the time of its appearance. As Professor R. H. Tawney, its recent editor, has remarked, this work is particularly instructive because its author was not a priest, withdrawn from worldly affairs, but a lawyer trained in Roman Law. He had held the positions of Master of Requests, English Ambassador to the Netherlands and Secretary of State to Queen Elizabeth, to whom the ways of the world were no closed book. In his book, Wilson propounds an imaginary discussion in which a lawyer trained in civil law and a clergyman named an "anti-usurer" (Ockerfoe) represent the author's side. They both violently spurn interest. The lawyer calls the usurer "the worst man that liveth", and would see him hanged. Under his own name in the Preface, Wilson says that he would like to have usurers exterminated like wolves. They should be either condemned to death or banished the country; at the very least, their property should be confiscated on their death. The clergyman's attitude is even more severe. The lawyer would have tolerated interest at least in cases where no obvious damage was done. But the priest—who had already, in an earlier passage in the book, wished all usurers to die of a murrain, because they lived like cattle and so should die like cattle—objected to this, and induced all the other participants in the discussion to agree to his unconditional condemnation of interest, in all cases and irrespective of its effects, for, as he said simply, it is against God's law. Wilson's personal attitude may be seen from a parliamentary debate on the maximum rate of interest, held in the year before the publication of his book, and it harmonizes completely with the views put forward in the latter. That a man in his position and at so late a period could defend such views and gain a great following by doing so is an adequate illustration that the conception pre-

[11] With regard to the more recent literature on these questions, the following references may suffice: Ashley, *Introduction to English Economic History and Theory* II ch. 6; E. v. Böhm-Bawerk, *Geschichte und Kritik der Kapitalzins-Theorien* (Jena 1884, 4th ed. 1921) ch. 3; G. Cassel, *The Nature and Necessity of Interest* (Lond. 1903) ch. 1; Tawney, *Religion and the Rise of Capitalism* (Lond. 1926) *passim.*—The most complete documentation, from partly the same points of view as those that follow in the text here, is Professor Tawney's Introduction to Wilson's *Discourse upon Usury* (Lond. 1925); see esp. 171.

vailing before mercantilism had created a new attitude. This may be asserted even if we add that Wilson, in true lawyer fashion, probably exaggerated the case for which he held a brief and that he makes an impression of general narrow-mindedness.[12]

It was not long before the mercantilists arrived at other conclusions. Bacon discussed interest without introducing almost any ethical or religious considerations. The essential point is not his acknowledgment that it was impossible to prevent "usury", for that merely illustrates his keen eye for realities. What was important is that he was guided in his condemnation of interest by economic and social standards. In this he distinguished himself profoundly from the theological formalism characterizing Wilson's argument of half a century before. Bacon drew up a list of the advantages and disadvantages of usury. This in itself is evidence of an attitude free from prejudice. But further it appears that all the seven disadvantages given were of an economic and not an ethical or a religious nature; and it is in this that the vital transformation is manifest. On the later development of ideas, another work was even more important. Sir Thomas Culpeper the elder, a contemporary of Bacon, wrote a *Tract against Usurie* (1621), a work which Sir Josiah Child reprinted in 1668 without knowing the author, and with which he closely associated himself. The introduction itself contains a declaration by Culpeper that he left the question of the propriety or illegality of interest to the clergy. What he limited himself to was to show that it was detrimental to a country without gold and silver mines, but with a plentiful supply of commodities. In the following discussion, also, Culpeper kept closely to this plan. He described it as a danger for the English that the Dutch, as neighbours of England, had a rate of interest of only 6 per cent, while the English paid 10 per cent. He then spoke of the effects on the country's ability to compete, the burden of state debt, agricultural rents, the period for the turn-over in afforestation, etc.—all purely economic arguments of greater or less accuracy, but without exception of a purely economic nature.[13]

As early as 1545/46 a statute regarding a maximum rate of interest had taken the place of a prohibition of interest. When the

---

[12] Wilson esp. 1 f., 183, 230, 285 f., 341 f., 350 ff., 363.—Wilson's observation in the 1571 debate: pr. (after d'Ewes, *Journal*) *Tudor Econ. Docs.* II 156 ff.
[13] Bacon *Essays*: No. 41 in the 1625 ed.: "Of Usurie" (ed. Wright 169).— Culpeper repr. as appendix to [Child], *Brief Observations Concerning Trade and Interest* (Lond. 1668) and contained together with the latter in his *New Discourse of Trade*.

prohibition had been brought into force again after some years, the legislation laying down a maximum rate of interest instead was made permanent by a law of 1571. It was this Bill which Thomas Wilson had attacked. It is true that several reservations were made in the statute regarding the validity of an agreement to take interest, but these were insignificant with regard to the application of the law. The early conception obviously did not disappear in the twinkling of an eye, but the new attitude gained more and more ground in the course of the 17th century. After the Puritan Revolution, public discussion no longer entered into the moral or ethical question of whether interest was permissible or not, but dealt with the practical economic problems of how *high* the rate of interest ought to be and whether its height should be limited by a legal maximum. Conservative opinion, with Sir Josiah Child as its most influential and convinced mouthpiece, answered the second question in the affirmative, putting forward the same arguments as Culpeper, i.e. by referring to the economic effects of interest. It is characteristic that the problem of interest, of all economic problems the one that was most calculated to provoke moral acrimony, was thus subjected to a purely economic discussion, even on the part of the advocates of a conservative policy. When at a later date the opposing forces, headed by Locke, with the assistance of an argument irrefutable in mercantilist eyes, won an intellectual victory over these advocates of a legal limitation in the rate of interest, this was in fact not a new step toward rendering economic discussion morally neutral; for the medieval moral conception of interest had already been outgrown —at least for the time being—by men active and influential in practical affairs. Not till well into the 19th century was the maximum limit to the rate of interest allowed to lapse in individual countries; but the "intellectual revolution" had already been ushered in by mercantilism.[14]

The sphere of *luxury* is equally typical. In this respect, too, mercantilism tended to substitute economic for moral considerations. It has already been observed in the third part (110,169) how mercantilism came to approve of luxury where it served to sell native commodities. Here we need only point out that this constituted a great revolution from the ethical point of view. Luxury was reprehensible to the medieval mind, for the striving after luxury took man out of his proper and religiously determined

[14] Statutes: 37 Hen. VIII c. 9; 5 & 6 Ed. VI. c. 20; 13 Eliz. c. 8.—Child, *New Discourse of Trade* (in the form of a collection 1692).—Locke, *Some Considerations of the Consequences of the Lowering of Interest*, etc. (1691).

"subsistence" and the standard of life corresponding to it. Like so many other medieval ideas, this persisted with great tenacity and often was victorious over the outlook of more recent times, as is shown in the innumerable sumptuary laws down to the 19th century. But in so far as the ordinances were based on such ethical foundations, they came into conflict with mercantilist ideals. From the mercantilist point of view, they could be justified only if they prohibited the use of commodities the consumption of which ought to be discouraged in the interests of trade and industry, i.e. usually foreign products. Mercantilism rejected in principle any ethical attitude towards luxury. The only consideration that carried weight was how far a particular measure furthered or obstructed economic life in the direction which mercantilism tried to lead it. Thus, finally, in strictest contrast to the medieval standpoint, there arose a conscious and frankly admitted tendency to justify luxury, indeed to stimulate it, quite irrespective of the status of the purchaser, in all cases in which it guaranteed a market for the country's products and "put money into circulation". Since economic policy set itself the task of building up native luxury industries, this consideration inevitably had to assert itself with greater and greater strength.

In one of his very first pamphlets, *Les trésors et richesses pour mettre l'Estat en splendeur* (1598), Laffemas thundered against people who objected to the use of French silks; those who exceeded in it damaged only themselves while their money remained in the country; and all purchasers of French luxury goods created a livelihood for the poor, whereas the miser caused them to die in distress.

The breach between the old and new outlook is better illustrated a little later in Montchrétien (1615). He began, in the first place, with a furious condemnation of the luxury which led to the shopkeeper to be dressed like the gentleman, and could only end in the overthrow of all order in society. "If Your Majesties," he complained, "do not lead us out of this confusion and external uniformity (*indifférence*) then all is at an end: all together they will result in the bankruptcy of true and convinced virtue: everybody will hunt after what is vain . . . brazenness will wax in the cities and tyranny in the country. Men will become effeminate because of the far too widespread opportunities for pleasure; through their endeavours to adorn themselves women will lose their modesty and their ability to manage their homes"— thus a purely moral evaluation. But further on, he comes to speak of the French luxury industries, which he would, of course, encourage by all possible means, and so he comes round to Laffemas' view. His reproach thus becomes entirely confined to foreign luxury goods: "Now since times and the world have changed," he observes, "I will not blame the use (of luxuries) altogether, provided that profit remains in the country, otherwise it becomes far too dear for us"—the degeneration of society no longer counts for anything.

In the later 17th century the new attitude was, without reservation, predominant. Petty (1662) justified "entertainments, magnificent shews, triumphal arches &c.," on the ground that their costs flowed back into the pockets of brewers, bakers, tailors, shoemakers and so forth; Fortrey justified "excess of apparel", and with regard to those that condemned it, said, "It rather ought to be maintained, and encouraged"—of course, assuming that the usual mercantilist demands were fulfilled. Von Schrötter (1686) directly attacked the regulations forbidding excessive display in clothing and declared that he would rather this was even greater. Barbon (1690) said, "Prodigality is a Vice that is prejudicial to the Man, but not to Trade . . . Covetousness is a Vice, prejudicial both to Man and Trade" and so on. The effect of this view in practice appeared, for example, in Sweden, where in the years 1708 and 1709, when the country had been involved for upwards of a decade in a war of life and death, the merchants were obliged to take over definite quantities of silks.

Thus the ground was well prepared for the most provocative and most widely discussed formulation of this mercantilist argument that it ever received, namely, for Mandeville's aphorism in the best-known title to his frequently quoted book, *Private Vices Publick Benefits* (1705, 1714 etc.), which was not only amoral, but was in fact immoral. In North European literature, too, the idea was put forward in the period immediately succeeding. The manner of its statement there is typical and demonstrates how very much this amoral attitude had already taken root, even among moralists. Holberg puts the following proof in the mouth of Henry, the pleasure-seeking domestic, in his comedy *Mascarade* (1724). The latter tries to convince Jeronimus, the old-fashioned father of his likewise pleasure-seeking master, Leander, that by giving alms, he merely supports the "lazy beggars", while he and Leander, the two masqueraders, were helping the "industrious beggars". He says, "The industrious beggars are tailors, shoemakers, huckstresses, confectioners and coachmen; to them we extend a helping hand. If all men lived so secluded a life as Herr Jeronimus, people of this kind would all die of hunger. You, sir, therefore reduce the whole nation to beggary by your almsgiving. But, as for us, we keep them from begging. If we are to help beggars it is better to help the diligent than the lazy." In a humorous way Holberg teaches exactly the same lesson here as Laffemas, Petty and several others had done in all seriousness. Anders Johan von Höpken, later Chancellor and at the age of twenty-eight president of the Swedish Academy of Sciences (1740), went so far as to select as the theme of his presidential address, "Of the Utility of Luxury".[15]

Equally typical is the development of English *tobacco policy*. There is a striking similarity between the fate of the tobacco policy and the change in attitude towards luxury as seen in the two-sided attitude of Montchrétien. When tobacco came into use as a luxury many serious men shook their wise heads, among them James I of England. The latter also published a small anonymous pamphlet called *A Covnterblaste to Tobacco* (1604), in which he demonstrated that the use of tobacco was morally reprehensible and medically harmful. In the same year he passed in his official capacity a proclamation concerned with imposing a duty on tobacco in the form of a fine, the reason given being perfectly typical. It was said in fact that this weed was formerly used only by the upper classes as a medicine, but that gradually it had become "through evil Custom and Toleration thereof, excessively taken by a number of riotous and disordered Persons of mean and base Condition, who . . . do spend most of their time in that idle Vanity, to the evil example and corrupting of others, and also do consume that Wages which many of them do get by their Labour and wherewith their Families should be relieved, not caring at what Price they buy that Drug . . . by which great and immoderate taking of Tobacco the Health of a great number of our People is impaired, and their Bodies weakened and made

---

[15] Laffemas, *Les trésors*, etc. 5 f., 11, 22.—Montchrétien, *Traicté de l'oeconomie politiqve* (1st ed. 83 f., 102).—Petty, *Treatise of Taxes*, ch. 3 (Econ. Writings, ed. Hull I 33).—Fortrey, *England's Interest and Improvement* (1st ed. 26, Repr. of Econ. Tracts ed. Hollander, 27).—[Von Schrötter], *Fürstl. Schatz- u. Rent-Cammer* ch. 56 (1st ed. 262).—Barbon, *Discourse of Trade* (1st ed., 62 f., Repr. of Econ. Tracts 32).—Sweden: K. Enghoff, *Tillståndet i Skåne . . . år 1707–1711* (Lund. 1889) 96; the basis is obviously a Letter Patent of 1695 (pr. *Samling Utaf. K. Bref. . . .*, ed. Stiernman, V 514).—Holberg, *Mascarade* Act 2, Scene 3.— Höpken, *Skrifter*, ed. C. Silfverstolpe, I (Sthlm. 1890) 160–70.—On the history of the literature: O. Wieselgren, *"Om yppighets nytta"* (Skrifter utg. av Humani- stiska Vetenskapssamfundet i Upsala XIV: III, Ups. 1912).—It was not easy to reconcile this argument with an admiration for Dutch thrift. Mandeville also believed that by their thrift the Dutch were simply making a virtue of necessity (1st ed. I 201–8, ed. Kaye I 185–90).

unfit for Labour", and so on and so forth. But it was no more than two decades later, by the year 1624, that the policy took a completely different course, without indeed the earlier attitude being given up in principle. The importance of tobacco-growing to Virginia and Somers Island was so great that imports from there were permitted, while tobacco production in England itself was forbidden later as earlier. In the very following year the colonial point of view was predominant. It was declared that by the infringement of the earlier ordinance, persons "have endeavoured as much as in them lieth to destroy so noble a work as the support of those Plantations which so much concerns our honour and the profit of our People". Gradually the tobacco policy became a major part of the old colonial system, without the moral objections put forward by James I being taken into further account. An Act of Parliament of 1660 declared without reservation that "Tobacco is one of the main products of several of those Plantations, upon which their Welfare and Subsistence and the Navigation of this Kingdom and vent of its Commodities thither do much depend". Mercantilism had thus won the day.[16]

Amoral means

What we have discussed above refers only to the amoral conception of the ends of economic activity, but in the choice of means for the attainment of these ends amoral considerations were likewise uppermost.

The underlying idea of mercantilism may be expressed as follows: people should be taken as they are and should be guided by wise measures in that direction which will enhance the well-being of the state. No one was more explicit in his statement of this view than Mandeville (1723). "Private Vices," he observed, *"by the dextrous Management of a skilful Politician* may be turned into Public Benefits" (my italics). What this meant primarily was that the individual's private economic interests were to be made serviceable for the ends of the state. Threats were to cease against anything that men were forced to aim at by natural necessity. At the same time, things ought to be arranged so cunningly that men aimed at something that was reconcilable with the interests of the state. The *Discourse of the Common Weal* goes into considerable detail on this point, "All things," says the author, "that should

---

[16] [James I], *A Covnterblaste to Tobacco* (repr. Engl. Reprints, ed. E. Arber, Lond. 1869).—Proclamations: pr. *Foedera* (ed. Rymer) 1st ed. XVI 601 ff., XVII 621–4, 668–72, Hague ed. VII: II 114 f., VII: IV 153–6, 186–9.— 1660 Act: 12 Car. II c. 34.—See for the rest Beer, *Origins of the Brit. Col. Syst.* ch. 4.

be done in a common wealth be not to be forced or to be constrained by the strait penalties of the law; but some so, and some
other by allurement, and rewards rather. For what law can compel
men to be industrious in travail, and labour of their bodies, or
studious to learn any science or knowledge of the mind? To these
things they may be well provoked, encouraged, and allured, if
they that be industrious and painful be well rewarded for their
pains, and be suffered to take gains and wealth as reward of their
labours . . . Take this reward from them, and go about
to compel them by laws thereto, what man will plough or dig
the ground, or exercise any manual occupation wherein is any
pain? Or who will adventure overseas for any merchandise? Or
use any faculty wherein any peril or danger should be, seeing his
reward shall be no more than his that sitteth still?" The author
did not return at all to the idea of direct compulsion. The same
tendency characterized the principles of practical statesmen.
Colbert wrote, on one occasion, "Very well do I know that the
merchants will never be forced in their trade and therefore do I
allow them also complete liberty; I am only anxious to assist
them in what they require and give them encouragement in the
form of their own advantage." The same was the view of Axel
Oxenstierna in a partially quoted utterance (1638); the Swedish
Government expressed the opinion that one should accomplish one's
ends "not with force, command or prohibition, but *consilio*", "not
interdicto, but *consilio*". In the first instruction to the Swedish Board
of Trade(1651), drawn up by the great Chancellor, the measures
against the export of raw materials and semi-manufactured goods
were detailed as follows: "Not that the export should be prohibited obviously and *per directum*, but that such prohibition
should be exercised *consilio*"—with friendliness and good will.[17]

In these activities *customs policy* was accorded a role which it
had never had in the Middle Ages. In the Middle Ages trade was
forced along the desired course by export or import prohibitions.
True the system of prohibitions persisted during the whole of the
mercantilist period and was only abolished in the 19th century,
so that the transition from prohibition to protection was, at the
same time, the first step towards a limitation of protectionism
itself. In mercantilism, however, there entered by the side of the
system of prohibition, a customs system which had not existed

[17] Mandeville, *The Fable of the Bees*, end of "A Search into the Nature of
Society" (1st ed. I 428, ed. Kaye, I 369).—*Discourse of the Common Weal* (ed.
Lamond, 57 ff.).—*Lettres de Colbert* II 577, note 1.—Oxenstierna: see above,
note 2, further *Samling Utaf. K. Bref.* . . . (ed. Stiernman) II 675.

before, and the new element was considered the orthodox one. Like so much else, the prohibitions were inherited from the previous period, for the existing powers here as almost everywhere were unable to eradicate the old remains root and branch.

On this point, too, a few utterances of the above-mentioned statesmen are typical, one of which has been mentioned in another context. Colbert declared in rather quaint terms (undated) that "The whole of trade consists in" granting customs freedom to raw materials imported and levying duties on manufactured goods, freeing re-export from duty and compensating export duties on domestic manufactures. Axel Oxenstierna believed (1636), "If anything is to be changed, the commodities leaving the country in unmanufactured form should be highly taxed, but the manufactured goods taxed very lightly." In the previous year, he had vigorously attacked the old economic policy in the following terms: "No further prohibitions should be drawn up by the Government, and the passing of such should not be allowed to governors, bailiffs or burgomasters with regard to any goods which might or should be imported or exported; for as common as such prohibitions are . . . so detrimental are they to the inhabitants and confusing to merchants, and are never maintained but misused by a few blowflies and self-seekers, to the nuisance and damage of many, and obstruct the industry of honest men both in the country and in the town." Neither Colbert nor Axel Oxenstierna were able even approximately to attain the ideal of a completely restriction-free state of affairs; but that such was their ideal, what has been quoted here can leave no room for doubt.

Henry Robinson was one among the numerous English writers who expressed the same view. Prohibitions of imports, in his view, led to reprisals, "wherefore a better course . . . would be with dexterity to lighten or lade either scale [in the balance of trade] in the custom and other charges which may insensibly make one dear and the other cheap". Lewes Roberts in the same year uttered similar sentiments, and the first important Swedish writer on economics, Johan Risingh, made them a central part of his recommendations, possibly under the influence of Robinson.

Roger Coke was emphatically on the same side (1675): "If my opinion were worthy to be admitted," he remarked, "no Goods of any sort should be Prohibited: but if any be imported which are Luxuriously consumed, with little or no employment of the people, as the wines imported are, they should pay the King the full value . . . But if an employment may happen to the People of the

Nation, if things were not imported, as in fine Linen, Lace, Points, Blacks, and Druggets, encouragement should be given to all people to instruct ours in those manufactures; and such duties for some time imposed on the Importation, that better hopes might be expected here, than otherwise, in working them."[18]

The "freedom of trade" had precisely this idea among the mercantilists: one was free to do what one wished without prevention or compulsion by governmental regulation, but the activity of the individual was to be directed along the right lines through economic rewards and penalties, the weapons of a wise government. Such an application of the term "liberty" must not be regarded as in any way inconsistent or lacking in honesty—at least not more so than any other application; for "liberty" is one of those concepts which scorn all attempts at consistent interpretation, as John Stuart Mill among others experienced to his cost.

The mercantilist conception of society appears in its most undiluted form in the attitude to the *movements of the precious metals*. The change of view characterized by the transition from "bullionism" to "mercantilism" consisted precisely in the fact that the pointless attempts at export prohibitions on precious metals were given up, and, instead, attempts were made to create a so-called favourable balance of trade by means of suitable measures in commercial policy; that is, to create an export surplus of goods which would induce the merchants by economic compulsion, which meant their own interests, to guarantee to the country an import surplus of silver and gold. For this reason, too, Mun in his most famous book dealt with all those measures advanced for the compulsory attainment of the desired result, and dismissed them one after the other as useless. The following conclusions headed a series of successive chapters in his book: "The enhancing or debasing our monies cannot enrich the kingdom with treasure, nor hinder the exportation thereof"; "A toleration for foreign

---

[18] *Lettres de Colbert* VII 284 note 2.—Oxenstierna, *Svenska riksrådets protokoll* VI 727, *Handlingar rörande Skandinaviens historia* XXXVII 181 f. re pectively.— Robinson, *Englands Safety in Trades Encrease* 51.—Lewes Roberts, *The Treasure of Traffike* (Lond. 1641) 39.—Johan Risingh, *Tractat om Kiöphandelen eller Commercierne* (unpub., written in 1650's and 1660's); cf. my *Sveriges ekon. hist.* I : 2 700. Coke, *Treatise* III 48.—Danielsson, *Protektionismens genombrott i svensk tullpolitik*, which likewise gives the quotation of Oxenstierna cited here, has (9) also referred to the agreement between the utterances of the two statesmen with regard to toll policy on the one hand, and a passage in Pieter de la Court, *Aanwysing der heilsame politike gronden en maximen van de Republike van Holland en West-Vriesland* (1669, 1671 ed. 95) on the other.

Coins to pass current here at higher rates than their value with our Standard will not increase our treasure"; "The observation of the Statute of Employments to be made by Strangers (*v.s.* II, 141) cannot increase nor yet preserve our treasure"; "It will not increase our treasure to enjoin the Merchant that exporteth Fish, Coin or Munition, to return all or part of the value in money"; "The under-valuation of our money which is delivered or received by bills of Exchange here or beyond the Seas cannot decrease our treasure." All the arguments given thus speak *against* compulsion and *in favour* of stimulation.

So far, all this may appear congenial to the modern mind, but the mercantilists were amoral in their choice of means in other spheres, too, where most people to-day would probably not consider them justified. This is particularly true with regard to the administration of justice, which was often looked upon simply as a means of producing economic gain for the state or society—"economic" taken here in its popular, material sense.

It is not surprising that the aim of organizing beggars and vagabonds in schemes of compulsory work was viewed as a means of increasing the wealth of the country. But it is interesting to find that the mercantilists regarded the exercise of judicial power throughout as a mechanism for providing society with labour and revenue under particularly advantageous conditions. This applies principally to Sir William Petty. In his most important theoretical work, *A Treatise of Taxes and Contributions* (1662), he suggested the substitution of compulsory labour for all penalties, "which will increase labour and public wealth". Even moral offences and heresy he proposed to punish with monetary penalties. "Why should not a man of Estate," he inquired, "found guilty of manslaughter, rather pay a certain proportion of his whole Estate, than be burnt in the hand?" "Why should not insolvent Thieves be rather punished with slavery than death? So as being slaves they may be forced to as much labour, and as cheap fare, as nature will endure, and thereby become as two men added to the Commonwealth, and not as one taken away from it." "And why should not the Solvent Thieves and Cheats be rather punished with multiple restitutions than Death, Pillory, Whipping? etc." He went through the whole scale of crimes in this way and was more courageous and consistent in his conclusions than most others. He believed it to be difficult, for example, to say by how much the penalty should exceed the value of what was stolen and proposed that the authorities consult "candid Artists in that Trade" on the subject, and suggested finally that a twenty-fold monetary penalty would be adequate. The idea as such had been already expressed long before Petty. Starkey, for instance, had put it forward in his dialogue between Cardinal Pole and Thomas Lupset (*circa* 1538); it was thus not peculiar to Petty's time. Even a much more antiquated author like Becher questioned why a thief who stole fifty guilders was hanged, if he could earn four-fold in the course of a year in Becher's projected workhouse.

In this respect, the mercantilists manifested many points of similarity to the utilitarians and more particularly to Jeremy Bentham, the actual progenitor of the latter. It was perhaps the greatest sorrow of Bentham's life that he failed to implement one of his cherished plans of a most original workhouse. He gave it the name of "Panopticon"; and its function was intended to be the employment of "convicts instead of steam, and thus to combine philanthropy with business", to quote Sir Leslie Stephens' summarized description or, to put it in Bentham's own words, "A mill for grinding rogues honest, and idle men industrious"—thus a new manifestation of Petty's arguments.[19]

It is true and very important that Bentham used Petty's argument with a difference. The utilitarians were humanitarians and wished to lessen the suffering in the world, an idea far removed from the mercantilists. In this respect the distinction was extraordinarily great. But the harnessing of justice for utilitarian ends was common to both. This was particularly evident wherever justice could be made serviceable to the state. The best example is the manning of the galley fleets through the activities of the law courts. This practice was pursued in many countries, but most vigorously and longest, probably, in France. In this matter Colbert did nothing more nor less than his predecessors and successors. But his activity throws particular light on this kind of economic policy.

In the innumerable letters of Colbert to the presidents of the Courts of Justice and to other persons, there is the continual refrain that they should "condemn as many criminals as possible to the galleys"—as one intendant put it in his letter to Colbert,

---

[19] On the treatment of vagrancy, etc.: Webb, *Engl. Poor Law History* I 102–14; Furniss, *Position of the Laborer in a System of Nationalism* ch. 4 and 5.— Petty, *Treatise of Taxes*, esp. ch. 10, "Of Penalties" (Econ. Writings I 67 ff.).— Starkey, *A Dialogue between Cardinal Pole and Thomas Lupset* (England in the Reign of Henry the Eighth, Early Engl. Text Soc., II, ed. Cowper, 197).— Becher, *Politische Discurs*, Part 2, ch. 26 (1673 ed. 246).—L. Stephen, *English Utilitarians* I 203.—J. Bentham, *Works*, ed. J. Bowring (Edinb. 1843) X 226 (Letter to Brissot); the book itself, *Panopticon* (written 1787, published 1791), *op. cit.* IV 37–172, as also the biographical part of the *Works*, show sufficiently what weight Bentham attached to his plan for this workhouse.

"In order to maintain this corps which is necessary to the state."
An *avocat général* at Toulouse said that judges who allowed themselves to be behindhand in this matter "should be ashamed of
themselves, that they served the King so ill in this respect, considering the great need for galley slaves". The condemned were
frequently kept in the galleys for tens of years beyond their
sentences; they were seldom set free at all unless they were
fortunate enough to buy a Turk or some other bird of ill omen
who then took their place, or unless they could buy themselves
free in some other way. In a letter to the Intendant of the galleys
in Marseilles in 1678, Colbert gave the latter detailed instructions
concluding, "His Majesty relies that you will have an eye to this
economy." An official list of sick galley slaves, whom the King
out of his graciousness and charity set free in the year 1674, is
characteristic of the system. One of the condemned mentioned
in the list had completed his sentence in 1650 and had thus
been kept twenty-four years beyond his time. Two others should
have been released in 1658, one in 1659, two in 1662, and finally
four in 1664. The number of these sick slaves who had been kept
at least ten years beyond their proper sentences was thus ten in
all, and they were then set free only because they were ailing,
which must have made them less serviceable. The same was true
of twenty-two others who had been kept less than ten years
beyond their sentences. In the year previous, the Bishop of
Marseilles, with typical respect for the maxim that might comes
before right, had written to Colbert saying, "The most vigorous
complaints come from those who have already served their time
twice or three times over and who find it difficult to contain themselves further in patience. If the King were to see his way to
liberating at least some of the oldest of them every year", in the
opinion of the prelate that would have a good effect.

The poor creatures who were thus treated were chained fast
by their oars, without trousers or shoes, sometimes kept alive only
by pieces of bread dipped in wine, bleeding from maltreatment so
that they often had to be whipped to make them move at all if
they had fallen asleep at their chains. Among them were such as
had come to grief for crimes which, in modern eyes, were of the
most trivial nature and some no longer punished at all. A large
proportion were recruited from the *faux-sauniers*, that is, people
who had extracted salt themselves from sea water and thus
transgressed against the government's salt monopoly. In Colbert's
time there was among them a Protestant gentleman who had been
condemned for attempting to leave the country. The important

point, however, is not this state of affairs in itself, for the abuses of the *ancien régime* were innumerable even in the eyes of those responsible for their administration. What was characteristic was that the representatives of the French monarchy considered this part of the administration of justice one of their honourable achievements. Thus in the longest of his state papers, a memorandum of 1663, Colbert pointed it out as a credit to his monarch—i.e. to his own credit—that they had succeeded in condemning so many men to the galleys.[20]

Similar examples are to be found in great number. In England, the French practice of recruiting galley slaves by the aid of the law had its counterpart in the practice of pressing people into the navy, indeed which lasted down to the beginning of the 19th century. It was one of the bases for the manning of the navy. If in doing so, justice was not prostituted in the French manner, to balance matters many people were taken who had not come into conflict with the law of the state at all. In addition, the slave trade, with its horrors long familiar to all, was one of the gems of trade which every true patriot had to regard as one of the foundations of his country's well-being. Population policy bore the same stamp, the slave trade being in many respects only one side of this policy. The innumerable letters with regard to the populating of the French colonies with young girls, who were sent thither by shiploads, usually from Houses of Correction, but sometimes also young country girls (*jeunes villageoises*), were almost of the nature of instructions for human breeding-studs. In the same breath mention is made of shiploads of women, mares and sheep; the methods of propagating human beings and cattle being regarded as roughly on the same plane. In other spheres, too, there were many interventions on the part of the states of which we have had occasion to speak in other contexts: e.g. the destruction of English tobacco fields by military power, in the interests of the colonies, which practice lasted in certain parts of the mother country for more than seventy years; similar measures in Sweden against such iron forges as competed for charcoal with the furnaces; against cities which it was desired to transplant from one place to another, and against Finns who would not relinquish their settlements in some parts of central Sweden and

---

[20] *Lettres de Colbert* III: 1: 1 1 ff. *et passim* (esp. III: 1: 1 142 f., III: 1: II 135); the list mentioned in the text III: II 680 f., report of 1663 II 51.—*Corresp. admin. sous Louis XIV* (ed. Depping) II 873–955 (Letter from the Bishop of Marseilles 939).—Clément, *Histoire de Colbert et de son administration* (Paris 1874) I 445–57.

therefore had their houses burnt down while they were themselves deported. We may further instance the "Political Lent", with prohibitions against the use of meat, for the encouragement of native fisheries; the compulsory wearing of woollen caps; the compulsory burial of the dead in woollen shrouds to create a market for the native cloth industry; the bitter and bloody crusade for the uprooting of cotton prints; the battle more grotesque than grim against stuff buttons, and so on and so forth; all of this in juxtaposition with a theoretical aversion to economic compulsion![21]

The amorality in the choice of means even more than in the choice of ends reveals the indifference of mercantilists towards the human element.

On the other hand there was a certain measure of toleration visible in the fact that what was regarded as an impossible ascetic ideal was abandoned and the weaknesses of human nature were taken into account as data upon which to base economic policy. This held good primarily in the *love of gain*. The literature is full of remarks such as "Every man is naturally covetous of lucre, and that wherein they see most lucre they will most gladly exercise". "No Laws are prevalent against gain." "Gain doth bear sway and command with most men." "Gain is the Centre of the Circle of Commerce." "So much hardship, so much trouble, so many men have no other objective than profit; around this centre point revolves the whole sphere of business," and so on.[22]

[21] Typical letters with regard to the population policy for the French colonies, apart from the sources given above (see above 161): *Lettres de Colbert* III: II 476, 481 note 1, 513; *Corresp. adm.* II 593 ff., 694.—Tobacco policy: Beer, *The Old Colonial System* I 144 f.; Lipson·III 169 ff., 181 f. It need not be emphasized that the contrast with modern conditions made here has had the achievements of the 19th century in view. How far recent tendencies will renew or even surpass the mentality here exemplified from mercantilism remains to be seen.

[22] The examples taken at random: *Discourse of the Common Weal* (ed. Lamond, 122, cf. 167 and Index under "Lucre"); Malynes, *Lex Mercatoria*, e.g. Part 2 ch. 9 part 3 ch. 10 (1st ed. Lond. 1622, 310, 419); *Center of the Circle of Commerce* 5, 68 *et passim* (it is the meaning of the title of the book); Sir R. Maddison, *Great Britains Remembrancer* (Lond. 1655) 14; Montchrétien, *Traicté* (1st. ed. Rouen 1615, 55).—More detailed is the introduction to a charter for French knitting manufacture of 1672, giving *inter alia* the following reasons, "connoissant . . ., après plusieurs expériences, qu'il n'y a rien qui fasse plus aimer à cultiver les Arts, ni qui puisse davantage contribuer à l'establissement & au progrès des Manufactures, que l'espérance de quelques avantages assûrés pour ceux qui s'y appliquent, à la vûe d'une récompense certaine à la fin de leurs travaux" (*Recueil des règlemens généraux et particuliers concernant les manufactures* IV 8).—Cp. Tawney, *Religion and the Rise of Capitalism* ch. 4.

The toleration did not, however, apply to the actual workmen. Their sin, as was shown at the end of the third part, was ineradicable sloth; the willingness to stimulate the interest of the *workers* by increased returns was indeed rare.

Irreligion

This brings us directly to the attitude of mercantilism towards religion. For reasons easily explainable this was similar to its attitude to ethics, and like this, was of great importance with regard to the practical shaping of economic policy.

The whole tendency of mercantilism made economic policy antagonistic to the church and priesthood, and on the other hand brought these into harness against mercantilism. Petty could seldom speak of priests without adding some malicious remark. Colbert from the start was in opposition to the interests of the church and this standpoint was to gain in importance in the course of development and finally leading to the victory of the church, annihilating the work of the great statesmen and driving the French Huguenots into countries competing with France.

In the first place efforts to increase the population were directed against celibacy. This consideration was mentioned in Protestant countries especially as a reason for the decline of Spain, but it was of practical importance in a predominantly Catholic country such as France. As early as a report of 1664, Colbert advised Louis XIV to lessen the number of monks and nuns. In accordance with this, the French practice of encouraging prolificacy by premiums was made conditional on the children not becoming monks or nuns. A higher age was prescribed for the monk's oath, and other measures, too, were taken to oppose celibacy.

In another important sphere of mercantilist activity, the opposition of mercantilism to religion and the church was equally pronounced. I refer to the struggle against idleness. Colbert was clearly very anxious as to the effects of monastic almsgiving on the diffusion of this, in his eyes, particularly detestable vice, and expressed his emphatic opinion concerning it on several occasions, the last being as late as 1680, when it had already become difficult to oppose the clerical tendencies in the court of Louis XIV and Madame de Maintenon. Colbert wrote to one of his intendants on "the host of beggars and idlers to be found in the neighbourhood of the monasteries, who give alms blindly without making any distinction between individual cases". One month later he returned to the subject of "these public alms which are given without reason or any knowledge of indigence". Conditions were not the same in the Protestant countries, but the Protestants were at one with the Catholic mercantilists in their dislike of the numerous holidays. The English pamphleteers calculated the number of days, and the millions, lost to industry in this way. Henry IV, and later more particularly Colbert, used all possible means to cut down the number of holidays.

As a politician in matters of colonial policy, Colbert was engaged in perpetual warfare with the priesthood in Canada, as well as with the Jesuits and various orders of monks. He himself instructed his intendants there to reduce their numbers as far as possible. The main cause for this was the fact that the priests wished to limit the retail licensing and sale of spirits to the Indians, while Colbert regarded this trade as the most certain means for inducing the natives to deliver the furs which represented one of the major economic interests of these colonies. The antagonism between commercial and ethical interests here was obvious. In his instruction to the intendants Colbert wrote, for example in 1668, that the intendant should confine the power of the priests, and should investigate whether they were really justified in suggesting that alcoholic liquor made the Indians lazy, or whether it was not true that on the contrary the prospect of it stimulated their hunting spirit. At the same time the intendant was to resist the Jesuits in their efforts to keep the converted Indians at arms length from the French. In another and later letter (1677) to the successor of this first intendant, Colbert was forced to put forward quasi-religious considerations which, however, proved a thin mask for his actual commercial motives. In his opinion the spirit trade should not be disturbed on trivial grounds, for it is a "commodity which serves to so high a degree to bring together commerce and the savages themselves with orthodox Christians such as the French". Indeed if the spirit trade were neglected it might well fall into the hands of the English or the Dutch and that would indeed be heresy! Finally in 1679, in spite of all his efforts Colbert had to yield, and forbid the trade in spirits with the Indians. This decree, however, remained purely nominal. The struggle against the efforts of the priesthood persisted.

Mercantilist economic policy came into conflict with religion more particularly where it was a question of the immigration of heretical craftsmen, or in general of religious toleration. Toleration was the unanimous demand of all theoretical and practical economic politicians under mercantilism. On no other question was there such complete unanimity. On the one hand the Dutch were referred to as the country to be imitated, and as the best illustration of the economic value of toleration. On the other hand, the expulsion of the Moors and Jews from Spain was exhibited as the pernicious result of intolerance. Colbert always took the part of the members of the reformed church, above all of the Dutch family of van Robais who had founded the textile works in Abbeville. However, he fought a vain contest, and tried to disarm his opponents by attempting to convert the Robais. But in this he was unsuccessful. On the whole Colbert was very careful that neither he nor his colleagues should press the priests and Jesuits too far, since, as he once wrote to an intendant, that would make them "almost useless for the service of the King". Of the direction in which his own desires lay, however, there can be no doubt.

In other countries where the clerical influence in politics was weaker, the reformers displayed greater courage. Petty went furthest with his worldly wise contempt for clerical considerations. We have already shown that he was in favour of commercializing the whole system of penalties. In agreement with this principle, he believed that heretics should be given complete freedom of religion in return for a decent payment. If they allowed themselves to be driven away from their faith by this measure, it proved, he thought, merely that their faith was of little consequence, but if this did not occur, that was just as fortunate an outcome. Such arguments were obviously far removed from the atmosphere of religious wars. But Petty was not content with this, and what he said in this connection constituted one of his most original contributions. In fact, he went so far as to assert that schismatics as such had a positive value from the economic point of view— a theory which Sombart, in our day, has taken up again. Petty stated, for example, "Trade is most vigorously carried on, in every State and Government, by the Heterodox part of the same." "Trade is not fixed to any species of Religion as such; but rather . . . to the Heterodox part of the whole." After proving this carefully, he concluded, "From whence it follows, that for the advancement of Trade, (if that be a sufficient reason) Indulgence must be granted in matters of opinion." That this in Petty's view was "a sufficient reason" may be clearly seen from the first part of the argument. All true mercantilists likewise attacked "Persecution as detrimental to trade". The whole problem acquired an effective reality, more particularly after the expulsion of the Huguenots from France, in those countries where the religion of the reformers differed from that of the particular country, i.e. especially in Lutheran countries. In most countries mercantilism, with its commercial viewpoint, won the day over the orthodoxy of the Church.[23]

The same tendency is manifested in the fact that the Jews were placed on a new footing in the 17th century in most western and central European countries. This should certainly not be regarded as a general pro-Jewish feeling on the part of mercantilists. No such sentiment was ever felt among those in power. The increased toleration was not moreover entirely the effect of economic considerations. Becher, who was generally strong in invective, spoke by preference of "Jews and canaille", and even found a mercantilist reason for his hatred of the Jews. He said, in fact, that they would not function as consumers of commodities, as the doctrine demanded, but preferred "to live in a slovenly and entirely mean fashion". A French intendant at the beginning of the 18th century believed, on the other hand, that the Jews were ideal citizens from a mercantilist point of view, because they did not invest their capital in land or other immovable things, but allowed it to circulate in trade. In spite of the incidental differences in outlook, which have always existed and will probably always exist where the Jews are concerned, this much is clear, that the leaders of mercantilist policy wished to extend toleration even to the Jews, and that this toleration was determined primarily by commercial considerations. At the same time, the purely financial requirements of the state also played their part, and sometimes even the religious interest in the mission among the Jews could work in the same direction.

The example of the Dutch was of specially great effect here. Dutch toleration of the Sephardic Jews who were driven from Spain and Portugal was an instance evident to all and furnished a

---

[23] The importance of celibacy as regards Spain: Child, *New Discourse of Trade* ch. 10 (1698 ed., 203).—Colbert and celibacy: *Lettres de Colbert* II 68 f., VI 3, 13 f.—Colbert and almsgiving: *ib.* II 714 and note 1.—Reducing holidays: "Polices to Reduce this Realme," etc. (1549): pr. *Tudor Econ. Docs.* III 323; later remarks collected in Furniss 44 f.; on France, e.g. Boissonnade, *L'organisation du travail en Poitou* II 138, 342–50, *Socialisme d'état* . . . (*1453–1661*) 301.—Sale of spirits in Canada: in gen. *Lettres de Colbert* III: II, esp. lxx f., 403 ff., 617–21, 641 note.—Examples of Colbert's attitude to the religion of the van Robais in the later period (1682) *ib.* II 738 f., 742; his quoted utterance III: II 403 f.—Of the English pamphleteers who advocated toleration, Child must be mentioned in the first place, but neither Coke nor the author of *Britannia Languens* were far behind him. Also the collection *British Merchant*, with its strong tendency to economic nationalism, is typical with its "arguments against persecution as detrimental to trade" (1713, Lond. ed. 1743, 148–51, 173–9).—Petty, *Treatise of Taxes* chaps. 2 and 10 Point 20; *Pol. Arithm.* ch. 1 (*Econ. Writings* I 22, 70, 263).—* See also below II 368, *Addendum* §13.

particularly powerful argument in a world dominated by envy and admiration for the Dutch. In English literature Child was foremost in making use of this argument; in the readiness of Holland to receive the Jews he saw one of the reasons for its superiority, and desired that Jews be naturalized in England like other foreigners. This was said after the Jews had been allowed once again to settle in England under Cromwell, where for three hundred and sixty years they had not been permitted—at least officially—to show themselves.

As usual it was in Colbert and his monarch again that the contrast between the claims of mercantilism, and religious intolerance in connection with the Jews, was expressed with particular clarity. In a letter of 1673 to the intendant in Aix, to which region Marseilles belonged, Colbert warned his subordinate not to lend ear to the complaints of the merchants against the Jews; nothing was more useful for trade than that the number of people engaged in it should be increased, even though the Marseilles merchants should not be able to comprehend this. "And whereas the settlement of the Jews," he said, "has certainly never been prohibited out of consideration for trade, since where they be the latter usually increases, but solely on the grounds of religion, and whereas *in the present case it is purely a question of trade*, you shall in no wise hearken to the proposals made to you against the said Jews" (my italics). In the colonies, too, Colbert showed favour to the Jews. Their "usury" was to be kept down, but he declared, also in the name of his King, they were to have complete freedom of conscience, with the proviso that the exercise of their religion did not shock the other colonists; otherwise they were to have the same privileges as the latter. Moreover the governors and intendants, acting on the ruling of Colbert, rejected the multifarious attacks made against the Jews. The pro-Jewish feeling manifested in France under Colbert at first went so far that Louis XIV, in a visit to the Jewish city of Metz, even visited the synagogue in his official capacity. But finally in this respect things went the same way that they did in many others. The last years of Colbert saw the triumphal return of intolerance which had won the day at Court and thus his last years saw the Jews numbered amongst those who were condemned for religious offences and the abuse of the sacrament. It was urged that they should be expelled from the French cities of the South and in point of fact this did occur to some extent. In the French West Indies, their good years likewise came to an end with Colbert's death. It is true that the French intendants still occasionally were sympathetic towards them, as is seen in the example (of 1709), which I have just quoted. In this respect, mercantilism in France was defeated and those who felt it most keenly were the Jews and reformed industrialists. But underneath all this there was still the fundamental tendency of the mercantilist economic outlook towards toleration.

Similarly in Germany. In the 17th and 18th centuries the Jews by favour of the princes gained a fresh foothold. Particularly well-known is the charter of the Great Elector allowing them in 1671 to settle in Brandenburg. A very valuable contribution to the history of the Jews of this time is the autobiography of Glückel von Hameln, a Jewish mother of thirteen children, who describes her experiences from the occupation of Altona by the Swedes under Charles X, until about 1720. In this book, practically two groups of characters occur to the exclusion of all others: Jews and Christian princes. The masters of small and great German principalities could not do without their "Court Jews". In this way the Jews found their niche in the mercantilist state order. Like Colbert in the first of the two letters quoted, *Kammerdirektor* Hille (1734), who, as we know, was Frederick the Great's instructor in economic affairs, declared, "*En matière de commerce* it is all one whether a gentleman or a Jew is the trader."

This clearly reveals the situation: altars were raised to other gods than those of religions. A concept such as that of Petty's with regard to criminal legislation, that monetary payments should take the place of all penalties, must have led directly to religious tolerance towards those who were blessed with worldly possessions.[24]

---

[24] Becher, *Politische Discurs*, e.g. Part 2 ch. 1 and 24 (1673 ed., 104, 218).— Intendant St. Contest to the French minister of finance 1709: pr. *Correspondance des contrôleurs généraux* (ed. Boislisle & Brotonne) III No. 209, note.— Interest in the Jewish mission, e.g. in Brandenburg under the Great Elector: M. Köhler, *Beiträge zur neueren jüdischen Wirtschaftsgeschichte* (Studien z. Gesch. d. Wirtschaft u. Geisteskultur, ed. R. Häpke, III, Berl. 1927) 9.—Child, *New Discourse of Trade*, chaps. 3, 7, and 10 (1698 ed. 103, 144, 197).—France: *Lettres de Colbert* II 679, 722, III: II 497, 522 f., VI 159 and note, 188 f., 193 (some of these also in *Corresp. administr.*, ed. Depping, IV); *Corresp. d. contr. gén.* I No. 567 (see, for the rest, index under "Juifs"); H. Wätjen, "Das Judentum und die Anfänge der modernen Kolonisation" (*Vierteljahrschr. f. Soz-. u. Wirtsch.-Gesch.* XI, 1913, 587 ff.); Martin & Bezançon, *L'histoire du crédit en France sous Louis XIV* 191.—Germany: Glückel von Hameln, *Denkwürdigkeiten*, ed. A. Feilchenfeld (4th ed., Berl. 1923); F. Priebatsch, *Die Judenpolitik des fürstlichen Absolutismus im 17. & 18. Jahrhundert* (Forschungen u. Versuche z. Gesch. d. M. A. u. d. Neuzeit, Festschrift D. Schäfer, Jena 1915, 564–651); S. Stern, *Der preussische Staat und die Juden* (Veröffentl. d. Akad.

3. SOCIAL CAUSATION

The same intellectual tendency was expressed also in the rationalism which characterized mercantilism to so high a degree. There was little mysticism in the arguments of the mercantilists. They certainly had many preconceptions; it would otherwise be difficult to explain why they looked upon economic life in the way they did. In general, however, they did not appeal to sentiment, but were obviously anxious to find reasonable grounds for every position they adopted. Moreover, their arguments, at least in many cases, were rather barren. This resulted primarily from their aims—material results for the state—without much interest being shown in individuals as such, and none at all in their spiritual welfare. In addition, the discussion of the application of means to ends—the use of material interests for purposes of state—usually revealed a lack of any exalted principles. Psychologically, the affinity between mercantilists and *laissez-faire* writers was marked in this respect, too, although the difference between interest in the state and interest in the individual, in power and humanity, makes itself felt throughout.

Already at an early date, this rationalism expressed itself in references to *nature*. Nature was conceived as a factor which also influenced the social sphere, social life being placed parallel to the physical life of the individual; and society was regarded as a body with functions similar to those of the physical body. The latter conception was linked to old traditions, and even early in the 16th century these traditions determined the form taken by the discussions. Starkey, for instance, in his dialogue between Cardinal Pole and Thomas Lupset was as tireless as he was tiresome in making use of this kind of metaphor (*circa* 1538). In this book of his, society suffers from consumption, paralysis, plague, frenzy and other "diseases of the body politic". The various parts of the body are identified with the various classes and organs of society, and so on. John Hales, the presumptive author of the *Discourse of the Common Weal*, in 1549 designated the revolt of that year as an attack of "civil frenzy". Malynes in particular was the victim of a fantastic nature symbolism. His *magnum opus*, *Lex Mercatoria* (1622), was built up on such a construction. The first book treated of

f. d. Wissenschaft d. Judentums, History Section, III, Berl. 1925) I: I–II, esp. I chaps. 3 and 4.—Hille's observation: Naudé, *Getreidehandelspolitik Brandenburg-Preussens bis 1740* (Acta Borussica, Getr.-handelspol.) 450.—On the whole question: H. Valentin, *Judarnas historia i Sverige* (Sthlm. 1924) 11–19 and for Sweden ch. 6.

"commodities, compared to the body of Traffic". The second of "Monies compared to the Soul of Traffic", and the third of "Exchanges for Money by Bills of Exchanges, compared to spirit or faculty of the Soul of Traffic".

Such physical or metaphysical phantasies as those of Malynes merely expressed what medieval preachers and writers might have put forward. However, this tendency to draw analogies from nature with regard to social phenomena was very important for the further development of social thought. But the result was different when the natural sciences made further advances and were believed to have discovered fixed rules for natural pheno-mena; for then the conclusion was tempting that this was also possible in the sphere of social events. For obvious reasons, these matters were manifested most clearly by Petty. He was not only an economist and statistician, but also a doctor and a natural scientist. With Becher, it is true, things were similar; but Becher in addition was an alchemist and, from the start, a visionary in everything that he undertook. He was therefore considerably less likely to import into social questions the ordered discipline of the natural sciences. Petty on the other hand went to extremes in his belief in the application of natural laws to the sphere of social phenomena. He quoted with approbation Horace's quip on nature that it could be driven out with a pitchfork and yet would always reappear. He was provoked by "that infinite clutter about resisting Nature, stopping up the winds and seas", and irritated by attempts "to persuade Water to rise out of itself above its natural Spring" (1662). Other authors of the 17th century were not so clear in their observation, but even in them was to be discerned the basic idea of a natural scientific nexus in social life. Here, too, Roger Coke was the most original —unfortunately in a fashion calculated to conceal the unusual independence and freedom from prejudice of his arguments. He wrote four connected pamphlets (1670/75), which he introduced with a lengthy series of "petitions" and axioms. He began with a discussion of the first axiom of Euclid, and then endeavoured to force the discussion into the same mathematical scheme. Certainly the only result of this was that he created a most bizarre impres-sion, entirely inappropriate to the content of his work. But still it is typical that he adopted such a method. Coke, of course, had the same attitude in principle as Petty, and said, for example, "I will never believe that any man or Nation ever well attain their ends by forceable means, against the Nature and Order of things." Davenant observed in 1698, "Wisdom is most commonly in the

Wrong when it pretends to direct Nature." These instances are by no means isolated.[25]

We must regard from the same point of view, many of the very numerous utterances to the effect that all interference by legislative means was unavailing. Sometimes they were certainly the expression of a by no means doctrinaire view, based on wide experience, of the corrupt and ineffective nature of state administration. But more frequently, and indeed at an early date, there appeared in addition to this a theoretical conception of a parallelism of the social world with the external phenomena of nature. This must have been so with Petty, when he said in 1676 that the lack of order in the administrative division of the country obstructs "the Operations of Authority in the same manner, as a wheel irregularly made, and excentrically hung neither moves so easily, nor performs its work so truly as if the same were duly framed and poised". It was quite natural for a member of the Royal Society in its early years to write in this way. But more than a century before Petty, William Cholmeley (1553) compared the quantity of goods in a country with the water in a spring, saying, "As they that stop the course of a river, and will suffer no man to fetch the water from them, shall have more discommodity by the keeping of the water than others can have by the lack of it, and yet in short time it will break from them, malgre their heads . . . ; even so, they that shall keep the commodity of their country from them that have the thing that it serveth for shall at the last (yea, and that within a short space) be glad to let it have the right course, and content themselves to be merchants to those where the utterance of their commodities lieth most best." The author of the *Discourse of the Common Weal* wrote roughly about the same time, "Every man will seek where most advantage is, and they see there is most advantage in grazing and breeding than in husbandry and tillage . . . So long as it is so, the pastures shall ever encroach upon the tillage, for all the laws that ever can be made to the contrary."

Curious as it may seem, in the course of the 17th century the idea grew common that it was impossible to influence the course of economic life by means of legislation. Expressed in varying terms and with changing emphasis, this is to be found in almost every mercantilist writing. Axel Oxenstierna, with his laborious

---

[25] Starkey (see above, note 19) 18 *et passim.*—Hales' statement: pr. *Discourse of the Common Weal* (ed. Lamond, lxvi).—Petty, *Treatise of Taxes*, ch. 6 (Econ. Writings I 60).—Coke, *Treatise* III 57.—Davenant, *Essay upon the East India Trade* (Appendix to *Discourses on the Publick Revenues* II) 35.

and latinized mode of expression, wrote in 1630 on the manifold disadvantages of the Swedish copper coinage, "They must well be suffered in silence, *propter edictum principis* [i.e. on account of the command of the prince], but do not change *opinionem hominum et communem sensum* [the opinion of human beings and sound common sense]. On the contrary, although they are occasionally hidden, they break out when the opportunity offers and then private individuals adapt themselves to them." Lewes Roberts connected the view with an apotheosis of the merchant who, according to him, regulated "tacitly in his Closet the disorders committed by mints and the oversights which the great affairs of Princes' necessities plunge them in; and thus creating to himself and others of his profession a certain Rule and public Balance, that shall serve as an equal Par and Standard of all Princes' coins whatsoever" (*The Merchants Mappe of Commerce*, 1638). Child expressed the idea of the binding force of economic powers much more generally and put it with his usual verbal elegance, "They that can give the best price for a Commodity shall never fail to have it, notwithstanding the opposition of any Laws, or interposition of any Power by Sea or Land; of such force, subtlety and violence is the general course of Trade." Davenant made the degeneration of the human race responsible for it, but was no less convinced of its validity; he said, "Nowadays Laws are not much observ'd, which do not in a manner execute themselves." The most lucid statement of this view is to be found in the report of an English committee of the year 1622, on the subject of the export prohibition on precious metals; it was probably written by Thomas Mun, a member of the committee, as the same typical formulation is to be found, in a somewhat weaker form, at the conclusion of his most famous book. The committee of course made the import surplus responsible for the export of the precious metals and said, "This is so necessarily true as that no law, no treaty, no loss to the merchant, . . . nor danger to the exporter, can prevent it, but if it be met with all in one part, yet it must out in another . . . But if this waste of foreign wares be kept within compass of our commodities vented in foreign parts, then though . . . the exchange go free at the pleasure of the merchants contracting it, though . . . all men be suffered to carry money wherever he will, yet this over-ballance of our commodities will force it *again with an increase* [of our stock by precious metals] *by a necessity of nature beyond all resistance*" (my italics).[26]

[26] Petty, *Pol. Arithm.* ch. 5 (Econ. Writings I 301).—W. Cholmeley, "The Requeste and Suite of a True-hearted Englishman"; repr. *Tudor Econ. Docs.*

These examples taken from an innumerable host of others demonstrate clearly the belief in the existence of a powerful, or perhaps even complete, social causality, in a connection between cause and effect which could not possibly be disturbed by any measures of the politicians. Even in the heyday of *laissez-faire*, when the "Heaven-ordained Laws of Supply and Demand" prevailed, it would be difficult to find a more extreme expression of the belief in the inexorable nature of economic laws as is evident in the last quoted extract from the report of the committee of 1622. This notion of the ineffectiveness of legislative interference was cherished not merely where it was believed that the latter stood in conflict with the inevitable course of nature; it was far more universal.

The idea as such was indeed old. In fact it has, perhaps, always existed in some form or another, but it grew in practical importance in the course of time. Sir Thomas More's *Utopia* (1516, English translation 1551), which did not represent a particularly typical mercantilist point of view, had already emphatically underlined the fact that repressive measures against theft, murder and vagrancy were useless, so long as the economic causes of these evils were not abolished: "Let not so many be brought up in idleness," he advised, "let husbandry and tillage be restored, let cloth working be renewed, that there may be honest labours for this idle sort to pass their time in profitably, which hitherto either poverty hath caused to be thieves, or else now be either vagabonds or idle serving men, and shortly will be thieves. Doubtless unless you find a remedy for these enormities, you shall in vain advance yourselves of executing justice upon felons." Sir Thomas More also came to the same conclusion as was advanced down through the ages as an argument against the infliction of the death penalty for theft; that, put briefly, the danger of murder was increased, because in this way the criminal lessened his risk without increasing the penalty. The same belief in the economic and social causes of crime lay behind the efforts of the Tudor and early Stuart periods to make the employers let the workers continue their work whether it paid the former to do so or not. The preoccupation with the causes behind social phenomena was also strong in other spheres in the 16th century. The earliest of the essays ascribed to

III 142.—*Disc. of the Com. Weal* 53.—*Oxenstiernas Skr. o brefv.* Ser. 1, I 345 f.—Roberts 48.—Child, *Discourse* ch. 8 (1698 ed., 147).—Davenant, *Essay upon ... Ballance of Trade* (1699) 55.—1622 report: extract in F. H. Durham, "The Relations of the Crown to Trade under James I" (*Trans. Roy. Hist. Soc. N.S.* XIII, 1899, 244 note 4); cf. Mun, *Engl. Tr.* ch. 21 (ed. Ashley 119).

Clement Armstrong, *A Treatise Concerninge the Staple* (*circa* 1519/35), states that the "lords in England", when listening to complaints regarding the evils in society, "never search to the original cause . . . what is the very root of the whole need, necessity and scarcity of the whole realm". In almost the same terms Starkey demanded (1538) that "we must study to cut away the causes . . . and not only punish the effect, as we do commonly". In the *Polices to Reduce This Realme of England unto a Prosperous Wealthe and Estate* (1549), the idea is applied to pricing policy: "It is not the setting of low prices that will any thing amend the matter. But it must be the taking away of the occasion of the high prices"— an insight into the facts which had evidently not yet been gained in the system of price regulation adopted during the first World War.

As usual the argument was expressed most clearly in the *Discourse of the Common Weal* (1549). The detailed philosophical theory of causation, with its practical application to economic phenomena, which forms the introduction to the third and last dialogue of this remarkable work, is really worth reproducing in full, but this would take up too much space. We extract the following passages in illustration: "As in a clock there be many wheels, yet the first wheel being stirred, it drives the next, and that the third, till the last that moves the Instruments that strikes the clock. So in making of a house, there is the master that would have the house made, there is the carpenter, there is the stuff to make the house withal. The stuff never stirs till the workmen set it forward. The workman never travails, but as the master provokes him with good wages [*sic*]; and so he is the principal cause of this house making. And this cause is of clerks called efficient, as that that brings the thing principally to effect; persuade this man to let his building, and the house shall never come to pass; yet the house can not be made without stuff and workmen." "Some think this dearth begins by the tenant, in selling his ware so dear; some other, by the Lord in raising his land so high; and some by those Inclosures; and some other, by raising of our coin and alteration of the same. Therefore some by taking some one of these things away (as their opinion served them to be the principal cause of this dearth), thought to remedy this; but as the trial of things showed, they touched not the cause efficient or principal, and therefore their device took no place. And if they had [penetrated to the main cause] the thing had been remedied forth with; for that is proper to the principal cause, that as soon as it is taken away, the effect is removed also." In this way the author came to demand the creation of favourable conditions for tillage.[27]

It goes without saying that such ideas did not peter out in the subsequent period. Remarks of writers in the later 17th century are so similar to these, that to reproduce them would almost amount to repetition. Cary (1695) regarded the prohibition against the import of Irish cattle as the cause for the institution by the Irish of woollen manufactures, which entered into competition with the English—the worst possible thing that could occur; "Since we refuse to take the Flesh," he remarked, "they chose to keep the Fleece." The author of *Britannia Languens* (1680) pointed out like his predecessors the uselessness of legislating against vagrants and criminals so long as the causes were not removed. Stagnation of trade, he believed, in agreement with Sir Thomas More, led to the outbreak of crime. Later still (1728), Defoe explained Algerian piracy on geographical and psychological grounds, which "made them Thieves and Robbers as naturally as Idleness makes Beggars". Child's analysis of the population problem, and more particularly his discussion of interest, shows how anxious were people to comprehend social life, and especially the economic side of it, as a mechanism bound fast by laws.[28]

To people of the time, there were two great outward reasons inducing them to search for a causal interconnection in the sphere of economic life. Their mental horizon, in fact, was dominated by two phenomena which appeared paradoxical to them. How was

[27] More, *Utopia* (Robinson's trans. 1551) Bk. 1 (Everyman's Library 26, 28).—[Armstrong], "Treatise": repr. *Tudor Econ. Docs.* III 94.—Starkey, *Dialogue* 171.—"Polices": repr. *Tudor Econ. Docs.* III 340, cf. 341.—*Disc. of the Com. Weal* 98–101.

[28] Cary, *Essay on the State of England* 101.—*Britannia Languens* chaps. 7 and 14 (1st ed. 97, 254).—Defoe, *Plan of the English Commerce*, Part 3 ch. 2 (repr. Oxford 1928, 239).—In my opinion Professor Tawney is therefore mistaken in the latter part of the following passage (*Religion and the Rise of Capitalism* 271): "Tudor divines and statesmen had little mercy for idle rogues. But the former always, and the latter ultimately, regarded pauperism primarily as a social phenomenon produced by economic dislocation. . . . Their successors after the Restoration were apparently quite unconscious that it was even conceivable that there might be any other cause of poverty than the moral failings of the poor." To my knowledge, there was no other distinction between the earlier and the later conception of the causes of pauperism than this, that unlike the earlier, the later did not blame it on to the moral shortcomings of the employers; moreover, they were perhaps even more inclined to quote poverty and vagrancy as a proof of the usefulness of their particular economic panaceas. Cf. also D. Marshall, *The English Poor in the Eighteenth Century* 21, 27, 37 ff.

it possible that Spain, in possession of the "treasure" of the whole world, could grow so poor that it had to see its "treasure" flowing away from it before its eyes; and how was it possible that being almost the only gold- and silver-producing country in the world Spain was forced on to a copper standard? And how, on the other hand, could the Netherlands, a tiny country without any natural advantages in production worth mentioning, which shortly before had appeared to be fighting a hopeless battle with the first power at that time in the world, acquire as if by the stroke of a magic wand the largest commercial fleet of the whole earth, and become superior in competition to all other nations in trade, shipping, fishing and colonial power? These two facts gave an extra-ordinary fillip to thought on economic matters in the 17th century.

In the first place, men were interested in nothing so much as in trade supremacy, and these two phenomena showed that it was impossible to deduce economic results in that field from the simple obvious facts. They illustrated how much a country could gain and how much it could lose, and how far such gain or loss could be independent of external circumstances. Men became conscious that every country was subject to the possibility of such changes. On the other hand, the fundamentally static outlook was so deeply rooted that these considerations stimulated no dynamic points of view. Nobody reflected that there was some-thing to be gained in the development of shipping, commerce, and colonization for all European countries together. The attitude to economic matters was national and not international. But fateful as was this limitation (discussed more fully in the second part of the present work), the contemplation of the inter-connected nature of economic phenomena had in itself effects of a general character. The contrast of the Netherlands and Spain stimulated speculation on more fundamental problems. It compelled people to think of economic phenomena as such. Thus, for example, the low level of interest in the Netherlands and the superiority which this appeared to give to the Dutch led to discussions on the problem of interest, which gradually paved the way to a better insight into the question. And even before this, the questions of what makes a country rich or poor in general were broached, in other words the effects on the wealth of nations of quite a host of important economic relationships, such as the quantity of money, the population total, industry, thrift, liberty of trade and toleration. Nobody can deny that, outward changes, connected with intellectual liberation, made people "think furiously" under mercantilism.

III

CONTRAST BETWEEN MERCANTILISM AND
LAISSEZ-FAIRE

After this survey of the constituent elements in the mercantilist conception of society, we now arrive finally at the problem broached at the beginning of this part. How was it possible that of two outlooks with so much in common as mercantilism and *laissez-faire*, the one stood for the most extreme state interference with economic life, while the other was opposed to any activity on the part of the state beyond that of protecting law and order? Or again, how could the belief in a naturally determined course of events, an almost mechanical causality, be combined with attempts at an all-embracing system of encroachments and regulation? And how were these endeavours reconcilable with the belief in social liberty?

There is no uniform reply to this complex of questions. The most important factors which can be marshalled in explanation are the following.

The freedom of trade and the harmony of interests of different countries, slogans which the mercantilist statesmen brought out when necessary, were obviously not always taken literally by them. Very often it was merely a question of beautiful phrases ready at hand to serve some particular interest or other. There can be no bridge over the gulf between the noble sentiments of trade as a means for the fraternization of mankind, to which Colbert referred in his company charters, and the idea of a perpetual trading war in which these companies, as he at the same time impressed upon his monarch, were to be the most important weapons. It is out of the question that Colbert himself could have been blind to so patent a contradiction. The correct and not very difficult explanation must be that the two points of view served different ends. The object of the first was to gain new participants and interested parties for the new structures, while the latter was the real motive behind the policy which was actually intended to be pursued in practice. The cosmopolitan utterances of Colbert merely demonstrate that with his theory he wished to evoke a response in certain quarters. In other words, the notion he expressed was widespread, even though it did not correspond to the opinion of the individual who uttered them.

But this is by no means the complete explanation of the problem.

In by far the majority of cases we gain the definite impression that the persons speaking or writing really believed what they uttered. This does not suggest that their outlook was free from contradiction; in many respects their arguments were contradictory and confused, for reasons that are not far to seek.

The first contradiction consisted in the connection of the attempts to increase trade in general and foreign trade in particular with the ceaseless striving to obstruct imports. The reason for it is this. It was believed to be possible to export without involving corresponding import, i.e. it was overlooked what effect an import surplus of precious metals must have on the exchange relationship of both countries, as explained in the fourth part. There was another contradiction when attempts were made to revive trade and on the other hand, equally ceaseless attempts were made to prosecute a commercial war. From a purely theoretical point of view this was not absolutely impossible, but in the actual circumstances, there was an equally great, and perhaps even greater, antinomy. The explanation for this dilemma was that the mercantilists were interested only in the trade of their own country, both that which it had already acquired and that which it still hoped to acquire from other countries, hardly giving a thought to world trade. In point of fact, however, the trade of all countries certainly suffered enormously from the blockading measures brought on by commercial warfare, the *bellum omnium inter omnes*. The obsession with power also had this result, that interest was taken not in the absolute total of commerce nor in the utility which it represented to the inhabitants of a particular country, but only in the superiority gained over other countries, irrespective of whether there was no absolute increase at all or perhaps even an absolute decline. They were satisfied so long as there was a relative increase. To this extent the interest in expanding trade was, so to speak, purely technical; in so far as real progress in trade was desired, the contradiction was mainly insoluble.

However, these two factors—hypocrisy and logical inconsistency—together do not yet explain the enormous contrast beween *laissez-faire* and mercantilism, in the practical results which they arrived at from the point of departure which was largely common to both. The true explanation lies in the fact that a belief in social causality permits of *both* conclusions alternatively, though contradictory to one another.

More particularly in its original form, but also later as a politically influential world outlook, economic liberalism meant literally the belief in physiocracy, φύσιοχρατία. the government of nature, or a *harmonia praestabilita*, a predetermined harmony inherent in the nature of economic phenomena themselves. Though few facts in the history of modern thought are better known, the idea may be summed up in a few sentences. The only requirement for the realization of this harmony was believed to be that it should not suffer interference from without. Even the somewhat later and more acute thinkers, such as Ricardo and Malthus, who perceived much disharmony in the unfettered evolution of economic forces, did not in general believe that anything could be gained by interference. The older and less sophisticated liberals still believed in an harmony as the outcome of economic phenomena, bound by immutable laws. Even before Adam Smith, Anders Chydenius in Sweden-Finland had stated, in 1765, that if all encroachment by the state were to cease, "the gain of the individual and of the nation would fuse in a common interest". Adam Smith himself reveals his opinion in his statement on the "invisible hand", through which every individual was made to serve the general weal, even though he pursued his own interest without any such end in mind. How *laissez-faire* arrived at this attitude, and to what degree such an attitude was uniform in it, belongs to the history of economic ideas and economic policy *after* mercantilism. What we are to do here is to point out the contrast between the mercantilist and the *laissez-faire* outlooks.[1]

Mercantilism embraced the opposite conception. According to one's attitude towards *laissez-faire* it may be said either that mercantilism did not penetrate to this view, or that it avoided this form of social superstitution. How was this possible? The reply is simple. If every social phenomenon is regarded as the working out of fundamental forces, this does not necessarily mean that those same forces bring about a *favourable result for society* without interference from outside or from above. This idea was expressed pregnantly by a late mercantilist, Sir Francis Brewster, in 1702. "Trade indeed," he said, "will find its own Channels, but it may be to the ruin of the Nation, if not Regulated."[2] The same idea was implicit in most observations with regard to social causation, e.g. in the statement presumably originating in Mun before the English commercial commission of the year

---

[1] Chydenius, *Den Nationnale Winsten* § 31 (Politiska skrifter, ed. E. G. Palmén, 133; Eng. trans., *The National Gain*, ed. G. Schauman, Lond. 1931, 88).—Adam Smith, *Wealth of Nations* Bk. 4, ch. 2 (Cannan ed., I 421).

[2] Brewster, *New Essays on Trade*, 61.

1622, quoted above (311). A *laissez-faire* adherent would certainly interpret it in the sense of a natural harmony, but the mercantilist by this argument meant nothing more than that interference should be directed at the causes and not against the effects, at the maladies and not against the symptoms; in other words, that the result intended could be obtained *on the assumption of suitable interference* but not otherwise. Petty said, in another quotation also reproduced above (309), that it was not possible "to persuade Water to rise *out of itself* above its natural Spring". The words italicized here show that he did not consider it altogether impossible, but believed that water could be induced to do this, if proper measures were taken. In this he was perfectly correct both literally and in the metaphorical interpretation.

Social causation in the eyes of the mercantilists was thus not automatic. On the contrary, there was an innumerable number of tasks awaiting the statesmen who wished to influence this causation in the direction of any objective which he had in view. Mandeville's observation, also quoted above (293), that private vices could be transformed into public benefits, be it noted, "by the dextrous management of a skilful politician", put the idea in a nutshell. Even a hundred years before, Bacon had made the same observation, and this, indeed, as a final outcome of his study on the greatness of states. "To conclude," said Bacon, "No Man can, by Care taking (as the Scripture saith) add a Cubit to his Stature; in this little Model of a Man's Body: But in the Great Frame of Kingdom, and Common Wealths, it is in the power of Princes, or Estates, to add Amplitude and Greatness to their Kingdoms. For by introducing such Ordinances, Constitutions and Customs, as we have now touched, they may sow Greatness, to their Posterity and Succession. But these Things are commonly not Observed but left to take their Chance." Becher, too, attacked the neglect to institute some regulation and the absence of any attempts to guide the effective forces along the desired road, and, indeed, he did this in a particularly interesting sphere—that of the choice and distribution of professions, a task which Elizabeth's Statute of Artificers had tried to solve in England. Becher's remark at the commencement of his greatest and most important work (1667) runs, "Nothing appears to me to be more remarkable than that no attention is paid in many places to these most difficult points and that every man carries on in the way he can, doing as he wishes, corrupting and causing a hundred others to corrupt; whether he succeeds to the good or ill, rise or fall, of the community, no one questions." That the desired choice of profession could be the effect of the natural free play of economic forces was an idea that apparently never entered Becher's mind.

And so finally the logical conclusion was reached over which the *laissez-faire* opposition of the 19th century made merry. An ordinance of the court chamber of Baden in 1766, for example, declared, "Our princely court chamber is the natural ward of our subjects. It is in its hands to guide them away from error and lead them on to the right path and to teach them, even against their own wills, how they are to institute their own households."[3]

The expression "liberty" naturally included, as we have already seen, entirely disparate things. Malynes gave the idea that liberty was entirely reconcilable with regulation by the state a happy expression when he wrote of the really fettered medieval trading organizations, "Such was the free trade of this kingdom in those days, wherein the subjects of all sorts upon all occasions might freely participate *under government*" (my italics).[4]

Likewise, the glorification of the merchant's calling did not mean that business men could be left to themselves. Sir Thomas Gresham, endowed with more commercial instinct than most of his contemporaries, expressed his view of their function in a letter to Cecil (1560) in the following terms, "As the merchants be one of the best members in our common weal, so they be the very worst if their doings be not looked unto in time; and forced to keep good order." Later it fell to Colbert in particular to temper his declarations on the blessings of freedom of trade with reproaches and warnings to the merchants for their incapacity in every respect. In particular he impressed upon them the necessity of subjecting their petty daily interests to the interests of the state or the whole, and even disputed their ability to see their own advantage. "We must overcome the opposition," he said, "which the merchants put forward against their own advantage." "The merchants think only of their own activity and of the facility for selling"; "it is also necessary that you (the intendant in Bordeaux) devote yourself to the study of the trivial interests of the merchants, who pay no attention to anything but their private trade, in order to see what is good and advantageous for the general trade of the kingdom" (all together in 1670), and so on.

Among the English writers of the 17th century, most of whom came from merchant circles themselves, the tone was naturally

---

[3] Bacon, *Essays*, No. 29 in the 1625 edn. (ed. Wright, 130).—Becher, *Polit. Discurs* Erster Vorsatz (1673 edn. 3 f.).—Ordinance of the Court Chamber of Baden: quot. Schmoller, *Umrisse und Untersuchungen*, 303.

[4] Malynes, *Lex Mercatoria*, Part 3, ch. 20 (1st edn. 496).

rather different. The underlying idea, however, was the same amongst practically all of them, that, in fact, the profit of the merchant in itself was no criterion of the profit of the country, but on the contrary, the profit of the individual could be the country's loss and vice versa. Mun distinguished carefully in his most famous book between the commercial gain of the country, of the merchant, and of the King, and reckoned with the possibility that any one of these three could realize a profit while one of the other two and even both suffered loss. Even so pure a representative of the merchant interests as Child started out from the anti-*laissez-faire* premise that "all Trade will be less gainful to Individuals, though more profitable to the Public". In another connection, he said that all classes of society participated more or less in the profit resulting from great trade, "whatever becomes of the poor Merchants". The latter were thus represented as the martyrs of society in most marked contrast to the view of Adam Smith and his "invisible hand". The German writers, who were further removed from practical activity in the business world, drove the view concerning this dissimilarity in interest to its extreme. Hörnigk, Becher's brother-in-law, believed, as was already stated in Part IV, that a mining concern which brought in only half the costs of production was a fifty per cent profit for the kingdom, although he made it quite clear that such an enterprise would lead to the immediate ruin of a private business man. The principal difference between the commercially-minded English and the suspicious continental mercantilists was, perhaps, that the former were rather apt to believe that merchants were sacrificed to state interests, while the latter feared the contrary.[5]

It is thus clear how the mercantilists could combine their view of a society determined by inexorable laws with their faith in the necessity of state interference, and why they did not hesitate for a moment to draw this conclusion. It may be asserted that it was precisely their general conception of society which led them to even greater ruthlessness than would have been possible without the help of such a conception. In their general view of society, they had rationalized the whole social tangle, but had not arrived at a belief in an immanent social rationality. Thus they believed themselves justified with regard to interference and, in addition, believed in its necessity, without being held back by a respect for such irrational forces as tradition, ethics or religion. The net

---

[5] Burgon, *Life of Sir Thomas Gresham* I 335 note.—*Lettres de Colbert* II 535, 573, 596.—Mun, *England's Treasure by Forraign Trade* ch. 7.—Child, *New Discourse of Trade*, ch. 1 & 9 (1698 edn. 69 and 165 f.).—Hörnigk: see above 194.

result was what we have shown, the precise contrary to a liberal economic policy, in *some* respects even more contrary to such a policy than the medieval had been.

This is not to deny that advanced *laissez-faire* arguments also occurred here and there even before the end of the 17th century, and this, indeed, even in authors who in other respects were purely mercantilists. And this is not unnatural; for however clearly it could be shown that social causation and state interference could go together, it was still but a small step from the conception of an existing social causal interdependence and a mastery over nature in social matters to the conception that such interdependence had an inherent rationality which ought not be disturbed. The general dominance of the idea of natural right was calculated to add fuel to such arguments.

Even around the middle of the 17th century there were occasional utterances arriving at this conclusion, one of them to be found in the remarkable pamphlet, *A Vindication of a Regulated Enclosure* (1656), written by J. Lee, a country clergyman during the Protectorate, to whom Professor Tawney has called attention. It is observed there that, "The advantage of private persons will be the advantage of the public." It was Sir Dudley North in 1691, with his epigrammatic brevity, who gave the clearest expression of this view before the end of the 17th century. His short pamphlet, however, remained entirely unknown; and it is not even certain that it was ever published. What it put forward, moreover, had really very little to do with mercantilism. It is much easier to see the struggle between old and new ideas in a typical eclectic thinker such as Davenant. He said (1697), "The Wisdom of the Legislative Power consists in keeping an even hand, to promote all, and chiefly to encourage such Trades, as increase the Public Stock, and add to the Kingdom's Wealth. Trade is in its Nature Free, finds its own Channel, and best directeth its own Course: And all Laws to give it Rules, and Directions, and to Limit, and Circumscribe it, may serve the particular Ends of Private Men, but are seldom advantageous to the Public. Governments, in relation to it, are to take a providential Care of the whole, but generally to let Second Causes work their own way; and considering all the Links and Chains, by which they hang together, peradventure it may be affirmed, That, in the main, all Traffics whatsoever are beneficial to a Country." The beginning and conclusion of this argument—which is possibly the one against which Brewster directed his attack—certainly do not hang together particularly well, and Davenant's hesitation is unmistakable. In general the new conception, which went so far in its belief in the domination of natural laws in society that it believed in an immanent reason in the free play of forces, belonged to a later period. It is a major factor in the struggle between mercantilism and *laissez-faire*, or, as we may say perhaps with equal justice, in the *transition* from mercantilism to *laissez-faire*.[6]

In addition, by no means all that characterized the above-described mercantilist conception of society was born of the same spirit as that of *laissez-faire*. The essential achievement of *laissez-faire* rested on the fact that it had an eye to the human. On this practical point it was poles apart from mercantilism, at least as much as it was in its specific economic theory. The humanitarian or philanthropic spirit growing towards the end of the 18th century, though it took it almost a century to prevail in legislation, was one of the powerful forces which put an end to the mercantilist system. In this there was in fact a fundamental harmony between —to keep to English names—political Liberals (or their equivalent) like Adam Smith, Bentham, Romilly, and Malthus on the one side and Conservatives like Wilberforce, Sir Robert Peel (the "cotton lord"), and Lord Ashley (later Lord Shaftesbury), on the other, struggling against pauperism, the Law of Settlement, the slave trade, negro slavery, the abuse of child labour in the factories and the mishandling of children in the sweat shops, the truculent criminal laws, and an infinity of other things, regarded with good will or indifference by an earlier age.[7]

Mercantilism had, as we saw, at any rate two aspects, the one pointing to liberalism and the other to its precise opposite. The question then arises which of the two was the more important; and there can certainly be no doubt that the *latter* was. Of the liberal aspect of mercantilism in its heyday, there were only a few factors actually operative, the interest in the new entrepreneur, the emancipation from ethics and religion, and the tendency to make private interests serviceable to the community. All these, however, faded into the background behind the conception that

[6] J. Lee, 'Ευταξία τõυ "Αγρου, or *A Vindication of a Regulated Inclosure* (Lond. 1656); cf. Tawney, *Religion and the Rise of Capitalism* 259.—North, *Discourses upon Trade*, Introdn. (1st edn. viii; Reprint of Econ. Tracts, ed. Hollander, 13). —Davenant, *Essay upon the East India Trade* (Appendix to *Disc. on the Publ. Revenues* II 1698) 25 f.

[7] Cf. esp. Dicey, *Relation between Law and Public Opinion* 106–10, 187 f., 402 f., and D. Marshall, *The English Poor in the Eighteenth Century*: "a new attitude towards the under-dog was coming into being" (53, cf. 53–6, 104, 153, 159 f.).

it was necessary to regulate economic activity according to certain doctrines of economic policy, a concept precisely most specific in mercantilism, and therefore at the antipode to *laissez-faire*. All talk of "liberty" was, in the main, music of the future. The reality consisted in enforced subjection to an economic system taken over from previous centuries and, over and above that, in mercantilism—to repeat the division of the foregoing parts—as a system of power, as a system of protection, and as a monetary system. However much the mercantilists themselves felt emancipated from tradition, in practice they were, generally speaking, caught in its net. In the general conception of society, as also in the striving after unity, liberalism was the executor of mercantilism. In the economic and humanitarian spheres, it became the conqueror—that is, of course, only for the duration of its own spell of power.

CONCLUSION

AFTER MERCANTILISM

Another book would be required, at least as extensive as this, to elucidate the history of economic policy after mercantilism. This brief conclusion does not aspire to such an end. It will only try to outline the contours of the development after mercantilism. More particularly will it show the fate of the ideology peculiar to mercantilism in the later period.[1]

Great power for the state, the perpetual and fruitless goal of mercantilist endeavour, was translated into fact in the 19th century. In many respects this was the work of *laissez-faire*, even though the conscious efforts of the latter tended in an entirely different direction.

The result was attained primarily by limiting the functions of the state, which task *laissez-faire* carried through radically. The maladjustment between ends and means was one of the typical features of mercantilism, but it disappeared once the aims were considerably limited. In *laissez-faire* they consisted, indeed, only in certain elementary and unavoidable functions of foreign policy, defence, legislation, and the administration of justice, nicknamed by Carlyle "Anarchy plus the Constable". Disobedience and arbitrariness, unpunished infringements of the law, smuggling and embezzlement flourish particularly under a very extensive state administration and in periods of continually changing ordinances and interference with the course of economic life. It was because the *régime de l'ordre* bore this impress that disorder was one of its characteristic features.

On the other hand, it is also evident that through the mere disappearance of mercantilism, the state did not indeed become stronger, but merely less pretentious. In actual fact, however, there was also a direct tendency making for increased power of

---

[1] The subject of these concluding remarks is naturally far too great for detailed reference. I may, however, call attention to an acute and stimulating, though not always well-founded or well-balanced, criticism of *laissez-faire* from the standpoint of the theory of cognition, by a Swedish economist, G. Myrdal, called in its German edition *Das politische Element in der nationalökonomischen Doktrinbildung* (Berlin 1933).—In the light of quite recent events, I have touched upon some of the leading ideas of these few pages in an article called "Planned Economy Past and Present" (*Index*, ed. Svenska Handelsbanken, May 1934).

the state. And to this *laissez-faire* contributed, even though it was not the sole deciding factor.

The achievement of *laissez-faire* in this respect consisted in its unifying work, already outlined in the concluding chapter of the first part. After all the thousand-year-old relics of medieval disintegration had disappeared and the territory of the state had been subjected to a uniform code of regulations, carried out, moreover, by common agents, it was so much easier for the organs of state administration to enforce compliance with their will.

At the same time, these agents themselves underwent a fundamental transformation through the rise of a paid bureaucracy or Civil Service, both in central as well as in local administration. On the continent, the foundations of this had been laid long before, particularly in France, Sweden, and Prussia, as the foregoing has illustrated. In these countries the metamorphosis really consisted in the uprooting of the confusion of the *ancien régime*, which had made itself felt in all spheres. But in England, the model country of the new era, conditions were different; there, there was still very much to be made up for in the field of administration. In central government it was only under *laissez-faire* that an effective bureaucracy was built up in the form of the Civil Service, although that had little in common with the conscious objectives of *laissez-faire*. In this was manifested a sound practical instinct. In local administration, the change in England did not, in the main, come about till after the period of *laissez-faire*.

In any case, the consequence was that the state, considerably limited in its functions, acquired far more efficient weapons than the more extensive state had ever had. For this reason, the last century is above all the century of effective administrative power. The experience of the first World War proved this quite clearly, for states were then in a position to apply even such measures as had never been considered possible under mercantilism. Witness to this the effective blockade of the Central European powers, which need only be compared with the ineffective Continental System of Napoleon, and similarly with the export prohibitions on precious metals, which in the earlier period had been regarded as entirely impracticable.[2]

To say that the organization of administrative power was not the conscious objective of *laissez-faire* is not to imply, as unfortunately it is so frequently made to do, that *laissez-faire* was antagonistic to the state. It was not; for to limit the scope of an institution is not to reject it. Such limitation is calculated rather to strengthen

[2] Heckscher, *The Continental System* 366–71.

it and in fact, *laissez-faire* did strengthen the state. There were two social phenomena, not one, of which *laissez-faire* approved and included in its calculations: the individual and the state. What it denied and overlooked were all the social structures *within the state* that stood between the two. In *this* respect it was "atomistic". This applied to the traditional corporations, local institutions and ordinary societies, professional and class associations, and monopolistic organizations. As a practical economic policy, *laissez-faire* attacked and rejected such institutions as purposeless and dangerous. It also condemned them in its capacity as an economic theory. It believed that they owed their existence only to irrational interferences, that people if left to themselves would recognize the uselessness of them—at least this was the English version of *laissez-faire* as expounded on these points. A most typical expression of this *laissez-faire* view of society is Ricardo's famous and epoch-making theory of foreign trade. Its point of departure, in fact, was the assumption that the factors of production within the limits of the state were freely and "atomistically" mobile, and capable of the most profitable application, but that they did not go beyond the boundaries of the state in any circumstances, i.e. had no international mobility at all. This furnishes an illustration of the conception of society which took cognizance only of the state and the individual.

It cannot be said that, in its condemnation of the corporations, *laissez-faire* distinguished itself vitally from mercantilism. This outlook on social life was a heritage adopted from the pre-*laissez-faire* era. The two tendencies parted in their judgment on the question of how far these corporations, disliked by both, could be done to death. In this *laissez-faire* was more radical, but it was seen that mercantilism showed more accurate judgment with regard to the general vitality of the corporate institutions.

It requires no elaboration to show that mercantilism and *laissez-faire* parted ways in their conception of the *relationship* between the state and the individual. But *laissez-faire* may easily be misunderstood also in this connection.

In mercantilism the individual was subordinated to the state unconditionally; he was solely a tool for the implementing of its aims. In *laissez-faire* he was *not* the reverse, although it might easily appear so. This is manifest in many points, first in the efforts to secure the integrity of the state's efficiency in the spheres reserved to it, in which connection Adam Smith's criticism of the colonial government of the trading companies is one example among many (*v.s.* I 453 f.). Secondly and more important "free" economic life, i.e. without the interference of the state, was by no means to become a playground of individual interests. The state and the individual each had its functions to fulfil. They were both equally in the service of a third party, the latter being the "community". This vitally important concept was thought of as the common interest of all the inhabitants of a particular social unit, which was not bound to any state or corporative organization. The slogan of Bentham and the utilitarians: "the greatest happiness of the greatest number", was a description of the interests of the community. "The Heaven-ordained Laws of Supply and Demand"[3] were to bring about the same result, and it was thought that they were capable of doing so by their own inherent powers. *Laissez-faire* was thus just as much preoccupied with the common interest as was mercantilism. But the collective good which it adopted as an objective was considered the sum total of the interests of all individuals, to be attained in a particular manner. Regarded in this light, even the state was to be subordinated to the community.

This provides the chief explanation for the attitude of *laissez-faire* towards the workers. It should by no means be denied that among the *laissez-faire*-minded employers, and the politicians greatly dependent upon them, class interests also played their great part. But to ascribe such considerations to the thinkers who established the foundations of *laissez-faire* is to distort the facts. This holds good both for the philosophic, primarily philosophico-legal, tendency initiated by Bentham, as well as for the school of *laissez-faire* economists. To keep to the latter, we need only quote Adam Smith. Again and again he expressed his frank sympathies with the workers and his preference for high wages, as for instance in the following passage: "What improves the circumstances of the greater part can never be regarded as an inconveniency to the whole: No society can surely be flourishing and happy, of which the far greater part of the members are poor and miserable." Malthus's practical programme was intended to raise the standard of living of the working classes by limiting the number of their children. With regard to the mercantilist ideal of a country becoming rich through low wages he exclaimed: "Perish such riches!" The idea underlying his remarks recurs in Ricardo, when he said, "The friends of humanity cannot but wish that in all countries the labouring classes should have a taste for

---

[3] "The Heaven-ordained Laws of Supply and Demand": J. Stirling, *Trade Unionism* (Glasgow 1869) 55. quoted in S. and B. Webb, *Industrial Democracy* (Lond. 1897) II 653.

comforts and enjoyments, and that they should be stimulated by all legal means in the exertions to procure them. There cannot be a better security against a superabundant population."[4] Both schools of early *laissez-faire* adherents identified themselves without reserve with the humanitarian tendency, which was a major point of contrast to mercantilism. In this respect, Malthus and Mandeville, for example, provide profitable comparison.

The new school sympathized with the workers, but only on the condition that they fulfilled their tasks in the service of the community and the general good. Everything was to be at the disposal of the nation as a whole in its capacity of consumer. All producers, and above all the workers, had to subject themselves to this higher common function. From this there proceeded a grand indifference towards all such individuals and groups as had nothing to offer in the service of this ideal; particularly hard were they on those who did not even want to offer anything. When, finally, the organizations of the workers and the interference by the state in their interest were regarded as useless and even harmful, it may easily be understood that the *laissez-faire* economists and philosophers were not very popular with the working classes. But we must beware of the serious historical errors which can easily arise from this.

The general aversion of *laissez-faire* to interference by the state emanated in the first place, among its theorists, from a purely economic interpretation of economic phenomena. Any one who reads Adam Smith without bias sees most strikingly the purely economic motives of the *laissez-faire* principles in him. He wrote, for example, "Every individual is continually exerting himself to find out the most advantageous employment for whatever Capital he can command. It is his own advantage, indeed, and not that of society which he has in view. But the study of his own advantage naturally, or rather necessarily leads him to prefer that employment which is most advantageous to the society."[5] The explanation is simple. The correlated factors usually discerned to-day in the theory of pricing can, in a simple economic theory, very easily appear ideal for the purpose. It is true we must assume

---

[4] Adam Smith, *Wealth of Nations* Bk. 1 ch. 8 (ed. Cannan, I 80).—Malthus, *Principles of Political Economy* (2nd edn., Lond. 1836) 214. The same trend of thought can be found amplified in the *Essay on the Principle of Population*, esp. chs. 4 & 13 of Bk. 4.—Ricardo, *Principles of Political Economy and Taxation* (3rd ed., 1821; *Works and Corresp.*, ed. Sraffa, Cambr. 1951, I 100)

[5] *Wealth of Nations* Bk. 4 ch. 2 (ed. Cannan, I 419).

for it that a social maximum arises if the objectives are achieved which each individual sets for himself and which they can attain with their given incomes. Here is not the place to discuss the validity of this idea. What we have to determine here is simply that this conclusion is very tempting when investigating elementary economic factors and that *laissez-faire* economists could easily believe that they deduced their economic policy directly from an analysis of economic phenomena.

The ideology fell into difficulties only when economic development, irrespective of interference from without, led to results which were disliked, or even regarded as a great misfortune for society. To the *laissez-faire* economists there were primarily two problems in this connection, both closely interdependent. The one was the tendency to over-population, demonstrated by Malthus. But the danger of over-population could not very well cause the problem of state interference to arise, for in the first place, over-population could be counteracted by individual action, and in the second place, any interference from above involved great difficulties. It was quite different in the second case, namely the theory of rent. Ricardo's view of economic development was dominated by the idea that where production and population were increasing, an ever-growing portion of the income of the community went into the pockets of landowners in the form of rent. One might have assumed that this view of the probable development would have led Ricardo to the practical conclusion brought forward later by Henry George and his school, i.e. the confiscation of all rents. It was all the more to be expected since, like the followers of Henry George, Ricardo regarded the development which he foresaw with particular alarm. But throughout his life Ricardo confined himself to attacking the duties on corn, which were calculated to raise rents unduly; he did nothing more than that, although he was a radical not only in matters of thought but also in party politics, and belonged always to the extreme left in Parliament. Why? It is difficult to find a more plausible explanation, than that he did not consider himself justified in instituting an attack on the unlimited right of private property. In any case this acquiescence in a result which he dreaded was almost the only point that was not susceptible of direct explanation from the economic point of view of *laissez-faire*. The explanation is to be sought, in this case, in something non-economic, in Ricardo's conception of what he considered serviceable to the general good. If the motive suggested was the true one, a direct application of natural rights was what prevented Ricardo from drawing the conclusion which otherwise lay nearest at hand in his study of purely economic phenomena.[6]

The same influence made itself felt in many other spheres, although nowhere, to my knowledge, was there so manifest a contrast between it and the obvious conclusions to be drawn from the examination of economic phenomena. If the economic thinkers of *laissez-faire* were already influenced in this way, among practical men of affairs and politicians it made itself infinitely more strongly felt. Free competition, individualism and the limitation of state encroachment often became pure dogmas to them, without any conscious rational foundations. That such a normative outlook existed is, in itself, by no means a criticism of *laissez-faire*. Some norm or other is always behind conscious action, for every action presupposes such a conception of the norm as, in itself, is not demonstrable. Here it was a question, in fact, not of science, but of economic policy, i.e. not thought, but action.

The fact that *laissez-faire* found support in the new science of economics also had other important consequences for the various aspects of mercantilism. With few exceptions, a better insight was gained, from the purely economic point of view, into the correlated factors of economic life. In addition, a practical policy was pursued supported partly by these elements of knowledge and partly from other sources. It would be an oversight to omit either of the two constituent elements.

Economic science consummated its most significant achievement within the sphere of practical economic policy in making an end to mercantilism as a monetary system, and in abolishing the whole jumble of notions discussed in the fourth part of the present work. This is perfectly natural, moreover, to the extent that in no other sphere did mercantilism rest on demonstrable fallacies to the same degree. True, the superstitions regarding the importance of the precious metals to the economic life of a country have not entirely disappeared. In this connection, the first World War, in fact, brought many purely mercantilist notions once again into broad daylight. Nevertheless, it cannot be denied that *laissez-faire* initiated a fundamental change in the conditions in this sphere. The return of foreign trade policy on many points to pre-*laissez-faire* ideas is, in fact, instrumental in showing that no parallel recrudescence has taken place in the sphere of mone-

[6] See the short Chapter 10 in Ricardo's *Principles* and cp. the illuminating description of "Ricardo in Parliament" given by E. Cannan (*Economic Journal* IV, 1894, repr. *The Economic Outlook*, Lond. 1912, 87–137).

tary ideas. For modern protectionism is no longer founded, like the mercantilist variety, on the necessity of an import surplus of the precious metals. The explanation is probably that mercantilist doctrine went much further in this respect than the popular conception, and that mercantilism therefore disappeared for the most part when the experts were convinced of the impossibility of maintaining it. It was precisely the acumen and discrimination of abstract thought characterizing mercantilist discussion on this point that allows the conclusion that this part of it was of a more esoteric character than the rest.

As is generally known, conditions were quite different concerning mercantilism as a system of protection. It is therefore necessary to devote some attention to this sphere with its particularly important practical effects. For the political victory of free trade under *laissez-faire*, Ricardo's theory of foreign trade was probably not of particular significance. From a theoretical point of view it was certainly one of the most remarkable achievements in the classical period of economic science. But it was far too difficult to grasp for it to be able to play a role in public discussion. On the continent it was hardly understood at all; and even in England, where its influence on theoretical conceptions was vital, popular discussions were based in the main on earlier expositions, more particularly on that of Adam Smith.

Adam Smith's achievement, again, was not particularly important in the pure theory of foreign trade, but of all the more importance in the practical policy of free trade. The major part of the voluminous fourth book of the *Wealth of Nations* was devoted to a criticism of mercantilism; it attacked its commercial policy (as well as its closely related colonial policy), and is an emphatic piece of free trade propaganda. Its basis, as usual with Adam Smith, was consumption or the community, and in addition, division of labour and exchange, which were hardly specific features of foreign trade. The following passage is characteristic of his particular kind of argument, "Between whatever places foreign trade is carried on," he said, "they all of them derive two distinct benefits from it. It carries out that surplus part of the produce of their land and labour for which there is no demand among them and brings back in return for it something else for which there is a demand. It gives a value to their superfluities, by exchanging them for something else, which may satisfy a part of their wants, and increase their enjoyments. By means of it, the narrowness of the home market does not hinder the division of labour in any particular branch of art or manufacture from being carried to the highest perfection. By opening a more extensive market for whatever part of the produce of their labour may exceed the home consumption, it encourages them to improve its productive powers, and to augment its annual produces to the utmost, and thereby to increase the real revenue and wealth of society."[7] If any economic arguments of a general character contributed to the victory of free trade, then they were arguments of this elementary kind. They were to be found in an even simpler form on the continent, particularly in the universally read works of French authors. In England, Cobden's uncommonly convincing eloquence contributed more than anything else to the diffusion of these points of view.

In addition *laissez-faire* attempted to overcome mercantilism as a system of power, and in doing so, drew cosmopolitan conclusions from what, in its premises, was so purely national a system. Every country, it was believed, derived a reciprocal value from prosperity, because the economic well-being of one country rendered it a better market for the products of another. A statement to this effect by Hume has already been quoted (*v.s.* II 14). It is to be found in practically the same form in Adam Smith.[8] In England, which had already become the principal industrial country in the world and the chief consumer of foreign corn, Cobden exerted himself to implement this idea in practice; while on the continent the argument was imitated without any independent additions.

How then did it happen that *laissez-faire* did not maintain itself in this sphere?

In this connection, the real defects in the theory of foreign trade as elaborated in the classical period, may be omitted. Ricardo's assumption that the factors of production were mobile within a particular country, but never crossed the boundaries, has come into increasing contrast with later developments, and the international mobility of the factors of production has in fact enabled one country to forge ahead economically at the expense of another, to an extent hardly reconcilable with the assertions of the *laissez-faire* economists. Many theoretical flaws in the free trade theory were also shown up during the course of time. But with regard to actual economic policy, this has not been of great significance. The cause for the shift in economic policy was more deep-seated. It arose from the general conception of society and the social psychology inherent in *laissez-faire*. What is peculiar is

---

[7] *Wealth of Nations* Bk. 4, ch. 1 (ed. Cannan, I 413).
[8] *Op. cit.* Bk. 4 ch. 3 pt. 2 (ed. Cannan, I 459).

that these defects were to be found precisely in those points which *laissez-faire* had in common with mercantilism, namely in its natural right, rationalist and atomistic features.

It was the conservative or historical spirit which overcame *laissez-faire*. That phenomenon is more recent than *laissez-faire*, even though it found support in, and to some extent in practice dated back from, earlier conceptions of the period before natural rights and rationalism. While mercantilism and *laissez-faire* originated primarily in England and France, the historical spirit had its specific home in Germany; such names as Hegel, Savigny, Stahl, and the German romanticists show that this was so. Only *one* great Englishman, Burke, and several Frenchmen of lesser importance need be included here in the development of economic ideas.

The most remarkable feature of the new tendency in theory, as pointed out, was that it presented no less a contrast to the mercantilist than to the *laissez-faire* conception of society. If it had no faith in "The Heaven-ordained Laws of Supply and Demand", it did not believe more in the "dextrous management of a skilful politician". Society was regarded as a growth in the highest degree naturally determined, to be changed only by slow and gently progressive treatment, bound to tradition, each individual nation containing inherent and more or less ineradicable peculiarities. The inherited and instinctive characteristics of men were accorded an entirely different importance from their conscious self-imposed objectives; their actions were interpreted not so much as an expression of a rational calculus, as an outward sign of unconscious sentiments. In the same way, the simplification in the scale of motives which had been fundamental both to mercantilism and *laissez-faire* was rejected. And with its disappearance there disappeared, too, the basis of the mechanistic outlook which had also been common to both. Economic policy could no longer add and subtract, but saw itself being referred to much more difficult methods. Like the opposing schools of thought, the conservative or historical spirit was, at the same time, both an interpretation and a demand, a doctrine and an economic policy. Its romantic and nationalist elements approved of the heritage of long bygone days, the relations with which, for lack of any precise knowledge, formed the basis of more or less fantastic efforts of the imagination; while in practice it demanded respect for all that was specifically nationalist, and enmity towards everything foreign, notwithstanding the apparently reasonable arguments that could be marshalled in its favour. In this, it was directed primarily against the rationalism of the immediately preceding centuries. But in addition, the new tendency developed an antithesis to the Middle Ages, since it was directed against super-state and universal tendencies.

Even to-day, it is not easy to estimate correctly the significance of this conservative or nationalist influence on the development of the last century. In many respects its victory has been complete. But it has certainly not brought about a convulsion similar to that of *laissez-faire* at its height; it is possible that that was not its intention at all. It is the best proof of the importance of *laissez-faire* that the form of society which it superseded has never been able to raise its head again and, indeed, that no one has tried to revive it. Herein lies the difference in the formative power of *laissez-faire* and mercantilism; mercantilism had not been strong enough to remove anything radically. But, none the less, *laissez-faire* in its historical form was also overcome.

This was primarily the case in the sphere of commercial policy. The idea of protection in mercantilism has undoubtedly been the most vital of all its ideas. It required the unqualified faith of doctrinaire *laissez-faire* to wipe out the "fear of goods". As has been shown in the third part, the "fear of goods" is the most natural attitude of the "natural man" in a money economy. Free trade denied the existence of factors which appeared to be obvious, and was doomed to be discredited in the eyes of the man in the street as soon as *laissez-faire* could no longer hold the minds of men enchained in its ideology.

The first universally read opponent of free trade in the 19th century, as is familiar, was Friedrich List. His criticism of free trade was based upon the general conservative objections to *laissez-faire*; his principal attack was directed against the mechanistic outlook of the latter, which was preoccupied only with the exchange of finished products. List's two main theses—that the theory of the "school" was a theory of exchange values instead of that of productive powers; and that the capacity to create wealth is more important than wealth itself—were both in greater conformity with an organic than with a mechanistic conception of society. But they also had many points of contact with mercantilist ideas, more particularly with those of Mun, as has been shown above. However, it can hardly be assumed that the theoretical content of List's theories were of great significance— his whole thesis was based upon opposition to agrarian protectionist policy. Free trade experienced more powerful attacks from another quarter.

Free trade loses its argumentative force as soon as an historically given form of economic life is regarded as justified, as conservatism regards it, by its mere existence. No doctrine can deny that foreign trade undermines the bases of many existing forms of professional and social life and many existing industries. If this is considered a disadvantage in itself, then an increase in international trade is, without further argument, likewise a disadvantage. It is true now that conservatism in this form postulates what is, in practice, an impossibility, in a state of society which changes at a rate as furious as was the case in the 19th century. But there is a great distinction between such changes as are regarded as the consequence of "development" and such as may be traced to the activities of other countries. To the first men believed that they had to bow, even though they were damaging to many private interests, and even in such cases where they might have been prevented. But the latter were the actions of enemies, and it would have been unpatriotic to climb down with regard to them.

With this we arrive at another weakness in *laissez-faire*. Even if it is justified in what it states concerning economic results, that is concerning the better provision of a country with commodities, this must not necessarily be taken as the final word. The idea of the "fear of goods" means, indeed, that it is better to keep goods at arm's length than to import them. If the goal of economic policy is determined by this idea, the free trade argument is left with nothing to recommend it. The same applies to the policy of power. The refutation of mercantilism as a system of power as put forward by Hume and Adam Smith is then no longer effective. In practice, national antagonisms are far more important to the economic system than economic antagonisms to the political. Because countries adopt an antagonistic attitude to one another, they turn sharply against competition which, in its economic effects, is no different from the competition within an individual country. To say that the well-being of another country is an advantage also to the native, because it creates a better market for the commodities of the latter, is then no longer to propound a convincing argument for international trade. For the well-being of the other country, the extension of its production into spheres regarded as particularly important or honourable is, in itself, a thorn in the flesh to many. So long as states remain imbued with a national consciousness, this remains almost unavoidable. Undoubtedly *laissez-faire* underestimated the strength of this feeling; and this criticism holds, whatever the judgment will be with regard to its value as a force in the direction of counter-acting it.

Finally, we come to the humanitarian influence represented in *laissez-faire* in contrast to mercantilism. In this respect, the conditions were particularly favourable for those who overthrew mercantilism, for an individualist outlook will easily support measures for the protection of the individual. Nevertheless, *laissez-faire* probably achieved least of all in this very sphere.

Laissez-faire extended its main protection only to the claims of the individual as against the state, and step by step abolished the often chaotic horrors which had collected in the repressive measures of the past millennia. But where it was a question of protecting human interests against the pressure of social con-ditions, which did not have their origins in definite measures of the state but which, on the contrary, demanded such measures if they were to be abolished, there the situation was different. On this point *laissez-faire* was obstructed by its belief in natural rights, i.e. its belief in a predetermined harmony, to which was added in practical policy the influence of employer and capitalist interests. It is true and extremely important that mercantilist traditions would likewise, and perhaps even more, have been useless for the purpose; but this does not change the fact that *laissez-faire* failed here in a vital task. Anything positive that was done in the sphere of social policy occurred on the conservative side—in England primarily through Lord Ashley, later Lord Shaftesbury, while in Germany through Bismarck. This, too, was perfectly explicable in principle, economic policy being bound up with the duty of the patriarchal state to care for the welfare of its subjects. Still more important were the results achieved by the independent action of the workers themselves, in trade unions and co-operative unions of consumers; the fear of their influence and the growing importance of socialism also goaded politicians into finding remedies.

While modern commercial policy is rightly represented as neo-mercantilism, this applies to socialism only to a very limited degree. The foregoing exposition has shown that mercantilism wanted *not* state activity in economic affairs, but private initiative and acquisitiveness stimulated by government measures in the supposed interests of the state. This interest of the state, determined by the policy of power and removed from any comprehension of the value of the human being, stood in most pronounced contrast to the socialist ideals of today.

This could also be said of the extremely interesting experiment which has been carried out in the communist "planned economy". The communist planned economy attempts to reach its goal by methods which are completely different from those of mercantilism to an even greater extent than does western socialism; for this very reason, the communist system may claim to proceed according to a fixed plan in a way which is in reality quite alien both to the practice and the mode of thought of mercantilism. There are few economic systems which have so few counterparts in history as the soviet economy.

Since the severe economic crisis of 1929-32 in Europe and America, the western economies also have turned away from their 19th century heritage in a far more fundamental sense and to a far greater extent than ever before, thereby drawing closer to the socialist and the communist ideal, though certainly without fully embracing either the one or the other. This transition was not merely quantitatively but also qualitatively of much greater significance than was the introduction of protectionism, and new social policies at the turn of the last century. A close study of the characteristics of the economic policies which are now dominant in almost every country west of Russia obviously lies beyond the bounds of this work. I must confine myself to the observation that what I have said about socialism and communism could also be applied to this type of political system and that it is similarly widely separated from the mercantile system.

This is not to deny that there are significant points in common between mercantilism on the one hand and all the tendencies which have superseded liberalism on the other. They agree in the rejection of two particular features of liberalism and in so doing align themselves with mercantilism rather than with opposite modes of thought.

In the first place, all non-liberal points of view agree on the deliberate repudiation of the liberal view that the unrestrained play of economic forces will result in a predestined harmony. Translated from philosophical doctrine into practical economic policy, this means that all systems other than the liberal require governmental interference with the course of economic life, although there are wide differences on the question of the ends and the means of such interference.

The second respect in which all non-liberal tendencies resemble each other is that they do not admit a supremacy to consumption over production—using both terms in the broadest possible sense. While non-liberals may not always consciously deny this supremacy, the liberals explicitly asserted it. Mercantilism, as we have seen, is characterized to a great extent by a view of production as an end in itself. To an even greater extent this appears to be true of so-called planned economies. Protectionism, socialism and the current system of government regulation are all dominated by a regard for different groups of producers, forcing consumers to make the most of whatever consequences follow from these considerations. It is undeniable that this is of fundamental importance in determining the directions of economic policy, and to this extent it may be said that mercantilist ideas have taken on a new lease of life. The present-day system of governmental regulation in practice presents innumerable similarities to mercantilism in practice. This is, however, not to say any more than that mercantilism gave way to liberalism which, after a period of dominance which represented a very short time in world history, gave way in its turn to newer systems.

Mercantilism cannot be resurrected in its entirety any more than any other historical phenomenon. We scarcely begin to exhaust the content of recent political ideologies by comparing them with the teachings and life of a past age. This does not mean, however, that the study of mercantilism may not contribute in various ways, either positively or negatively, whether as a foundation or as a historical parallel, towards a more profound insight into the problems of political economy both in the present and in the future.

KEYNES AND MERCANTILISM[1]

I

John Maynard Keynes paid considerable attention to mercantilist doctrine in his celebrated *General Theory of Employment, Interest and Money,* devoting the greater part of one chapter to an attempt to rehabilitate the doctrine. This is not at all surprising since Keynes' view of economic relationships is in many ways strikingly similar to that of the mercantilists, despite the fact that his social philosophy was quite different from theirs—to some extent, indeed, its very opposite. For Keynes, it may be said, the interests of the workers were of central importance; for the mercantilists, considerations of general national interest almost entirely took precedence over concern for the lower classes. Keynes' exposition of the mercantilist interpretation of economic phenomena is, as he generously acknowledged, to a very large extent based on the first edition of the present work. My only objection to his reproduction of the picture I drew, is to point out that it only includes those parts of mercantilist theory that happen to coincide with his own analysis of economic behaviour.

I do not intend, therefore, to discuss Keynes' summary of mercantilist doctrine in full but shall concentrate on those sections where he claims to find support for his own theories. A complete discussion of Keynes' treatment of mercantilism would involve consideration of his whole theory and this is obviously out of the question here. Still less would it be appropriate—even were my knowledge adequate for the task—to consider the enormous discussion provoked by Keynes' book. Unfortunately I must limit myself to an examination of those parts of Keynes' presentation which appear to me to be weak. Let me also say, however, that if we were discussing the validity of Keynes' strictures on the shortcomings of classical economic theory, my judgment would be rather different. It is possible that Keynes did not himself attach decisive significance to his remarks on mercantilism. If he had lived longer, he might have expressed opinions substantially different from those of the book. Indeed, one of his most valuable attributes was his ability to free himself from earlier statements of opinion; views we find at the end of his

---

[1] The contents of this chapter first appeared under the title "Något om Keynes' 'General Theory' ur ekonomisk-historisk synpunkt." (*Ekonomisk Tidskrift,* 1946.)

posthumous essay on the American balance of payments[2] are difficult to reconcile with those found in *The General Theory*.

Unfortunately the nature of Keynes' whole theory is such that it is almost impossible either to verify or to disprove the supposed facts on which it is founded. Keynes may have been aware of this since he repeatedly warned his readers not to draw too sweeping conclusions from his theory and then to apply them to the formulation of policy; these warnings, as we know, have been largely ignored. This has, however, little relevance to the present discussion. The important point is that Keynes was working with purely psychological categories in a way which had largely been abandoned in theoretical writings since about the time of the outbreak of the first world war. The very adequate index of *The General Theory* indicates that his doctrine is based on such concepts as "the propensity to consume, to hoard or to save" and, still more important, "liquidity preference" and the absence of its converse "the inducement to invest". It is clear *a priori* that these are phenomena which cannot be verified by means of studies of the world about us; similarly, it is obviously impossible to apply psychological tests to past generations.

Keynes was seemingly aware of these difficulties since, except in isolated instances, he refrained from attempting to produce statistical evidence in support of his theories. Indeed, he did occasionally pass the comment that observable data cannot be found to correspond to his concepts. His whole theory of interest —with the conclusion that interest is a payment for the loan of money and not of capital—may be said to rest on the concept of the "propensity to hoard", which is after all nothing more than "liquidity preference". Keynes himself emphasizes that it is not the actual extent of hoarding but the "propensity" with which he is concerned. This he justifies by saying that the amount of hoarding—"so long as we mean by 'hoarding' the actual holding of cash"—must be equal to the quantity of money and is thus independent of the behaviour of individuals. (*General Theory*, 174). Obviously, it is impossible to verify this postulate by studying the actual amount of hoarding. It is without doubt a striking fact that the great extension of the scope of economic statistics in recent years and the growth in the importance of econometrics, as these studies are called, are of no help at all when we attempt to evaluate Keynsian theory—a theory which is regarded by so many scholars today as fundamental and universally applicable. With

[2] "The Balance of Payments of the United States" (*Economic Journal*, 1946. 185).

the best will in the world and with access to far greater resources than those at my command, any attempt to test that theory would still remain completely inadequate. Keynsian theory can be nothing more than pure hypothesis, resting on assumptions which can neither be proved nor disproved.

II

In other respects, Keynes has simplified matters for his critics by stating his propositions boldly and with healthy scorn for reservations or ambiguous formulations.

Let us take as our starting point a positive statement from the *General Theory* which will serve admirably as a means of examining Keynes' views on mercantilism. After having commented on three points in mercantilist reasoning which he considers to be correct, he goes on to say:

It is impossible to study the notions to which the mercantilists were led by their actual experiences without perceiving that there has been a chronic tendency throughout human history for the propensity to save to be stronger than the inducement to invest. The weakness of the inducement to invest has been at all times the key to the [sic] economic problem. *(General Theory, 346-8)*.

One has to view with some degree of envy a great scholar —and I would be the last person to deny that Keynes was such— who can perceive eternal truths throughout the whole of human history with such light-hearted ease. But let us first look closely at the assumptions from which these conclusions are drawn.

Keynes apparently does not find it necessary to prove that mercantilist conceptions are either correct or even probable; he evidently assumes that they follow, quite simply, from the writers' perception of "actual experiences". It has always been supposed— and rightly so—by people who take the trouble to reflect on these things, that the "actual experiences" of separate individuals cannot be used as a guide to the behaviour of society as a whole. The observations which individuals are able to make with their own eyes represent an infinitesimal part of the total activity of the community. If we attempt to draw general conclusions from personal experiences, we are generalizing from extremely limited observations; conclusions arrived at in this way can have no *a priori* claim to universality. An essential prerequisite to accurate knowledge of social phenomena is mass observation. Keynes should have asked what possibility the mercantilist writers had of conducting such mass enquiries, to what extent sources of appropriate information were available to them and, if they had the information, to what extent they made use of it. It is inconceivable that he wished to imply that facilities for mass observation of social phenomena were better during the mercantilist age than during the time of the liberal writers; yet otherwise he could not have avoided the conclusion that the mercantilists had at least no greater means of reaching the truth than the classical writers. But his conclusion was precisely the reverse.

If the mercantilists had in fact given definite evidence of an interest in empirical observation or of a willingness and ability to set aside their preconceived notions, we would obviously have scrutinized their assumptions with the greatest care. Keynes however produces no evidence whatsoever to show that the mercantilists did allow themselves to be influenced by "actual experiences". Is it entirely impossible to suppose that, on the contrary, their minds might have been so dominated by preconceptions that they were led to conclusions which in no way corresponded to the realities they should have been able to observe? Since Keynes pronounces that the classical theorists were completely devoid of the ability to draw correct conclusions from their "actual experiences", his failure to raise the same doubts about the mercantilists is all the more inexcusable. One can only suppose that in his considered opinion the ability to draw correct conclusions from experiences existed until 1776 but suddenly and mysteriously vanished in that year.

Over and above all this, the mercantilist view of actuality is made to apply "throughout human history". Here Keynes cannot support his case with anything the mercantilists themselves ever said or intended. They claimed no timeless universality for their doctrines; it was not of the slightest interest to them.

So far our criticisms have been purely methodological; now we can go a stage further. I suggested earlier that "propensities" and "inducements" were concepts which cannot be scientifically studied. But it is not impossible to examine the accuracy of the information which our forefathers—mercantilists included—had about those aspects of their society for which evidence was available. We can ask how they used the data they were able to acquire and to what extent they allowed their thinking to be influenced by their observations. Most of the following examples have been taken from my paper[3] to which I have referred earlier (II, 182, n.6). Here I shall be using only a small part of that material.

As I have suggested many times in this work, one of the most independent and intelligent of the mercantilist writers was Roger

Coke. Keynes makes use of a reference I made to one of Coke's statements. Coke wrote in 1675 that:

"The Dutch . . . . send yearly 1,500 Sail of Ships into the Sound . . . . yet in a year we (the English) send not above seven into the Sound (two whereof are Laden with Woollen Manufactures, the other five with Balast only) . . . ."   (Roger Coke, *Treatise III*, 54).

Here we have a precise statement of fact; thanks to the publication of the records of the Sound dues, we can easily test its accuracy.

The first impression is that the true figures for outward vessels from Holland and England bear no resemblance at all to those presented by Coke. If we examine the figures of ships sailing under Dutch and English flags, however, we can see how Coke produced his statement. Admittedly, such a high figure as 1,500 for Dutch vessels is nowhere to be found, but the figure for one year about this time (1669) was 1,005 which is not too far from the truth. Moreover the records show that in three isolated years (1666, 1672 and 1673) the number of English ships passing through the Sound was even smaller than Coke stated; in 1666 there were none at all. This shows at once how Coke derived his figures and how misleading they are. These three years were war years and the Dutch vessels declined in numbers—to 460, 163 and 359—as well as the English. Coke simply compared the highest Dutch figure available—increasing it incidentally by about 50%—with one of the lowest English figures. Furthermore, he overlooked the fact that, as he wrote, the number of English ships was rapidly increasing, absolutely as well as relatively. He obviously could not have known that this trend was to continue through the succeeding years, but this point itself illustrates how little his version reflects the true facts of the situation. In the three years 1674, 1675 and 1676 the number of ships entering the Sound under the Dutch and English flags were respectively, 652 and 120, 434 and 364, 467 and 403. These figures tell quite a different story from Coke's 1,500 and 7.

It may be instructive at this point to examine contemporary views of the balance of trade, since this was a central feature of mercantilist doctrine and figures almost as prominently in Keynes'

[3] "Samhällshistoria och statistik", in a collection of my essays *Historieuppfattning materialistisk och annan* (Sthlm. 1944). Similar essays appeared earlier in the Danish *Nationaløkonomisk Tidsskrift*, 1937, 153-173 ("Statistikens Anvendelse indenfor økonomisk-historisk Forskning") and in the *Quarterly Journal of Economics*, LIII, 1939, 167-193 ("Quantitative Measurement in Economic History"). The references to the Swedish Royal Commission on Foreign Trade during the 1680's are taken from C. Danielsson, *Protektionismens genombrott i svensk tullpolitik* (Sthlm. 1930, 62). See also my *Sveriges ekonomiska historia*, II, 2, 556.

treatment of it. Here, however, we have to turn to Sweden rather than England for evidence. Throughout the 1660's, 1670's and 1680's, it was repeatedly asserted in current discussions that Sweden's so-called unfavourable balance of trade should be transformed into a favourable balance. At the end of the 1680's, an important official trade commission stated with great emphasis that there could be no doubt that Sweden's balance of trade was passive; there is no reason to suppose that smuggling was the explanation. Yet official balance of trade figures which survive from this period—for 1661, 1662 and 1685—all show an export surplus. There is only one conclusion to be drawn: people sometimes didn't trouble to consult evidence which was both available and perfectly clear.

The same failure to take account of factual evidence—whether from inability to observe it or from indifference towards it—betrayed itself in even more significant matters. Throughout the early years of the industrial revolution, English political leaders were agreed that the population of the country was declining, although simple reflection should have persuaded them of the opposite; all the available evidence indicates that population was rapidly increasing. Similarly, it was taken for granted in Sweden during the "Era of Liberty" (1719-72) that "multitudes of the Swedish people are leaving the country every year", to quote from the title of the prize essay set by the Academy of Science in 1763; no fewer than 30 entries were received. Pehr Wargentin, the first statistician in Sweden with any claim to be scientific, at first agreed, but by 1780 his more detailed examination of the population statistics had led him to the conclusion that emigration from Sweden was insignificant or nil.[4] At a later date Gustav Sundbärg investigated the same material more thoroughly and concluded that the annual rate of emigration must have been less than one per thousand.[5]

But, as is well known, Sweden is the only country in which the population statistics for the period before 1800 are at all reliable. The mercantilists had practically no statistics whatever at their disposal. Even the Swedish investigators were affected by current fancies and prejudices in their own field; it was stated for example in 1761 in an official report of the Board of Statistics, which was responsible for population statistics, that "several examples could be given of children born in this country to women of over sixty years of age."

[4] See my Sveriges ekon. hist., II: 1, 63 ff.
[5] Sundbärg, Emigrationsutredningen: Betänkande (Sthlm. 1913) 57 and tab. 1.

Since Keynes is claiming to be able to identify a trend which
persists through the whole of human history, it may be appropriate
to conclude with an example from the Middle Ages. In 1371 the
English Parliament decided to levy a tax which was to be collected
in fixed equal sums for every parish. The amount per parish was
assessed on the assumption that there were 40,000 parishes in the
country. It is not unreasonable to expect that the King and his
parliament would have had at least a vague notion of the number
of parishes in the country; the correct number, however, turned
out to be 8,600. The consequence of the original ingenuous
mistake was that the amount of the tax per parish had to be
increased five-fold.

I hope that these examples have shown how little weight
can be given to statements made by writers in the past—and for
our purposes by the mercantilists in particular—concerning social
conditions in their own time. In view of their grotesque mistakes
in matters of measurable data, the idea that their "actual
experiences" gave them any insight into less tangible aspects of
social behaviour is indeed very far from the truth.

The main reason for the apparent ignorance of their
contemporary society shown by earliest writers, in comparison
with those of more recent times, was the absence both of systematic
mass observation and of systematic statistics. It is important to
remember also that even the limited data available was usually
inaccessible to the mercantilist writers. The sort of information
they needed was regarded as *arcana*, secrets of state: the Swedish
population statistics were thus regarded from the very beginning.
I drew attention earlier (II, 181, n. 6) to complaints by Davenant
in 1698 and 1699, that it was only with extreme difficulty that he
had managed to secure some of the accounts of public revenue
after all the important government offices had refused his requests
to be given access to the information. In the absence of statistical
data, writers resorted to so-called "political arithmetic",
calculations which, though sometimes undoubtedly ingenious and
skilful, were much more often dependent upon arbitrary
generalizations from casual observations or were without any
factual basis whatever. Such was the nature of the statistical
material, if any at all, on which the mercantilist writers generally
relied. Naturally this was reflected in their work, a fact which other
contemporary writers did not fail to point out.

Finally, it may be asked if there could be anything in the idea
that early economic writers—and especially the mercantilists—
possessed unique qualities of insight into reality, distinguishing

them from the classical writers who were pure theorists, blind to reality. It is presumably some notion of this sort that explains Keynes' greater faith in the former. If so, he evidently credited the mercantilists with a prodigious clear-sightedness and an intuition for economic truth which were denied the classical economists whose insight was doubtless marred by the depth of their meditation. I think it may be said that this is a false view of the mercantilists. They used methods which were just as orthodox, they were just as willing to pursue preconceived ideas to their logical conclusion, as any other group of writers. I showed this earlier in quotations from Petty and Asgill (II, 201ff., 213). When Petty advocated making imported silver into silver plate, he was certainly not led to this view because he had observed a shortage of silver plate; and when Asgill indicated that his system would allow land values to rise to infinity, it is not to be supposed that he had ever seen land of infinite price. In both cases, these were purely theoretical conclusions drawn from the writers' *a priori* notions of economic relations.

I think we can now leave the sentence from Keynes with which this discussion began. There are no grounds whatsoever for supposing that the mercantilist writers constructed their system—with its frequent and marked theoretical orientation—out of any knowledge of reality however derived. There is nothing to indicate that they were any different in this respect from the classical economists. Keynes asks us to believe that it is impossible "to study the notions to which the mercantilists were led by their actual experiences" without accepting their results as correct; I suggest that nothing could be easier than to reach exactly the opposite conclusion.

III.

So far my criticisms have been mainly negative. It is much more difficult to present in a constructive fashion the factual evidence which is relevant to the assumptions on which Keynes bases these aspects of his theory. So little research has been done on this problem—or rather these problems—that definitive answers cannot be given; in any case any answer which is made to apply to all human behaviour must be a dubious one. It is in the nature of the problem that the investigation must leave the psychological plane where Keynes dwelt. Appropriate facts have to be looked for in any aspect of economic life that is relevant to the problem. My next step is therefore to examine whether there are any indications of a general tendency towards purely monetary saving, i.e. a preference to hold savings in monetary form rather than to invest them; to examine past price trends; and finally to discuss the significance in past centuries of unemployment of the factors of production—of labour in particular—and if so what type of unemployment it appears to have been.

Before the commercial revolution, which occurred towards the end of the middle ages and during the period of the great geographical discoveries—indeed, even later still—saving was presumably confined to a small number of people, and not necessarily the wealthiest. The great incomes were those of monarchs and noblemen—but their pretensions were probably greater than their incomes. The large retinues they maintained, the ostentation considered to be appropriate to their rank, must generally have made them spenders rather than savers, buyers on credit rather than lenders. The modern notion that savings come from the rich dates from a time when the differences in the conspicuous material standards of living between the different classes in society have virtually disappeared; only then have the wealthy been able to become the chief source of savings—and only to the extent that they have not been turned into milch-cows by the confiscatory tax policies of governments. At the present day, who can guess whether a man one meets in the street is a millionaire or a manual labourer? There could have been no mistake about it in the Middle Ages; a nobleman could not possibly have been mistaken for a serf or an artisan.

If, as Keynes would have us believe, economic expansion depends upon the existence of a sufficient readiness to consume and a strong enough aversion to saving, then no period in the history of western civilization should have been so propitious for economic progress as the Middle Ages. His conditions were then fulfilled as in no subsequent period. The savings of both Christian and Jewish merchants were absorbed extensively by governments and princes either in free or enforced loans or in outright extortion. In either event they were used to increase the consumption of the rulers above the level for which they could pay out of their own incomes.

As commerce expanded, there came into being new social classes with a disposition to save; an increased number of people came to have incomes which were greater than they needed to meet their normal demands or to satisfy their existing living standards. There is every likelihood that the excess of their incomes over their expenditures grew as their incomes increased. There subsequently followed an expansion of industry which in its turn probably accelerated the same process still further. If one wishes to deny that economic expansion proceeded parallel with the growth of savings, one must assert either that there was no economic expansion or that there was no saving. I for one cannot see how either fact can be denied.

This does not preclude the possibility, of course, that there might have been a gap between savings and investment. A great deal of money was certainly hoarded. There is only one sense of "hoarding"—the word which perhaps appears more frequently in Keynes' book than any other—which can be submitted to the test of history; that is, the literal one. I shall persist in using the word in its literal sense despite the fact that Keynes' own concept of "liquidity" is, as he says himself (240ff.) extremely vague. As far back as we can go, from the earliest period about which history has been written, we find material evidence in the form of many discoveries of hoards of coins; and there is every reason to suppose that far into the nineteenth century people continued to hoard great quantities of money in bottom drawers, stockings or the like. Quoting from a source which so far as one can tell is completely reliable, Macaulay relates how Sir Dudley North was very irritated to find, on his return from a long business trip to the Levant in 1680, that all his acquaintances deposited their funds with the London goldsmiths. North stubbornly continued to keep his cash at home.[6]

If we examine more closely the facilities for the disposal of savings, it becomes clear that a very large part of the total saving never saw the capital market but went directly into the saver's own business. We may assume that this is what happened to the savings of merchants though they often accepted deposits from other savers; primarily their accumulations were from their own savings and they placed them in long-distance trade and in those industrial establishments which continued to be financed by merchant "putters-out" well into the eighteenth century. The most obvious example of the re-investment of savings in the saver's own business is that of the large landowners who must have required large supplies of funds to finance the almost revolutionary conversion of agriculture during the 17th century in Holland and, most of all, during the 18th century in England. A third example is to be found in the need for further investment in the continuing expansion of industry in the years after the industrial revolution. It is almost certain that these needs were met primarily from the savings of the entrepreneurs out of the large unconsumed profits

[6] Macaulay, *History of England.* (1st ed. London, 1855) IV, 491 ff.

derived from their businesses.[7] In none of these examples are there any grounds for suspecting that there was any inclination to withold savings from investment.

The very fact that so much of the saving went into investment without recourse to the capital market must have tended to make it more difficult for the *pure* savers, without their own businesses, to find outlets for their savings; more difficult also perhaps for banks and bankers to place the private savings which they received. As long as the capital market was inadequately organized, there must have been in many sectors a considerable amount of hoarding that was in no way indicative of any sort of "propensity" on the part of the savers. On the other hand, there undoubtedly was a growing tendency which might reasonably be labelled "liquidity preference"—namely a reluctance to part with savings because of the fear of losing them; this is what was stated to have worried Dudley North. Both these motives for hoarding became less and less operative as the organization of the capital market improved and the whole economy became increasingly more stable. The essential fact is that more and more funds for investment clearly became available during the course of the 19th century.

Two conclusions may now be drawn from this outline with some degree of confidence. Economic activity increased at the same time as savings were expanding; the two were not opposing forces. Secondly, insofar as there existed a tendency to hoard, i.e. insofar as investment was not equivalent in amount to savings, the gap between the two was very far from widening; on the contrary, it narrowed continually, except during short periods of disturbance.

We must now turn our attention to the question of the supply of money. When, as with Keynes, interest is expressly regarded as interest on money and the level of the interest rate as determined by the quantity of money, then the actual supply of money, or purchasing power, must be taken to be the historically determining factor. If there is an adequate supply of the means of payment, then, no matter how great "liquidity preference" may be, according to this line of thought the needs of the economy will always be satisfied; in accordance with Asgill's formula, the pure interest rate should then sink to zero. As far as I can see, Keynes gives no indications which would help one to decide what he regards as positive criteria of an adequate supply of the means of payment, other than changes in the rate of interest itself; but in order to use this as a criterion, it is necessary to start by assuming

[7] T. S. Ashton, *The Industrial Revolution, 1760-1830* (London, 1948) 94-100.

what we are trying to prove, i.e. by accepting the validity of the theory itself. This is obviously unsatisfactory. It might be possible to detect in Keynes' words at one point a clue to his views, but since his intention is not clear, I shall refrain from further comment. There is one factor, however—the movement of prices—which no modern theorist, certainly not Keynes, can deny has a close relationship to purchasing power, despite the complexity of the relationship between prices and the quantity of money. Accordingly it is to price movements that we must now turn and I propose to begin with an outline of price changes since the time of the great geographical discoveries. Here we are on fairly solid ground.

There is presumably no need for me to document the well-known facts of the great influx of precious metals—gold and especially silver—and the ensuing veritable revolution of prices, which continued through most of the 16th century, starting only a few decades after the discovery of America. The price trends of the next two centuries are not so generally known nor so clearly evident. The first part of *Nederlandsche prijsgeschiedenis* (1943) by N. W. Posthumus provides continuous price series based on quotations at weekly or shorter intervals on the Amsterdam bourse, long the foremost commodity market in Europe. We find a somewhat irregular trend from the 1620's to the 1680's in which may be distinguished a relatively weak rise followed by a more marked decline. Violent price fluctuations occurred in the decades around the turn of the century, but prices rose steadily thereafter with only minor disturbances until the 1790's when revolution and war brought much more violent increases. It seems possible to conclude from the different indices drawn up by Posthumus that prices increased by about one third between 1705/09 and 1785/89; the increase between 1789 and 1815 varied very greatly from one commodity to another; according to the unweighted series which appears to me the most plausible one, prices seem to have doubled between 1790/94 and 1810/14.

If we are to test the validity of the Keynesian thesis, we must look further for evidence of the trend in other countries. Thanks to the fact that the Bank of Amsterdam maintained its character as a deposit bank without note issue almost uniformly for only slightly less than two centuries, we have a situation down to the Revolutionary Wars in which the general price trend in the leading financial centre in Europe corresponded very closely to the movement of the price of silver and was not subject to severe disturbances. This was seldom true in other countries. Even before the advent of inconvertible paper currencies, persistent depreciation occurred from the Middle Ages onwards, with consequent increases of prices.

Relevant source material is relatively accessible in England and Sweden, making it possible to follow the price trends in these two countries. It is reasonable to suppose that Swedish monetary history corresponded in effects—though not always in form—to that of continental countries and that prices were more stable in England than elsewhere, though less stable than in Holland. Karl Åmark has compiled an index of Swedish prices based on *markegångstaxorna* ("assessed average market rates"), which therefore relates primarily to agricultural prices. This index shows a fifteen-fold price rise from the 1730's to 1815. The rise was continuous for eighty years, although irregular and, of course, with occasional slight setbacks; the only important exception to the trend was the well-known severe fall in prices between 1764 and 1768 or 1769 which was the consequence of a deliberate deflationary policy. The English price trend can be clearly seen if one draws a graph from the data in Beveridge's *History of English Prices;* the curve appears fairly steady, especially at first, although rising quite perceptibly. The rise becomes marked during the phase of inconvertibility in the last years of the 18th century and continued so for the next decade, although it was by no means as violent as in Sweden; by 1814 prices were at a level about three times higher than that of the early 1730's.

Naturally we know the most about the price trends of the 19th century. In the main, prices tended to fall from 1815 until just before the middle of the century when gold was discovered in California and Australia, and then to rise until the mid-1870's; the next twenty years saw a sharp decline, but the rise began again in the late 1890's and continued until the outbreak of the first World War.

From this it may be seen that the periods in which the supply of money in the western world was restricted to a level which worked against price increases were relatively short compared with those with the opposite tendency. There have been only two periods of predominantly falling prices since the beginning of the 18th century, namely, the years from the end of the Napoleonic Wars to the middle of the 19th century, and the years from the mid-1870's to the mid-1890's The decline in prices which occurred at times in the course of the 17th century was mild, while the 16th century was characterized by a pronounced rise in prices.[8]

[8] The literature on price history is much too extensive to be cited here

Keynes does not challenge this generally accepted view of the trends. On the contrary he states himself that in the very long run, prices have always tended to rise and that even in the 19th century—when the periods of falling prices were undoubtedly more significant than in the preceding centuries—prices were comparatively stable. He quotes Sauerbeck's index to show that "the highest quinquennial average. . . . between 1820 and 1914 was only 50 per cent. above the lowest." (*General Theory*, 308). The question at once arises therefore of reconciling this interpretation with Keynes' basic premise that "throughout human history the propensity to save [has been] stronger than the inducement to invest."

It would be difficult to decide from historical evidence alone whether an increase in prices of about 15 times in 80 years, such as that in Sweden between the 1730's and 1815, fulfils Keynes' requirements for a "true inflation" (*General Theory*, 303) or not; it is really of little consequence. It can be maintained that the monetary situation in Russia and Central Europe after the first World War—which Keynes described as "very abnormal circumstances" (*General Theory*, 207)—differed only in degree from conditions which were normal in many, if not most, countries for long periods of time before the second half of the 19th century. We only need to observe the tendency in post-war Europe to return to conditions of barter, as happened on many occasions in earlier history in times of severe depreciation; to quote one example: The town clerk of Stockholm about the time of the death of John III (1592/93) wrote in the city *memoranda*, "Swedish coins were so debased in these times that no person would accept money for his goods; prudent people traded only goods against goods."[9]

It seems to me to be symptomatic of present-day tendencies that Keynes does not mention anywhere, as far as I can discover, the real reason for the excess of currency which has been

in detail. For Sweden, see my *Sveriges ekon. hist.* I: ii, second part ch. V for the 16th century, I: ii, second part ch. IX, for the 17th century, diagrams iv-xiii for both centuries, II: ii, ch. XI, and diagram xxxiv ff. for Sweden and England in the 18th century. For the post-1815 period, see my article "Evig Inflation?" (*Balans*, 1950, 222-28 and diagram.)

See also K. Åmark, "En svensk prishistorisk studie" (*Ekonomisk Tidskrift*, 1921, 147-70 and tables); G. Myrdal, *The Cost of Living in Sweden, 1830–1930* (Stockholm Economic Studies 2, 1933, 25-32) on "markegångstaxor"; N. W. Posthumus, *Nederlandsche prijgeschiedenis*, I (Leiden, 1943); W. Beveridge, *Prices and Wages in England from the 12th to the 19th century* (London and New York, 1939).

[9] *Sveriges ekon. hist.* I: i, 82, similar quotation from same source, 219 ff.

characteristic of such a large part of the history of western civilization. This was of course quite simply that governments needed money to finance wars and other state expenditures. Nine times out of ten—to be quite conservative—this was the reason both for the debasement of coinage and for the over-issue of paper. The effects on general economic life were generally unexpected and only intended in exceptional cases. The Swedish example of 1592/93 seems to indicate precisely the opposite to an inadequate propensity to invest; it leads us to suppose that a continuous inflation had resulted in a "flight to real values". I am inclined to assume that this was a usual consequence in many countries of disturbances in the monetary system. That wages generally lagged behind prices was undoubtedly a rule to which there are but few exceptions. For example, the long period of rising prices in Sweden in the 18th century was accompanied by a marked decline in the real wages of workers in the iron industry, and, it may be presumed, an even greater decline in the real incomes of handicraftsmen. The only large class which seems to have derived any benefit was the peasantry, apart from various groups of speculators whose gains were far larger. These effects followed quite incidentally from monetary policies which were based only to an insignificant extent on any regard for economic growth.

It is surely a striking fact that Keynes' attempt to rehabilitate the mercantilists did not have its roots in the simple fact that, after the price revolution of the 16th century, the 17th century was in the main a period of steady prices. This viewpoint was put forward in a doctoral thesis, *The Theory of the Balance of Trade in England, a Study in Mercantilism,* (1923) by Bruno Suviranta. My own view is that it is not very plausible to say that mercantilist theory can be explained by the conditions of the time for the simple reason that the roots of mercantilism go back at least to the middle of the 16th century when monetary conditions were exactly the reverse. Nevertheless, there is more to be said in support of this interpretation than can be said in favour of one which extends its validity throughout the whole of human history.

IV.

The whole of Keynes' work is dominated by the problems of employment and unemployment. So far as I know, there has been very little research into the factors historically determining the level of employment, and thus the rate of unemployment. It is highly desirable that this subject which is so important in economic history should be treated in a series of monographs. In the present state of our knowledge, we must proceed cautiously, although there can be no doubt about certain fundamental facts.

Until 1900, though to a decreasing extent in the later years, agriculture was the dominant economic activity of Sweden and many other countries. In these economies, unemployment was about as independent of monetary and market conditions as it is in modern Russia where the possibility of allowing the unemployed to stream back into agriculture, at least at times, is regarded as having been quite important. The determining factor was the harvest. The hordes of beggars on the highways described in early Swedish sources were driven there by crop failures. In some parts of Sweden a serious crop failure could force entire villages out upon the roads to beg. It should not be necessary to explain that no "planned investment" could have done anything to remedy that kind of unemployment—if indeed that word is at all appropriate.

These comments obviously do not apply to early industrial activity. In western and some parts of central Europe, industry was from an early date much more important than in countries like Sweden which remained predominantly agrarian. In these economies, unemployment was a more tangible fact. It is quite likely that many of the "sturdy beggars" referred to in English Poor Law legislation were workers who had at one time or another been engaged in some sort of industrial activity. Nevertheless, even in such cases, discussions which proceed along Keynsian lines are almost always wide of the mark.

In the early stages of development, the industrialized sector of an economy was subject to repeated dislocations which have very little in common with the kind of disturbance we now call the business cycle. They were dislocations resulting from wars, state interference of various sorts and changes in market conditions, especially abroad. As industrialization became more widespread, people spoke in England of "the firm basis of land and the fluctuating basis of trade." One of the examples which Keynes claims as evidence of the clear-sightedness of the mercantilists (*General Theory*, 347, quoting me) is taken from a parliamentary debate in 1621 on the "scarcity of money". The situation was largely the outcome of an intrigue which had resulted in the transference of the old privileges of the Merchant Adventurers' Company—and with them the charge of handling England's chief export, cloth—to a completely new and rootless company;

this enterprise had collapsed and an economic crisis had resulted. This was a not uncommon situation; it seems to reflect a normal state of affairs in which there is nothing at all to suggest that there was any unemployment existing as a result of insufficient investment. The predominant type of industrial unemployment before the industrial revolution was mainly, if not wholly, of the old, well-recognized classical type which Keynes calls "frictional". This certainly did not mean that its effects were not at times extremely severe. In many cases, we may suppose that sensible governmental intervention could have warded off the causes of the unemployment; in several cases, the unemployment only arose because of foolish governmental intervention in the first place. I know of no single example in which it might be suggested that the difficulties were brought on by a general inadequacy of the "inducement to invest". This is not to deny that an increase in credit could not possibly have improved matters.

I think that it is permissible to suggest that this remained true for as long as a century after the start of the industrial revolution (in the popular sense of the term)—that is, until the 1860's and 1870's. So far from being a "general" theory, Keynes' theory is appropriate to a situation which could scarcely exist in the absence of fixed capital investment on a large scale and perhaps also in the absence of strong labour organizations.

But Keynes' view was quite opposed to this, since he believed that he had discovered a trend running through all human history. He is in reality merely putting into words the same sort of conception as has so often and for so long been regarded as characteristic of the classical economists. Adam Smith has often been reproached for his talk of "a certain propensity in human nature".... "to truck, barter, and exchange one thing for another". Smith at least attempted some sort of sociological explanation (in the introduction to the second chapter of Book I); there is no counterpart to this in Keynes' assumptions of his many "propensities". A final and much more important point is that the human propensity to trade indisputably has existed for thousands of years longer in mankind's history than the propensity to save too much and to invest too little.

V.

The new exposition of economic relationships, of which Keynes is without question the pre-eminent leader, is therefore to be regarded essentially as a product of the increased significance of fixed capital investment. The Keynesian theory, moreover, is intimately bound up with factors which are even more limited in time; it might well be called a product of depression. The origins of this mode of thought lay in the severe fall in prices and the twenty year depression from the mid-1870's to the mid-1890's. These years saw the re-introduction of protection in its new forms, protection for agriculture and the Bismarckian *Solidaritätssystem*. They gave the stimulus to those two warriors in "the brave army of heretics" to whom Keynes devoted a great deal of space, Silvio Gesell and J. A. Hobson. This change in the intellectual climate was not brought about in any sense by stagnation but occurred in conditions of falling prices created by new revolutionary developments, primarily in transoceanic commerce, drawing America much closer to Europe than ever before. American wheat now enabled the people of Europe to satisfy their hunger for almost the first time in history but at the same time threw European agriculture into very serious difficulties.

The main point which concerns us here, however, is that fixed capital investment, plus the accompanying increase in the size of the unit of operations, gave real significance for the first time to what I have called "intermittently free goods"—unused resources of productive factors, whether material or human, which, in themselves, are "scarce". It must be emphasized strongly that this constitutes a practical problem of great importance. However, not merely is it a problem restricted to our own era, but also its fundamental essence is quite different from what Keynes supposed it to be. It makes necessary a fundamental revision—or more correctly an amplification—of the classical atomistic theory. Keynes himself used the analogy of Euclidian versus non-Euclidian geometry (first used so far as I know by J. M. Clark); at least to the non-mathematician the comparison seems apt, with the extremely significant reservation that one has temporal limitations and the other is universal. But it is certainly quite untrue that non-Euclidian geometry has made Euclidian superfluous. An extension to the edifice of economic theory built according to this plan would in my opinion preserve much of the old and give a much less constrained and a more correct impression of the new than is to be found in many existing constructions. To pursue this matter further would, however, carry me far beyond the limits of this chapter.

Let me conclude by emphasizing that Keynes' remarkable book should be read in its historical context. It may have been influenced by the changes in circumstances and ideas which I have mentioned above; but its *specific* motivation is to be found in the persistent unemployment in England between the two World Wars, a phenomenon with which Keynes seems almost to be obsessed. Seldom has a work with pretensions to universal applicability been based to such an extent on a single narrow point of view. It became in consequence the opposite of a "general" theory and became instead a theory of quite limited applicability. Until the second World War it had been the view of Keynes—and of others—that, in the absence of planned investment, war alone could create full employment. I do not know whether Keynes had the opportunity to reconsider his views in the light of conditions immediately after the war, when all productive resources, material and human alike, were strained to the breaking-point. But, in any event, this has nothing to do with the history of mercantilism.

ADDENDA

Addendum §1: (Replaces and supplements text from last paragraph, 16, to and including line 41, 17.) What was it that differentiated the mercantilists and their views on power as a factor in economic policy from Adam Smith and liberalism in general? In the first edition of this work, I maintained that the difference lay in opposite views concerning ends and means. Thus for the mercantilists power was a goal in itself, though certainly not the only and final goal. For Adam Smith, however, as is consistent with the title of his great work, power was only a means to the end of welfare, admitting, of course, that some degree of welfare must be sacrificed in order to make the remainder secure. It is against this thesis that Jacob Viner has written the essay cited in the footnote on p. 13. Here he has included an imposing array of quotations from contemporary English writings and from other contemporary comments. The implication of these expressions is, in general, that power, commerce and welfare (plenty) were placed side by side as equally desirable and mutually compatible goals. It seems quite clear to me that Viner has concerned himself too much with the phraseology of these expressions and too little with the wider issues which determined the views of the various authors and politicians. Nevertheless, his evidence impresses me as being sufficiently strong to make me abandon my original thesis on this issue. After a careful consideration of his work, I have come to the conclusion that in the great majority of cases the difference between the mercantilist position and that which succeeded it was a difference of degree and not a difference of kind. On the other hand, I am still of the opinion that this difference of degree was both great and significant, and that it played an important role both in the mercantilist theory and in mercantilist policy, since it was naturally associated with both. The following discussion deals with certain economic measures in the sphere of power politics; that these measures ceased, for all practical purposes, after the decline of mercantilism impresses me as being of great importance. It seems apparent that Viner does not take issue with me on this.[1]

[1] "That the mercantilists considered power as an end in itself and as an important end, and that they considered wealth to be a means of power need not be examined here, since there is no ground for disputing these propositions and, as far as I know, no one has ever disputed them. That the mercantilists overemphasized these propositions I would also not question." (The choice of the word "overemphasize" appears to me to be unfortunate, since it presupposes a non-existent criterion with which to measure the dose of the policy

In order to achieve an adequate understanding of the influence
wielded by the concept of power on the economic doctrine of
mercantilism, it may be well to begin with a detailed account of
the ideas of two leading statesmen, one an Englishman and the
other a Frenchman.

Most accessible among the English mercantilists in this matter is
Francis Bacon, a thinker from whom one would hardly expect an
extreme approach. Bacon was not a radical thinker; in his breadth
of understanding and capacity to survey general problems he
exceeded most if not all of his contemporaries. On this topic
however, he reveals a degree of extremism and one-sidedness
more pronounced than is to be found in most contemporary
writings. Nevertheless his views on this issue as well as on many
others are of particular interest and are likely to have been shared
by others. I have quoted one of his statements above; there can be
no doubt that in his admiration for Henry VII he saw a great
advance in the transition "from consideration of plenty to consideration of power", which he understood to be the significance of
the king's economic policy. I propose now to give some account of
the longest of his Essays and to supplement it by quotations from
some of the others.

of power which should have been the right dose—an assumption which is
clearly unjustifiable.) Further: "It is doctrine, and not practice, which is
the main concern here." (Viner, "Power versus Plenty . . ." 6 and 20 resp.)
Since my discussion is concerned both with doctrine and with practice, my
interpretation and his may be expected, to some extent, to take separate
courses. However, his theses in the form he has given them here should in
the main be quite compatible with the first edition of this book. That Viner
directs his criticism against me seems to depend on the fact that time after
time he attributes to me the conception of power as the sole end for the
mercantilists. This is an interpretation which I fail to understand and which
is nowhere supported by any quotation. In the first edition, as in the present
edition (I 25), the following statement appears: ". . . wealth as such was
the centre of interest and dominated economic thought and dealings to an
equal degree in both [mercantilism and liberalism], far more in fact than the
question of its ultimate application." Finally, it should be mentioned that
a German critic, H. Rachel, in diametric opposition to Viner, upbraids me
for not having given the power aspect sufficient space: "Zutreffend wird die
Kombination von Einheits- und Machtstreben als charakteristisch für den
Merkantilismus hervorgehoben, nur hätte der Machtgesichtspunkt dabei
durchaus vorangestellt und stärker betont werden sollen." ("The striving
for the combination of unification and power as characteristics of mercantilism
are rightly given prominence but the power aspect should have been underlined and more strongly emphasized throughout." *Forschungen z. brdb. u.
preuss. Gesch.* XLV, 1932, 180). This characteristic opposition depends in
part on the fact that Viner and Rachel have two very different countries
in mind.

In his edition of Bacon's Essays, Aldis Wright expressed the opinion that the Essays contained Bacon's most mature and carefully selected thoughts; we may thus assume them to be representative of his views. For present purposes the most apposite essay is No. 29 in the 1625 edition. The subject had long been of interest to Bacon; there exists a fragment from 1608 which constitutes an introduction to an essay and which was included in the 1612 edition, and later in the Latin edition, reputedly translated by Hobbes. The title, "Of the True Greatnesse of Kingdomes and Estates" might suggest that the essay comprises Bacon's views on the factors contributing to all aspects of a state's greatness. On the other hand, the Latin title is "De proferendis imperii finibus", ("on the extension of the state's frontiers") and thus presumably indicates that he was emphasizing one particular aspect of the subject. Other statements, including that already cited, make it quite clear that he thought along the lines developed in the full essay. The text with which the present work is prefaced (I, 7) is a quotation from this essay. What follows here is an outline of the basic argument, largely in its original form, but omitting the mass of historical, mainly classical, examples.

After an introductory paragraph, Bacon turned to the difficulties involved in measuring the power of states. My prefatory quotation comes from this section and is symptomatic of the main tendency in his exposition. The external implements of power are but sheep in lion-skins, he wrote, while the disposition of the people is "stout and warlike". The first principle of greatness is to have a race of warlike men. Money is not the sinews of war, as it has been trivially said, if in a base and effeminate people the sinews in men's arms are failing. States which would achieve greatness must be on their guard not to let their nobility and gentry become too large a class, for in such a case the common man becomes enslaved and not one head in a hundred has the strength to bear a helmet. This is of particular importance to the infantry, the army's nerve; otherwise the result will be a large population but only relatively little strength. With admirable forethought, Henry VII therefore created an agricultural system based on prosperous and independent owners, a yeoman class which produces good soldiers. Free servants of the nobility could fill the same role, and the nobles ought therefore to be encouraged to maintain a large retinue, practice hospitality and generosity since that would unquestionably contribute to military greatness. States which generously naturalize foreigners are "fit for Empire" for the trunk of the tree which they have thus come to nourish will not be too weak to support its branches. Indoor employments are not for a war-like people which loves danger more than work; thus it was to the advantage of the peoples of antiquity to have slaves; now that slavery has disappeared with the coming of Christianity, the same end should be served by limiting a population to groups of farmers, free servants and artificers.

Without practice, continued Bacon, there is no proficiency, and no country achieves greatness without practice in the use of weapons. A state must utilize justifiable situations—which they can pretend arise—to go to war. Countries which strive for greatness are not slow to take up a challenge, and no state can be great which does not arm itself at every justified occasion. A just and honourable war is the best practice. A civil war is the heat of fever, but a foreign war is the heat of physical motion which helps to maintain bodily health, while courage is dissipated and habits decay during an apathetic peace. Finally, Bacon dwells on the special significance of sea power.

Here one finds an obviously strong feeling for the superiority of quality over quantity, but this, like all else, has been made the basis for open recourse to a policy of power which reminds us of the most violent theories of power in our own century, of Nazism and Fascism, with which west-European mercantilism had little else in common. There are, moreover, differences from the type of mercantilism which later became common, such as the warning against indoor employments. But, in what might be called his everyday views on events, Bacon was a mercantilist. It is thus striking that he gave welfare and commerce not so much as a sidelong glance; even the demand for yeoman agriculture was determined by considerations of pure power-politics.

Amongst Bacon's other essays there certainly exist statements not stamped with the same extreme one-sidedness, but which in principle are fully compatible with those given above. In one essay ("Of Empire", §19 in the 1625 edition) he advises princes to be on their guard "that none of their neighbours do overgrow so by increase of territory, by *embracing of trade* [italics mine], by approaches, or the like, as they become more able to annoy them than they were". Commerce appears here with its characteristic purpose—its contribution to power. In a third essay (§15: "Of Seditions and Troubles"), he writes that the export of a country's natural resources, its produce and its transport services cause "riches to stream in like a spring flood", but the approach is that indicated by the title—to avoid seditions and troubles—not to create plenty. These quotations are not a biassed selection but are intended to provide a fair summary of those parts of Bacon's essays which are relevant to this discussion.[2]

Undoubtedly Bacon trod a lone path in many respects and, as I have already noted, he cannot be looked upon as a representative spokesman for mercantilism in general. That is not the case with the exponent of mercantilism to whom I now turn, namely, Colbert. More than any other contemporary statesman, Colbert belonged to mercantilism in letter and spirit, positive and negative. To this extent the name Colbertism given to the whole phenomenon of mercantilism is largely justifiable. As has often happened, the philosopher showed a greater propensity to exaggerate than did the practical statesman, though Colbert had all the French proclivity for blending logic with epigram; examples of such expressions could be taken from a number of his official writings.

In a report to Louis XIV in 1664, Colbert wrote that in order to reach the great objectives which the king had set as his goal, it was necessary to "limit the occupations of all of Your subjects as far as possible to those which serve the lofty aims: they are agriculture, trade (*les màrchandises*, i.e., trade and manufacture), war at sea and on land." All else should be set aside. In a letter to a cousin who was Intendant at the naval base at Rochefort, Colbert wrote two years later: "Trade is the source of [public] finance and [public] finance is the vital nerve of war." This attitude emerges more explicitly in discussions of concrete problems than in general pronouncements of this kind, although even here, Colbert's statements are surprisingly fruitful.

Addendum §2: The extent to which Colbert's words and deeds were determined by this one single consideration may easily be exaggerated. The correspondence concerning the choice of an alliance for France in 1669, referred to above, gives some indication of this, as Viner has also noted. The concern there is not for power, but above all else, foreign trade, in particular foreign trade by sea, which is referred to flatly as "the most important subject in the world." The English in particular, it is said, are not moved more strongly by anything else. According to Colbert's opinion on that occasion, only commerce can "create a surplus for the country's subjects, and as a result provide for the satisfaction of princes." An interest in the people's welfare is also indicated in this formulation, otherwise quite foreign to Colbert's official writings, and it is even more strongly expressed elsewhere in the same document, thus: "Although the welfare of their subjects is

[2] *Essays* and *Colours of Good and Evil*, ed. W. A. Wright (reprinted, Lond. 1920): Wright's comment, 292; essays in order cited: 118–30, 77, 59.

the last, it ought nevertheless to stand first in the thoughts of good princes." Welfare for subjects comprises in part the maintenance of internal peace, and princes should endeavour "by means of commerce to make available to their needy subjects better opportunities for maintaining life and for the rich, a greater surplus." This latter should properly be seen as further evidence for the enormous value of commerce.

Addendum §*3*: Napoleon's "war against the English" in this connection was, of course, the Continental System. From many points of view this constituted the most consistent example of the mercantilist policy of power. Since it lies outside the period dealt with in this investigation, I shall only mention it in passing at this point. The idea behind the Continental System was much older than Napoleon, and was essentially the desire to "vanquish England by excess", to force her to her knees by cutting off the continent from her products and those of her colonies. Economic warfare was used here, perhaps with greater consistency than ever before, to serve a purely political end. They were one of the main weapons—perhaps the main weapon—in the struggle which lasted two full decades and ended only with Napoleon's fall. What was paradoxical in this situation was the use of curious and conflicting measures, such as the extension of trading with the enemy, a phenomenon which stands in sharp contrast to the policy of the first World War and stresses the basic differences in economic conceptions. Extensive transactions between enemies could be allowed so long as it was believed that the relationship would leave the other side poverty stricken. It was only after this policy of Napoleon had been unmistakably proved a failure that it degenerated into a gigantic system of extortion, from which the original purposes had largely disappeared. The formal plan underlying the Continental System marked the zenith of the mercantilist policy of power, despite the fact that Adam Smith's doctrines had been propounded several decades earlier.[1]

Addendum §*4*: Both trade and welfare, the aims with which power was customarily associated, must also be understood in their specific mercantilistic meaning. A "favourable" balance of trade implied the necessity of assuring an excess of exports over imports, thus diminishing the level of internal consumption. The "fear of goods" was fundamental to the doctrine of mercantilism, and the "economy of low wages" was at least a widely accepted doctrine. A typical mercantilist of orthodox views was thus in no position

---

[1] See my book, *The Continental System* (Oxf. 1922, Swedish ed: *Kontinental-systemet*, Sthlm. 1918), which is concerned with the relationship indicated here.

to regard the welfare of the broad masses as a desirable goal. Much the same attitude prevailed with respect to trade, though with certain qualifications. There is no doubt that the promotion of trade—especially overseas trade—ranked first among the achievements after which the mercantilists strived. Their eagerness on this point was qualified: trade was not to bring the country more goods than it took out; on the contrary, the aim was to create an excess of exports. In addition, care should be taken that as many vessels as possible were maintained and a maximum number of seamen and fishermen employed. This latter policy was precisely in line with the interest in power: it would guarantee naval strength without setting up a competing occupation. Thus there are two reasons why trade and welfare cannot be regarded as equipollent to power. On the other hand, Viner is undeniably correct in maintaining that they were mutually compatible goals.

Addendum §5: Concern with the supply of saltpetre for the production of gunpowder created considerable difficulty in France as well as in England. Special measures taken to assure an adequate supply of saltpetre appeared as early as the middle of the 15th century in France and followed the normal pattern for such measures there. According to a statement of 1601, saltpetre production was a state monopoly, as was the right of coinage. Final responsibility was placed on a high administrative officer— for 11 years, Sully—with a hierarchy of subordinates. For a time production was allocated *pro rata* to the various provinces. In general, private interests carried out the actual production, but under strict government surveillance. Because of the usual obedience shown by the French population under the *ancien régime* the regulatory system does not seem to have met any serious opposition, although illegal private production was never completely stamped out. The French regulations were subject to much less discussion than the English, thereby rendering them rather less interesting. The system was more thorough than the English and administered more intensively. (See Nef, cited above, I, ch. 6, *Addendum* §3; for France: 59-68; England: 88-98).

Addendum §6: Thomas Hobbes strikingly expressed his thoughts on money in 1651 when he wrote that gold and silver "have the priviledge to make the Common-wealths move, and stretch out their armes, when need is, into forraign Countries; and supply, not only private Subjects that travell, but also whole Armies with Provision." (*Leviathan*, 1st ed., part 2, ch. 24, 130; ed. Waller, Cambr. 1904, 180).

Addendum §7: E. A. J. Johnson was probably the first to elucidate the line of thought which had perhaps the most serious consequences for the usual mercantilist doctrine. Briefly, this involved replacing the doctrine of the balance of trade with what might be referred to as the doctrine of the "balance of work", that is, the conception that the decisive factor determining the value of a country's foreign trade was the amount of labour which went into its exports relative to the amount of labour represented by its imports. This approach was particularly clear in the contents of *The British Merchant,* a rather superficial but politically influential publication, first brought out as a periodical and later as a series of books. This reasoning coincided largely with the usual eagerness to export manufactured goods and to import those which, like raw materials, represented as little expenditure of labour as possible. Further analysis shows clearly that this increased the demand for labour and thus led to higher wages. It is unlikely that mercantilists in general were aware of this effect, since they were ordinarily proponents of an "economy of low wages". Even the ordinary view of the role of precious metals came to be reviewed from the same angle. (See E. A. J. Johnson, *op. cit.,* last chapter: "The Export of Work and Foreign Balances".)

Addendum §8: Sweden had an indefatigable counterpart in the contemporary Christopher Polhem whose suggestions in widely different technical fields indicate that he was in all probability a greater inventive genius than the others mentioned here, although most of his inventions were never applied practically. (The literature on Polhem is extensive; see my *Sveriges ekon. hist.* II:2 504 ff. for an evaluation of Polhem's significance.)

Addendum §9: One of the more surprising criticisms of my work is directed against my treatment of Mandeville's views on "the Poor", and the necessity for keeping them at the lowest possible standard. The criticism is to be found in a review by A. Meyendorff in *Baltic and Scandinavian Countries* III, 1937, nr. 1 (5) 134. He quotes a statement which is intended to illustrate that Mandeville looked with disfavour both upon wages which were too low as well as those which were too high. Meyendorff does not give the precise quotation and consequently it has been impossible for me to find the statement to which he alludes. I do not believe, however, that there can be any doubt about the general tenor of Mandeville's writings in this respect. In particular his "Essay on Charity and Charity Schools" which has been appended to later editions of his book (see above, 167), constitutes a diatribe against the demands of servants and labourers. The latest editor of Mandeville's writings, F. B. Kaye, maintains in the introduction to his edition (I, lxix-lxxii) that this point of view "is apt to impress the modern reader as almost incredibly brutal", and that, despite the honest desire to do him justice, he has no other comment on the criticism directed against Mandeville on this point than to note that he shared the opinion of his contemporaries and differed from them only in that he did not play the hypocrite.

Addendum §10: There are but few examples of direct protest against this identification of money and wealth. In addition to that ascribed to Papillon and cited in the text, another should be mentioned, curiously enough also concerned with the question of East India trade. Although it has since acquired a considerable reputation for its early espousal of liberal ideas, it seems less certain that it received any attention when it was published in 1701. Its author is unknown; its title: *Considerations upon the East-India Trade*. The development of the author's reasoning runs as follows: the true and primary wealth both of individuals and of the whole people consists of meat, bread, clothing and houses—the conveniences as well as the necessities of life; progress and improvement lie in the secure possession and the enjoyment of these things. They are wanted for their own sake; money is regarded as wealth because it will buy them. Precious metals are secondary and dependent; clothing and goods are real and primary riches.... This reasoning appears so clear that misunderstanding seems impossible. This is not so, however, for the pamphlet continues to the effect that everything which is consumed in England is loss—it can reap no profit for the country .... The author's talk of meat, bread, clothing and houses as the real riches is forgotten; such things are intended for use within the country and, indeed, this is scarcely to be avoided.

Addendum §11: On the basis of another set of the many notes from the debates of 1621 (*Commons' Debates 1621*, ed. W. Notestein, F. H. Relf, H. Simpson, New Haven 1935, II 30f., Yale Hist. Publ. XV), Lipson (II lxxix) has maintained that one comment indicates that goods were considered as riches. Read in its context, however, this expression takes on another significance. The speaker in question was as eager as any of the others to investigate the causes of the shortage of money and wished to summon the silversmiths and the Merchant Adventurers before Parliament to ask their advice on how to keep the precious metals in the country. The argument, to use Lipson's quotation, was: "It is a general opinion that any kingdom that is rich in staple commodities must needs be rich." It ought therefore to be investigated whether goods could not be sold or had been forced down in price, for "if so, then there must needs be a want of coin." Not only was the speaker in full accord with the others in thinking that the scarcity of money was the reason for their difficulties, but the most obvious interpretation of his comments about riches is that the abundance of commodities required money and should have attracted it.

Despite the fact that there are certainly many who feel that the two preceding sections represent an obsolescent economic theory, I have left them unchanged because I do not share this opinion. With respect to Keynes' interpretation of the contribution of mercantilism, I refer the reader to the supplementary chapter in this edition.

Addendum §*12*: (Supplement to footnote 6, 251.)

In his essay on the theory of international trade before Adam Smith, Viner cites another pamphlet in addition to the one mentioned in the footnote above. It is that of Isaac Gervaise, *The System or Theory of the Trade of the World,* published in 1720, and hitherto unknown to me. Judging from Viner's exposition (79-83), the work presents a discussion of the issue which is uncommonly lucid for that time. This impression is strengthened by the more detailed reference by J. M. Letiche, "Isaac Gervaise on the International Mechanism of Adjustment", *Journal of Political Economy* LX, 1952, 34-43. Since I have not had access to Gervaise's work, and since it apparently attracted no attention before Viner discovered it, I shall be content with the reference to the discussions of it quoted here.

Addendum §*13*: James II's declaration of indulgence (1687), promulgated to favour his fellow Roman Catholics, was camouflaged under the interest "for the increase of trade"; to coerce people in matters of mere religion "has always been directly contrary to our inclination, as we think it is to the interest of Govt. [*sic*], which it destroys by spoiling trade, depopulating countries, and discouraging strangers". See J. Paget, *The New " Examen "* (1861, repr. Manchester 1934, 211f.).

INDEX TO BOTH VOLUMES

INDEX

All page numbers without volume indication refer to Volume I of the present work. Where they refer to Volume II they are preceded by the Roman numeral "II". References to two consecutive pages are followed, as a rule, by the letter " f.", while " ff." denotes three consecutive pages. For more than three, the first and last pages are given. An asterisk after a number indicates a footnote, but where something is mentioned both in the text and in a footnote, only the former is indicated.

Names of people are printed in small capitals, titles of books, pamphlets and articles in italics. Works of known or presumptive authors are to be found under the authors' names; collections of documents, collective works and writings of unknown authors are to be found under their respective titles. Names of anonymous authors are in square brackets. Under the name of the publisher or editor reference is made to the particular work.

Abbeville: van Robais' cloth factory, 188, II 304

Åbo: monopoly in foreign trade, 135

Absolutism, 296, 456, 474, II 277

Académie de peinture et de sculpture, 177, 185

Acta Borussica, 59*, 71*, II 92* f.; cf. SCHMOLLER, G.

Act of Union: between England and Scotland (1707), 53; between Great Britain and Ireland (1800), 54.

Acts and Ordinances of the Eastland Company, 374*, 379*, 381*, 383*, 414*, 424*, 450*

Acts and Ordinances of the Interregnum, II 37*

Acts of the Privy Council, 268*, 269*, 328*

Admission fee: in the regulated companies, 386 f.; in the joint stock-companies, 396, 411 f.

Aerarium, II 211.

Affaires extraordinaires: French fiscalism, 180

AFFO: *Storia della città di Parma*, II 140*

Africa Company: *v.* Trading companies

African trade: Portugal, 341 f.; England: partnerships, 390

Agents (factors), II 76

Agrarian protection: combined with industrial protection, 225 f.; comparison between England and continental countries, 300; Denmark and Brandenburg, II 93; List's attitude towards, II 335

Agriculture: France: supply of labour, 156; industry favoured in preference to agriculture, 211; unique example in favour of agriculture, 212*; England: peculiar position in the English system of industrial regulation, 224-232, 238, 239, 250, 272; connection with quantity of money according to Hume, II 236; according to Locke, II 240

Aides: connection with the tolls, 94, 97, 124

Aix, II 306

ALBION, R. G.: *Forests and Sea Power*, II 40*, II 43*

ALBRECHT of Hapsburg, 62

Aldcaldamentos, II 141

Alençon: its cloth industry, *règlement*, 159; warden with gild organization in the neighbourhood of the town, 207; child-labour, II 156

Algiers: piracy, II 314

Alingsås manufactures (Sweden), 191*, II 147

ALMQUIST, H.: *Göteborgs historia*, 37*

ERRATUM

The head of this page should be numbered 372 in place of 342, et seq.

339 f., 367, 381, 392, 408 f.;
permanence and durability in
industry and mining, 336-339,
388, 392; for shipbuilding, 403 f.;
for political and military purposes, 340, 360, 390, 403-410;
connection with the development
of different forms of enterprises,
332, 339 f., 368 f., 404, 410.—
v. also Enterprise capital, Capital,
association of
Capital (Stock), II 190, II 196-199;
synonymous with money, II 199;
circulation considerations, II 218;
credit security, II 221-231
Capitalism: modern, 23; not a cause
of the closed nature of the gilds,
175, 182 f., connection with war
and luxury, 191; in English
economic life, 221 f., 303; need
for greater mobility, 304.—v. also
Anti-capitalism
Caps: duty to wear woollen caps in
England, 265; cappers, English,
265
Carcassonne: Draperie Royale de:
discs in cloth manufacture, 163
CARLYLE, T., 42, II 325
Carmarthen, 259, II 109
Carnarvon, II 109
Carolingian monarchy, 38, 52; uni-
form measures, 114; coinage,
119; coinage of system, 467
Carpenters: in Limoges: levy on a
table brought in privately, 177
CARR, C. T., 396*, 428*, 444*, 449*,
451*; v. further *Charters, Select,
of Trading Companies*
Carta Mercatoria (1303), II 84; v.
further Statutes, English
Cartel, 364, 383 f., 391
CARUS-WILSON, E. W.: *Origins and
Early Development of the Mer-
chant Adventurers*, 331*, 377*,
421*
CARY, J.: commodities and money,
II 99; connection with Locke,
II 119; wage policy, II 169 f.;
opposed to thrift, II 209; English
import prohibition, cause of Irish
competition, II 314; *Essay on the
State of England in Relation to*

its Trade, 270*, 320*, II 99*, II
120*, II 125, II 127, II 154, II 170
f., II 194*, II 314*
Casa: de Contratación, 344, II 70; *di*
S. Giorgio, 335
CASAUX DU HALLAY, Sieur DES:
Deputy for Nantes in the 1701
Board of Trade, 84, 106, II 39*,
II 40
Case of monopolies: v. Cases, English
Cases, English—
1365: (judge, Finchden): against
restraint of trade, 281
1376/77: Peachey's Case: monopoly or competition, 282
1409/10: Gloucester Grammar
School Case: monopoly or
competition, 282
1414/15: (judge, Hull): against
restraint of trade, 281
1590/1: Chamberlaine de Londres Case: craft freedom
against monopoly, 283
1590/1: Anonymous: appren-
ticeship in one trade sufficient
for all, 292, 293*
1599: Davenant v. Hurdis: craft
freedom against privileges,
283
1602/3: Darcy v. Allen or Darcy
against Thomas Allin (Case
of Monopolies): against royal
patents of monopoly, 288,
290
1610: Case del citie de Londres
(Waganor's Case): for customary rights, 284, 286, 290 f.,
307, 308*
1612: Sutton's Hospital Case:
features of a corporation,
444*
1613/14: Rogers v. Parrey:
restraint of trade, 261*
1614: Le Case des Tailleurs des
Habits, etc., del Ipswich
(Clothworkers of Ipswich
Case): against monopoly,
283; period of apprentice-
ship, 305 f.
1615: Rex and Allen v. Tooley
(Tolley's Case): tapestry
work outside the Statute of

INDEX

GEORGE ALLEN & UNWIN LTD
London: 40 Museum Street, W.C.1

Auckland: 24 Wyndham Street
Sydney, N.S.W.: Bradbury House, 55 York Street
Cape Town: 58-60 Long Street
Bombay: 15 Graham Road, Ballard Estate, Bombay 1
Calcutta: 17 Chittaranjan Avenue, Calcutta 13
New Delhi: 13-14 Ajmere Gate Extension, New Delhi 1
Karachi: Haroon Chambers, South Napier Road, Karachi 2
Toronto: 91 Wellington Street West
São Paulo: Avenida 9 de Julho 1138-Ap. 51